Religious
LYRICS
of the
XVth Century

Oxford University Press, Ely House, London W. 1

GLASGOW NEW YORK TORONTO MELBOURNE WELLINGTON
CAPE TOWN SALISBURY IBADAN NAIROBI LUSAKA ADDIS ABABA
BOMBAY CALCUTTA MADRAS KARACHI LAHORE DACCA
KUALA LUMPUR HONG KONG TOKYO

FIRST EDITION 1939

REPRINTED LITHOGRAPHICALLY IN GREAT BRITAIN
AT THE UNIVERSITY PRESS, OXFORD
FROM SHEETS OF THE FIRST EDITION
1952, 1962, 1967

Religious
LYRICS

of the

XVth CENTURY

Edited by

Carleton Brown

OXFORD
At the Clarendon Press

PREFACE

THE appearance of the present collection carries to completion the plan projected in the Spring of 1920 of a series of three volumes devoted to the Lyrics of the thirteenth, fourteenth and fifteenth centuries respectively.

In assembling the fifteenth-century material and preparing it for the press I have received helpful suggestions from many persons whose friendly assistance cannot be formally acknowledged. I wish, however, to express special thanks to Sir William Craigie for his kindness in carefully reading the proofs and solving a number of the textual problems presented by the lyrics in Arundel MS. 285, to Professor Anna J. Mill of Mount Holyoke College for collating the text of No. 78 with MS. 19.3.1 in the Advocates Library, Edinburgh, to my friend Professor Charlotte D'Evelyn of the same College for undertaking several errands on my behalf at the British Museum, to Professor F. W. Baxter of the University of Belfast, who made available for my use his photographs of Lant's print of No. 159. I wish also to thank Captain R. B. Haselden, Curator of MSS. at the Henry E. Huntington Library, for obtaining permission to print several texts from manuscripts in that Library, and for his courtesy in replying to inquiries concerning them; also to thank the Dean and Chapter of Westminster Abbey for leave to print No. 175.

Finally, I wish to express my obligations to my friend Dr. Rossell H. Robbins for generously allowing me to collate a number of my texts with his own transcripts of them. C. B.

NEW YORK UNIVERSITY,
December 1938.

CONTENTS

Contents

Contents

Contents ix

SONGS AGAINST FORTUNE.

SONGS OF THE DECADENCE OF VIRTUE.

SONGS AGAINST VICES.

PROVERBS AND MORAL SENTENCES.

Contents

INTRODUCTION

In compiling this selection of lyrics of the fifteenth century it has not proved feasible to arrange the pieces according to manuscript order, as in the case of the thirteenth-century lyrics, or according to chronology, as with the lyrics of the fourteenth century. The materials for the present volume, instead of being grouped in manuscript collections, occur for the most part as separate items scattered through a large number of manuscripts, which yield little definite information as to date and provenience. In these circumstances it seemed advisable to follow a purely topical arrangement, which at least serves the convenience of the reader by placing side by side pieces which treat identical or similar themes.

Of the fifteenth-century verse here assembled, somewhat over half has hitherto been virtually inaccessible. Seventy-four of these pieces have never been printed previously, and five others have appeared only in the *Register* or in Catalogue descriptions of manuscript. Also, the texts of twenty-six pieces previously printed are here presented from manuscripts which (as in the case of Nos. 6, 136, 154, and 172) are so far superior that they may be considered as new texts. Nos. 68 and 178 were printed over a century ago (in the *British Magazine* and *Censura Literaria* respectively) but have not subsequently been reprinted.

Although this collection of fifteenth-century lyrics includes 192 pieces, as compared with 135 in the *Religious Lyrics of the Fourteenth Century*, the task of selecting them has been more difficult owing to the far larger amount of material which was available. For the volume of extant fifteenth-century poetry, contrary to the impression which one receives from handbooks of literature, is many times larger than that of the preceding century. Indeed, from the material available a collection ten times the size of the present volume would have been possible. In view of this situation, some rigorous and even arbitrary limitation became necessary.

The works of the well-known poets of the century being readily accessible in recent editions, it seemed advisable to omit these altogether. Consequently the reader must turn elsewhere for the lyrics of Lydgate, Hoccleve, Awdley, Henryson, Burgh, Ryman, Dunbar, and Kennedy. The only exception to this rule was the inclusion of two Prayers against the Pestilence by Lydgate, which were overlooked in MacCracken's edition of the *Minor Poems*.

As a result, the present collection consists almost wholly of anonymous poems, although in a few instances names of authors are preserved. There is a quatrain by Bishop Pecock (No. 119) and a Lament of the Soul of Edward IV (No. 159) by Skelton; Squire Halsham, the author of No. 171, has been identified by Dr. Helen South (*PMLA*, l. 362–71); as to the possible identity of R. Stokys, named as the author of No. 181, see *Mod. Lang. Notes*, liv. 131–3. Concerning the other persons whose names are connected with pieces here printed— H. Bowesper (No. 40), Richard Spaldyng (No. 31), Robert Harman (No. 64), A god whene (No. 169), William Hammer (No. 56), Robert Peet (No. 162), and Rate (Nos. 129 and 151)—we know little or nothing.

Lacking the work of the best-known poets of the century, the present collection falls far short of being an anthology of fifteenth-century religious verse. But it should serve the better on this account to indicate the general level of poetic tendency and achievement, since it reflects the prevailing taste and interest of the period instead of the literary accomplishment of a few individuals.

Another question which presented itself was whether the selection should be restricted to poems of a certain standard of artistic excellence. By applying the standards of the nineteenth and twentieth centuries, the lyrical product of the fifteenth century could unquestionably have been reduced to a volume of distinctly smaller proportions, though much pure gold would remain. But such an anthology, however useful it might be in other respects, would not correctly or adequately represent the poetic taste of the century, nor would it give proper emphasis to its special characteristics; and the fundamental aim in the present volume was to offer the reader a fairly representative collection of religious lyrics from the fifteenth century, which should exhibit their defects as well as their excellences.

In the lyrical development of the century perhaps the most characteristic feature was the rise of the carol. Whereas the *Religious Lyrics of the Fourteenth Century* present only a solitary example of the carol (No. 88), with the turn of the century we meet with them in considerable groups. The number of carols printed in the present collection might easily have been increased. However, the appearance, while the present volume was in preparation, of Dr. Richard Greene's *Early English Carols* made it possible to restrict the number of carols somewhat by admitting only a representative selection. Twenty-eight of the texts here included (although not all of these in my opinion can be classed as carols) are also printed by Dr. Greene.

No century can be sharply marked off from the one which precedes or the one which follows. Consequently

the reader will expect to find among these pieces many
themes which mark the continuance of fourteenth-century tradition. Conspicuous among these are the Hymns
to the Virgin, the Complaints of Christ, the Marian
Laments, and the Songs of Mortality. No less than 38
hymns and songs to the Virgin are here included—as
compared with the 14 or 15 in the fourteenth-century
collection. This number, however, is not disproportion-
ate in view of the greatly increased volume of these hymns
and songs during the fifteenth century, although these
expressions of devotion, it must be said, when compared
with those of the preceding century, show a certain loss
of fervour and tend to become formal exercises.

This is well illustrated by the poems on the Joys of the
Virgin. Whereas in the fourteenth century these, with
their recital of the Annunciation, Nativity, and Resurrection, concerned themselves with the terrestrial joys,
the scene in almost all the fifteenth-century pieces is
transferred to heaven, and the praises of the Virgin are
sung by cherubim and celestial choirs. One misses the
touch of human reality also in the Songs of the Assumption
and the Coronation of the Virgin, in which the sense of
artificiality is increased by the pomposity of the aureate
style. A considerable group of these songs are based upon
the Latin hymns *Ave regina celorum*, *Salve regina*, and
Regina celi letare. But the Latin original is often farced
by tedious repetition, and instead of spontaneity we have
the verbal ingenuity of an acrostic.

In sharp contrast to pieces of this type are Nos. 40–4,
in which devotion to the Virgin is expressed in simple language charged with real feeling. The concluding pieces in
this section—Nos. 45–9—are of particular interest through
their employment of the phrases of the secular love lyric.
'I Have now Set my Heart so High' repeats the title of No.

129 in the *Fourteenth-Century Lyrics*, though in that case
the song was of love to Christ instead of to the Virgin.
But in the 'Love Message to My Lady', 'I Will Serve my
Lady until Death', and 'I Will Have no Other Spouse',
the language parallels the phrases of the courtly song so
closely that one must read the text carefully to be certain
that the devotion expressed is directed toward the Virgin.

Among the songs relating to the Virgin, the type which
reached its highest development in the fifteenth century
was the Marian Lament. As examples one may cite
Nos. 6 and 7, which in imaginative description and human
pathos surpass all earlier treatments of this theme. The
explanation is probably to be found in the fact that in
character these laments are dramatic quite as much as
lyrical, and the fifteenth century was marked by a rapid
growth of interest in the religious drama. Professor
George C. Taylor has called attention to the direct
influence of the religious lyrics upon the drama, but no
one, so far as I am aware, has suggested the converse,
namely: that the drama may also have served to stimu-
late and vitalize the lyric. Certainly this appears un-
questionable in the case of poems treating of the Virgin's
sorrow and the sufferings of the Crucified.

The harrowing scene of the Crucifixion had been so frequently described in the fourteenth-century Complaints
of Christ, usually with emphasis upon the physical tor-
tures, that in the case of this theme a fresh lyrical
impulse might seem scarcely possible. But whereas in
Nos. 102–4 the Appeals to Man from the Cross repeat
essentially those in the *Lyrics of the Fourteenth Century*,
in No. 105 one recognizes a new note. Though in this
piece the refraid line, *Quid vltra debui facere?* continues
the tradition of the fourteenth-century *Populi meus quid
feci tibi?* in its tone this lyric owes much more to the

Appeal of the Virgin in the well-known '*Quia Amore Langueo*'.[1] Even its phrasing shows some reminiscences: compare, for example, ll. 25 and 27,

> I must love þe, I maye none oþer
>
> .   .   .   .
>
> Or ellys þu art an vnkynde broþer,

with lines 9 and 11 of the *Quia Amore*:

> I longe for loue of man my brother
>
> .   .   .   .
>
> I am hys moder—I can none other.

Unless I am much mistaken, Christ's appeal to man in this fifteenth-century poem was consciously designed as a counterpart to the Virgin's appeal in the *Quia amore*. That it does not rise to the superb height of the earlier lyric every one will concede—imitations rarely equal their models—but what is really significant is that an attempt was being made to infuse into this appeal of Christ to mankind something of the human yearning and tenderness which are so remarkable in the *Quia Amore*.

The first three Complaints of Christ (Nos. 106–8) continue without essential change the tradition of the fourteenth century. But 'Brother, Abide' (No. 109) gives to the old theme a new treatment which one will not find in the earlier poems on this subject. This is something more than a recital of the details of the Passion: and the emphasis is less upon the physical sufferings than upon the anguish of the spirit and the human feelings of Christ in his yearning compassion for the soul of man. The poet visualizes the narrative by adding homely details:

> I lede my yought wyth children in the strette,
> Poorly a-rayed in clothes bare and thyne,
> Suche as my mother for me dyde make & spyne.

[1] *Religious Lyrics of the Fourteenth Century*, No. 132.

The scene in the judgement hall of Pilate is compressed drama:

> 'Speke, manne,' qd pylate, 'how ys thy lyf convayed?'
> And wyth that worde, wattur to whasche he callde,
> And I stode styll, seke and sore appalled.

When Jesus was led forth from the judgement hall,

> Some pulled me forwarde & tare my powur a-ray,
> And by the here some plukkyd me bake a-gayne.
> Often I stomelled & felle to the grounde for payne
> And, wythout pyte of my grevance or hurte,
> They spornned me vp, all betrodene in durte.

The arrival at the summit of Mount Calvary is graphically portrayed:

> When I came vp my breth was at an ende,
> I cowde not speke, in me no powur ther was,
> But as in a mane redy for to passe.

After his final cry, 'Heli, heli', the death of Jesus is described as a painter would have seen it:

> And wyth that worde, I layde myne hede a-syde,
> And dolfully gave vp the spret & dyed.

In the Complaints of Christ, then, as in the Marian laments, the lyrics of the fifteenth century show a distinct heightening of the poetic imagination which, as I have said, appears to be due, in part at least, to the quickening influence of the religious drama with its notable development during this same period.

The besetting sin of Lydgate, as of his contemporaries generally, was prolixity; and, if the work of the monk of Bury be taken as representing the lyrics of the century, one must pronounce them prolix and wanting in variety, particularly the more formal pieces, which are propelled mechanically along traditional grooves. Others there are, however, with no trace of hackneyed phrases or

conventional formulae. Tucked away on the fly-leaves
and in spare pages of manuscripts, one finds stray bits of
verse remarkable for their epigrammatic conciseness and
for their unaffected and uninflated diction. Such, for
example, are 'The Wounds as Wells of Life' (No. 100)
and 'Christ Triumphant' (No. 111), of eight and six lines
respectively. These assure us that even the fifteenth
century had not lost the faculty of natural, spontaneous
expression. The notion that the religious poetry of the
century lacked variety is likewise based on a misappre-
hension. The truth is that the lyrics of this period exhibit
a diversity equal at least to those of the thirteenth and fourteenth centuries. With some of the songs and hymns to
the Virgin already noticed as examples of the aureate style,
one may compare the fervour and simplicity of Richard
de Caistre's hymn (No. 64). In his petition to Jesus,

> Chomfort hem þat carfull ben,
> And helpe hem þat ar woo begone,

we may perhaps recognize an echo of a line in *Piers
Plowman*:[1]

> Conforte þi careful, cryst, in þi ryche.

The language of 'An Evening Prayer' (No. 127) is almost
as simple as the modern 'Now I lay me'; and two of the
lines have a ballad swing:

> Owre lorde is the frwte, oure lady is the tree;
> Blessid be the blossome that sprange, lady, of the!

Unpretentious and direct also is the 'Morning Prayer'
by Rate (No. 129) which begins:

> Ihū, lord, blyssed þu be!
> ffore all þis nyght þu hast me kepe
> ffrome þe fend & his poste,
> wheþer I wake or þat I slepe.

[1] B-Text, xiv. 179.

This devotion concludes with a petition to the guardian angel:

> My gode Angell, þat arte to me send
> ffrome god to be my gouernour,
> ffrome all euyll sprytis þu me defend,
> And in my desesys to be my socoure.

In the three prayers to the Guardian Angel (Nos. 132–4) one finds the same directness and absence of rhetorical ornament.

Much study has been devoted to the popular ballad and the problem of its origins, but comparatively little to the popular lyric, though this presents problems essentially similar and affords no less authentic testimony as to the characteristics of folk poetry. Without committing ourselves to any theories as to their origin, we may recognize the popular character of 'Maiden Makeles' (No. 81), 'Adam lay i-bowndyn' (No. 83), 'The Child that Died for Us' (No. 99), and 'By a Chapel as I Came' (No. 116). In these pieces the lyric touches elbows with the popular ballad.

Contrasting sharply with these, on the other hand, is the group of theological lyrics (Nos. 118–20), which are sophisticated in tone and are characterized by verbal conceits and clever paradox. Lyrics of this type owe no kinship to the ballad, but look forward, instead, to the poetry of the metaphysical school. And yet popular and theological lyrics alike were the product of the fifteenth century.

Nos. 130 and 131 were called forth by the same historical occasion, namely, the departure of the young king Henry VI for France in the spring of 1430. The first of these, 'Speed Our King on His Journey', is a prayer for the safety of the king, while the second, 'Mary, Take in Your Hand this Dread Voyage', is a prayer spoken by the king himself. The mention in the former of the 'precyouse pastour, seynt erkenwalde' gives strong indication that it was composed at London. The references to current events in these pieces and the fact that they can be definitely dated make them of particular interest. Both are written in 8-line stanzas, but the lines in the first are of four stresses, while those in the second have five stresses.

The ten Songs of Penitence (Nos. 137–46) are for the most part of the conventional type, without individualizing touches or evidence of personal feeling. A conspicuous exception, however, is No. 139, which expresses realistically the state of mind (and body) of a person suffering from an attack of acute indigestion—a lyric which, oddly enough, is provided in the manuscript with a musical score. In No. 141 we have a very unusual instance of English verses translated directly from a prayer in Latin prose—the text of which immediately precedes in the manuscript. Though it follows the original closely, the translation is surprisingly smooth and idiomatic. 'A Song of Sins' (No. 146), the last of these penitential lyrics, is chiefly notable as an example of metrical ingenuity, the same rimes being carried through the twenty-six lines of the poem. It may be compared in this respect with the 'Song of "Goods"' (No. 189).

Old Age and Mortality—common themes in the lyrics of any century—are liberally represented in the present collection (Nos. 147–64). These pieces, as one would expect, repeat the familiar *Memento Mori* of the earlier lyrics. But the lesson is presented not merely in the form of exhortation, but also dramatically, as, for example, in No. 149:

> ffare well, this world! I take my leve for euere,
> I am arested to apere at goddes face.

> To-day I sat full ryall in a cheyere,
> Tyll sotell deth knokyd at my gate,
>
> .   .   .   .
>
> Speke softe, ye folk, for I am leyd aslepe!

This tendency towards dramatic monologue is seen also
in No. 158, in which we have personifications of Knight,
King, and Clerk translated from the Latin *Vado Mori*.
But though these Latin verses date from the early fourteenth century, their influence upon the English lyric
begins, apparently, in the fifteenth century. And it is to
the fifteenth century also that the closely related 'Dance
of Death' belongs—another illustration of the infusion
of the spirit of drama in the lyric. Skelton's 'Lament of
the Soul of Edward IV' (No. 159) is from first to last a
dramatic monologue. The moralization is spoken by the
king's own lips—the poet does not intrude himself either
to praise or blame. The inevitable *Ubi sunt* motive finds
expression in passing, but the emphasis is laid upon
specific incidents in the reign of the deceased king, with
explicit mention of his taxation of the 'commynalte', and
of the wars with France—

> I was youre kyng and kepte yow from youre foo,—

of strengthening the fortifications of Dover and London, of
the castles built at Tattersall, Nottingham, Windsor, and
Eton. His farewell to his queen is charged with true pathos:

> Lidy besse, for me long may ye call,
> Whe be departyd vntyll domus day!
> I lovyd you, lady, my souerayne ouerall.

And the words which Skelton puts into the mouth of
Edward,—

> I haue pleyd my pagent   now am I past,—

make an almost startling approach to Elizabethan
dramatic metaphor.

One of the most remarkable poems on the Mortality theme is that 'On the Untimely Death of a Fair Lady' (No. 153), in which the speaker mourns an actual personal loss.

Then sorwed I   .   .   .   .
And mourned for my maystresse, here marred in molde.

.   .   .   .

O myghty lord   .   .   .   .
Haue mercy on the soule of my dere maistresse!

.   .   .   .

Deliuere here, gracious lord, fro peyne and distresse!
Endowe here in thi place of plesaunt paradise,

.   .   .   .

Of lordis lyne & lynage sche was, here sche lyse!
Bounteuus, benigne, enbleshed wyth beaute,
Sage, softe and sobre an gentyll in al wyse.

We appear to have in these verses, then, an instance of the true personal elegy—a type of poem excessively rare in Middle English. In fact, with the exception of *Pearl*, the interpretation of which is still disputed, this poem is, so far as I am aware, the earliest personal elegy in the language.

'The Mirror of Mortality' (No. 154)—unlike the preceding poem—does not spring from the grief of bereavement. None the less, it was called forth by a particular situation and has a special personal application, although in the text of this piece printed by Varnhagen these local and personal references were lacking. With these restored to the text, we are now able to fix the date of composition and also to localize the manuscript at Tattershall, Lincolnshire.

The friendly aspect of Death presented in No. 163 stands out in sharp contrast to the tone of the earlier lyrics treating mortality. The attitude of the poem does not, of course, conflict in the least with the doctrine of

the medieval church. Indeed, it is interesting to observe
that the author depended for the substance and even for
some of the phrases of his poem upon Book III of the
Pricke of Conscience.[1] The significant fact is that the
author of the present poem ignores completely the terrors
of death and centres attention instead upon the hopes of
heaven. Such a shift of emphasis is hardly to be found
in the religious lyrics of the fourteenth century.

Still more unmistakable testimony to the changing
tone in the fifteenth century appears in the 8-line stanza
which immediately follows, 'Death, the Port of Peace'
(No. 164). In the lines

> Here ys the reste of all your besynesse,
> Here ys the porte of peese, & resstfulnes—

we recognize clearly the spirit of the Renaissance. At the
threshold of the sixteenth century we are already looking
forward to Spenser.

The last twenty-eight pieces are, strictly speaking,
moral rather than religious, though in the manuscripts
they stand side by side with religious poems and many
of them are pervaded by a homiletic flavour. The six
lyrics on Fortune (Nos. 165–70) continue the fourteenth-
century tradition without essential variation. 'Good
Rule Is Out of Remembrance' (No. 172), notable throughout for its pithy, sententious style, is crammed with a
host of proverbs and old saws—such, for example, as
'A bare berde wyl sone be shaue', and 'Þe pot is esy for
to kepe þer þe fatte is ouer-blowe'.

The topical or 'sentence' lyrics, of which the series in
the Vernon MS.[2] offer the best-known examples, maintained their popularity in the fifteenth century. In the

---

[1] Cf. especially ll. 2086–119 and 2162–205 in Morris's edition.
[2] See *Religious Lyrics of the Fourteenth Century*, Nos. 95–120.

present collection Nos. 177, 178, 182, 183, and 186 are
'refraid' poems, written in the same measure as those in
the Vernon MS. 'Þei may wytyn hem-self her owyn woo',
'Yeve vs lycence to lyfe yn ese', 'Whate euer thow sey,
A-vyse the welle', 'Euer more for the better a-byde',
'Mesure is best of all thynge', are refraid lines wholly
similar in tone to those in the earlier models. But even
the theme of the Deadly Sins (No. 178) takes on a certain
sprightliness through the quaint use of medical termino-
logy. No. 181 enlarges on the mischief wrought by
gossiping and malicious tongues, and No. 182 is a warning
to consider carefully before speaking, what you say, about
whom you speak, where, to whom, why, and when. If
every man had borne this in mind, the author remarks,
many things that have been wrought in England would
never have been begun. No. 183 counsels prudence and
patience and No. 185 enjoins against being either too
proud or too humble. Similar is the lesson in No. 186:

> In ilke manere of mans mode
> Mesure is best of all thynge.

The author of No. 188 describes man's labour 'to gadre
goode and grete Riches':

> We trow thus to level the see—
> It may nat be by none ymagynacoune!

In these pieces one finds no great originality, though
much shrewd observation and well-pointed advice. On
the other hand, the concluding piece (No. 192) is pitched
in a wholly different key. It sets forth in terms of
Christian Stoicism a philosophy of life, beginning—

> The law of god be to þe thy rest—

and concluding

> for here-in of al wynnyng lyth crosse & pile,—

that is, herein consists the sum of all good.

The fifteenth century has suffered in literary reputation through the very fact that it intervenes between Chaucer and the Elizabethan Age. The literary historian is disposed on this account to treat it chiefly as a period of hibernation. Rather, it is a period of transition, and in the history of living forms transitions are phenomena of the utmost importance, for only by closely observing these can the emergence of successive types be rightly understood.

Even a casual reading of these fifteenth-century lyrics is sufficient to demonstrate that no real line of cleavage exists between the fourteenth and fifteenth centuries. When one crosses the threshold of the sixteenth century the continuity may seem to the reader somewhat less obvious. However, the lyrics of the century, if studied attentively, supply evidence of a development from the fifteenth to the sixteenth century almost as constant as that traceable from the fourteenth to the fifteenth. The apparent break in continuity was to a large extent the result of new external conditions—the extension of printing, the introduction of the new learning, and the change of religion. And, though changes in external conditions materially modified conventional forms, they did not quell the essential spirit of the earlier lyrical tradition, but merely opened new channels for its expression.

THE TEXTS

THE texts here printed have been collated in every case
with the original manuscripts or photostatic reproduc-
tions. The manuscripts have been followed in ortho-
graphy and capitalization; and the Middle English cha-
racters Þ and ȝ have been retained. On the other hand,
the punctuation of the texts is editorial, and hyphens
have been introduced, chiefly in compounds and after
prefixes, which in the manuscripts are often separated.
Also, the ordinary manuscript contractions have been
expanded without the use of italics.

In some cases, in order to make the texts intelligible,
it has been necessary to correct obvious scribal errors,
but in every instance where an emendation has been
introduced in the text the reading of the manuscript is
recorded at the foot of the page.

1.   *Dear Son, Leave Thy Weeping*

Porkington MS. 10

XPē qui lux es & dies, / noctis tennebras   [fol. 202ʳᵒ]
detegis / lucisque lumen crederis, / lumen
Beatum predicans.

A Baby ys borne vs blys to bryng;
  A mayddyn I hard loullay synge:
'Dyre son, now leyfe thi weppng,
Thy fadyre ys þe kyng of blys.'   4

Precamur sancte domine / defende nos in hac
Nocte / sit nobis in te requies / quietam
Noctem tribue.

'Nay, dere modyre, for yow weppe I noȝt,
But for þingis þat schall be wroȝt
Or þat I have mankynd I-boȝt;
Was þer neuer payn lyke yt I-wys.'   8

Ne grauis sompnus erruat / nec
Hostis nos surripiat / nec caro illi con-
senciens / nos tibi reos statuat.

'Pes, dyre sone, say þou me not soo!
Thow art my chyld, I have noo moo.
Alas! þat I schwld see þis woo,   [fol. 202ᵛᵒ]
Hyt were to me gret heyuenys.'   12

OCuli sompnum capiant / cor ad te semper
vigilet / dextera tua protegat / famulos
qui te diligunt.

'My hondys, modyre, þat ȝe now see,
Thay schall be nayllyd one a tre;
My feyt all-soo fastnyd schal be—
fful monny schall wepe þat hit schall see.'   16

DEfensor noster aspice / insidiantes
reprime / guberna tuos famulos /
quos sanguine mercatus es.

'Alas! dyre son, sowerov now ys my happe;
To see my chyld þat sovkys my pappe
So rwthfully takyn ovt of my lape,
Hyt wer to me gret heyuenys.'   20

MEmento nostri domine / in graui isto corpore /
qui es defensor anime / ad-esto nobis domine.

'Alsoo, modyre, þer schall a speyre
My tendure hert all to-teyre;   [fol. 203ʳᵒ]
The blud schall keuyre my body þer—
Gret rwthe yt schall be to see.'   24

DEo patri sit gloria eiusque soli filio
cum spiritu paraclito et nunc & in-
perpetuum amen Et C.

'A! dere sone, þat is a heyvy cas;
When gabrell cnellyd before my face,
And sayd "heylle lady full of grace",
He neuer told me nooþing of þis.'   28

Gloria tibe domine qui nattus [es hodie].

'Dere modyre, peys, nowe I yow pray,
And take noo sorrow for þat I say;
But synnge þis song "by by lowllay",
To dryfe away all heyuenys.'   32

2.   *Here I Sit Alone, Alas! Alone*

B.M. Addit. MS. 5465

Alone, alone, alone, alone, alone;
Here I sitt alone, alas! alone.   [fol. 48ᵛᵒ]

AS I walked me this endurs day
    to þe grene wode for to play
& all heuyness to put away
    my-self alone.   4

As I walkyd* vndir þe grene wode bowe   *[fol. 49ʳº]
I sawe a maide fayre I-now;
a child she happid, she song, she lough—
    þat child wepid alone.   8

'Son,' she sayd, 'I have þe borne   [fol. 49ᵛº]
to saue mankynd þat was forlorne;
therfor I pray the, son, ne morne,
    but be still alone.'   12

'Moder, me thynkith it is ryȝt ill
that men [me] sekyth for to spill.
for them to saue it is my will;
    therfor I cam hither alone.'   16

'Sone,' she sayd, 'let it be In þi thought,
for mannys gilt is not with-sought;
for þu art he þat hath all wrought,
    & I þi moder alone.'   20

3.   *It is my Father's Will*

Bodleian MS. Add. A. 106
(Sum. Catal. No. 29003)

Lullay, lullay, my lityl chyld, slepe & be now styll;   [fol. 14ᵛº]
If þu be a lytill chyld ȝitt may þu haue þi wyll.

'HOw suld I now, þu fayre may, fall apone a slepe?
    better me thynke þat I may fall apone & wepe
Fore he þat mad both nyght & day, cold & also hette,
now layde I ame in a wispe of hay I cane noder go nore
    crepe   4
Bot wel I wate as well I may—slepe & be now styll—
                  [fol. 15ʳº]
Suffre þe paynes þat I may; it is my fader wyll.

7 MS. heppid.   11 MS. no more.
18 sought] MS. stone.   19 all] MS. all well.

Seys þu noȝte, þu fayr may, & heris þu noȝte also
How kynge herod, þat keyne knyght, & of his peres mo 8
þat be a-bowte nyght & day my body fore to slo?
þai seke me both nyght & day at werke me mekyll wo,
  bot well I wate as well I may—slepe & be now styll—
  Suffre þe paynes þat I may; it is my fader wyll.   12

How suld I now, þu fayre may, how suld I now myrth
  make?
My songe is mad of walaway; fore dred I begyne to
  whake,
Fore drede of þat ilk day at I my deth sall take
& suffre þe paynes þat I may fore synfull man sake.   16
  Fore well I wate as well I may—slepe & be now styll—
  Suffre þe paynes þat I may; it is my fader wyll.

bot ȝitt me thynk it well besett If man haue of me mynd,
& al my paynes well besett If man to me be kynd.   20
þare is no deth at sall me let, & I hym trew fynd,
One þe rode fore to sytt, my handis for to bynd.
  bot well I wat as well I may—slepe & be now styll—
  Suffre þe paynes þat I may; it is my fader wyll.'   24

4.   He said Ba-Bay, she said Lullay

Harley MS. 2380

Þis endres nyght A-bout mydnyght   [fol. 70ᵛᵒ,
  As I me lay for to sclepe,   col. 1]
I hard a may syng lullay
for powaret sor sco wepe.   4
    He sayd Ba-Bay;
    sco sayd lullay,
    þe virgine fresch as ros in may.

4 MS. scow wrypt.

Sare sco soght Bot fand sco nought   8
To hap hyre sone Ihū fro cold.
Iosef sayd belif, 'scuet wyfe,
Tell me wat ȝe wald,
Hartly I ȝou pray.'   12
    He sayd ba-bay;
    Scho sayd lullay,
    þe virgine fresch as ros in may.

Scho sayde, 'scueit spows, Me thynk greuus   16
Myn child sud lig In hay,
Sene he is kyng And mayd al thyng,
And now Is powrest In aray.'   [col. 2]
    He sayd bay-bay;   20
    Scho sayd lullay,
    þe virgine fresch as ros In may.

'Hire he Is þat bers þe prys
In all thyng þat he as wrowght;   24
To hap my Barne Som clas I ȝarne,
Bot wat It I ne rowght,
þis yoles day.'
    He sayd Ba-Bay;   28
    Sco sayd lullay,
    þe virgine fresche as ros In may.

'Modere dere, amend ȝoure chere'—
þus says hire sone Ihū hir till—   32
'Al-of I be In poure degre,
It is my ffadris wyll
And sud be obay.'
    [He sayd ba-bay;]   36
    sco sayd lullay,   [fol. 71ro]
    þe virgyne fresche as ros In may.

      35 obay] MS. hay.

'A crown o thorne for sawll-is lorne
Opone my hed me most ned were,　　　　40
And till a tre So nayled be;
þare payns þay wyl me dere
þoron a-say.'
　　　He sayd ba-bay;　　　　44
　　　Scho sayd lullay,
　　　þe virgin fresch as ros In may.

'Þe trewght sal fal hout of þe postill hall
vnto 3ou, modere, all-oon to duell;　　　48
Wyll I call fro þe fends thrall
Adam out of hel
to py verray.'
　　　he sayd ba-bay;　　　　52
　　　sco sayd lullay,
　　　þe virgin fresch as ros In may.

Sco sayd, 'sweit sone, wen sal þis be [don],
þat 3e sal suffir al þis vo?'　　　　56
'Moder fre, al sal 3e se
With xxx 3er & thrio—
It is no nay.'
　　　He sayd ba-bay;　　　　60
　　　sco sayd lullay,
　　　þe virgin fresch as ros In may. [fol. 71ro, col. 2]

'Sone, I yow ix qwen sal þu ris?'
'Moder, verray apone þe thyrd day　　　64
þat Iudas has me sald t'outray.'
　　　He sayd ba-bay;
　　　Sco sayd lullay,
　　　þe virgin fresch as ros In may.　　　68

'I sall vp steiien þat 3e ma se,
Apon my fader ryght hand,

In blis to Be, and so sal ȝe
To were A croune garland   72
In blis for hay.'
 He sayd ba-bay;
 Sco sayd lullay,
 þe virgin fresch as ros In [may].   76

'Syng me ere, My moder dere.'
'Wet souet vois I ȝou pray,
Wep no more, ȝe gref me sor,
ȝour morninge put a-way—   80
Sing and say lullay.'
 He sayd ba-bay;
 Sco sayd lullay,
 þe virgin fresch as ros Ine [may].   84

5. *She Sang, Dear Son, Lullay*

MS. Ashmole 189
(Sum. Catal. No. 6777)

Thys yonder nyȝth y sawe A syȝte, [fol. 106ᵛᵒ]
A sterre As bryȝth As ony daye
& euer A-monge A maydene songe,
'by by, lully, lullaye.'

THys mayden hyȝth mary, she was full mylde,
she knelyde by-fore here oune dere chylde.

She lullyde, She lappyde,
she rullyde, she wrapped,   4
 She wepped wyth-owtyne nay;
She rullyde hym, she dressyde hym,
she lyssyd hym, she blessyd hym,
 She sange 'dere sone, lullay'.   8

She sayde, 'dere sone, ly styll & slepe.
What cause hast þu so sore to wepe,

Wyth syȝhyng, wyth snobbynge,
wyth crying & wyth scrycchynge   12
   All þis londe daye;
And þus wakynge wyth sore wepynge
Wyth many salt terys droppynge?
   ly stylle, dere sone, I þe pray.'   16

'Moder,' he sayde, 'for mane I wepe so sore
& for hys loue I shall be tore

Wyth scorgyng, wyth thretnyng,   [fol. 107ro]
wyth bobbyng, wyth betyng   20
   for sothe, moder, I saye;
And one A crosse full hy hanggyng,
And to my herte foll sore styckynge
   A spere on good frydaye.'   24

Thys maydene Aunswerde wyth heuy chere,
'Shalt þu thus sovere, my swete sone dere?

Now y morne, now y muse,
I All gladnes refuse;   28
   I, euer fro thys day.
My dere sone, y þe pray,
thys payne þu put Away,
   and yf hyt possybyll be may.'   32

6.   *Filius Regis Mortuus Est*

MS. Douce 78
(Sum. Catal. No. 21652)

A S Reson Rywlyde my Rechyles mynde,   [fol. 3ro]
  by wayes & wyldernes as y hadde wente,
a solempne cite fortunyd me to fynde;
to turne þer-to wes myne entente.   4

    27 MS. Now morne y.

I met a mayde at þe citeys ende,
snobbynge & syȝynge sche wes ny schente,
a fayrer foode had y not kende.
hurre herre, hure face, sche all to-rente,   8
Sche tuggyd & tere with gret turment;   [fol. 3ᵛᵒ]
sche brake hure skynne boþe body & breste,
and saide þese wordys euer as sche wente,
'filius Regis mortuus est.'   12

'The kyngis sone,' sche saide, 'is dede,
and kynge of kyngis his fadur is,
and y am his modur, þe well of rede.
my sone is go, my Ioy & my blys.   16
Alas! y sawe my dere chylde blede;
he may not speke to modur his.
I lullyd hym, y lapped him, y wolde him fede—
so cruelly wes neuyr childe slayn y-wys.   20
Ther wes neuer modur þat hedde sayn þis
but sche wolde wepe, þawe she louyd him leste.
no wondur þawe y be full of carefulnys,
for filius regis mortuus est.   24

Ther wes neuer modur þat lefte suche a fode be-hynde,
so petuesly slayn withoute trespas,
but sche wolde haue loste hur mynde,
and often tymes haue cryedde "alas!"   28
And y, þat knywe neuer of man-is kynde,
y bare him in my body, clene mayde as y was.
suche be þer no mo as clerkis canne fynde;
þan am y sche þat mooste cause has.   32
Throwe Ierłm stretis a man myȝte trace
þe blode of my childe like a beeste.   [fol. 4ʳᵒ]
suche wes myne happe, suche wes my grace,
for filius regis mortuus est.   36

9 turment] MS. turnement.

ffilius Regis, myne owne dere chylde,
y say him honge on þe crosse in my syȝte;
y lokyd on hym and hym behylde.
sone, se þi modur, a woful wyȝte.   40
I sownedde, I fyll downe in þe feelde,
I wolde haue spoke but y ne myȝte.
I snobbudde, I sykyd, I kowde not welde;
sorowe smote at myne herte, y fyll downe ryȝte.   44
My sone sawe his modur þus y-dyȝte,
so rufully his yes on me he keste,
as who seyth "fare wel, my modur bryȝte,
ffilius Regis mortuus est."   48

I cried þo died myne owne sone dere;
I swette, y sownydde, y saide "alas!"
no wondur þowe y carefull were—
my fadur, my broþer, my spouse he was,   52
Myne helpe, myne socour and all my chere.
nowe without broþer and spowse y moste hens pas,
fadurles & modurles y am lafte here,
as a woman forsake þat no goode has.   56
Gabriel, þu dedeste calle me full of grace;
nowe full of sorowe þu me seyste!
þe terys tryllyd downe be my face,
ffilius Regis mortuus est.   60

[I l]okyd upp on-to my childe,
y criede one þe Iues & bade hange
þe modyr by þe childe þat neuer was fylyde.
o dethe, a-lasse! þu doyste me wrange!   64
My sone þu sleyste, alasse þe whyle!
come, sle his modur, why taryeste so longe?

46 keste *first written* caste *and then cancelled.*
47 *On margin in same hand, marked for insertion.*
54 out *interlined above.*   61 to *above the line.*

þu morþer-man, why arte þu so vyle?
come to his modur þat dethe wolde fonge.   68
Thow sleyste my sone with paynys stronge,
come sle his modur at my requeste,
for y may synge a sorowfull songe,
filius Regis mortuus est.   72

[*Lines 73–108 supplied from MS. Rawlinson C. 86*]

Thou erth, I reclayme & appele,   [fol. 75ᵛᵒ]
That thou recewedst that gentill blod!
Thou stone, howe durst thou be so frayll
To be a mortes wherin his crosse stode?   76
Stone he made & erth eche dele
That bene regementis to the Rode.
Your maker ye sle; ye knowe righte well
he did neuer evill but euer did good.   80
He was euer meke & myld of mode,
Nowe lieth he wounded like a best.
Alas! my babe, my lyves fode
That filius Regis mortuus est.   84

Thou tree, thou crosse, howe durst .thou be   [fol. 76ʳᵒ]
The Instrument to hong thy maker soo?
Vnto his ffader [y] may appele the.
Thou were the cause of my sonnes wo—   88
No cause, but help that it so be.
Tre, Cry mercy, that art my ffoo!
Had thei ordeyned A rode for me
To haue hanged me thei had well doo   92
[But what may y seie, whidir schal y go?]
A Tree hath hanged A kyng full prest—
Suche kyngis there be no moo—
ffor filius Regis mortuus est.   96

85 MS. trees.
93 This line, skipped by the Rawlinson scribe, is supplied from
the Lambeth MS.

Thou scourge, with cordis thou brak the skyne
With hard knottis, I crye vpone the!
Ye bete my sonne that neuer did synne;
Why bete þou hym & spare me,   100
Made he nott the? thou woldest not blyne,
Thou teryst hys skynne & wold nott letţ.
Thou myghte nott sett the poynt of a pyne
Vpon hole skynne, so thou hym bett.   104
All blody was the brighte of his blee
Thou madist it blak or thou woldest sest.
ffader, one thi sonne haue pety,
ffor filius Regis mortuus est.   108

Cursyd Iues, why dude ye þusse?   [fol. 4vo]
how durste ye sle youre savyoure?
When he schall deme þen schall ye curse;
ye canne not hyde you from his scharpe schoure.   112
All oþer creaturys þey ar petuvsse:
þe sone, þe clowdys, for his doloure,
yn tokenynge þei changyd & mornyd tyll vsse
When ye dide hym þis dyshonowre.   116
The erthe quakyd, bothe temple & towre,
þat bare you synfull proude & preste.
þe planetis changed & made dolowre—
filius Regis mortuus est.   120

Mortuus est my soveren lorde,
ded is my dere childe, alasse!
nowe y may walke in þis falce worlde   [fol. 5ro]
as a wrecchyd wyȝte þat wantyth grace.   124
All þis y say to be recorde;
y myȝte no lengur loke hym in þe face.
And þus y came from caluarye-warde
Wepynge and waylynge þat y bore wasse.   128

    123 worlde *first written* worde *and then cancelled.*

yf eny man love me len me a plase
þat y may wepe my fylle and reste,
and euer more to crye "alasse, alasse!
filius Regis mortuus est".   132

Nowe, fadur of heuyns & celestiall leche,
y comende all my gydance to þi grete myȝte,
þi grace and power, hertely y beseche
onys or þat y dye, of my swete sone to have a syȝte. 136
þo sownyde a voice from heuen in fay,
yn-to þat vertuys virginis breste,
"þu schalte se þi swete sone and say,
ffilius Regis is a-lyve et non mortuus est."'   140
                                Explicit.

7.   *An Appeal to all Mothers*
                Cambridge Univ. MS. Ff. 5. 48

(1) OFf alle women þat euer were borne   [fol. 73ʳᵒ]
       That berys childur, abyde and se
How my son liggus me beforne
Vpon my kne, takyn fro tre.   4
Your childur ȝe dawnse vpon your kne
With laȝyng, kyssyng and mery chere;
Be-holde my childe, be-holde now me,
ffor now liggus ded my dere son, dere.   8

(2) O woman, woman, wel is the,
Thy childis cap þu dose vpon;
þu pykys his here, be-holdys his ble,
þu wost not wele when þu hast done.   12
But euer, alas! I make my mone
To se my sonnys hed as hit is here;
I pyke owt thornys be on & on,
ffor now liggus ded my dere son, dere.   16

         134 my *interlined above.* MS. degydance.

(3) O woman, a chaplet chosyn þu has
Thy childe to were, hit dose þe gret likyng,
þu pynnes hit on with gret solas;
And I sitte with my son sore wepyng,   20
His chaplet is thornys sore prickyng,
His mouth I kys with a carfull chere—
I sitte wepyng and þu syngyng,
ffor now liggus ded my dere son, derẹ.   24

(4) O woman, loke to me agayne,
That playes & kisses your childur pappys.
To se my son I haue gret payne,
In his brest so gret gap is   28
And on his body so mony swappys.   [fol. 73ᵛᵒ]
With blody lippys I kis hym here,
Alas! full hard me thynk me happys,
ffor now liggus ded my dere son, dere.   32

(5) O woman, þu takis þi childe be þe hand
And seis, 'my son gif me a stroke!'
My sonnys handis ar sore bledand;
To loke on hym me list not layke.   36
His handis he suffyrd for þi sake
Thus to be boryd with nayle & speyre;
When þu makes myrth gret sorow I make,
ffor now liggus ded my dere son, dere.   40

(6) Be-holde women when þat ȝe play
And hase your childur on knees daunsand;
Ye fele ther fete, so fete ar thay
And to your sight ful wel likand.   44
But þe most fyngur of any hande
Thorow my sonnys fete I may put here

43 *So in Chetham MS. and Ff.* 2. 38: *the reading in Ff.* 5. 48
is hopelessly corrupt: 'He fele þerfor fittys or day.'

And pulle hit out sore bledand,
ffor now liggus ded my dere son, dere.   48

(7) Therfor, women, be town & strete
Your childur handis when ȝe be-holde,—
Theyr brest, þeire body and þeire fete—
Then gode hit were on my son thynk ȝe wolde,   52
How care has made my hert full colde
To se my son, with nayle and speyre,   [fol. 74ʳᵒ]
With scourge and thornys many-folde,
Woundit and ded, my dere son, dere.   56

(8) þu hase þi son full holl and sounde,
And myn is ded vpon my kne;
thy childe is lawse and myn is bonde;
Thy childe is an life & myn ded is he—   60
Whi was this oȝt but for þe?
ffor my childe trespast neuer here.
Me thynk ȝe be holdyne to wepe with me,
ffor now liggus ded my dere son, dere.   64

(9) Wepe with me, both man and wyfe,
My childe is youres & lovys yow wele.
If your childe had lost his life
ȝe wolde wepe at euery mele;   68
But for my son wepe ȝe neuer a del.
If ȝe luf youres, myne has no pere;
He sendis youris both hap and hele
And for ȝow dyed my dere son, dere.   72

(10) Now, alle wymmen þat has your wytte
And sees my childe on my knees ded,
Wepe not for yours but wepe for hit,
And ȝe shall haue ful mycull mede.   76

49 MS. towm.   75 *Before* wepe *an* s *crossed out.*

He wolde agayne for your luf blede
Raþer or þat ʒe damned were.
I pray yow alle to hym take hede,
ffor now liggus ded my dere son, dere.   80

(11) ffare-wel, woman, I may no more   [fol. 74ᵛᵒ]
ffor drede of deth reherse his payne.
ʒe may lagh when ʒe list & I wepe sore,
That may ʒe se and ʒe loke to me agayne.   84
To luf my son and ʒe be fayne
I wille luff yours with hert entere,
And he shall brynge your childur & yow sertayne
To blisse wher is my dere son, dere,   88

Explicit fabula

8.   *O Thou, with Heart of Stone*

MS. Ashmole 189
(Sum. Catal. No. 6777)

THou synfull man of resoun þat walkest here vp &
downe,   [fol. 109ʳᵒ]
Cast þy respeccyoun one my mortall countenaunce.
Se my blody terys fro my herte roote rebowne,
My dysmayd body chased from all plesaunce,   4
Perysshed wyth þe swerd moste dedly of vengaunce.
Loke one my sorofull chere & haue ther-of pytee,
Be-wailynge my woo & payne, & lerne to wepe wyth
me.

Yf þu can not wepe for my perplexed heuynesse,   8
Yet wepe for my dere sone, which one my lap lieth ded
Wyth woundis Innumerable for þy wyckednesse,
Made redempcyoun wyth hys blood, spared not hys
manhed.
Then þe loue of hym & mornynge of my maydenhed   12

78 MS. dāmed.

Schuld chaunge thyne herte, & þu lyst behold & see
Hys deth & my sorow, & lerne to wepe wyth me.

Thyne herte so indurat is þat þu cane not wepe
ffor my sonnes deth ne for my lamentacyoun? 16
Than wepe for þy synnes, when þu wakest of þy slepe
And remembre hys kyndnes, hys payne, hys passioun,
And fere not to call to me for supportacyoun.
    I am thy frend vnfeyned & euer haue be; 20
    Loue my son, kepe well hys lawes, & come dwell
    wyth me.

9. *Who cannot Weep come Learn of me*

Rylands Lib. Manchester, Lat. MS. 395

Sodenly afraide, half waking, half slepyng   [fol. 120ʳᵒ]
and gretly dismayde, A wooman sate weepyng,

With fauoure in hir face ferr passyng my Reason,
    And of hir sore weepyng this was the enchesone:
Hir soon in hir lap lay, she seid, slayne by treason.
Yif wepyng myght ripe bee it seemyd þan in season. 4
    Ihesu, so she sobbid,
    So hir soone was bobbid
    and of his lif robbid,
Saying þies wordis as I say þee, 8
'Who cannot wepe come lerne at me.'

I said I cowd not wepe I was so harde hartid:
Shee answerd me with wordys shortly þat smarted,
'Lo! nature shall move þee thou must be converted 12
Thyne owne fadder þis nyght is deed',—lo þus she
        Thwarted—

13 MS. chaumce.   14 my *interlined above*.   18 MS. byndnes.
21 MS. som, *with a light stroke across the third minim of the* m.
MS. dewll.

'So my soon is bobbid
& of his lif robbid.'
forsooth þan I sobbid,   16
  Veryfying þe wordis she seid to me.
  Who cannot wepe may lerne at þee.

'Now breke hert, I the pray, this cors lith so rulye,
So betyn, so wowndid, entreted so Iewlye,   20
What wiȝt may me behold & wepe nat? noon truly!
To see my deed dere soone lygh bleedyng lo! this newlye.'
    Ay stil she sobbid
    so hir soone was bobbed   24
    & of his lif robbid,
  Newyng þe wordis as I say thee,
  'Who cannot wepe com lerne at me.'

                                                    [fol. 120ᵛᵒ]
On me she caste hire ey, said 'see, mane, thy brothir!'
She kissid hym & said, 'swete, am I not thy modir?' 29
In sownyng she fill there, it wolde be non othir;
I not which more deedly, the toone or the tothir.
    Yit she revived & sobbid,   32
    so hire soon was bobbid
    & of his lif robbid.
  'Who cannot wepe,' this was the laye,
  & with þat word she vanysht Away.   36

10.   *Our Lady's Imprecation*
           Cambridge Univ. MS. Ff. 5. 48

(1) Listyns, lordyngus, to my tale   [fol. 71ʳᵒ]
       And ȝe shall here of on story,
Is bettur then ouþer wyne or ale
Þat euer was made in this cuntry,   4

      23 Ay] MS. An. *Trin. Coll. MS.* Euer.

How iewys demyd my son to dye.
ychan a deth to hym þei drest.
'Alas!' seyd Mary þat is so fre,
'þat chylde is ded þat soke my brest.'   8

(2) 'O Judas how durst þu be so bolde
To betray my son to any iewe?
ffor xxx d. þu hym solde,
fful wel þu wist hit was not dewe.   12
Sore of þat bargan þu may rew,
þer-for þi saule in hel is drest.
Wo worth þe tyme þat I þe knew!
the childe is ded þat soke my brest.   16

(3) 'þer-for þi sorow shall never slake,
Traytur, for þi fals trayng.
þu made þe Iewys my son to take,
Caytef cursid, with þi kyssyng;   20
þer-for in hell shalle þu hyng,
þe fendis in fyre þi flessh shall fest.
Euer wo worth þi vpspryngyng!
þe childe is ded þat soke my brest.   24

(4) 'Among fendys þat be felle
Thy body bonys shal be brent,
þi dwellyng þer-for shalbe in hell,
With lucifere þi life is lent.   28
þu made my son on rode be rent,
þer rewth it was to se hym rest.
thus, traitur, þorow þi falles assent
the childe is ded þat soke my brest.   32

(5) 'Therfor, iewys, worth yow shame!   [fol. 71vo]
Off my richnesse ȝe haue me robbyd,
ȝe thoȝt ȝe hade a full gode game,
When ȝe my son with buffettes bobbyd,   36

He feld riȝt sore, no thyng he sobbyd
ffor alle your werkis full well he wist.
My ioy, my hert, ȝe al to-robbid,
the childe is ded þat soke my brest.   40

(6) 'Vn-to a pyler wondur sore
ȝe bonde hym þer to abyde.
ffor he leuyd not on your lore
ȝe bete hym both bak and side.   44
Vn-to pylot prest ȝe cryed
Þat on a crosse he shulde be fest.
Thus, trayturs, þorow your fals pride,
The childe is ded þat soke my brest.   48

(7) 'O wriȝt, how durst þu make þat tre—
Welaway! why did þu so—
Þer-on my son nayled to be
And for to suffur alle þis woo?   52
Alas! why was þu his foo?
He greuyd þe neuer þat I wist.
Now sones get I neuer moo,
The childe is ded þat soke my brest.   56

(8) 'With sharpe scourgis þei hym bete
And rent his flessh fro þe bon,
Till his blode stode at his fete,
With-in his body lefte þei non.   60
ffull stille he stode as eny ston
And lete yow bete hym as a beest.
Mourne I may & make gret mone,   [fol. 72ro]
The childe is ded þat soke my brest.   64

(9) 'O Iewys, how durst ȝe do þat spyte
To thirle my sonnes hert with a knyfe?
Mych of my woo I may yow wyte,
Owt of his brest ȝe bare þe life.   68

Thus to deth ȝe can hym drife,
To spoyle þat prince ȝe were ful prest.—
Dere son, þu myȝt haue stynt her strife—
The childe is ded þat soke my brest.   72

(10) 'The sonne hit sett alle at þe none,
The erth hit made a dolfull dyn—
Ther-by myȝt ȝe wete wrong had ȝe don,
ȝe had slayne þat lorde þat alle shall wyn—   76
The see to rore þen can begynne,
The clowdis ouer-cast, all liȝt was lest.
His myȝt was more þen ȝe may mynne,
He rose agayn þat soke my brest.   80

(11) 'With armyd knyȝtes ȝe can hym kepe,
And wende to haue holdyn hym in your holde,
But when he list þei were a-slepe
(ffor to wakyn þei were on-bolde)   84
The ston ouer hym he can vp-folde
And trad vpon þe pruddist prest,
And went his way wher-so he wolde—
The childe is risen þat soke my brest.   88

(12) 'Then to hell he toke þe way,
With wondis wyde and al blody.
The foule fendis to affray,   [fol. 72ᵛᵒ]
With hym he bare þe crosse of tre.   92
Helle ȝatis fel vpyn to þat fre
When my son with hande hym blest.
The fendis roryd when þei hym se—
The childe is risen þat soke my brest.   96

(13) 'Adam and eve with hym he toke,
Kyng Davyd, Moyses and salamon,
And harrowid helle euery noke,
With-in hit lefte he sowlis non   100

82 holdyn *interlined*.

But fendis in hit to dwell allon.
lucifer þer bonde he prest,
þer-in to bide as stille as ston—
The childe is risen þat soke my brest.'   104

(14) Thus scunfett he þe fendis fell,
And toke his pray þat he had boȝt,
And put hem in-to endlesse welle
Ther ioy and blisse faylis noȝt.   108
Now pray we to hym with hert & thòȝt,
That prince þat soke oure lady brest,
Owt of this worde when we are broȝt
With hym and hir in heuyn to rest.   112

Explicit

11.   *Stabat Mater Dolorosa*

MS. Ashmole 59
(Sum. Catal. No. 6943)

Here nowe filoweþe next a devoute Invocacioun to oure Ladye
[By þe Priour of Bridlington][1] with þe þe [sic] refrayde Stabat
mater dolorosa.

H Eyle! goddes moder dolorous,   [fol. 64ʳᵒ]
   By þe crosse stonding forwepped,
While þy sone hong ful pitous,
þe swerd of sorowe þyne hert kitte.   [fol. 64ᵛᵒ]   4

O howe muche sorouful drede
þowe sufferd, goddes moder, þoo,
To se þy sone pitously blede!
þe stremys of blode þane rane him fro.   8

[1] The ascription to the Prior of Bridlington stands at the top
of 64ᵛᵒ and 65ʳᵒ.
        2 *Read* for-grette *and thus restore the rime.*

O what is he þat may not weepe
Noþer with eghe nor with hert,
Þat seeþe þe, lorde, so lowe crepe!
Þou sykest and qwakst with smert.   12

O whane [he] taste bitter galle,
And gaf his goste til heven kynge,
He forgaf heos enmys alle
And þeire sore turmentyng.   16

O þou woful moder & mayde,
Þat hadest deþe in þy dolour,
Make my gooste with þee faste tyed
To him þat is my saveour.   20

O dolorous mayde so bright,
Make me to mowrone with þee,
Þat never by daye ne night
Youre stronge sorowe forgote be.   24

O glorious þou mayde mylde,
Make me to mowrne not to misse,
Þat arte glorefyde with þy chylde,
Þat of þi love I ne misse.   28

O þou virgyne mylde & meke,
Make me to weepe and wayle,
Þy childes peyne and þine eke,
Þat I no love chaunge for his.   32

O þou, ladye of ladyes alle,
ffor þy worþy names three:
Qwene of heven þe saintes calle,
And lady of þis worlde þou be.   36

27 blisse *dotted for deletion after* with.

O Emparyse of helle, þy name is kouþe
To þe Ioye of al man-kynde.
þer-fore homely nowe with mouþe
þowe mayst prey heven kynge.   40

O þou blest virgyne clere,
Beo redy, aye bytwene god and man
fful medyate, with þy prayer,
Ay, at moste neode of synful man.   44

O ladye, my sight most fayle
At þe blacnesse of my deth ;
My soule þane behoveþe wayle
ffor defaute of tonge & breth.   48

O howe myne herte þane wol qwake
ffor enmys to leye þeire lyne !
Now ladye, for þy childes sake,
Nowe helpe me, ladye, þat same tyme.   52

O glorious ladye ful of grace,
vowch nowe sauf to helpen me
And to withstonde þ'enmys face
And to destroye þeire gret poweste.   56

O ladye, remembre my preyer
þe whiche I make nowe vn-to þee,
And prey þy sone þat haþe no peer
To haue my sowle in his lovely eie.   60

O fayre ladye of aungelle floure,
In prophet and patryake desyre,
Dyademe of Martre and confessour,
Beaute of virgynes & sainte in feere.   64

60 MS. lovesy.

O ladye, þat arte so bright   [fol. 65ʳº]
As is þe sunne in þe ffirmament,
ffor þe gret ioye þou hadest in sight
whane þow were to heven went.   68

O ladye, come, þat dredful houre
Whane derk deþe shall m'assayle,
And beo to me sikur sokoure
þat alle þe feondes of me shal fay[l]e.   72

O lovely lady bright and sheene,
Kepe me þane frome ferdnesse,
ffrome þ'orryble sighte and kene
þat feondes make in þeire foulnesse.   76

O ladye of heven, þou mylde qwene,
And ladye of þis worlde þer-to,
And Emparyce of helle to beon
þe sayntes calle þee, þer fro.   80

O ladye, for þat gret honoure
Þat þou haste for synners sake,
Þowe helpe me in þat stronge stour
Whane þey frome hens wolde me take.   84

12. *Hail, Mother and Virgin Immaculate*

B.M. Addit. MS. 20059

ALl haile! lady, mother & virgyn immaculate,   [fol. 98ᵛº]
Haile! mary, most precious that bare our savyour ihū
Haile! clarified cristall, haile! wife mundificate.
Haile! rote of grace, our ioy thow did renewe   4
ffor the holy gost did clerely in the yssue.
Our soles for lacke had ells perresshed sore
Nere throȝ the helpe of our highe redemptour.

All haile! whose solempne glorious concepcioun   8
ffull of glorie and hye ioye tryumphaunte,
Bothe celestyall & terrestriall gif laude with Iubilacioun
Of new ioy & gladnesse with solace incessaunte.
Alhaile! whose natiuite to vs is solempnysaunte,   12
fferens lucem vt lucyfer, lux oriens,
Dyademe Angelicall, verum solem preveniens.

Alhaile! be thy mekenes sine viro fecunditas,
Whose Amyable Annunciacioun to vs was redempcion. 16
Ioye therfore be to the, tu summa suavitas,
And glorified be the houre of thy incarnacioun,
By whome we advoyde the infernall dampnacioun.
So dulcour was the ground in whom crist hym planted. 20
O mater most illuminate, we my3t not the haue wanted.

Haile! true chast virgyn & mother immaculate,
Whose pure purificacion to vs was purgacion.
Haile! replete with all virtue Angelicate,   24
Whose celestiall hye Ascendaunte Assumpcion
Was oure gret ioye and glorificacion.
Wherfore, dere lady, solistrice be for grace
That we with thy son in heyven may haue a place.   28

13. High Empress and Queen Celestial

MS. Arch. Seld. B. 24
(Sum. Catal. No. 3354)

O Hie Emperice and quene celestiall,   [fol. 137ᵛᵒ]
  Princes eterne and flour Immaculate,
Oure souerane help quhen we vnto the call,
Haile! ros Intact, virgyne Inuiolate,   4
That with the fader was predestinate
To bere the floure and makar of vs all,

9 hye *interlined above.*

And with no spue of crime coinquinate,
Bot virgyne pure, clerare than Cristall.   8

O blissit ros, o gemme of chastitee,
O well of beautee, rute of all gudenace,
O way of bliss, flour of virginitee,
O hede of treuth, o sterr without dirknace,   12
Graunt me synfull, lyuing In vnclennace,
To sew the path of parfyte cheritee,
And to forsake my synnis more and less,
Ay serving him þat sched his blud for me.   16

O blissit lady, fillit of all gudenace,
Sen all my hope and traist is in ȝour grace,
Beseke ȝour sone for ȝour hie gentilnace
To grant me laisar or I dee, and space,   20
All vicious lyf out of my saule to race;
And euer to lyve in vertew and clenace.
Out of the fendis bandis and his brace,
Now, glorious lady, help of ȝour gudenace.   24

ffor rycht as phebus with his bemys brycht
Illuminate all this erd In longitude,
Rycht so ȝour grace, ȝour beautee, and ȝour mycht
Anournyt all this warld in latitude: 28
Tharfore to me now schaw ȝour gratitude,
Off ȝour magnificence, þat day and nycht
ȝour benigne grace be to me lyvis fud;
And me to saue from euery maligne wicht.   32

ffor though Leuiathan, the ald serpent, [fol. 138ro]
Dissauit had oure parenes prothoplaust,
That In this warld doune has, Indigent,
Maid him to be put till at the last   36

33 serpent] MS. spent.

Eternale deth, quhilk euer suld haue last.
Knawing 3our pure and Incorrupt entent
Incomparable, the holy gaste als fast
Into 3our Innocence doune has sent,   40

And 3ow Illumynit with that blisful lycht
I mene the sone of the hie deitee
That on a croce suspendit was on hicht
ffor the redemption of humanite.   44
Quharfor throu 3ow, my souerane lady free,
Mankynde redempt was; tharefore day & nycht
In euery place blissit mote 3e be
Eternaly, abufe all erdly wicht.   48

                              Qd Chaucere.

14.   *Thou shalt Bear the Fruit of Life*

Harley MS. 2251

(1) **A**L hayle, Mary ful of grace!   [fol. 1ᵛᵒ]
        Oure lord of heven is with the;
His mansioun in the made he has,
Also of the borne shal he be.   4
His glorious body shaltow see,
Naked lyeng in an oxe stalle;
And til hym present shal kynges thre
Gold, Mirre and Incence Royall.   8

(2) Blessed be thow among wymmen alle!
Thow shalt be mayde, moder and wyf—
Al cristen men so the shal calle,
ffor thow shalt bere the fruyt of lyf.   12
That blessid child shal breke the stryf
Betwene the devil and al mankynd;
Man shal he bryng from al myschief,
The wey to hevene than shal he fynde.   16

(3) Seynt Anne, thy moder, ful blessid is she,   [fol. 2ro]
ffor she the bare by myracle dyvyṇe;
An aungel hir warned, sent fro the Trynite,
The fruyt of hir shuld right ferre shyne,   20
ffor to sconfite the snake serpentyne
Whiche of manhod had dominacion—
Man shuld be delyuerd from al tribulacioun.

(4) O mary, moder of al consolacioun,   24
Nempned so thow were—th'aungel bare witnesse—
Of Anne; thow were deliuered a grete confortacioun
ffor man, to bryng hym owte of distresse,
Both pure and clene set in al holynesse,   28
Ihesu, thy sone, hym lyked wele thy gouernaunce;
Replenysshed were thow with vertu of mekenes—
Of thi pappis sowkid he for oure sustinaunce.

(5) Whan hym lyked he made purviaunce,   32
Mankynd for to bryng vnto saluacioun,
ffor of man he had a goode Remembraunce—
To suffre deth, that was his conuersacioun.
Of his peynes he made a demonstracioun   36
Whan he tolde his Apostels of his peynes sore:
To save mankynd, that was his entencioun,
Ellis al the world had be forlore.

(6) Thow wrecchid man, leve thy pride   40
And thynk from erth that thow came;
Here thow mayst nat long abyde.
Bowe thy knees,—spare for no shame—
Whan thow herist Ihc̄, oure lordis name.   44
Wele art thow bounde so for to do,
Sith aungelis and devils knele therto.

19 the *interlined above.*

15.   *A Salutation to the Virgin*

Corpus Christi Coll. Oxf. MS. 155

Aue

HAile be þou! hende heven qwene   [fol. 250ᵛᵒ]
    þat thurgh chastite was chosen with
        childe,
Mary, most to þe I meene,
Moder meke and mayden mylde,   4
With-owten wem or wo I wene,
Oure herte of bale in þe gun belde,
Clens me owte of cares kene
And wreke awaye my warkes wylde.   8

Maria

Mary, ihū darlynge dere,
þus I thynke in my thoghte,
Wele I wate if synne ne were
Goddes moder ware þou noght,   12
ffor synne he fanged þe to fere,
To wyn & wele he haues þe wroghte.   [fol. 251ʳᵒ]
Helpe, hende, to I am here,
þat I be his þat me dere boghte.   16

Gracia

Of grace is graunted þe þat gate,
þat na gude will for-gete,
Heghly hende, heuen ȝate,
þat syttes be-syde þy sun sete,   20
þere my ȝernynge þou ne hate,
When dede sall founde my flesche to fete ;
ffor, than to luf is to late,
When wormes make of me þere mete.   24

Plena

ffull was fillyd þy flesche,
And derly dyghte, þrogh deyte ;
And sythen with nayles nayled was,
And forthe þan was taken to a tre.   28

15 to = till, ' while '.

            Þe water & blode, þy wemmes it wesche,
            Of þat body was borne of þe;
            My rede is noght worthe a rysche
            Bot mary haue mercy on me.   32

Deus   Oure lorde lyked forto lende
            And man be made in myddell erthe;
            Sone his sonde gun he sende,
            To þy will his wyrschyp werde.   36
            ffor his loue helpe me, hende,—
            Of folyes fell I fele me a-ferde—
            & fecche me fro þe fende;
            I doute on domesdaye to be a-deryd. 40

Tecum   With þe he was and ay sall be, [fol. 251ᵛᵒ]
            ffader & sone & haly gaste
            Trewly taken in trinite,
            And þou, moder & mayden chaste,   44
            Þe serten sothe I teche þe,
            Of all menskes þis was the maste.
            ffor his loue þat lightyd in þe,
            Þan saue my sawle in haste.   48

Benedicta tu Blyssed be þou euere and aye
            In lede þat þe þat luf lente.
            Moder, if þou þy sone will praye
            Þat neuere no sawll sall be schente, 52
            fforsothe þy sone will noght saye naye—
            It was his awen commaundemente;
            He will be buxome to þe aye
            ffor in þy worschep wome he wente. 56

In mulieribus In women wate I none þin ewen,
            God tempill, trewe to tell,
            Lady of erthe, qwene of hevene,
            And holden emprice of helle.   60

            57 MS. þi newen.

Stable sterne, here my stevene
ffor all my frendes whare so þay dwelle,
ȝif I þere names I ȝow noght nevene,
Defende þam fro the fendes of hell.   64

Et benedictus Blyssed be þou eueremare,   [fol. 252ʳᵒ]
Mayden moder, mary mylde,
Þy sone of þy body þou bare
And þy fayred was neuere fylde.   68
I byseke þe with ȝernynge ȝare
Þat þou praye to þy blissed childe,
Of this werlde when I sall fare,
ffro þe foule fende þat ȝe me schelde. 72

ffructus The frute of þe makes me bothe full & fede,
Swete ihū mylde of mode,
Till his bredyr gan he bede
Als brede & wyne his flesche & blode. 76
Mary, for thy maydenhede,
Þou gif me grace to fang þat fode
Before my dede þat I drede,
He graunte me grace of gates gode.   80

ventris tui Of þy body þan was he borne,
And þou with hym wroght wemles,
ffor folyce fell oure fader byforne
Ihū þe to moder he chese,   84
Rede ros with-owten thorne,
Þat byrde þou bare, þe Prince of pes.
Ne lat my saule neuere be lorne
Bot wyssed whare þy will es.   88

Ihesus Amen Ihū, ware noght þy mercy were, [fol. 252ᵛᵒ]
My gude ware noght worthe a bene.
Thorugh meuynge of þat mayden mere,
Þat mediatur is made in men.   92

62 MS. ffor all my foes for all my frendes.   90 MS. abene.

Now to lof lystens and lere,
Swylke loue in lede I may ȝow lene
Als present ȝe þis prayere here,
Hayle be þou, heven quene!   96

16.   Mary, Pray thy Son for us

Caius College Camb. MS. 383

Virgo rosa virginum tuum precare filium [p. 68]

ALle ȝe mouwen of ioye synge,
  fro heuene ys come god typynge,
mary mylde, þat gode þyng,
      Iam concepit filium.   4

Quene of heuene, wel þe be!
Godes sone ys borene of þe
forte make vs alle fre
      Ab omni labe criminum.   8

Wanne þat he of her bore was,
In a crache wyt hey & gras,
& for houre synne diede on cros
      Surexit die tercia.   12

Aftur hys ded, in hys vp-rysyng
To heuene he toc hys vp-styyng,
Þer he dwellus wyt-oute lesyng,
      Deus super omnia.   16

Marie, modur wyt-oute wemme,
Brytur þan þe sonne-bem,
Þe has taken wyt hym
      ad celi palacia.   20

6 MS. beroñ.

To þe we makun houre mone,
Pray for vs to þy sone,
Þat we mowene wyt hym wone
    In perhennum Gloria.   24

17.   *Enixa Est Puerpera*

MS. Ashmole 1393
(Sum. Catal. No. 7589)

Enixa est puerpera

A lady þat was so feyre & briȝt   [fol. 69ᵛᵒ]
    velut maris stella
Browȝt forth ihū full of miȝt,
    parens et puella.   4

Lady, flor of all þing,
    rosa sine spina,
Þat barist ihū heuyn king,
    gracia diuina.   8

All this world was for-lore,
    eua peccatrice,
til þat ihū was y-bore
    de te genitrice.   12

Of al wymmen þu art beste,
    felix fecundata,
To al wery þu art reste,
    mater honorata.   16

Wel I wote he is þi sone
    ventre quem portasti;
Then wol grant þe þi bone,
    Infans que[m] lactasti.   20

            21 MS. Tho þe.

Hou swete he is, hou meke he is,
    ullus memorauit ;
In heuyn he is & heuyn blys
    nobis preparauit.   24

Of all wymmen þu berist þe price,
    mater generosa,
Grawnt vs all paradys,
    virgo gloriosa.   28

18. *Ave Maris Stella*
Sloane MS. 2593

AUe maris stella, þe sterre on þe see,   [fol. 27ʳᵒ]
  dei mater alma, blyssid mot Xe be,
atque semper virgo, prey þi sone for me,
felix celi porta, þat I may come to þe.   4
Gabriel þat archangyl he was massanger,
so fayre he gret our lady with an aue so cler.
heyl be þu, mary! be þu, mary,
ful of godis grace & qwyn of mercy.   8
Alle þat arn to grete wiþoutyn dedly synne,
forty dayis of pardoun god grauntyt hym.

19. *Hail, Star of the Sea*
B.M. Addit. MS. 37049
Aue maris stella dei Mater Alma.

HAyle! se sterne, gods modyr holy,   [fol. 27ᵛᵒ]
  pray þu þi swete son safe vs fro foly
þat walks in þis warld lyke vn-to þe se,
Ebbyng & flowyng ful of vanyte.   4

In the MS. lines 5, 6 follow immediately after lines 1, 2.
2 MS. 'And' *crossed out before* 'pray'.

ffor to al wretches þat wil for-sake þair syn
þow schynes as a sterne þaim redy to wyn,
And euer-more redy for vs to pray
To gytt vs forgyfnes withouten delay,   8
Of al oure synnes & gret trespes
þat we hafe done both more & les.
Now, swete lady both meke & mylde
And moder of god, mayden vnfyled,   12
Crowned abofe al angels, qwene of heuen,
Blyssed art þu þerfore euer-more to neuen.
þow pray þi son to gif vs grace our lyfe to mende
And his byrnyng luf in-to vs sende.   16
Thynk on gode, lady, þus for vs to praye,
þat we with þe may dwelle for euer & ay. Amen.

20.   *Mary, Bright Star of Heaven and*
Holy Church

Univ. of Edinburgh. Laing MS. 149

O farest lady, o swetast lady,   [fol. iv]
o blisful lady, hewynnis quheyne.

O Sterne so brycht, þat gyfys lycht
til hewyne & haly kyrk,
þi help, þi mycht grant ws ful rycht.
Raik throw þire clowdis dirk;   4
fra hel sa fel conwoy ws clene.
one þe, mare, þus most I meyne.

thow ruby red, þat rasis ded
and grantis synnarise þare lyf,   8
for til remeid þe fendis pleid
quha can þi help discrif?

6 MS. 'redy for to' *with* 'for' *crossed out.*
7 MS. 'vs for to' *with* 'for' *crossed out.*   1 MS. streñ.
8 MS. 'synnes oure'.

but þe, lady, quha may sustene
þare warldly lustis bath scharp & kene?　　12

Þow wel of grace, ostend þi face
quhen ded sal ws persew.
away þow chase of fendis þe brase;
ask at þi sone Ihū,　　16
one ruyd his blud þat bled betwene
for oure traspass, before þin eyne.

now, lady myne, þi ere inclyne
to me þi seruitour.　　20
quhen I go hyne, hef my saul fra pyne.
þow keip it in þi cwre,
In place quhare grace ay growis grene,
foreuer In ioy þar-til contein.　　24

　　O farest lady, o swetast lady,
　　o blisful lady, hewynnis quheyne.

21.　　　　　*Hail, Queen of Heaven*

Arundel MS. 285

HAill! quene of hevin & steren of blis;　　[fol. 196vo]
Sen þat þi sone þi fader Is,
How suld he ony thing þe warn,
And thou his mothir and he þi barne?　　4

Haill! fresche fontane þat springis new,　　[fol. 197ro]
The rute and crope of all vertu,
Thou polist gem without offence,
Thou bair þe Lambe of Innocence.　　8

18 MS. þi neyne.　　　　25 *first* lady *interlined above.*
　　　　　　1 MS. steren^t.

22.   *Ave Gloriosa*

Arundel MS. 285

Ane deuoit orisoun   To oure Lady The Virgin mary, Callit
Aue Gloriosa   [fol. 193ro]

Haill! Glaid and glorius,   [fol. 193vo]
    Haill! virgin hevinnis queyne,
Haill! grane maist glorius
That Is or euer hes bene—
Off the, mary, I mene.   5

Haill! plant maist Precius   [fol. 194ro]
ffor manis medicyne,
Thow wesche all vicius
The flesche for to refrene
And keipe our conscience cleyne.   10

Haill! cumly cristell cleir
Abone þe ordouris nyne,
Als blith as bird on brer,
On ws synnaris to schyne
Off thy deuoit doctryne.   15

HAill! CRistis mothir Deir
And doctrix maist diuine,
Oure harmes for till heir
Thy eir till ws inclyne,
And saife our saulis fra pyne.   20

Haill! Seder Scheyne, Haill! virgin cleyne,
Ay glemmand into glore,
Haill! cipros greyne, Haill! fra the, Soleyne,
Our saullis saif fra Sore,   [fol. 194vo]
To synnaris send Succour.   25

18 MS. harnes.   21 MS. cleyne virgine.
                  23 MS. Spleyne.

Haill! well I weyne Off grace bedeyne,
Till cairfull creatour;
To the we meyne Oure caris keyne,
Thou art our trew tressour,
Off bewte the mirrour.   30

Thow flagrant flour Off sueit Sapoure,
Haill! deir Dochter of Ann,
In thy closour our Saluiour
Wes Iounit god and man,
In the oure grace began.   35

Haill! brichtest Sterne, Haill! licht lucern,
Off vertu well but vice,
Thow ws gouerne ffra feindis Inferne,   [fol. 195ʳᵒ]
O port of parradice,
Thou precius perle of prise.   40

O mary meik, we the beseik,
Befor þe Iuge quhen sall meit,
Off thy prayer we þe require,
Defend ws fra our fa
On dreidfull domesday.   45

O madin myld That bur þe child,
Quhilk for the gilt
And gret misdeid He sore did bleid
On croce on gude friday
And wesche ws fra all wa.   50

Thow art the band of our blising,
Doun discending fra dauid king;
Our souerane of þe did spring,
The way of verryte,
O mothir of mercy.   55

42 sall meit] ? *read* we sall ga.
47 *Defective; rime word missing.*

PErfit plesand and moist benyng,   [fol. 195ᵛᵒ]
But pryde, pacient attour all thing,
Thy haly hand to bliss ws bring,
Thou trone of Salomone,
Thou fleis of Iedeoun,   60
Thou mothir and mad allone,
But carnall corrupcioun.

Thou cheif of chaistite,
Thow well of virginite,
At the we seik suppley   65
Agains our enemye.

BEfor our Lord Meis all discord,
Thou be our beild fra blame ;
We be restord To ferme concord,
Beseiking his haly name.   70

HAill! wilsum wicht Thow counsall richt [fol. 196ʳᵒ]
ffra falset and defame,
Mothir of mycht, Baith day and nicht
Scheild ws fra Syn & schame.

Thow cleir clarite Off Sapour sueit,   75
The haly spreit The purifyit,
And maid the meit Our blis to beit,
Specull of pulcritude,
Thou seid of Sanctitude.

ffor grace we greit Befor thy feit,   80
With teris weit And hert contret,
Thi mirthis meit In hevinnis streit
Schawand thy Celsitude   [fol. 196ᵛᵒ]
With glore and gratitud.

70 MS. nane.   74 MS. schame & Syn.

Haill! fairest forme of face,   85
To saulis succour send,
And Len ws tyme & space
Oure mis for till amend,
ffra dewillis ws defend.

Haill! ground of all our grace,   90
We ws to the commend;
The blis of hevin ws brace,
Off þis warld quhen we wend.

      Amen finis.

23.   *Ave Regina Celorum, I*

        Trinity College Dublin MS. 516

A deuowte[1] salutacion of Aue regina celorum   [fol. 23ᵛᵒ]

HAile be þu, maide, modir of crist!
  Haile be þu, blessidest þat euer bare childe!
Haile! comeli quene, mari þu hight,
    Haile! nory of goodnesse, maide so milde,   4
    Haile! fairest floure, þat neuer was defilid.
      Haile! wit and welle of al visdom,
    Haile! loueli lely þat syne exilid,
      Aue Regina celorum.   8

Haile! rose ryal, comfort of care,
  Haile! blessid ladi bothe faire & bright,
Haile! swete salue for al maner sare,
    Haile! lanterne of light brening light,   12
    Haile! blessid berde in þe is pight,
      Haile! ioye of mankynde boþe al & sum,
    Haile! pynacle precious in heuyn be right,
      Mater regis angelorum.   16

      [1] deuow *struck through before* deuowte.

Haile! crownde quene, fairest of alle,
  Haile! flouer on þe feld, ouur blisse on-brad,
Haile! to whom women do calle,
  Altyme þat þei ben hard be-stad,   20
Haile! whom al þe fendys drede
  And euer schul in-to þe day of doum.   [fol. 24ro]
With maydenis milke þi sone þu fed,
  O Maria flos virginum.   24

Haile be þu, fairest þat euyr god fand!
  Haile be þu rechest of al tresoure!
Haile! lampe euyr lightand,
  To hie & lowe, riche and poure,   28
Haile! spices swettest of al sauoure,
  Haile! of whom oure ioye gan coum,
Haile! of alle wemen frute & floure,
  Velut Rosa vel lilium.   32

Haile be þu, godely ground of al grace!
  Haile! blessid sterre shini[n]ge on þe see,
Haile! counfortable counfort in euury case,
  Haile! aftur god chefe of charite,   36
Haile! wit and welle of al merce,
  Haile! þat bare oure lord ihū al & sum,
Haile! tabernacle of þe trinite,
  ffunde preces ad filium.   40

Haile be þu, virgyn of al vertues!
  Haile! blessid modir þat al may wilde,
Haile! noried norse of swet Ihesus,
  Haile! mari, mode[r] & maide milde,   44
Now lady to thi sone þu say,
  That we may come to his kyngdou[m].
ffor me and al cristen þu pray,
  pro salute fidelium.   48

24.   *Ave Regina Celorum, II*

Porkington MS. 10

OFf all þe bryddus þat euer ȝeyt were,   [fol. 88ᵛᵒ]
    so fayre, so freche as þer is wone,
Was neuer ȝeyt myȝt be here pere,
    Made of fleche, blode and boñe.   4
This bryde sche ys wittouttyne pere,
    And perles euyre-more schall be;
Wherefore I þynke, in good manere,
    To hayle here witt an aue.   8
A blessyte frut schew forthe gane bry[ng],
    ffor vs dethe soffyrde alle & somme;
There-fore to hure now wyle I synge,
    Ave regyna celorume.   12

hayle be þu! mare, bleyssyd foode,
    And blessyd mot þu euyre be!
Thow se þy sone vppon þe rovde;
    ffor owre syne dethe soffyrd he—   16
he was full mercyfull & ful good,   [fol. 89ʳᵒ]
    When he for vs syche payne wold dre;
His mercy passytȝ all erthely good.
    þer-fore we pray þe with hert fre,   20
þu helpe vs, lady, as þu may beste,
    And gravnt vs þat we may come
There þu art callyd, witt most & leste,
    M[a]tere regys angelorum.   24

Hayle be þu! now wyrgyne clere,
    The holly gost lyȝt þe witt-In;
Thow bare a chyld of gret powere,
    A neuer was fylyd witt no syne.   28

7 þynke] *corrected from* þynge.   8 MS. So hayle.
9 schew] *read* sche.   18 MS. dur'

Thow stod full stylle witt myld chere
  And hyme consaywyd. witt mykyl wynne.
He perssyd þi wombe as son soo clere,
  And ȝeyt þu was a cleyne wyrgyne.   32
Of alle wyrgyns, þu art callyd modyre,
  þat euer bare lyfe vndyre-nethe þe sone.
I say by þe & by no nodyre,
  O mater flos virginum.   [fol 89ᵛᵒ] 36

Haylle be þu! quene moste comely,
  þat euyr was formyd both fare & nere!
Therefore I hayle þe worschypfully—
  In all þe world was neuer þy pere.   40
Thy sone ys kynge moste worthy & myȝty,
  ffor ouer alle thyngus ys his powere.
And welle I wote & lefe fully
  he wylle deme þe best prayere;   44
þerefor þu pray þat bleyssydfull kynge,
  þat þe blys in-with þe may wonne,
þere as þu art euer, with ray schynnyng
  Velud rosa wel lylyom.   48

hayl be þu! now fayrryst of face,
  Thyn eerys to vs þu wolt inclyne.
We pray þe pray for ovre trespas,
  þat we be sawyd frome helle pyne.   52
þu gravnt vs for þi mekull grace,
  as þu arte emprys of helle & heyuyn,
Defend vs frome þe ffeynndus mallys,   [fol. 90ʳᵒ]
  And lete vs neuer with hyme be evyne.   56
To þe, lady, now dewoutlye
  We aske hit witt dewocyoune,
That þu pray for vs full herttely,
  ffunde preces ad felium.   60

  51 *Before* ovre *the scribe wrote the first stroke of* v.

Hayle be þu nowe! most worthy flovre
    That euer was vppone þe grovnde,
ffor þu arte emprys of þe heyȝthyst tovre
    That euer ȝete was I-fond.   64
In þat hyþe place þu hast hovnowre,
    As þu arte worthy, of fre & bond,
ffor þer ys Ioy with-ovte dolovre,
    And blyse euer-more I vndure-stonde.   68
Vnto þat blys, lady, vs brynge,
    Where þu art quene of alle and some;
þu pray þi sone, þer he his kynge,
    Pro salute fydellium.   72

þu grant vs, lady, ovre askynge,
    As we can to [non] nodyre calle;   [fol. 90ᵛᵒ]
But when we euer eyllys anny þinge
    One þe we cry, bothe one & alle.   76
þer-for, lady, make herkenynge
    Vnto vs synfull or þat we falle,
That we may at oure hyndynge
    To dweylle with þe in þi hyȝe halle.   80
Now, lady, make vs þis be-heste,
    That we may come to þe alle & some—
Then may we synnge, bothe Most & leste,
    Ave regyna celorome.   Et C.   84

25.   *Salve Regina*

MS. Bodley 423
(Sum. Catal. No. 2322)

Salue regina

HEyl! comely creature curteys of kynde,   [fol. 164ʳᵒ]
    Chaast quene of konnyng, of comfort & counsail,
The moderhed of thy mercy to oure soules sende,
Worthily to thy worship that we may say 'al heyl'.   4

Lijf & likyng in the lay allone
Whan þe swetnesse of our saueour þe dide assaile,
Now helpe vs, our hope in oure mykel mone,
Meue up our myndes to the, & merciful moder, al
    hayle!   8

As careful caitifs & combred we crye,
Outlawes & outcastes, the sones of synne,
As the heires of eue to thy pyte we preie,
Weilyng & wepyng, thy welthes to wynne.   12

In this dale of dolour dresse vp our dedes,
Holyest of halowes hyghe, the we preye,
 Our speker & our spye, specialy now spede vs,
Turne towarde trespassours thin almesful eye.   16

And ihū that is gentel, bountiful & blessed,   [fol. 164vo]
the fruyt of oure feith & fode of þy wombe,
shewe vs his shinyng after þis exile wrecched,
Merciful maide, helpe vs wiþ thyn honde.   20

Mary, moder & mayden, cherissher of þi chirche,
euerlastyng gate of ioye and of eese,
refresshe vs wiþ þy refute, wel þat we may wirche,
the fader & thy fode graunte vs to plese.   24

Meke mayde & mylde, softe & right swete,
the praiers of thy peple gadere with thy grace,
the lust of oure leudenes lere vs to lete,
teche vs þe trewe way to take & to trace.   28

Oure sorwe & our siknes shewe to thy sone,
that pricked was & peyned & clenched on þe cros:

to dryue downe our deth his manhod he nome
that doolfully dyed and richely aroos.   32

After þe birthe verrely clene maiden þu were;
goddys moder, mary, haue mynde on our preiere.

26.   *An Expansion of Salve Regina*

B.M. Addit. MS. 37049

Salve Regina

Salue	HAyl! oure patron & lady of erthe, [fol. 29ᵛᵒ]
Regina	qwhene of heuen & emprys of helle,
Mater	Moder of al blis þu art, þe ferth,
Misericordie	Of mercy & grace þe secunde welle. 4
Vita	lyfe come of þe, as þe sownde of a bell
Dulcedo	Swetnes, þu art both moder & mayde,
Et spes n̄ra	Oure hope with þe þat we may dwelle
Salue	Hayl! ful of grace as gabriel sayd. 8
Ad te	To þe oure socour, our helpe, oure trust,
Clamamus	We crye, we pray, we make oure complaynt,
Exules	Exylde to pryson fro gostly lust.
ffilij	þe childer of adam, þat so was ataynte 12
Eue	Of eue our moder, here, ar we dreynte.
Ad te	To þe, þat byndes þe fendes whelpe,
Suspiramus	We sighe, we grone; we wax al faynte
Gementes	Wepyng for sorow, gode lady, now helpe! 16

16 for *interlined above.*

Et flentes	Wepyng for syn & for oure payne,
In hac	In þis derknes oure tyme we spende;
Lacrimarum	Of teres þe comforth is a swete rayne,
Valle	In þe wayle of grace it will discende.

[fol. 30ʳᵒ]

Eya	Hafe done, gode lady, grace is þi frende; 21
Ergo	þerfore send vs sum of þi grace.
Aduocata	Oure aduocate, make vs a-fore our ende
Nostra	Oure synnes to wesche whils we hafe space. 24

Illos tuos m. o.	þi mercyful eene & lufly loke
Ad nos conuerte	Cast opon vs for oure disporte.
Et Ihesum	And Ihū, þi babe, þat þi flesche toke,
Benedictum	So blyssed a lord, make vs supporte, 28
Fructum	þat fruyt of lyfe may vs comfort.
Ventris tui	Of þi wome þe fruyt may suffyse
Nobis	To vs, whorby we may resorte,
Post hoc	Aftyr þis exyle, to paradyse. 32

Exilium	Exyle is greuos in þis derk werre;
Ostende	Schewe vs þi lust, þe stronger to fyght.
Benignū	Benygne lady & our se sterre,
O clemens	O buxum lanterne, gyf vs þi lyght. 36
O pia	O meke, o chaste, o blistfull syght,
O dulcis	O swete, o kynde, o gentyll & fre,
Maria	Mary, with Ihū þat Ioyful knyght,
Salue	Hayle & fare wele! & þinke on me!
	Amen. 40

17 *Before* payne *a word* (? rayne) *has been cancelled.*
18 derknes] *interlined above; on the line,* deʳknes.
39 Ioyful] *supplied in margin to replace* gentyl, *cancelled.*

27.   *Regina Celi Letare*, I

MS. Laud Miscell. 213
(Sum. Catal. No. 1045)

Regina celi letare &c. Nota quod in ista antiphona sumitur alleluya 4 modis scilicet quod 4 ibi sunt alleluya. Quia alia alleluya tamen valet sicut lauda deum creatura, alia lux vita & laus, alia saluum me fac deus, alia pater & filius & spiritus sanctus; sic autem est ista antiphona intelligenda.

> Quene of heuen, mak þu murth,   [fol. 186ʳᵒ]
> & prays god with all þi myght,
> for of þe he tok hys burth,
> þat is heele, lyf & lyght.   4
>
> He rose fro deth so sayd he.
> Save vs gode, in nede moste!
> pray for vs þe trinite,
> ffader & sone & holy gost.   8

28.   *Regina Celi Letare*, II

Pepys MS. 1236
(Magdalene Coll. Cambridge)

> [R]Egina celi and Lady, letare,   [fol. 98ᵛᵒ]
> Lemyng lely & in place of lyght,
> Quia quem meruisti portare
> Ve ben sett sempiterne in his syght.   4
> Resurrexit as he sayde to the
> By myracle of his grete myght.
> Into heuyn ascendyd with humanyte,
> Aboue the orders of Angelys bryght,   8

6 MS. gerte.

Gloryouse lady, gete vs that ryght
    To thi ryall mansyon vnto be nome,
After the deth when we be dyght,
    Maria virgo virginum.   12

O kynde curatrix, to thi caytif kyd,
    To cure oure sore þou keptyst a corn.
With-in thy bowelys thow bare a bryd,
    The blessedyst blossum þat euer was born,   16
Oure holy lorde on the was hydde.
    By hyrying of a Angels horn,
A mansuete message was the amydde,
    Godys moder to be callyd at euyn & morn.   20
    Lykly, lady, we were to be lorn,
        And cast in seruage all & sum;
    Make vs be founde thy face beforn,
        Maria virgo virginum.   24

O pia, precyous, pure princes,
    Pynnacle of price of thre persones,
Too bemes of blysse is thy bryghtnes,
    Y-blessyd be ye in blode & bones!   28
Thy louely lyppys of bryghtnes
    Lappe me fro longyng, lady, ones;
As ye be mayde of all myldenes,
    & ther-to ryght, agayn all mones.   32
    Thy dwellyng is in worthy wonys,
        Exaltyd into þat heye solum.
    Good lady, gouerne us fro gronys,
        Maria virgo virginum.   36

O clemens, castell of chastyte,
    Coruna cristi, comely thyng,
Tabernakyll of the trynyte!
    Full tendere was thy trewe louyng.   40

O Ioye, generosa of Iesse,
  Ihū, thy Iewell, is oure Ioyyng.
O spes nostra, specyous to see,
  Salue regina, to the we syng!   44
    O mons, swete mary, when þat we myng,
      The Fendys malyce hit doth ouercom.
    Pray for vs to cryste, oure king,
      Maria virgo virginum.   48

O dulcis diamounde, deyre damesell,
  Domina mundi, thow delykat dame,
Tronus dei thow art to tell,
  Intemerata, turtyll tame.   52
O speciosa, syttyng in selle,
  þou saue vs sothly fro Satanas is shame,
Crist for vs, þat Iewys didde kelle,
  þat kyndely of thy cloyster came,   56
    That babe hath bought vs fro oure blame,
      Hys eyre to be euer in eternum.
    Godis moder, gare vs to haue heuynly game,
      Maria virgo virginum.   60

O oryens splendryx, in syght specius,
  As the splendaunt sonne sytth in space,
So shewyth your symylytude most glorius
  To euery gost growyng in grace.   64
O prudent, puella precius,
  The patron of heuyn pleyd in thi place.
O very Virgyn most vertuus,
  & worshep ouer all wymmen þou hase,   68
    Thyn humylyte exaltyd hase
      Thy blod, þat wyll be to thy chylde bocsum,
    Neuer to dwelle in hell duras,
      Maria virgo virginum.   72

O sancta saluatryx, sett in saluacion,
　　Se to thy seruantys þat thei ben sure,
& put hem fro preuarycasion ;
　　After ryȝtfullnys do not reddure.　　　　　76
Lett noȝt creaturys of thy chyldys creacyon
　　Be vnder the caytyuys of hell cure.
The well of mercy mayᵣmake mediacyon,
　　Agayn all mysse that passyt mesure.　　　　80
　　O quene, full queme to euery creature,
　　　　Pray that we may to the com,
　　To se thy trone & thy tresoure,
　　　　Maria virgo virginum.　　　　　　　84

29.　　*Regina Celi Letare, III*

Cambridge Univ. MS. Kk. 1. 6

REgina celi, letare,　　　　　　　　[fol. 201ᵛᵒ]
　　Where-thourgh the worde was wrought þan,
Whan Gabriell grete þe on his knee,
　　In whome fyrste þis worlde began.　　　　4
　　'Aue,' he seyde to þe sertayne,
'Gracia plena, god is with the,'
　　Where-thourgh þou conseyuedyste god & man,
Regina celi letare.　　　　　　　　　　8

Quia quem meruisti portare
　　Kyng, Emperour of heuene & helle,
And þou, moder & mayden clene,
　　That neuer was ffyled in flesche ne ffele.　　12
　　Thy pyte spryngeth, lady, as doth a welle,
Vn-to alle synfull þat serue the,
　　Where-fore, lady, to þe we melle,
Regina celi letare.　　　　　　　　　　16

2 MS. worde I was. *In MS. lines 2 and 4 are transposed.*

Resurexit sicut dixit,   [fol. 202ro]
  That for vs lay dede in a stoone,
And resyd he was from deth to lyth,
  And al to saue vs ffrome oure foone.   20
  Than were þou, lady, wel be-goone,
Whan þat þy sone to Heuene gan flee,
  Wher-fore þe Angeles Ioyede echoone,
Regina celi letare.   24

Ora pro nobis ad deum,
  As ȝe are sche þat neygheth hym nere,
Vn-to þy blisse þat we may come,
  What þat þou seyste he wyl þe here;   28
  Wher-fore we pray þe, lady dere,
Oure Auoket þat þou wylte be,
  As ȝe to-geder were bounden in fere,
Regina celi letare.   32

Here enduth regina celi.

30.   *The Five Joys of Our Lady*

Cotton MS. Caligula A. ii

Quinque Gaudia

1. HEyl! gloryous virgyne, ground of all our
    grace,   [fol. 135ro]
Heyl! modere of crist in pure virginite,
Heyl! whom the son of god ches for his place,
Send from above down from the faders see.   4
Heyl! with thyne ere conceyvynge, send to the
The message be gabryell, in this wyse seynge,
'Heyl! full of grace, oure lord ys with the.'
Heyl! with thyne humble hert to it obeying.   8

2. Heyl! that with god so priuy art and pleyne,
   Among all wymmene blessed most þu be.
   Heyl! that conceyved and bere with-outen peyne
   The second person in the trynyte,   12
   Heyl! chast lyly descended from Iesse,
   Heyl! cristall clere, Heyl! closet of clennesse,
   Heyl! blessed burioun, Heyl! blome of all beaute,
   ffayrest of fayre, aye flowryng in fayrnesse.   16

3. Heyl! emperyse of heuen hyest of astate,
   Heyl! mayden makelesse, heyl! moder of pyte,
   Heyl! queene of counfort, of counfort desolate
   When thou thy chylde sawe dying on a tre.   20
   Heyl! whos vprisyng full shynyng was to þe,
   Heyl! that oure mescheves old hast new redressed,
   Heyl! be whos meene this lord hase made vs fre,
   The fruyt of thy wombe, ay be he b[l]essed.   24

4. Heyl! stydfast sterre with stremys lemyng ly3t,
   Heyl! that beheld full clerely with thyne eye
   Thy son ascendynge be his propre myght,
   Peersyng the clowdes in-to heuen hye,   28
   Wher it was sayde to hem of Galelye:
   'Why merveyl ye thus lokyng vp in veyne?
   This lord þat thus Ascended my3tylye,
   Ry3t as he stey, he shall come doun Ayeyn.'   32

5. Heyl! floure of vertu, whos feyrnesse may not fade,
   Heyl! rose on ryse most holsom of odoure,
   Heyl! whom the holy gost can Ioye, and glade
   In the assumyng vp in-to his toure.   36
   Heyl! comely queene, there crowned with honoure,
   Heyl! mediatrice and mene for man-kynd,
   Heyl! salue to seke vs synners send socoure,   39
   These Ioyes fyve empryntynge in oure mynd.   Amen.
                      Explicit.

31. *The Five Joys of Our Lady, with Acrostic*

MS. Bodley rolls 22
(Sum. Catal. No. 30445)

Sancta Maria

[M] Yldyste of moode & mekyst of maydyns alle,
     O modyrs mercyfullyst, most chast þat euer
        was wyfe,
Worschypfullyst of women þat were, ȝet be, or schalle,
Parfytst of a prayowre, þe best þat euyr bare lyue,   4
Whose salutacyon was fyrste Ioye of thy fyve,
Whan gabriel seyde 'hayle mary ful of grace'—
wyth þe wheche worde þe holy gost as blyue
Wythyn þi chest hath chosyn a ioyful place.   8

[A] Secunde Ioy hadyst þu whan cryst ihū
     Of þe was borne & ȝet was þu a mayde;
ffor company of man thou nevyr knewe.
Chylde forth þu brynge, but wyth wordes þat wer
     sayde   12
Of þe aungel; whom of þu wher a-frayde
Tyll he seyde, 'mary, loke þu drede nowte,
Plucke vp thyn herte and be no thyng dysmayde,
ffor thys hye werke almyghty god hath wrowte.'   16

[R] ysyn from dethe to lyf that ys eterne
     ys thy swete son, ascend vp on hye
In-to a trone above the stremyng sterren,
Wher aungellys syng a-bowte þe chererchy,   20
Lovyng þat lorde wyth heuynly melody,
As kyng of kyngis, whose regne schal euer endure.
Lo! gracious lady and modyr of mercy,
Thys was thyrde ioy of thy blest auenture.   24

    14 MS. *after* mary, dere *underpointed for deletion.*

[I]n solempne wyse assumptyd wyth a songe
　　Of cherubyn, thy forthe ioy to atteyne,
was þi body and thy sowle aungellys amonge,
vnto thy son browte vp yn febus wayne,   28
wher personys three yn O god sytte certeyne.
Of whose presens ryght ioyful mayste thow be,
ffor, as scrypture in holy bokys sayn,
Thow conceyuydyst clene that holy trinite.   32

[A]nde they alle three of on affeccion
　　haue chosy the cheffe, the quene for to be
Of heyvyn and erthe, wos coronacione
wes thy fyffte ioy wyth grete solempnyte.   36
Now blyste lady, flowre of virginite,
Graunt vs thy grace oure lyvys to a-men[de],
That we may come here-aftyr vnto the,
Vnto þat ioye whyche nevyr schal haue ende.   40

[p]ryncese, pray to thy sone,
[i]n worschyp of þi salutacyon,
[p]erpetually þat we may wone
[w]yth hym, yn hys hy domynacione,   44
[e]uyr lastyng to lyue yn þat mancione.
[l]lady, graunt vs thys sayde supplycacione.

32.　　*An Orison to Our Lady by the Seven Joys*

Cambridge Univ. MS. Ff. 1. 6

[M]Ost glorius quene, Reynyng yn hevene,　　[fol. 146ro]
　　Stere of the se, of all this worldell lady,
I be-seche you for all youre Ioyes Sevene,
In this grete nede sende cumforte and mersy.   4
And ther as mane can schape no remedy,

29 MS. certeyte.　　34 MS. te quene.　　36 MS. fyrste.

Schew ye youre myght, youre grace & your goodnesse
To youre sarvant that lythe in grete dystresse.

Preves I-now ther ben of youre pete,   8
ffor ye fayle none that can haue afeccyun
Vn-to youre grase; so larche is your bownte
That all the worlde by you hath consolacyun.
Youre blessed sone hyryth youre orysoun   12
And grantyth you all thyng ye woll hym pray;
What 3e desyre, þat can he not gaynesay.

Hertes sorow and verry ynvarde drede
Maketh me fle to youre grace for socowre,   16
ffor ye neuer yit faylid none at nede—
your grete mercy so fre is euery owre.
Now swete lady, ryght as 3e be the flowre
Of all womene, the chef helper in dystresse,   20
Torne all my woo into Ioy and gladnesse.

33.   A Salutation by the Heavenly Joys

Royal MS. 17. A. xvi

HAyll be þu, qwen of gret honour!   [fol. 29ʳᵒ]
     our lord þi hert has fild wyth grace.
Of mede & ioy þu bers þo flour
     þu pas all santis be-for gods face.   4

Haill be þu, spouse of gods chesyng!
     Os son today in erth gifs lyght,
So my clernes gyfs lyghtynyng
     Til all þo courte of heuen full bryght.   8

Hayll! wessell full of all godnes,
     All heuenle courte dos þi byddyng
& worchyps þe wyth gret suetnes,
     Os qwen of all wyth-oute irkyng.   12

Hayll be þu, may of hegh lifyng!
  Whos will & godis ar ay both on,
Þer-for he grauntis þe þin askyng,
  ffor whom þu prays he warns þe none.   16

Haill! oure comforth, alway at nede   [fol. 29ᵛᵒ]
  after þi will þi seruand her,
our lord reward & gife þaim mede
  in heuen & erth wyth santis seyr.   20

Haill! fair moder of criste Ihū,
  Þat sitis nest god in trinite
Schinand in flech, of all vertu
  is non þe like ne neuer sall be.   24

Haill be þu, flour of women all!
  þu art sikyr þat þes ioes sewen
Sall neuer decres ne ȝhit doune fall
  bot last in blis alway in heuene.   28

ffor þes sewene ioes, for hus þu pray,
  moder of criste þat hus has boght,
Þat he hus kepe both nyght & day
  & set in hym our luf & thoght.   32

Criste ihū, lord of maieste,
  Þat has in heuen wyth gret lowyng
Worchipt & set þi moder fre
  in ioy & blis of all likyng,   36

Þu graunte hus grace thorgh her prayer,
  þi will to do all oure lifyng,
& kepe hus ay fro perels here,
  & graunte scho be at our endyng   40

hus to defend fro our enmys,
  & comforth hus wyth þi mercy,
So þat we may in paradice
  Wyth þe & her duell endlesly. Amen.   44

34. *The Seven Joys of the Virgin in Heaven, I*

Henry E. Huntington Library, MS. HM. 127

Hit is y-founde and y-write þat oure lady apered to seint Thomas
of caunterbury[1] and badde him and tauȝt him to worschipe here
for þe seuene ioyes durable and euerelastinge þat sche haþ now in
heuene as wel as hede[2] ede now for þe five temperal ioyes þat he[3]
hadde on erþe þe which beþ passed and þese beþ þe seuene þat
folweþ.

[fol. 53ʳᵒ]

B E glad, of al maydens flourre,
   Þat hast in heuene swich honoure
     To passe in hye blisse
Aungelys and oþur seintȝ also;   4
Þe ioye is nouȝt like þer-to
     Of eny þat þer isse.

Be gladde, goddis spouse briȝt,
Þat ȝeuest þer gretter liȝt   8
     To þe heuenli place
Þan euir dede sunne on erþe here   [fol. 53ᵛᵒ]
When hit was briȝtis and most clere
     In þe midday space.   12

Be glad, of vertues vessel clene,
To whom obeiþ as riȝt quene
     Þe court of heuen on hyȝe,
And worschipeþ wiþoute stynting   16
Þorwe þankinges and be blessing
     And endeles melodie.

Be glad, moder of ihū dere,
Þat spedist alle way þi prayere   20
     By-fore þe Trinite.

---

[1] 'Thomas of caunterbury'—cancelled by a Protestant censor.
but still legible.

[2] hede—*corrector divided this word* 'he de' *and added* 'ede'.

[3] he—*corrected in margin to* 'sche'.

As god wil, suich is þi wille;
Þere may no wiȝt sinful spille
    On whom þou hast pite. 24

Be glad, moder of heuene king,
Swich he wol, aftir plesing,
    To þi seruaunt trewe
Graunt boþe mede and reward 28
Here and also aftirward.
    In Ioye þat euer is newe.

Be glad, mayden and moder swete,
Next þe sone þou hast a sete, 32
    I-glorified blisfulli.
And þis we saddely beleue,
But how, openly descriue
    Ne may no þing erþeli. 36

Be glad, of oure gladnesse welle,
Þat art seker ay to dwelle
    In mirþe þat haþ non ende,
Which schal neuer were ne wast; 40
Þer-to bringe vs, moder chast,
    When we hen wende.

Þus, þou blessed quene of heuene,
I worschipe þe wiþ ioyes seuene 44
    In alle þat y may.
When y schal leue þis soreful lyf,
Be to me redy in þat strif,
    Lady, y þe pray. 48

Lady, for þese ioyes seuene
And for þi gladnesse fiue,
Bringe me to þe blisse of heuene
Þorwe grace of clene lyfe. 52

35. *The Seven Joys of the Virgin in*
Heaven, II

Henry E. Huntington Library, MS. HM. 142

Septem gaudia beate marie

GAude, of uirgins þe freshest floure,   [fol. 19ro]
  In maydenhede a launtern of odour,
In reuerence, worschippe and honour,
        Transcendens splendiferum,   4
The princes of aungelis in Ierachie,
The beaute of blessed seyntes so hiȝe,
Passynge also by alle clergye
        A dignitate munerum.   8

Gaude, spouse of god, so clere
As the lyȝt of þe day þat schynethe here,
By cours of þe planetis in the spere
        Solis datur lumine.   12
So þou makest þat glorious cite
In pees Ioye by the syght of the,
Schinynge and schewynge in alle degre
        Lucis plenitudine.   16

Gaude, uessel of alle uertu,
Schinynge as heuen in hyde and hewe,
At whos commaundynge hangeth ful trewe
        Tota celi curia,   20
The blessediste and benigneste þat euer grewe,
Worthyeste and clenest þat euer man knewe,
Moder and norice of criste Ihū,
        Veneratur in gloria.   24

18 MS. Schnynge.

Gaude be þe, bonde of ful good wille,
As loue to loue that neuer þouȝt ille
In parfyte charite and pite þer-tille
      Iuncta sic altissimo,   [fol. 19ᵛᵒ]
That what so euer thi wille be   29
May don for man to make us fre
Aske and þou haste graunted the
      A ihū dulcissimo.   32

Gaude, moder of wrecches wilde,
The fader of heuen þat gat þi childe
As a fre kynge to his douȝter mylde
      Dabit te colentibus   36
A couenabel rewarde to his mede
And ordeyned so him þat he schal spede,
A sete for thy loue where is no drede
      Regni in celestibus.   40

Gaude, mayden cristes moder,
Thow art oure voket and he oure broþer—
Oonly þou seruyd þis and noon oþer,
      O virgo piissima,   44
Aboue alle creatures for to bee,
In sight, astate and dignite,
That thow art þe holy trinite
      Sessione proxima.   48

Gaude, mayde and moder clene,
Siker and sure, fayre lady schene,
Be graunt of þe godhede—þis I mene,
      Quod hec septem gaudia,   52
Thei schal neuer sclake, thei schal neuer sece,
Nor neuer fade ne neuer decrece,
But be freshe and dure and euer encrece
      Per eterna secula. Amen.   56

36.   *The Seven Joys of the Virgin in Heaven*, *III*

Harley MS. 372

Gaude flore virginali [fol. 55ro]

I Oy, blissid lady, with pure virgynal floure!
   And honoure special, transcendyng vp on hee
In-to the ioyful heuenly toure
Where prynces of aungels inhabite bee.   4
Above all seyntis there pight is thi see,
Thorowh dignyte of thi giftis, evire to dwell,
the which be so grete that tong none can tell.

Gaude sponsa cara dei

Ioy, derword spouse of god almyght!   8
for as the sonne the day lightyns with his beemys clere,
So plentevously, of peace thou givys the light
to thoo þat in this world bene leuyng heere.
Derknesse is noone where þu art neere,   12
O glorious lanterne, euyre shynyng bright;
thi sone to love and drede, optene vs will & myght.

Gaude splendens vas virtutum [fol. 55vo]

Ioye, vessel pure of vertuous shynyng!
to whos bekenyng & call, both more & lesse,   16
al the heuenly court is euyre inclynyng,
the to honour & worship as weel worthi is.
The, ihū modire, wele & gladnesse
with laude & glory, euyre on the call   20
Angels archaungels & oþer seyntis all.

Gaude nexu voluntatis

Ioye with þe, bande of blissid wilfulnesse,
& with þe, bande of parfytt luf & charite!
So to that god ioyned þat most myghti isse   24

that þi askyng graunte euyre wil he.
Ihū þi sone, most of benygnyte,
ay to þi desyres wil accord & assent,
and hym euyre to please is þi will & entent.   28

Gaude mater miserorum
Ioye, pytevous moder of syners! þat one þe call
for releyse of þer synne & þer trespace:
for þi luf, þe fadur of þeise worldis all
graunte to theme pardone, mercy & grace,   32
& after in heuyne both seete & place
With him in blisse euyre to be.
thus synners be sauyd, lady, thorogh help of the.

Gaude virgo mater x̄p̄i
Ioye, blissid lady modire of crist Ihū!   36
for þu, most blissid virgyne, deseruyd hath alone
þat þi seete gloriously piyht shuld be nowe
all-ther next ioyned to þe holy trynytees trone;
Where þe seyntis of heuyne þe worschip euerychone, 40
With ympnes & canticles & organs emang,
& oþer melodies moo than mans hert think kane.

Gaude virgo mater pura
Ioye, blissid virgyne, cristis modire pure!
Euyre dwelling sure & in certante   44
Þat theis Ioies to þe schal euer stand sure,
& neuer more decrece ne neuer lessyned be,
but fresshly florissh & encrece in eternyte.
þus in endlesse blisse ay shal thow dwell,   48
queene of heuene, lady of erth, Emperice of hell.

O Sponsa dei electa
O, thou chosyne spouse of god, blissid moder also
of oure lord ihū crist þat vs ful dere hath boght,

44 MS. certane.

Sett vs in þe right way, þat we may surely go   52
vp to eternal blisse, þer-of þat we fayle noght,
where peace is & glory newe dayly in broght.
And with þi pitevous eeris here vs whan we call,
And suffir vs neuer to þe fend to mak oure soulys thrall.
  Amen.   56

37.   *A Song of the Assumption*

Cotton MS. Caligula A. ii

Veni Coronaberis

SUrge mea sponsa, so swete in syȝte,   [fol. 107ᵛᵒ]
And se þy sone in sete full shene!
Thow shalte a-byde with þy babe so bryȝte
   And in my glorye be, & be called a qwene.   4
Thy mamelles, modur, full well I mene,
   I hadde to my mete, I myȝte not mysse.
Aboue all creatures, my modur clene,
   Veni Coronaberis.   8

Cum, clene Crystall, to my cage.
   Columba mea, I þe calle,
And se þy sone, in seruage
   ffor mannus sowle was made þralle.   12
In þy place þat ys princypall
   I playde pryuely wyth-owte mysse.
My herytage, modur, haue þu shall,
   Veni coronaberis.   16

ffor macula, modur, was neuur in þe,
   ffilia syon, þu arte þe flowre!
ffull swetely shalte þu sytte by me,
   And were a crowne wyth me in towre;   20

And all myn angelles to þyn honowre   [fol. 108ro]
  Shall þe worshyppe in heuen blysse.
Thow, blessed body þat bare in bowre,
  Veni coronaberis.   24

Tota pulcra es to my plesynge,
  My modur, princes of paradys!
A watur full swete of þe shall sprynge,
  Thow shalte aȝeyn my ryȝtes ryse.   28
  The welle of mercy, modur, in þe lyys
    To brynge þy blessed body to blysse.
  And all my sayntes shall do þe seruysse,
    Veni [coronaberis].   32

Veni, electa mea, to myn an hyȝe,
  Holy modur & mayden mylde,
On sege to sytte me bye,
  That am þy kynge & þy chylde,   36
  Holy modur, with me to bylde,
    Wyth þy blessed babe þat ys in blysse—
  That virgyn þat was neuur defylde,
    Veni [coronaberis].   40

Vox tua to me was full swete
  Whene þu me badde, 'babe be stylle'.
ffull goodly gone oure lyppes mete,
  Wyth bryȝte braunches, as blosme on hyll.   44
  ffauus distillans þat wente wyth wylle
    Oute of þy lyppes whene we dede kysse.
  Therfore, modure, þys ys my skyll,
    Veni [coronaberis].   48

Veni de libano, þu lylye in launche,
  That lappes me louely wyth loulynge songe!
Thow shalte a-byde wyth þy blessed braunche
  That so solemply of þe spronge.   52

Ego, flos campy, þy flowre, was fonge,
  That on Calverye cryede to þe ywysse.
Moder, ȝe knowe hyt ys no wronge,
  Veni [coronaberis].   56

Pulcra ut luna, þu bere þe lambe,
  As soone þat shyneth moste clere.
Veni in ortum meum, þowȝty damme,
  To smelle my spyces & erbes in fere.   60
  My place ys pyȝte for þe plenere,
    ffull of bryȝte braunches & blomes of blysse.
  Cum now, modur, to þy derlynge dere,
    Veni [coronaberis].   64

Que est ista so vertuus,
  That is celestyall for oure mekenesse,
Aurora consurgens gracyous,
  So benygne a lady of fyne bryȝtnesse,   68
  That ys þe colour of kynde clennesse.
    Regina celi, þat neuur shall mysse
  Thus enþeth þys songe of gret swettenesse,
    Veni coronaberis.   72

38.   *The Coronation of the Virgin, I*

B.M. Addit. MS. 20059

THe infinite power essenciall,   [fol. 99ʳᵒ]
  Me thoght I sawe verrement,
Procedyng from his trone celestiall
To a dere damsell that was gent.   4
Songes melodious was in their tent,
Of Angells synging with gret solemnyte
Before a quene whiche was present,
  Ecce virgo Radix Iesse.   8

Tota pulcra, to the lille like,
She was set withe saphures celestiall;
The odour of hir mowthe aromatike
Dyd coumford the world vnyuersall,   12
Moche clerer she was then the cristall,
She is the flowre of all formosite,
Devoide of actes crymynall,
 Ecce virgo Radix Iesse.   16

Oleum effusum, to languentes medsyne,
O maria by denominacioun,
Fulgent as the beame celestyne,
Called vnto hir coronacioun.   20
Phebus persplendent made his abdominacioun,
Devoidyng all in tenebrosite,
ffor gret love of hir exaltacioun,
 Ecce virgo Radix Iesse.   24

Ryght diligent were the mynstrells divine, [fol. 99ᵛᵒ]
Trones and dominaciones for to expresse,
Angells, Archangells dubbit in doctryne,
To mynystre to þat regall arayed in rychesse.   28
The prynce perpetuall spake to that pryncesse,
Smylyng in his suavyte,
'Columba mea, the Cloystre of clandnesse
 Ecce virgo Radix Iesse.'   32

'Surge, true tabernacle of virginite,
Bothe mother and maiden inculpable,
Cum furthe of thy consanguinite
Vnto glorie incomparable.'   36
Then kneled this oryent & amyable
Before the pellicane of perpetuete,
And he crowned that Regyent venerable,
 Ecce virgo Radix Iesse.   40

21 MS. abhominacioun.

By the spectable splendure of hir fulgent face
My sprete was rauesched, & in my body sprent,
Inflamed was my hert with gret solace
Of the luciant corruscall resplendent,   44
Then this curious cumpany in-contynent
Withe the seraphynnes in their solemnyte,
Solemply sang this subsequent,
   'Ecce virgo Radix Iesse.'   48

O Deifere delicate and doghter dyuyne,   [fol. 100ʳᵒ]
Mother of mercy and meyden melleffluus,
Devoide of dysseyte, dubbet in doctryne,
Trone of the trinite, treite thow for vs.   52
Vs defende from the dongeon dolorous,
And bring to abide in blisse withe the,
There to love our godd most glorious,
   Ecce virgo Radix Iesse.   56

Dulcis amica dei, rosa vernans, stella decora,
Tu memor esto mei dum mortis venerit ora.
   Spes nostra Iesus maria.

39.   *The Coronation of the Virgin, II*

Harley MS. 2255

VNdir a park ful prudently pyght,   [fol. 150ᵛᵒ]
  A perillous path men passyd by,
There herd I a melody of myght,
Scandaunt on skalys above the sky,   4
Aungellys EXALTANT, bothe lowde and hih,
Tenours, trebelys, many a meene ther was:
they sett ther song ful sapiently,
'BENEDICTA SIT SANCTA TRINITAS.'   8

      41 MS. spectacle.

The Clowdys they cleeff, the sky to clere,
The day fro dirknesse made devisioun,
byrdis they buskyd fro breere to breere—
thus fyned the firmament at his avisioun.   12
The day-sterre, ellect froom alle illicioun,
to mynistre and meene his chaunte he chas:
Than Countryd the queer with this conclusyoun,
With 'BENEDICTA SIT SANCTA TRINITAS'.   16

A melodious myrthe it was to me,
fful pure and precious be poyntes passaunt,
So shynyng vpward the excelcite,
With obediaunt beemys bryghtly abundaunt.   20
ANGELLYS, ARCHANGELLYS, froom vicis advertaunt,
Moore gloryous than euere was gleem or glas,
THRONYS, DOMINACIOUNS, thus CRIST COLLAUDAUNT,
With 'BENEDICTA SIT SANCTA TRINITAS'.   24

Euere kneelyd and Clepyd on my Creature,   [fol. 151ro
To haue knowlage of the glorye that glood;
So was I enspyred froom the speculat splendure,
That my spirit was ravysshed, my boody a-bood,   28
than sawh I my makere in his manhood,
Aboute the PRINCIPATUS that nevir shal pas,
The POTESTATES presentis ther BEATITUDIS abrood,
With 'BENEDICTA SIT SANCTA TRINITAS'.   32

The Choys of the CHERUBYNNES, they were cherable
To synge with SERAPHYNNES in here suavite,
Vertuously devidyng ther voysis venerable,
The IERARCHYES Ioyed with greet IOCUNDITE.   36
Than knelyd a queen of fair femyninnyte,
Seyng ful seyntly INTER FILIAS,
'ffor Coronacioun of my sanguinite
BENEDICTA SIT SANCTA TRINITAS.'   40

'Now, come on, my COLVIR,' than seid Oon Kyng,
'And flour, of flours moost fortunat,
My tent, my troone, my tresour towchyng,
My merrour, my moodir INMACULAT,   44
My shyning selecture not SUPERAT,
but above alle women that evir was.'
Than seid this turtyl, thus translat,
'BENEDICTA SIT SANCTA TRINITAS.'   48

Thus was she sett CELESTIALLY
and Ioyned in Ioyes with Cryst IHŪ
In a paall powdryd with clene perry,
With SAPHIR, shynyng bryght and blew.   52
Ther-to full of pacience and of vertu,
fful pure in peerle hire Clothyng was.
All Ordrys of Aungellys singing new,
'BENEDICTA SIT SANCTA TRINITAS.'   56

Here face, moost splendaunt than the SONNE,
hire Colour as Cleer as CRISTAL bryght—
Thus ordynatly, hire lyve is ovir-ronne,
that tyl hevene and erthe she may geve lyght,   60
Thus magnifyed is our moodir of myght,
by preposicioun that nevir shall pas,
And of the godhede to haue a sight,
With BENEDICTA SIT SANCTA TRINITAS.   64

Hire ORYENT heer lay ovir the nekke
To counforte vs in our CAPACITE.
Alle Ordrys of Aungellys bowyd at a bekke,
And fyl to this flour of fair felicite.   68
Crownyd she is in hire benignyte;
A sceptre in hand seyntly she has,
Disposyng our deth daily be dignyte—
BENEDICTA SIT SANCTA TRINITAS.   72

57 moost] *read* more.

40.   *Fresh Flower of Womanhood*

Royal MS. 6. B. ix

RYht godely, fressh flour of womanhode,   [fol. 198ʳᵒ]
   My lyues Ioy, myn hertes plesance,
Example of trouth and rote of godelyhode,
   And verayly my lyues sustenance—   4
And, with al þe hool, feythful obeisance
   That seruant can thenk or deuyse,
To you þat haue myn herte in gvuernance,
   Me recemande in all my best wyse.   8
      Quod H. Bowesper.

41.   *Mary, Be our Succour and Help*

B.M. Addit. MS. 39574

MArye, goddis modir dere,   [fol. 57ᵛᵒ]
   Socoure & helpe us while we ben here,
   Gouerne, wisse and rede.   3
As þou art modir, mayden and wijf,
Clense us fro synne and graunte good lijf,   [fol. 58ʳᵒ]
   And helpe us in oure nede.   6

42.   *Keep Us a Place in Paradise*

Harley MS. 1022

QUene of parage, / paradyse repayred I-wysse, [fol. 61ᵛᵒ]
   lyth of linage, / lere me of heuenly blysse,
ffor þat es wage / þat lastet & neuer may misse.   3

lady Ioynge, / reioyce vs Ioyles abydynge,
þat of al thynge / comfort is & refreschynge.
Pray þou our kynge / he kepe vs in heuen a wonynge. 6
      Amen oremus.

   5 MS. yng' *interlined after* comfort.

Mary so milde,
ffor luf of þi childe
here þo wylde
   þat prayen þe now.   10

Grace to vs hylde,
with blysse þou vs bylde,
ffro synne þou vs schilde—
   Amen, for our prowe.   14

43.   *Our Lady and all the Angels, Pray for Me*

MS. Rawlinson B. 408
(Sum. Catal. No. 11755)

I Pray þe, lady, þe moder of crist,   [fol. 6ro]
Praieth ȝoure sone me for to spare,
With al angels and Iohn Baptist,
   And al ȝoure company þat now ys thare,   4
   Al holichurch, for my welfare.
      Graunt me of ȝoure merites a participacion,
      And praieth oure lorde for my saluacyon.   7

44.   *Mary, Remember Me at my Last Day*

MS. Douce 1
(Sum. Catal. No. 21575)

B Lessed mary, moder virginall,   [fol. 77ro]
Integrate mayden, sterre of the see,
Haue remem*braunce at the day fynall   [*fol. 77vo]
On thy poore seruaunt now prayng to the.   4

Myrroure without spot, rede rose of Ierico,
Close gardyn of grace, hope in disparage,
Whan my soule the body parte fro
Socoure it frome myn enmyes rage.　　　　8

45.　*I Have now Set my Heart so High*

Trinity College Camb. MS. 652

I Haue nowe sett myne herte so hye,　[fol. 170vo]
My luff alone is one oone lente
the whiche is fayre, fecunde and fre,
the myldeste may that euer was mente.　　　4
She hase myne herte in yche degre,
She is so generus and so gente,
And I hir chose for chastite
eternally trewluff to tente.　　　　8
Hyr dulcede is indesinente
ffor she is rote of all recreaunce,
Hyr frute is indeficient
to luff wyth-owte varyaunce.　　　　12

Tota pulcra and principall
of plente that is plenitude,
Castell of clennes, I hyr call,
that beldith in beatitude,　　　　16
beyng as clene as clere crystall
Whose meuynge is mansuetude.
hyr sete is sett sempeternall
In excelsis so celsitude.　　　　20
O pierles princes, thy pulcritude
Was so indewed wyth dalyaunce,
thy fortune was so felicitude
to luff wyth-owtyn varyaunce.　　　　24

17 beyng as] *a single letter written above* as.
21 *A single letter written above* thy.

46.   *A Love Message to My Lady*

MS. Douce 326
(Sum. Catal. No. 21900)

GOe, lytyll byll, & doe me recommende [fol. 14ro]
Vn-to my lady with godely countynaunce,
ffor, trusty messanger, I the sende.
Pray her that sche make puruyaunce ;   4
ffor my love, thurgh her sufferaunce,
In her Bosome desyreth to reste,
ssyth off all women I loue here beste.

sshe ys lylly off redolence,   8
Wych only may doe me plesure ;
she is the rose off conffydence,
Most conffortyng to my nature.
Vn-to that lady I me assure,   12
I wyll hur loue and neuer mo—
Goe, lytyll byll, and sey hur so.

she restyd in my remembraunce,
Day other nyght wher-so I be ;   16
It ys my specyall dalyaunce
for to remembyr hur bewte ;
she is enprentyd in ych degre
With yftis of nature in-explycable,   20
And eke of grace incomparable.

The cause þerfor, yf she wyll wytt,
Wyll I presume on sych a flowre
ssay, off hyr, for yt ys I-wrytt,   24
she is þe feyrest paramour
And to man in ych langour

23 Wyll] ? *read* Wy (= Why).
25 'Pulcherrima mulierum. canticorum. h^o. c^o.' *added in margin
in same hand.*

Most souerayne medyatryce.
Ther-ffor I loue þat flowre of pryce.   28

Her bewte holy to dyscryve   [fol. 14ᵛᵒ]
Who is she that may ssuffyce?
ffor-soth no clerk þat is on lyve,
ssyth she is only withowtyn vyce;   32
Her flauour excedith the fflowr-delyce.
Afore all flowris I haue hur chose
Enterely in myn herte to close.

Hyr I beseche, seth I not feyne   36
Butt only putt me in hur grace,
That off me she not dysdeyne,
Takyng regarde at old trespace;
seth myn entent in euery place   40
sshall be to doe hur obeysaunce
And hur to loue saunce varyaunce.

47.   *I will Serve my Lady until Death*

MS. Bodley 939
(Sum. Catal. No. 27691)

[fol. 116ʳᵒ]

[E]Uery man delytyth hyly in hijs degree
Hym for to stand in hys ladyys grace,
And i am one off them—I say for me—
That wyll be besy in euery maner place   4
Her for to serue beningli & purchace
Her mercy, & ther-vppon a-byde
Unto deth me do sett a-syde.

30 she] ? *read* he.
40 *Added in margin in same hand and marked for insertion.*
41 to *interlined above.*

[A]Nd vn-to yow, myn lady dere,   8
With humble hert & lowly obseruance
I yow besech & hyly yow requere
Me for to haue in your remembrance,
Wych may me wele preserue & auavnce   [fol. 116ᵛᵒ]
The rathyr throw thys prayer that i make,   13
And to yow, good lady, my body I do betake.
                                        Amen.

[W]Yth hertte trew whyl my body wyll indure
Truly in yowre seruyce I wyll a-byde,   16
B[e]sechyng yow of soch grace & vre
As yt lyk yow for me to prouyde,
ffor vn-to me þow be best gyde,
Reuerent lady, that euyr I dyd fynd,   20
And vnto me best lady and most kynd.

[A]Lso, good lady, one thyng i yow besech,
That thys prayer* may be to yow acceptable,
                                      *[fol. 117ʳᵒ]
And that þow be to me my soule leche,   24
ffor neuyr i fownd yow variable.
Now, gracyus good lady, mak me so able
That thys prayer may passe to yowr presence,
And mercy to haue for myne offence.   28

[I]N yow, good lady, soch affiance I fynd
That I yow chese to be souereyn off all
And me purpose yow ta have in mynde
Euery day & mercy to yow calle.   32
Now, gracius lady, with hartt, lyffe, lust & alle,
I yow besech in euery heuynesse
Me for to helppe & in euery distresse.
                                        Amen.

48.   *I Will Have No Other Spouse*

Cotton MS. Caligula A. ii

Pon a lady my loue ys lente,   [fol. 91ʳᵒ]
 With-owtene change of any chere,
That ys louely & contynent
And most at my desyre.   4

Thys lady ys yn my herte pyght;
Her to loue y haue gret haste.
With all my power & my myȝth,
To her y make myne herte stedfast.   8

Therfor wyll y non oþur spowse,
Ner none oþur loues, for to take;
But only to here y make my vowes,
And all oþur to forsake.   12

Thys lady ys gentyll & meke,
Moder she ys & well of all;
She ys neuur for to seke,
Noþur to grete ner to small.   16

Redy she ys nyght & day,
To man & wommon & chylde ynfere,
ȝyf þat þey wyll awȝt to here say,
Our prayeres mekely for to here.   20

To serue þys lady we all be bownde,
Both nyȝth & day yn euery place,
Where euur we be, yn felde or towne,
Or elles yn any oþur place.   24

Pray we to þys lady bryȝth,
In þe worshyp of þe trinite,
To brynge vs alle to heuen lyȝth—
Amen, say we, for charyte.   28

11 MS. vowe.   17 MS. nygh.

49. *God in Trinity, Give Me Grace*

Cambridge Univ. MS. Ii. 6. 43

[L]Orde, þat art of myȝtis moost,   [fol. 120ᵛᵒ]
ffadir & sone & holy goost,
  God in trynyte,
Thou ȝeue me grace daye & nyȝt   4
The to serue with all my myȝt,
  lord, y be-seke þee.

And out of synne my lyf to lede,
That y þe fende mow not drede   8
  Whan y schall hennys wende.
In heuen blys þou ȝeue me grace
The to see face to face,
  Worlde withouten ende.   AmeN.   12

50. *A Petition to Father and Son and
       Holy Ghost*

Harley MS. 2406

ALmyghty god, fadir of heuene,   [fol. 8ᵛᵒ]
ffor cristis loue þat dyde on rode,
I praye þe, lorde, þou here my steuene,
  And fulfill my will in gode.   4

Crist, thi fader for me praye,
  ffor hir loue þou lighted inne,
He yeue me myght, or þat I dye,
  Me to amende of all my synne.   8

The holy gost, þou graunte me grace,
  Wiþ such werkes my lif to lede,
That I may se god in his face
  On domys day wiþouten drede.   12

No. 49. *Ll. 8 and 9 marked in the margin for transposition.*

Marie, þi sone for me þou praye,
  He yeue me grace, or þat I wende,
Þat I haue after I dye ·
    þe blisse of heuene wiþouten ende.   16

ffader and sone and holy gost,
  All one god and personys .iij.,
Almyghty god of myghtes most,
  Lord, þou haue mercy on me.   20

And on alle that mercy nede for charite.
          Amen par amore Amen.

51.   *A Prayer to the Three Persons in the Trinity*

B.M. Addit. MS. 20059

O Radiant luminar of light eterminable,   [fol. 100ᵛᵒ]
  Celestiall father, potenciall god of myght,
Of heyven & erthe, o lorde incomparable,
  Of all perfeccions essenciall most parfight!   4
O maker of mankynd thow formed day & ny3t,
    Whose power imperiall comprehendithe every place;
My hert, my mynde & all my holl delite
    Ys, after this lyf, to se thy glorious face,   8

Whose magnificens is incomprehensible—
  All argumentes of reason truly hit dothe excede—
Whose deite dowteles ys indiuisible,
  ffrom whome all grace & godenesse dothe procede. 12
  Of his support all cryatures haue nede;
    Assist me, gode lorde, & graunte me thy grace
To lyve to thy pleasure in worde, tho3t & dede,
    And, after this lyff, to se thy glorious face.   16

O benygne Ihū, my soveraigne lord & kyng,
  The onely son of God by filiacion,
The secunde person without begynnyng,
    Bothe god and man, our faithe makith playne relacion—
    Mary, thy moder by wey of incarnacion—   21
      Whose glorious passion our soles dothe revyue,
    Agaynest all bodely & gostly tribulacion.
      Defende me, withe thy petious woundes fyve.   24

O pereles prince, peyne᷄d unto the dethe,   [fol. 101ʳᵒ]
  Rufully rent, thy body wan & blowe
ffor our redempcion gave vp thy vitall brethe—
    Was neuer sorow like to thy dedly woo.   28
    Graunt me, out of this world when I shall goo,
      Thy endles mercy, my chefe preseruatyve.
    Agaynst the world, the flesshe and the devyll also
      Defend me with thy petious woundes fyve.   32

O fyre vervens, enflammed with all grace,
  Enkyndlyng hertes with brondes most charitable,
The endles reward of pleasure & solace,
    To the fader & the son thow art coniunctable   36
    In vnitate whiche is inseparable.
      O water of lyfe, O well of consolacion,
    Agaynst all suggestions dedly & damnable
      Rescow me, gode lord, by thy preseruacion.   40

To whome is approched, the holy gost by name,
  The thrid person, one god in trinite,
Of parfite loue thow art the gostly flame.
    Emperour of mekenes, pease & tranquyllite,   44
    My coumford, my counsell, my parfite charite,
      O water of life, O well of consolacion,
    Agaynst all stormes of hard aduersite
      Rescow me, gode lord, by thy preseruacion.   48

33 vervens=fervens.

52. *In One is All*

Harley MS. 1022

1. THurgh grace growand, in god almyght [fol. 65vo]
        Mekle maked for to spring,
    A song ful soth & ful of lyght
        our conscience consels for to syng.   4
    ffolk þat is faythful, & loth for to fayle,
        þei fall to þis song both grete & small;
    ffor þaim think it wil a-vayle
        þei sayn oft-syth, In one is alle.   8

2. Off one I syng, & wil not spare,
        þat made al thynges both lest & most;
    ffor of oure bales he makus vs bare,
        fadur & son & holy gost.   12
    In hym es alle & alle he is,
        god & man he es to be calle;
    Wyse men, thynken ful wele of þis
        & euermore sayn, In one es alle.   16

3. Almyghty god, almyghty sone,
        Almyghty are þo persones thre,
    With-oute begynning, o god in trone,
        With-outen qwam no thyng may be.   20
    He come doun to mary, þat may,
        & made vs fre þer we were thralle,
    To suffur pyne os I þe say
        & þus we profe, In one is alle.   24

4. And sythen he hang apon þe rode
        With wondus wyde, wondur ffelle,

4 MS. vs *dotted for deletion after* conscience.
10 MS. most & lest.

þat gart hym [gyld] þo gost so gode—
  þo passioun vs profers for to telle—   28
And suffred more þan I may say,
  for we suld stande & noght falle.
& be his seruandus both nyght & day,
  & þus vs thinke, In one es alle.   32

5. Trayst in þo trinite þat al thyng can,
  & noght in golde, for þat wil wayst;
ffor gold makus many a man
  In gode or euel to haue no tast.   36
Trayst not trewle bot in one,
  qwen al is gone he abide schalle
þat al thyng made, os seyt sent Ione:
  qwar for me thynk, In one is alle.   40

6. Helle is hedus on to se,
  & vgle to neuen to any wyght;
þarfor pray we þo trinite
  þat we be neuur þedir dyght,   44
ffor þat had bene our ful ryght,—
  qware pyne is bittur os is þe galle—
Nad ihū died, þat comele knyght,
  & þus we profe, In one is alle.   48

7. If we wele do wele schal vs be,
  os holy men vs has kende;
loue we þen þo trinite
  þat made þo blysse þat neuer sal ende.   52
he bring vs vnto hys blysse
  & hery vs hye in-to hys halle,
þo hole trinite he graunt þisse
  & alle þat trowes, In one is alle.   56

27 *After* þat *the word* spere, *dotted for deletion.*   28 for *inter-lined above* þus, *dotted for deletion.*   29 may *written above* kan, *dotted for deletion.*   39 thyng *deleted after* al.   53 ˉabove vs, *written more faintly*, you.

53.   *The Pater Noster*

Univ. of Edinburgh MS. Laing 149

ALmychty god, our fader of hewyne abuf,   [fol. 87ro]
  blyssyt be þi name with ws allowit alway,
come mot þi kynrik til al þat can þe luf,
done be þi wil in erd as in hewyne ay;   4
Oure dayly bred þu gyf til ws to day;
forgyf oure dettis as we our dettowris men;
lat nocht temp ws mare na we suffer may,
bot fra al ewil deliuer ws, amen.   8

54.   *Our Father, Have Pity on Me*

Cambridge Univ. MS. Add. 5943

PAter noster, most of myȝt,   [fol. 167vo]
  þat al þys world hast wrot,
help me, synful wrechyd wyȝt,
for synne þat I perysche nowt.   4

Pater noster, haue pety on me,
and helpe me synne for to flee
and euer to worch þy wylle.   7

Pater noster, yblessyd mote þu be,
ffor þyn sone þat deyd on tre,
help me, wreeche, þat y ne spylle.   10

1 hewyne] hewynis *written before this word and a line drawn
through it.*
    5 *Before* dayly *a stroke cancelled, as though the scribe had begun
to write* b.
    6 *Before* our *two letters, probably* ar, *cancelled.*

55.   *Salvum me fac, Domine*

MS. Ashmole 189
(Sum. Catal. No. 6777)

FAdyr & sone & holy gost,   [fol. 105ʳᵒ]
  Grete god in trinite,
As þu art lord of myȝtis most,
  Saluum me fac, domine.   4

Fadyr of heuyne, mercy of my gost!
  Swete god, þu rew one me!
Vanite we bene, well þu wost,
  Saluum me fac, domine.   8

In vanite we lyve yne
  That mene call ryalte,
To þe, lord god, hyt ys All synne—
  Saluum me fac, domine.   12

Graunt vs, lord, þy blysse to wynne,
  The fendis temptynge euer to fle.
In holy lyuynge, þu stabyl me yn—
  Saluum me fac, domine.   16

My flesche, þu lerne me to chaste
  and worly lofe put fro me;
In my endyng att þe last,
  Saluum me fac, domine.   20

A domysday, whene I shall a-peyre
  In þat dome þy face to see,
Put a-wey fro me All fere,
  Saluum me fac, domine.   24

56.   *God Guides All Things*

MS. Hatton 2
(Sum. Catal. No. 4130)

GOd is a substaunce foreuer dureable,   [fol. 168ᵛᵒ]
  Eterne, omnipotent, mercifull & iuste,
Which gideth all thinges in order conuenable—   3
A god in whome eche man ought to truste,
Who for praire geue grace to mortifie eche lust,
In whose feare & loue all that shall here endure   6
Shall after this life of better life be sure.
    Per me, gulielmum molleum manu propria.

57.   *God Governs for the Best*

Henry E. Huntington Library, MS. HM 501

BLessid god, souereyn goodnesse,   [fol. 147ᵛᵒ]
  mercy to me, thy synfull creature!
though fre wyll be graunted me at largess[e],
  3ett this freell body, of wrechid natur[e],   4
  That my slepy soule hath vndir cure
    is so asayled with sotell treson
    þat fre will is often venquessched, & resone.

whi woldest [þu], lord, mankynd make   8
  the worthiest Creature of all this werkes?
nou3t to dampn hym ne to forsake,
  but for þu lovist hym, as witness clerkis.
  þu knowist my 3erus, dayes and werkis,   12
    what I haue done, now do, or schall—
    my hert, my wyll, my purpose and all.

8 þu *supplied from the Cambridge MS.*
9 this] Camb. MS. þi.

then, good lord, wilt þu Constren   [fol. 148ʳᵒ]
  my wykked wil fro wrong gouernance.   16
I am bridelid, þu holdist the reyne—
  then rule me, lord, at thi ordenaunce.
    thy wyll, good lord, be don & þi plesance,
      þat after thi wyll euer be my wyll,   20
      & my will after þi wyll, & þat is skyll.

for thu wilt euery mannes sauacioun ;
  for no thing in this worldis space
is half so dere in reputacioun   24
  as mannes soule, before thi face.
    then wilt þu, goodly, graunt vs grace
      So to do her to yeve the enchesoun
      for to save vs by mercy & resoun.   28

than mercy, lord, my savioure,
  of al my synnes & wickidnesse,
from my begynyng in-to this oure,
  ȝet oones mercy ! I ask for-yeveness,   32
    not of deserving, lord, but of þi godness.
      graunt me schrift of mouþ, gret repentaunce,
      satisfaccioun, and perseueraunce

of al angers and aduersite,   [fol. 148ᵛᵒ]
  losse of frindes and worldly richesse,   37
hunger, thurst, myscheff or pouerte,
  labour, travell, bodely sekenesse,
    wrong defamacioun or gret distresse,   40
      sklaunder, repreff or vylonye,
      dispyt, perell or wicked Company,

of perell on see, water or lond,
  hurtes, fallis, or wrong in-presonyng   44
for wreth or Envy falsly borne on hond,
  of stryvis, scornes, fals bakbyting,

23 no *interlined above.*   43 or] MS. on ; Camb. MS. or.

sorow of hert, pensyfnes, wrong demyng,
    and of al oþer dissese or stryff   48
    þat I haue had seþ I had first lyff.

I thanke þe, lord, with al my hoole entent,
    with hert, soule and good effeccioun,
lord goromercy, of all þat þu hast sent   52
    as for my merit & my Correccioun;
    for I trust hool with out Susspeccioun
        al is for the best seþ I was borne,
        as þi wyll is, as I haue seyd aforne.   56

for bettur is to ly seke in my bed   [fol. 149ʳᵒ]
    then, hoole, to be drenched in the see;
& better wer þat my fingger bled
    þen in foly stryff fully slayn to be;   60
    and better wer al aduersite
        in þis world þat eny tong can tell
        then, after þis Ioye, for to go to hell.

this, lord god, of this disposisscioun   64
    is thi will don, for þi will is best.
þat litell dissese is remyssioun
    of gret disseses be-forne kest,
    for after werr comyth pes & rest,   68
        and often, for þe gretter aduerssite,
        after-ward the gretter prossperite,

wher ellis in pride our herttis wold rise,
    and oft forffet thi graciouse wyll.   72
me þerfor, lord, I pray the Chastice,
    but sle me not, lord, þouȝ þu haue skyll,
    Seþ I am submyt hooly to thi wyll,

50 al *interlined above.*
64 of this] Camb. MS. off þi.   72 Camb. MS. forgett.
74 *Written in margin, marked for insertion*   þouȝ] MS. þouþ.

kneling for mercy be-fore thi face.   76
for body and soule I ask thi grace,

that al sorowes and trybelacion
  ꝥat I haue suffred her be-fore
mot suffice, lord, for my savacioun.   80
   [bu]t now I pray þe, ho, lorde, no more   [fol. 149ᵛᵒ]
   [bu]t þat thu wilt my soúle restore
    [to] verrey pes and cherite,
    [to] love þe, lord, for þu lovust me.   84

[lo]rd, after [as] it is nessesary
  [for] al Cristen in þis world found—
[fo]r my frend, for my aduerssary—
   [a]fter as I love, and am I-bound   88
so to do, in this worldis ground,
   [th]ey may haue grace, þour wyll of the,
   [as] best may avayle to euery degre,

[f]or body & soule, under thy law ;   92
  [th]at euery bad purpose & wicked entent
[ha]ue not his Course but be with-drawe,
  [&] euery good hert, þat well haþ ment
   [a]fter thi Chirch & þi Comaundement,   96
   [In] word & werk well to spede,
   [&] in Charite so forth to procede

that, with oone hert in love & vnyte,
  [a]fter this schort worldly passage,   100
[t]hrough þi passcioun þat is mene & mot be,
  [that] we may Come to þat heritage,
  wher we may be-hold thi bryȝt visag[e],   [fol. 150ʳᵒ]
   with angellis & senttis synggung in kynd,   104
   'sc̄s, sc̄s, sc̄s, lord god with-out ynd.'

85 as *supplied from the Cambridge MS.*

58.   *The Seven O's of Christ*

Harley MS. 45

O Sapiencia que ex ore altissimi prodisti Attingens a fine usque
ad finem fortiter Suauiter disponensque omnia Veni ad docendum
nos viam Prudencie.   [fol. 168ʳᵒ]

O Sapiencia of þe ffader, surmountyng all thyng,
   Procedyng from his mowthe his hestis to fulfill,
Alpha and Oo, both end & begynnyng,
ffrom end so to end dost atteyne and tylle,   4
Disposyng ich werk swetly at his wyll,
We the besiche, lord, with humble reuerence,
Come þu and teche vs þe ways of prudence.

O Adonay & dux domus Israel qui moysi in igne flamme rubi
apparuisti & ei in syna legem dedisti veni ad redimendum nos
in brachio extento.

O adonaye, chieff duke of Israell,   8
Which them conduced from thrall captiuite,
Apperyng to Moyses madist hym of counsell
In þe mount of syna, ther shewyng thy maieste,
Tokyst hym thy law in a bushe fire flamme,   12
We lowly be-sich the, lord omnypotent,
Come and redeme in thy powre most extente.

O Radix Iesse qui stas in signum populorum super quem con-
tinebunt reges os suum quem gentes deprecabuntur veni ad
liberandum nos iam noli tardare.

O Radix Iesse, most Souerayne and excellent,
Stondyng in godly signe of euery nacion,   [fol. 168ᵛᵒ]
Tofore whome all kyngys þer mowthys shalle stent,   17
Beynge ryghte mywet and styll as any stone,
Shall knele in þi presence & mak deprecacione,
Them to delyuer & vs all in a throwe,   20
Sprakly, blyssyd lorde, be nott ther-in slowe.

Heading: MS. disponens *repeated.*   7 Come *corrected from* Cume.

O clauis dauid & septrum domus israel, qui aperis & nemo
claudit, claudis & nemo aperit, veni & educ uinctum de domo
carceris sedentem in tenebris et in umbra mortis.

O clauis dauid, of whom Isaias tolde,
Hote septure & key, to eche look welle mett
Of Israelle—I meane of Iacobus howsholde— 24
Thowe opynyst lokes whiche no wyghte can shett,
And closist a-geyn þat cannott be vnshett;
Lowse vs, þi presoners, boundene in wrechidnesse,
Off synne shadowed with mortalle derknesse. 28

O oriens splendor, lucis eterne & sol iusticie, veni et illumina
sedentes in tenebris & umbra mortis.

O oriens splendor of euer-lastynge lyghte,
Whos bemys transcende þe commyn clerenesse
Of sonne or mone, for we of very ryghte
The clepe þe bryght sonne of trowth, ryghtwysnesse 32
With iustise & mercy eche wrong to redresse,
To þe we clepe with alle owre hert & brethe,
To lyght vs þat sytt in þe derknesse of dethe.

O rex gencium & desideratus earum, lapisque angularis, qui
facis vtraque unum, veni [et salva] hominem quem de limo
formasti.

O rex gencium, whom alle people disire 36
To honour & love with herty affeccione,
The corner stone þat craftly browȝth nyre [fol. 169ʳᵒ]
The both testamentis, makyng þem one,
Oold & newe madest lawfully vnyon, 40
Saue, lord, mankynd, thy most noble creture,
Made of vile erthe to resemble þi fayre figure.

22 MS. dauid *interlined above*.
31 MS. kyndnesse *crossed out after* very.
33 With . . . to] MS. Which . . . do.

O emmanuel rex & legifer noster, expectacio gencium & saluator
earum, veni ad saluandum nos domine deus noster.

O emanuel, owre souerayne lord & kyng,
In whom we crystene mene trust in especiall,   44
Geue to thy suggetis grace, by good lykyng
Wele to perfourme þi preceptis legalle,
And saue vs, thy seruauntis, fro myscheff all.
Thus we pray, owre graciouse sauyowre,   48
Owr lord, owre good, owre louyng redemptore.

O uirgo uirginum, quomodo fiet quia nec primam similem, uisa
es nec habere sequentem, filie ierlm̄ quid me admiramini diuinum
est misterium hoc quod operata est in me.

O uirgo uirginum, alle pereles in uertu,
Wymmen of ierlm̄, muse on þis mater,
How þu, a maydyn, art the moder of Ihū.   52
Natheles, if ony of them þis secretly enquire,
Swet lady, then shortly make to þem þis an-swere:
'The hye myght of god þis mystery first be-gane.
Ʒe dameseles of Ierlm̄, why wonder ʒe so thane?'   56

59.   *Jesus, My Lord and Protector*

MS. Bodley 939
(Sum. Catal. No. 27691)

(written as prose)

IHū almygty, and mary, maydyn fre,   [fol. 12ᵛᵒ]
By the mediacion off court eternall,
Preserue my liffe in such felicite   3
That uertu may increce & vyce may haue a falle.
ffor to none odur wul i neuyr calle,
But only to the, my lord & protector,
Aʒenst alle myn enmys to be my defendor. amen.   7

60. *Christ, Defend Me from My Enemies*

Corpus Christi Coll. Oxford, MS. 274

[N]Ow rightwis Iuge, crist lord Ihū,   [fol. 1ᵛᵒ]
   of kyngis kyng and lord also,
With thi fadir þow regnes so trew
   the haly gost & elles no mo.   4
Gudely þow take my praier now,
   and twrne noght þin ere þer fro.

To erth when þow come downe fro hevene,   [fol. 2ʳᵒ]
   & cled þe in a virgyne clene,   8
þe verray flesch þow tuke full evene,
   & visitt all þis warld be-dene,
and clensed vs of oure synnes sevene—
   With þi blude þi luffe was sene.   12

Thi glorius passioun I þe beseke,
   gracius god, þat marked all,
Defend my saule I be noȝt seke
   fro all perilles þat may be-fall;   · 16
in thi servis for to be meke,
   & duelle with þe in stede & stall.

Thy vertew, lord, ay be me nere,
   of thy defence þat I noȝt faile,   20
myne enemyse þat my saule noght dere
   When þat þai seke forto assaile:
body and saule þow kepe infere,
   þat þaire frawdis neuer me prevaile.   24

Thow þat, with þi myghty hand,
   brake vp þe ȝate of hellys pitt,
breke myne enemyse þat þai noght stand;
   and all þaire waytyngis þow vnknytt,   28
       6 MS. þi nere.

be þe whilk þai ere all way wirkand
  me fro þe right way for to flytt.

Criste, me criand now þou here,
  Wrich vmsett with synnes fele,   32
Askand þi pite with hevy chere.   [fol. 2ᵛᵒ]
  Of thi solace send me some dele
þat myne enemyse rise noȝt to dere
  ne of my schame me to apele.   36

Destrued be þai þat me wald spill!
  Welke þai oway right vnto noght!
ffalle þai in gildre þai will
  thurgh envy thai for me wroght.   40
Ihū, meke withoutyne ill,
  fforsake me nevir þat þow dere boght!

Be my defendour and my scheld
  & my protectour be all-way!   44
Vnder þi baner þu me beld,
  þat thurgh strengh gayne-stand I may,
and myne detractours make to held
  &, þai oure-commyne, be glad for ay.   48

Send me fro þi sete aboue
  þe haligaste es comfortour
to clere my counsell, þat es in drove,
  thurgh his counsell & his splendour;   52
and all my haters hy to reprove,
  and þaire hatered turne to dolour.

The figure of þi crosce haly
  all my wittis vmbelappe,   56
With þe baner of þi victory
  ourecome my fo—grawnt me slike happe,

39 MS. galdre; *after this word* at *crossed out.*   42 þat] MS. at.
55 crosce] MS. cosce.
56 wittis] MS. wittis þai—*erroneously, as shown by the Latin text.*

and putt hem to þe vilany,   [fol. 3ʳᵒ]
    als þow with crosce gaffe hym a knappe.   60

Crist, þu haue mercy on me now,
    of lifand god þe Sone allone,
mercy, I pray! on þe I trow,
    lord of Angelles, sittand in trone,   64
mynde on me, lord, evir haue þow,
    gifer of grace, take þu my mone!

God þe fadir & þe Sone infere
    and þe haligaste also,   68
þat lord ert called lefe & dere
    and onefald god withoutene mo,
endeles vertew ay be þe nere
    and wirschippe þat sall neuer say ho. Amen.   72

61. *Jesus of Nazareth, Have Mercy on Me*

Cambridge Univ. MS. Ii. 6. 43
Oracio bona de ihū xⁱ

[I]Hū crist of Naȝareþ,   [fol. 89ᵛᵒ]
      That for vs all suffriddist deþ
Vpon þe rode tree,   3
Thorow vertu of ȝowre woundis v.
    That ȝe suffryd in ȝoure lyue,
    Haue mercy on me!   AmeN.   6

62.   *A Prayer by the Wounds against the Deadly Sins*

Balliol Coll. Oxf. MS. 316 A

[I]Hū, for thi blode þou bleddest   [fol. 108ʳᵒ]
      And in the firste tyme þu sheddest
In thy membre pryve,

Clense me oute of lecherye,   4
And oute of all Maner folye,
    And haue Mercy on me.

[I]hū, for the dropus swete
That þou swettest on olyvete   8
    ffor drede all to thy dethe,
Oute of wrath clense my life,
Haue mercy on me, synful caytife,
    Ihū of nazarethe.   12

[I]hū, þi peynes weron ful stronge
When the scorges, both smert & longe,
    Made thy body to blede.
On thee, Ihū, mercy y crye   16
To clense me oute of glotonye
    And helpe me at myn nede.

[I]hū, for thi þorny crowne
That made þi blode to renne a-downe   20
    Aboute thi fayre face,
Let no pride my soule drecche ;
Haue mercy one me, synful wrecche,
    Ihū, for thi grete grace.   24

[I]hū, as y vndurstond,
Thou bleddist blode at boþe þine hond
    When þat þei were nayled ;
Clense me oute of covetise   28
And graunte me grace sone to ryse,
    Of synnes when y am assayled.

[I]hū, þu bleddest more blode
When þou were nailed on þe rode   32
    Thoru þi fete with nayles.

Let me nevere in slowthe synke,
But graunt me grace for to swynke
    Thynges that me avayles.   [fol. 108ᵛᵒ]

[I]hū, blessid be thi bones!   37
Blode and watire ran at ones
    Oute of þi precious herte;
Oute of envy clense þou me,   40
And graunte me loue and charite,
    Ihū, for thy woundes smerte.

[H]aue mercy on me, ihū criste,
ffor thi dethe and þine vpriste,   44
    And for thi modere loue,
And for thi strong passioun,
Of al my synnes pardoun
    And bryng vs to hevene aboue. A. M. E. N. 48

At the beginning of each stanza a small letter is written, with
space left for an illuminated initial.

63.   *Let not the Fiend Overcome Me*

Royal MS. 17. C. xvii

I Hū cryste, þat dyed on tre   [fol. 96ᵛᵒ]
  And sofurred pyne for Adam syn,
Gyf me grace to worschepe þe,
    For þe to plese I wolde begyn.   4
Swete Ihū, of mercy fre,
    Graunt me grace þi luf to wyn,
And fleschely luf þu do fro me,
    For Mary luf þat þu lyght in.   8
Lord, for þat ded þu dyed for me,
    Late me neuer no luf begyn
Ware-thrugh þu suld dysplesyd be,
    Nor I be blemyst wyt schame or syn.   12

Ihū, begynnere of my wele
   And coueryng of my cares colde,
Me, soro-full, I pray þe hele,
   Þat syn as wondyd many folde.   16
As þu had for me wondys fele,
   And of þi sogette was þu salde,
Wen dede sall my days dele
   My saule þu take into þi halde.   20
Swete Ihū, my luf lele,
   Þat sofurd for me bothe hungur & colde,
Lat neuer þe ffend so wyt me mele
   Þat he ouercome ȝong nor olde.   24

Ihū, thynk, þu boght me dere
   Wyt harde payns & wondes sore,
Ryghtwys prince wytoutyn pere,
   Lat me noȝt rest in syn no more;   28
And gyf me grace, hwyles I am here,
   Wyt hert & wyll to do þi lore,
And wyt þi grace my saule þu clere,
   Þat þe ffend as fyled wyt syne sore.   32
Swete Ihū, þu stand me nere
   Wen he assayles me any more,
And lat hym neuer ourecome here,
   To gar me syn as I dyd ore.   36

64.   *Richard de Caistre's Hymn*

MS. Harley Charter 58. C. 14

Oracio venerabilis viri Richardi de Caystre quondam vicarius
Sancti Steffani Norwyc quam oracionem ipse composuit.

IHū lorde, þat madest me
   And with þi blyssyd blode hast bowght,
fforyeue þat I haue greuyd þe
   In worde, werke and thowght.   4

15 Me] MS. My.

Ihū, for þi woundys smerte
  On fote and handys too,
Make me meke and lowe in hert,
  And þe to loue as I schulde doo.   8

Ihū [criste], to þe I calle!
  As þu art god full of myght,
Kepe me clene, þat I ne falle
  In fleshely synn as I haue tyght.   12

Ihū, grante me myn askyng,
  Perfyte pacyonis in my desesse,
And neuer I mot doo þat thyng
  Þat schulde yn onythyng dysplese.   16

Ihū, þat art heuene kyng,
  So[þ]-fast boþe god and man also,
Ʒeue me grace of [gode] endyng
  And hem þat I am beholdyn to.   20

Ihū, for þoo dulful teris
  Þat þu gretyst for my gylt,
Here and spede my preyorys,
  And spare [me] þat I be not spylt.   24

              Pater noster Aue Maria

Ihū, for hem þat I beseche
  That wrathyh þe in ony wyse;
Withhold from hem þi hande of wreche
  And lete hem leuyn in þi seruyse.   28

9 criste] *the reading of nearly all MSS.; clearly a scribal mission.*
16 yn] *Probably we should amend to* þe, *as in most MSS.*
19 gode] *omitted in Harley and Trinity; found in all the other MSS.*
24 me *occurs in nearly all MSS.*
25 þat I *should be corrected to* I þe, *the reading of most MSS.*

Ihū, yoyfull [for] to sen
  Of all þi seyntes euerychone,
Chomfort hem þat carfull ben,
  And helpe hem þat ar woo begone.   32

Ihū, kepe hem þat ben goode,
  And mende hem þat han greuyd þe,
And sende men frutes of erdely foode,
  As eche man nedyth to hys degre.   36

Ihū, þat art withowteyn lese
  Almyghty god in trynyte,
Cese þise werrys and send us pees,
  With lestyn[g] loue and cheryte.   40

Ihū, þat art þe gos[t]ly stone
  Of all holy cherche and erde,
Bryngge þi foldys floke in one
  And reule hem ryghtly with on herde.   44

Ihū, for þi blyssyd blode,
  [Bryng tho soules in-to blys]
Of qwom I haue had ony goode,
  And spare þat þei han done amysse. Amen.   48

    Pater noster aue maria qd Robt. Harman.

65. *Make Me Loathe Earthly Likings*

B.M. Addit. MS. 37788

Swete Ihū

GOod god, make me for þi love & þi desyre   [fol. 88ro]
 ley doune þe birden of fleshly myre
And erthly lykingis to lothe: 3
My wille of þe flesh haue ladiship,
Reson of my wille haue lordship,

    29 for *a scribal omission; found in nearly all MSS.*
    46 *This line supplied from the Merton MS.*

& þi grace be lorde vppon them boþe;　　6
And so throw me withinne & withowte
to be soget ondir þi wille alle abowte
to alle þat is reson Right & soþe.　　9

66. *Grant Peace to Thy True Lovers*

Henry E. Huntington Library, Ellesmere MS. 34. B. 7

A deuoute prayer

O Ihū, to all thy true louers
　Graunt peace of hert and stedffast mynde;
To theym that þi loue dothe seke
Thou graunt theym thy grace and solas eke.　　4

O ffader dere, most of powere,
Gyff thy children thy loue in fere,
And grace to keepe the same.

O Ihū, flowre moste of honour,　　8
O swete sapoure, moste of dulcoure,
Blessed be thy name!　.

O spirit, inspire loue and desire,
Accende thy ffyre, defende frome ire,　　12
And keepe vs from blame!

O Lady bryght, launterne of lyght,
Swettist wyght, moder of myght,
And mayden of goode fame!　　16

O true loue, true, knytt in vertue,
Thy loue to grow in vs euerr newe
Gyff vs grace withoute reclame.

O blessed mary, virgyn of nazareth   20
And moder of almyghty lorde of grace,
Which his peple saued hase [frome deth
And] frome the paynes of the infernall place.

Nowe, blessed lady, kneele afore his face,   24
And pray hym soone my sowle to saue from losse
Which with his blessed bloode bought hase
thorow hys great passion nailed on the crosse. Amen.

67.   *Close in My Breast Thy Perfect Love*

B.M. Addit. MS. 37049

I Hū, my luf, my ioy, my reste,   [fol. 24ʳᵒ]
  þi perfite luf close in my breste
þat I þe luf & neuer reste;   3
And mak me luf þe of al þinge best,
And wounde my hert in þi luf fre,
þat I may reyne in ioy euer-more with þe.   6

68.   *Lord, I long after Thee*

Trinity College Dublin MS. 155

I Hū, for þe mourne I may   [fol. 8ᵛᵒ]
  As turtel þat longeþ boþe nyȝt & day
  for her loue is gone hyr froo,
for aftur þe, lorde, me longeþ ay;   4
And þat is al my myrþe & pley,
  Where I sitte or goo.

No. 68.   3 gone] MS. loue.

þerfore, lord, þou rewe on me [fol. 9ʳᵒ]
And helpe me sone, þat I may see   8
þe feyerhe[d] of þi face
With angelys þat byn bryȝt & clere
And holy soules þat þou bouȝtes dere
Into holy place.   12

69.   *Ave Gracia Plena*

B.M. Addit. MS. 20059

Aue gracia plena dominus tecum. luce. 1.   [fol. 97ᵛᵒ]

AVe gracia plena, devoide of all trespace,
  Ryght well knowen to god before the world began,
Promysed of prophetes for oure chyefe solace,
  Annunciat by Aungell was thy concepcioun,   4
  Without originall synne as diuerse maketh men-
     cioun—
    Bothe gotene and borne, non in like case—
    Wherfore, haile! glorious lady, mary full of grace.

Ecce concipies et paries filium. luce. 1.
Orietur stella ex Jacob. Numero. 24.

Haile! gracious virgyn, in materno vtero   8
  Sanctified also, or euere thou wast borne
Esayas prophesyed, withe diuuer other moo,
  þat þu shuldest conceyve which most helpe men for-
    lorne,
   The blessid ster of Jacob promysed long beforne,   12
    The swete flowre of Naȝareth, most feyrest of face—
    Wherfore, haile! glorious lady, mary full of grace.

10 clere] MS. clepᵒ.
11 *After* þat *is written* þᵘ *with dots for deletion.*

Spiritus sanctus superueniet in te et virtus altissimi obum-
brabit tibi. luce 1.

Haile! generouse lady, in thy tender age
  Inuiolate, vnto god of most hye devocioun,   16
Beawtefyed with vertue and voide of all owterage,
  O fresshe fragraunt floure, of greatest discrecioun
  Ab inicio predestynate, by diuine eleccioun,
    In whome our sauyour crist chose his dwellyng
      place—   20
    Where-fore, heile! glorious lady, mary full of grace.

Ego dixi dij estis et filij excelsi omnes. psal. 81.

Haile! pure virgyn, mary, in thy childes byrthe—
  Of carefull payne and woo, there was non in the
Whiche women do suffre—þu haddest all ioye &
      myrthe,   24
  Therfore þu maist be called a goddes; yf any be
  Other in heven or erthe, then surely thow art she—
    One spyryte and will with cryst in his palace.   27
    Wherfore, haile! glorious lady, mary full of grace.

Quum autem adheret deo vnus spiritus est. 1 Cor. 6.
Oculi domini super iustos et aures eius ad preces   [fol. 98ro]
eorum. Psal. 33.

Haile! precellent lady, bothe quene & empresse,
  The chosen spowse of god his promyse to fulfyll,
Pray for vs, pore wretches þat lyve here in distres,
  O flowre of virginite, whiche neuer thoghtist yll; 32
  Thy son will performe what so euer is thy will.
    Loke! for whome thow prayest, released is his
      trespace—
    Wherfore, haile! glorious lady, mary full of grace.

21 MS. fore *interlined above.*

Quia respexit humilitatem Ancille sue. luce 1.

Haile! rubicounde Rose, of womenhod the flowre,   36
   Synes thy fyrst begynnyng our lord was with the,
Of thy carnall substaunce he became our sauyoure.
   Perceyvyng thy gret godenesse & humilite,
   Thow optayndest grace before the deite,   40
     Or euer cryst did come into thy palace—
     Wherfore, haile! glorious lady, mary full of grace.

Quia fecit mihi magna qui potens est. luce 1.

Haile! serene princesse, shynyng in vertu clere,
   Pray for vs suche grace here presently to optayne. 44
O carbuncle of chastite, in gyftes þu hast no pere;
   Kepe vs from heresyes and all opynyons vayne,
   Desyre cryst, thy son, that we may remayne
     Aboue with hym in syon, þat ioyfull heyvenly
       place—   48
     Now here I do conclude, haile! mary, full of grace.

Dulcis amica dei, rosa vernans, stella decora,
Tu memor esto mei dum mortis venerit hora.

        Amen
    Spes mea   Jesus Maria.

70.   *Ecce! Ancilla Domini*

       Cambridge Univ. MS. Add. 5943

'ECce! ancilla domini'—   [fol. 182ᵛᵒ]
   thus seyde the virgine by-thute eny vyse,
Whan gabryll grett hure gracyously:
'hayle be thu, virgine! I-preued on prys,   4
thu shalt conceyue a swete spyce.'
then seyde the virgine so myldely:
'Ther-to I han ful lytel of prys,
   ecce! Ancilla domini.'   8

hayle be thu, gracious! by-thute eny gult,
mayden I-bore alther best,
Al en thy body schal be fulfullyd,
That profythes haueþ ypreched ful prest;⁣   12
he wyl be bore of thy brest.
Then sayde the virgine so myldely:
'he ys to me a welcome gest,
    Ecce! ancilla domini.'   16

Then sayde that Angel: 'conseyue þu schalt
With-in þyn holy body bryȝt
A chyld þat Ihesus schall be I-callyd,
Þat ys þe gryte godes sone of myȝt;   20
þu ert hys Tabernacle fayre I-dyȝt.
Then seyde þe virgine mildely:
'Syþ he wroȝt neuer a-ȝeyn þe ryȝt,
    Ecce,' &c.   24

Kalle hym ihesus of nasaret,
god & man in on degre,
that in the rode schalle suffre deth
and regne schalle in dauidys dignite,   28
wel goude tydynges hath sente to the.
then seyde the virgine so myldely:
'he schal be dyre welcome to me,
    Ecce! Ancilla domini.'   32

71. *Gabriel Came Down with Light*

MS. Ashmole 189
(Sum. Catal. No. 6777)

Alma redemtoris mater

SWete lady, now ȝe wys,   [fol. 105ᵛᵒ]
   As ye bene quene of heuen blys,
Why þat yowre name callyd ys
         Redemtoris mater.   4

I saw gabryel cum doune with lyȝth,
To me he seyde, þat swete wyȝth,
'Aue maria, þu shalt hyȝth
        Redemtoris mater.'   8

'Man to safe þat was for-lore,   [fol. 106ʳᵒ]
As prophetis seyde here be-fore,
Ihūs of þe now wyll by bore,
        Redemtoris mater.'   12

Oure ladye merwaylede al yn here þoȝth,
How þat þe angele seyde myȝt be wroȝth,
Syne mane she knewe nott,
        Redemtoris mater.   16

'Now drede þe nouȝt, my lady bryȝth,
The holy gost one yow ys lyȝth,
And werke so þat ye shall hyȝth
        Redemtoris mater.'   20

Worþy lady, & quene of blysse,
Off þy mercy lete vs not mysse,
Thynke þat þy name called ys
        Redemtoris mater.   24

By prophetis hit was seyde be-forne,
To safe mankynde þat was for-lorne,
Ihūs of þe now shalbe borne,
        Redemtoris mater.   28

Lete þy mercy now spring & sprede,
ffor-sake not man for hys mysdede,
To þe men call in euery nede,
        Redemtoris mater.   32

14 Al *deleted before* angele.

Lyft vp þy hert, man, & see
The frout of lyfe she beryth to þe.
Withoute ende here name shall be
       Redemtoris mater.   36

I wyll & shall Att my conynge
Seken & seruen þat worþy thynge,
ffor she was clepyd in here chyldynge,
       Redemtoris mater.   40

An Angele seyde to þe mayden fre,   [fol. 106ᵛᵒ]
'The holygost shall com to the
And þorowe hys werkyne þu shalt be
       Redemtoris mater.'   44

Maydene & modyr yn on persone.
was neuer non fownde but ye Alone;
Pray we All to heuyne kynge A bone,
       Redemtoris mater.   48

72. *My Thought Was on a Maid so Bright*

Trinity Coll. Camb. MS. 1230

Alma redemptoris mater   [No. III]

AS I lay vp-on a nyth
My þowth was on a berd so brith
That men clepyn marye ful of myth
       Redemptoris mater.   4

[T]o here cam gabryel wyth lyth
and seyd, 'heyl be þu, blysful wyth!
To ben clepyd now art þu dyth
       Redemptoris mater.'   8

37 MS. comynge.

At þat wurd þat lady bryth
Anon conseyuyd god ful of myth
Than men wyst weel that sche hyth
    Redemptoris mater.   12

[Q]wan ihesu on þe rode was pyth
Mary was doolful of that syth
Til sche sey hym ryse vp rith
    Redemptoris mater.   16

Ihesu that syttyst in heuene lyth
Graunt vs to comyn beforn thi sith
wyth that berde that is so brith
    Redemptoris mater.   20

73. *Sapiencia Sent to Redeem Man*

Lansdowne MS. 379

Mirabilem Misterium   [fol. 38ro]
þe sone of god ys mane be-cume

A Mervelus þyng I hafe musyd in my mynde,
  Howe þat veritas spronge owȝte of þe gro[u]nde,
And Iusticia for all mane-kynde,
ffrom heuene to erthe he came a downe.   4
    Mirabilem Misterium & ce

Than misericordia, that mercyfull maye,
Seyng mane was dampnde for hys trepas,
hathe sent down sapiencia, þe sothe to saye,
Mane to redeme and bryng to grase.   8
    Mirabilem misterium & ce

Celestyall Cyteȝens, for vs þat yowe praye
To hyme þat ys bothe alpha and oo,
That we maye be sauyd one domus daye,
And browȝte to þat blysse he bowȝte vs to.   12
    Mirabilem Misterium, þe son of & ce

Heading: MS. Misteriiȝ.   5 MS. mĩa.

74. *Honour to Him Who Descended from Heaven*

Trinity Coll. Camb. MS. 652

Honour be euer withowtyne ende   [fol. 169ᵛᵒ]
To hym that fro the hevyne discende

THat was Ihū, oure saueour,
   The oonly sone of god myghty,
That beldyt in that bygly bowre,
Whiche is the wombe of mylde mary.   4

Mylde that maydene may be cald,
ffor with fylthe was she neuer fylde;
ffull wele was hyr that had in wolde,
In hyr chief chawmbre, suche a chylde.   8

She is the chief of chastyte,
the conclaue and the clostre clene,
Of hym that hyr humylite
Commendyth, amonge his sayntys bedene.   12

ffull worthy is she to com-mende,
ffor hir mekenes as wytnes wele
that was the cause god sone descende,
ffor to be borne here, for oure sele.   16

75. *Mary Bore Both God and Man*

Trinity Coll. Camb. MS. 1230

Haile mary ful of grace Modyr in virgynytee   [No. I]

THe holy gost is to þe sent
   ffro þe fadyr omnypotent;
Now is god wyth-in þe went,
   The aungel seyd, 'aue'.

Qwan the aungel 'aue' began,
fflesch & blood to-gedyr ran;
Marye bar boþe god and man,
  Thorw vertu & þowr dyngnyte.   8

So seyth þe gospel of seynt ion,
God & man is mad but on,
In flesch & bloyd, body and bon,
  o god in personys thre.   12

And þe prophete Ieremye
Told in hys prophecye,
That þe sone of Marye
  Schuld deye for vs on rode tre.   16

Meche ioye to vs was graunth,
And in erthe pees I-plaunth,
Qwan þat born was þis faunth
  In þe lond of galyle.   20

Mary, graunth vs þe blys
Ther þi sonys wonyng is;
Of þat we han don amys,
  Prey for vs pur charyte. Amen.   24

76.   *Born is Our God Emanuel*

Trinity Coll. Camb. MS. 1230

Nowel nowel nowel To vs is born owr god emanuel
(No. II)

IN bedlem þys berde of lyf
Is born of marye, maydyn and wyf;
he is boþe god & man I-schryf. Nowel nowel
Thys prince of pees xal secyn al stryf,
  & wone wyth vs perpetuel.   5

This chyld xal bey vs wyth hys bloyd
And be naylyd vp-on þe royd,
hys raunsum pasyth al erdly goyd. Nowel nowel
allas! qwat wyth dar be so woyd,
    To sle so ientyl a iowel.   10

Be hys powste he his emprys
Schal take fro helle at hys vprys,
and saue mankende vp-on þys wys. Nowel nowel
Thus tellþ vs þe prophecys,
    Þat he is kyng of heuen & helle.   15

This maydenys sone to hys empere
Schal stey to heuene be his powere;
hys holy gost vs alle xal lere. Nowel nowel
[Ther] þei and þe fadyr in feere
    Schul regne, o god—þys leue I weel.   20

Pray we þys chyld wyth good entent,
In our deying he vs present
On-to hys fadyr omnypotent. Nowel nowel
The ferst tydyng of þys testament
    browth to vs seynt gabryel.   25

77. *A Maid Hath Borne the King of Kings*

A. MS. Ashmole 189
(Sum. Catal. No. 6777)

REgem regum A mayde hath borne,   [fol. 104ᵛᵒ]
To Sawe mankynde that was forlorne;
And ȝyt ys sche as sche was be-forne,
    Res miranda.

Angelus consilij
Was borne of þis blessyd ladye,
Virilis ignara consorcii
   Sol de stella.   8

Cedrus Alta libani,
þat grewe on þis hylle so hye,
Yne oure valey he doyth Aplye
   Carne Sumpta.   12

Verbum ens Altissimi,
Persawynge mischefe so nye,
ffor our synnes he cam to dye
   Valle nostra. amen.   16

Ysayas cecinit   [fol. 105ro]
þat a chylde schalle be borne,
Synagoga meminit
þerof longe tyme beforne;   20

Set non suis vatibus
þer-of þay take no Affiawns,
Sibiliniis versibus
þat borne was of oure Aliawns.   24

Infelix propera te, þe y saye,
Leste þu be dampned a domys daye;
þane shalt þu synge welawaye,
but þu belyve hec predicta.   28

     B. MS. Arch. Selden B. 26
      (Sum. Catal. No. 3340)

G Lad & blithe mote ȝe be,   [fol. 19vo]
  All that euer y here nowe se,
     Alleluya!

10 MS. yrewe.
  11 MS. yuoure *with* yu *cancelled*. Aplye] Alp *first written and*
then cancelled.   16 MS. Valle nram̃.

Kynge of kyngys, lorde of alle,   4
borne he is in oxe stalle,
        Res miranda.

The angel of consel, now borne he is
of a maide ful clene y-wys,   8
        Sol de stella—
The sunne þat euer shyneþ bry3t,
the sterre þat euer 3eueth his ly3t
        Semper clara.   12

Ry3t as þe sterre bryngth forth his beme,
So þe maide here barn teme,
        pari forma.
Nother þe sterre for his beme,   16
noþer þe maide for here barne-teme,
        ffit corrupta.

The cedur of liban, þat growyth so hye,
vnto þe ysope is made lye   20
        Valle nostra.
Godys sone of heuen bry3t,
vn-tyl a maide is he ly3t,
        Carne Sumpta.   24

Ysaye saide by prophecie,   [fol. 20ᵛᵒ]
the Sinagoge hath hit in memorye,
3yt neuer he lynneth maliciusly
        esse ceca.   28
Yf they leue not here profetys,
þen lete hem leue ethen metrys,
In Sibylinys versiculys
        hec predicta.   32

Un-happy iewe, come þu nere,
By-leue ellys thyne eldere.
Why wolt þu, wrecche, y-dampned be
        20 lye] *read* alye.

Whomme techeth þe letter ?   36
By-holde the childe þe better—
Hym bare a maide, moder, marye.

78.   *Verbum Caro Factum Est*

Advocates MS. 19. 3. 1

Verbum caro factum est.   [fol. 94ᵛᵒ]

I Passud þoru a garden grene,
   I fond a herbere made full newe—
A semelyour syght I haff noght sene,
   O ylke treo sange a tyrtull trew—   4
There-yn a mayden bryȝt off hew,
   And euer sche sange, & neuer sche sest:
Thies were þe notus þat sche can schew,
   Verbum caro factum est.   8

I askud þat mayden what sche mentt,
   Sche bad me byde & I schuld here;
What sche sayd I toke gude tent,
   yn hyr songe had sche voice full clere: 12
Sche said, 'a prynce withouten pere
   Ys borne & layd betwene to best;
Therefore I synge as ȝe mey here
   Verbum caro factum est.'   16

And þoroght þat frythe as I can wend,
   A blestfull [song] ȝit hard I mo;
And þat was of threo scheperdus hend,
   'Gloria in excelsis deo.'   20

4 treo] *perhaps* tree.   6 sest] MS. sesest.
13 sche] *blot over final letter.*
18 song *in the text of Sloane MS.* 2593.
19 threo] *perhaps* three.

I wold noght they had faren me fro,
   And eft-hyr þem full fast I prest;
Then told þei me þat þei sange ssoo
   ffor verbum caro factum est.   24

They said þat songe was þis to sey:
   'To god a-bouun be joy & blysse!
ffor pece yn erth also we pray,
   Tyll allmen þat yn goodnesse ys.   28
   þe may þat is withouten mysse
      hasse borne a child be-twene to best;
   Sche is þe cause þer-off Iwysse
      That verbum caro factum est.'   32

I fared me furthe yn þat frythe
   I mett threo commely kyngis with crone;
I spod me furth to speke þem with,
   & on my knees I kneled done.   36
   þe ryalest of home to me con rone
      And said, 'we farred wele at þe fest,
   ffro bethleem now ar we bone
      ffor verbum caro factum est.   40

'ffor we seo god be-comun yn mannus flech,
   þat bote hasse broght off all oure bale,
A-wey oure synnus forto wesche;
   A mey hym harburd yn hur hall,   44
   Sche socourd hym sothly yn hur sale,
      & held þat hend yn hur a-rest;
   ffoll trewly mey sche tell þat tale
      That verbum caro factum est.'   48

---

26 *A single letter deleted after* To.   30 MS. best⁹.
34 threo]. *perhaps* three.   35 spod] *possibly* sped.
36 s *deleted before* kneled.   41 seo] MS. sě.
47 sche] *blot over final letter.*

Vntyll þat prences wyll we pray,
  Als sche is bothe moder & mayd,
Sche be oure helpe als sche wele mey
  To hyme þat yn hur lappe was layd;   52
To serue hyme we be prest & payd,
  And þer-to make we oure behest,
ffor I hard when sche sange & said
  'Verbum caro factum est.'   56

    Explicit pro John hawghton.

79. *Make Ye Merry for Him that is Come*

MS. Ashmole 189
(Sum Catal. No. 6777)

Alleluya Alleluya deo patri sit gloria

SAluator mundi, domine,   [fol. 107ro]
  ffader of heuene, yblessyd þu be!
þu gretyst A mayde with one Aue,
  Alleluya, Alleluya!   4

Ad-esto nu[n]c propicius,
þu sendyst þy sonne, swete Iesus,
Man to be-cum for loue of vs,
  Alleluya deo!   8

Te reformator sensuum,
lytyll & mekell, All & some,
make ye mery, for hym þat ys ycom,
  Alleluya deo!   12

Gloria tibi, domine,
Ioy & blysse A-monge vs be!
ffor Att thys tyme borne ys he,
  [Alleluya, Alleluya!]   16

    14 & *repeated.*

80.   *The Lord that Lay in Asses' Stall*

MS. Arch. Selden B. 26
(Sum. Catal. No. 3340)

I-Blessid be þat lord in mageste   [fol. 28ᵛᵒ]
qui natus fuit hodie

THat lord þat lay in asse stal-le,
   cam to dye for vs al-le,
to mak vs fre þat erst were þralle,
   qui natus fu-it hodie.   4

This lorde þat lay in asse stalle,
Come to dye for vs alle,
To make vs fre þat erst were þralle,
   Qui natus, &c.   8

Wel mowe we glad & mery bee,
Sith we were þralle & nowe be free;
The fende oure foo he made to flee,
   Qui natus, &c.   12

And sith oure foo is fled fro vs,
We mowe wel synge & say ryʒt þus:
'Wel-come he be, this lorde iesus,
   Qui natus,' &c.   16

Nowe blessyd be this lord benynge,
That nolde his cruelle dethe resynge,
But for man-kynde to dye endynge,
   Qui natus fuit hodie.   20

19 endynge *probably a corruption of* undigne, *as indicated by the rimes.*

81.   *The Maiden Makeles*

Sloane MS. 2593

I syng a of a myden þat is makeles   [fol. 10ᵛᵒ]

I Syng of a myden   þat is makeles,
kyng of alle kynges   to here sone che ches.

he cam also stylle   þer his moder was
as dew in aprylle,   þat fallyt on þe gras.   4

he cam also stylle   to his moderes bowr
as dew in aprillè,   þat fallyt on þe flour.

he cam also stylle   þer his moder lay
as dew in aprille,   þat fallyt on þe spray.   8

moder & mayden   was neuer non but che—
wel may swych a lady   godes moder be.

82.   *Her Son Recovers Us from Adam's*
Fall

Lansdowne MS. 379

Ihc̄   [fol. 38ʳᵒ]
Tydyngis, tydyngis þat be trwe,
Sorowe ys paste and Ioye dothe renwe.

Q Whereas Adam cawsed be synne
Owre nature thus to be mortall,
A maydene sone dothe now begyne
ffor to repoyse vs frome þat fall,   4
And þat ys trwe—
The name of hyme ys Cryste Ihū.

Sume of oure kynde hathe hadd suche grase
That syne hys byrthe they dyd hyme se—   8

Bothe sonne and mother, fase to fase—
  In þe chefe Cyte calde Iude,
  And þat ys trwe—
  bothe kyngis and shepardes þey yt knwe.   12

The prophettis þer-of ware no þyng dysmayde
  Of þat tydyngis before þat þey hadde tolde,
ffor nowe yt ys fall ryȝthe as þey sayde:
  A clene mayde hathe borne a kynge,   16
  And þat ys trwe—
  ffor he ys borne to ware þe purpull hwe.

The refrains are written at the side opposite each stanza.

83.   *Bless the Time the Apple was Taken!*

Sloane MS. 2593

ADam lay I-bowndyn, bowndyn in a bond,   [fol. 11ʳᵒ]
  fowre þowsand wynter þowt he not to long;
And al was for an appil, an appil þat he tok,
As clerkis fyndyn wretyn in here book.   4

Ne hadde þe appil take ben, þe appil taken ben,
ne hadde neuer our lady a ben heuene qwen;
Blyssid be þe tyme þat appil take was,
Þer-fore we mown syngyn, 'deo gracias!'   8

84.   *A New-Year Song of the Nativity*

Sloane MS. 2593

A New ȝer, A newe ȝer a chyld was I-born,   [fol. 16ʳᵒ]
  vs for to sauyn þat al was for-lorn,
so blyssid be þe tyme!

  14 *Read:* Before þat hadde tolde of þat tydynge.

þe fader of heuene his owyn sone he sent, 4
his kyngdam for to cleymyn,
   so blyssid be þe tyme!
al in a clene maydyn our lord was I-lyȝt,
vs for to sauyn wiþ al his myȝt, 8
   so blyssid, &c.
al of a clene maydyn our lord was I-born,
vs for to sauyn þat al was for-lorn,
   so blyssid, &c. 12
lullay, lullay! lytil chyld, myn owyn dere fode,
how xalt þu sufferin be naylid on þe rode?
   so [blyssid, &c.]
lullay, lullay! lytil chyld, myn owyn dere smerte, 16
how xalt þu sufferin þe scharp spere to þi herte?
   so [blyssid, &c.]
lullay, lullay! lytyl child, I synge al for þi sake.
many on is þe scharpe schour to þi body is schape 20
   so [blyssid, &c.]
lullay, lullay! lytyl child, fayre happis þe be-falle,
how xal þu sufferin to drynke ezyl & galle?
   so [blyssid, &c.] 24
lullay, lullay! lytil chyld, I synge al be-forn,
how xalt þu sufferin þe scharp garlong of þorn?
   [so blyssid, &c.]
lullay, lullay! lytil chyld, qwy wepy þu so sore 28
& art þu boþin god & man—quat woldyst þu be more?
   so [blyssid, &c.] [fol. 16ᵛᵒ]
blyssid be þe armys þe chyld bar abowte,
& also þe tetis þe chyld on sowkyd, 32
   so [blyssid, &c.]
blyssid be þe moder, þe chyld also
Wiþ bene-dicamus domino,
   so blyssid be þe tyme! 36

85.   *A Song for the Epiphany*

Henry E. Huntington Library, MS. HM 147

Welcum welcum welcum Xe redemtor omneum.

Now ys cum owre saue-owre,   [fol. 114ro]
   And now hathe mare borne a flowre,
To al this wordill a grete soccowre,
   celi terreque dominum.   4

Now be þe Iuys fallyn in fyȝte
of Seynt stevyne, þat nobull knyȝte;
be-cause he sayde he saw a syȝte,
   lapidauerunt stephanum.   8

Seynt Iohñ, that was a martyr fre,
on crystis lappe a-slepe lay he,
of hevyn he saw þe preuete,
   aduocatur conviuio.   12

Erode, that was so full of syne,
let sle þe chyldryne of israell kyn,
of too yere age & eke withyn,
   In bethelem confinio.   16

Seynte Thomas, þat was a marter good—
Ther came knyȝtis bothe ferse & woode,
They steryde his brayne & schede his blode;
   sic passus est martyrrium.   20

Ther came thre knyȝtis with rache presens,
Offryde golde, myrre, franke-andsence—
Offryng with grete honnowre & reuerens,
   adorauerunt puerum.   24

    14 Before *chyldryne* the scribe wrote *s* and afterwards struck
it through.
  16 MS. ? conviuio.

86.   *Angels, Star, and Magi*

Advocates MS. 19. 3. 1

Ihū almyghty kyng of blys   [fol. 59ʳᵒ]
Assumpsit carnem virginis.

AS holy kyrke makys mynd,
   Intravit ventris thalamum;
ffro heyuyn to erthe to save monkynd
   Pater misit filium.   4

Of mary mylde cryste wolde be borne
   Sine virili semine,
To save monkynd þat was forlorne,
   Prime parentis crimine.   8

To mare come a messenger
   Ferens salutem homini,
Sche aunswerd hym with mylde chere,
   'Ecce! ancilla domini.'   12

Mekely on þe, þo holy goste
   Palacium intrans uteri—
Of althyng meknes is moste
   In conspectu altissimi.   16

When he was borne þat made all thyng,
   Pastor creator omnium,
Angellis þei began to syng,
   'Veni, redemptor gencium.'   20

Thre kyngis come on goid xij day,
   Stella mycante previa;
To seche þat chylde þei toke þo wey,
   Portantes sibi munera.   24

A sterne forth ladde þeis kyngis all,
   Inquirentes dominum,
Lyyng in a nasse stall
   Invenerunt puerum.   28

ffor he was kyng of kyngis heghe,
   Rex primus aurum optulit ;
And allso lord and kyng ful ryght
   Secundus rex thus protulit ;   32

ffor he was god, mon and kyng,
   Mirra mortem retulit ;
He hus all to heuyn bryng
   Qui mortem cruce voluit.   36

87.   *The Journey of the Three Kings*

Porkington MS. 10

The ster he schynythe boþe nyȝte & day,   [fol. 199ᵛᵒ]
To lede iij kyngis þer Ihū lay.

IHu whas Borne in Bedlem Iude,   [fol. 200ʳᵒ]
  Alle off a mayden, so fyndythe whe.
Owte off þe Este com kyngis iij,
Wythe ryche presente as y yow say.   The ster 4

The stuarde whas Bolde off þat contre
And Bade Errod schollde come and see
lyke as þey wentyn, all ye iij,
Goyng ffurthe yne þer Iornay.   The ster 8

ffurthe þey wentyn, pas for pas,
And Euer þe ster schone one þer ffase,
lyke as þe sone doþe throw þe glas,
And yne-to Bedleme þey toke þer way.   þe ster 12

31 kyng ful ryght *supplied in the MS. by a later hand. Cf. the
text of this with Harley 275, fol. 146 b (cf. Greene).*

Whene þey com yne-to þe plas,
Ihū wythe hys modyr whas,
þey knelyd a-downe & made solas,
And euer kyng tyll oder gan say—   þe ster   16

Whene þey had made vp hyr offeryng,
gollde and myr and ryche thyng,
they lay a-downe & toke restyng,
ffor alle a nyȝte and alle a day.   þe ster   20

As þey lay in þer slepyng,   [fol. 200ᵛᵒ]
Ther come a angell & browȝte tydyng,
And Bade theme wende nat by errod þe kyng,
But Bade þeme take a-noþer way.   þe ster   24

Errod off þis he wyxyd fful gryll,
þa þis iij kyngis Came nat hyme tylle,
Alle to ffull-ffyll hys false wylle,
And tyll hys knyȝteys he gane say—   þe ster   28

Errod Bade hys knyȝtes a-none
That þey schollde in-to bedleme gone
And sle þe chyllderyne euery-chone—
And yet he faylyd off hys pray.   þe ster   32

Angellys Come owre lady a-none,
And bade hyr in-to Egypte gone,
ther-yne to wonny, þer yne to dwelle.
yne tyme hyt wer errod-ys endyng day.   þe ster   36

Herrod dyyd and went to hell,
þer yne to wonny, þer yne to dwell,
And yne þe depyste pytte he fell—
And þer he ys ffor euer & ay.   þe ster   40

18 MS. ryhe.
37 hell] MS. dwell.

88.   *Balthazer, Melchior and Jasper*

Sloane MS. 2593

OUt of þe blosme sprang a þorn,   [fol. 12ʳᵒ]
    quan god hymself wold be born—
he let vs neuere be forlorn,
            þat born was of marie.   4

þer sprong a welle al at here fot,   [fol. 13ʳᵒ]
þat al þis word it turnyd to good—
quan Ihū cryst took fleych & blod
            of his moder marie.   8

Out of þe welle sprang a strem,
fro patriarck to jerusalem—
til cryst hymself a-ȝen it nem
            of his moder, etc.   12

In wynter quan þe frost hym fres,
a powre beddyng our lord hym ches;
betwyin an ox & an as
godes sone born he was
            of his, etc.   16

It was vp-on þe twelwe day
þer come þre kynges in ryche aray,
to seke cryst þer he lay
            & his, etc.   20

þre kynges out of dyuers londe
swyþe comyn wiþ herte stronge,
þe chyld to sekyn & vnder-fonge
            þat born was of marie.   24

Stanzas 6 and 7 marked in MS. to be inserted after stanza 5.
6 MS. trnyd.   21 MS. dyues.

þe sterre led hem a ryte way
to þe chyld þer he lay—
he help vs boþe ny3t & day
   þat born was of marie! 28

Baltyzar was þe ferste kyng, [fol. 13ʳᵒ]
he browte gold to his offeryng,
ffor to presente þat ryche kyng
   & his moder marie. 32

Melchiar was þe secunde kyng,
he browte incens to his offering,
for to presente þat ryche kyng
   & his, etc. 36

Jasper was þe þred kyng,
he browte myrre to his offeryng,
ffor to presente þat ryche kyng
   & his, etc. 40

þer þey offerid here presens, [fol. 13ᵛᵒ]
wiþ gold & myrre & francincens,
& clerkes redyn in here seqwens,
   ephifanye. 44

Knel we down hym be-forn,
& prey we to hym þat now is born:
'& let us neuer be for-lorn,
   þat born was of marie!' 48

89. *The Three Kings and Herod*
St. John's Coll. Camb. MS. 259

QWan crist was borne in bedlem, [fol. 4ᵛᵒ]
 þer rose a stere os bryth [os lem],
þat gafe so glorius a glem
  ouyr dale and downe. 4

Oure dale and downe it sprong and sprede,
þat made iij kynges to be a-drede;
In-to an unchoud lond it hem lede,
   into a towne—   8
þer were iij kyngys of grete renowne.

þe cam to seke herowd þe kyng,
and askyd hym of all þat thyng,
And speryd aftyr þe chyld so ȝyng,   12
   þat xuld be kyng—
þat schud be kyng of all Iury.
'we saw a stere secyrly,
þer-for we worchyp him for-þi,   16
   þat chyld so ȝyng;
Here gold and homage we hym bryng.'

'Wend ȝe forth, all thre in-fere,
And of þat chyld if ȝe may here,   20
þat ȝe wyll com agen in-fere,
   I ȝou beseke.
I ȝou beseke þat ȝe me say,
Os ȝe com homward agen in ȝore way,   24
þat I my-selfe hym woyrchyp may,
   þat chylde so meke;
on my bare fete I wold hym seke.'

þe kyngys no lenger þer abode,   28
but forth to bedlem þan þe rode,
and þe stere before hem glode
   Vn-tyll þie were—
Vntyll þie were þer ihū lay,   32
woondyn in a cryb of hey.

5 MS. sperde.   7 MS. unchŏd.   17 ȝũg.
21 MS. cum ȝen he.   25 MS. wyrchyp *with* o *interlined above.*

þem thowt it was a pore aray

.   .   .   .

Of prins of pes þat hast no pere.   36

Now knele we downe, all iij in-fere,
And offyr to þis derlyng dere
Gold soree and rekyls clere,
    and myre al so—   40
and myre al so in tokenyng
þat he is ueri man and kyng,
Soffarond prins ouyr all thyng,
    oon and no moo,   44
for holy wryth bere wyttenes al so.

An angell warnyd hem in here slepe,
þat þie xuld hem for herowyd kepe;
þei thankyd god with deuocion depe,   48
    and hom þie wente—
and hom þie wente on here Iornay.
quan þie-of herowd hard say,
he sayd 'alas! and welaway,   52
    for I am schente;
þis chyld he wyll my kyndam hente.'

þen erowd was both wode and wroth,
with mekyll Ire he made hys othe,   56
þat all þe londe it xulde be loth
    þat he was borne—
þat he was borne þat xuld be kyng.
he bade to doo a spythfull thyng,   60
to slee chyldẏrn both elle and ȝyng,
    in bedlem borne
with-in ij wyntrys þer beforne.

39 MS. Glod.   46 MS. selpe.   52 MS. þe.
55 MS. þe rerowd.   *57 In the MS. this line follows 59.*
60 bade] MS. dyde.   61 ȝyng] MS. thayng.   63 MS. before.
2025·16

þe chyldryn sprongyld an þe sperys,   64
þe moderys wept ful bytyr terys
þat herowd dyd hem gylte-les derys,
   þat fend so felle—
þat fend so fell, fowle mut hym befalle!   68
þat þus þeis chyldyrn martyryd all;
On-to marie we crye & calle,
   þer in blys well,
to scheld us from þe pyth of helle.   72

90.   *Hostis Herodes Impie*

Sloane MS. 2593

hostis herodis impie, Xpm̄ venire quid times; non   [fol. 32ᵛᵒ]
  eripit mortalia.

ENmy herowde, þu wokkyd kyng,
  qwy dredes þu þe of cristes comyng?
he deȝyryt here non erþely þing
þat heuene haȝt at his ȝeuyng.   4

ibant magi quia videant stellam sequentes preuiam lumen.

þre kynges þer saw a sterre ful bryȝt,
þei folwyd it wiþ al here myȝt;
bryȝtnesse þei saw þrow þat lyȝt,
þei knewe god wiþ here ȝyftes ryȝt.   8

lauacra puri gurgitis selestis angnus attigit peccata nostra.

þe welle haȝt waschyn vs fro wo,
þe lomb of heuene is comyn vs to;
he þat synne neuere wold do
haȝt waschyn clene our synnys vs fro.   12

70 MS. marte. MS. gye.
72 MS. schend us ferm. MS. *transposes ll. 71 and 72.*

nouum genus potencie aque rubescunt idrie vinumque.

> his my3t is chawngyd of newe maner, [fol. 33ro]
> þe water wyx red in pecher;
> þe water is turnyd to wyn ful cler,
> ageyn þe kynde þow it were.   16

Gloria tibi domine qui aperuisti hodie cum patre et sancto spiritu
in sempiterna secula amen.

> louyng, lord, be to þe ay!
> þat ha3t schewyd þe to vs þis day,
> wiþ fader & holy gost veray,
> þat in þe word neuer fayle may.   20

91.   *The Story of the Passion*

Arundel MS. 285

The Passioun of Christ

COmpatience persis, reuth & marcy stoundis [fol. 159vo]
  In myddis my hert, and thirlis throw þe vanis.
Thy deid, Ihū, þi petuous cruell woundis,
    Thy grym passion, gret tormentis, grevous panis,   4
In-grauit sadlie in my spreit remanis.
    Sen me of noucht þou hes boucht with þi blude
My ene, for doloure, wofull teris ranis,
    Quhen that I se the nalit on þe rude.   8

In Symon lepros hous of bathany,
    Thy feit anoyntit mary magdalen,
With precius balme & nardus-specatyve,   [fol. 160ro]
    Scho passit fra tyme hir synnes wer forgevin.   12
Thy flesche and blude in breid and wyne betuen
    Gaif thy disciplis, & Lawlie wosche þair feit.
Thy manheid dred thy passioun to sustene,
    Quhen þat þou prayit on monte oliveit.   16

            6 Sen] MS. Se.   10 MS. anonytit.

To gyde the Iowis, come Iudas scariot
    And kist þe, christ—all þe disciples fled.
To ane wraichit man Cayphas & Pylot,
    Bund as ane theif, so wes þou harlit & led   20
Till Herod had in purpor habit cled,
    ffor hethin halsit, blasphlemit, with mony blaw
Beft at ane pillar, blaiknit and forbled
    At Locostratus, quhair þai leid þe law.   24

Cuttis for þi cot þai keist, was never sewit,
    Out-throw þi hernis, þe croun of thorn þai applyit,
Wailland þin ene, into þi visage spittit,
    And for derisioun 'King of Iowis' þai cryit.   28
That nycht þi name Sanct peter thris denyit.
    Drownit in dule myrk was þi mynd, mary,
To wonder on, throw Ierusalem þou hyit
    To se thy awin sone, þat þou fosterrit, de.   32

Ruffit on croce, thir wordis did repeit,   [fol. 160vo]
    'Scicio'; richt sone þai seruit þe with gall.
Scharpe wes þe speir, þe nalis Lang & gret.
    Thy ribbis rakkit, þi face oure-spittit all,   36
To golgatha, godis sone celistiall,
    Thy croce with force þou bure, with cure & heit.
Thy tender hid and flesche virginall
    Werry, forwrocht in watter, blude and sueit.   40

Throu maryis saule þe suerd of dolour thrist,
    Quhen þat þou said, 'se þair thy sone, woman',
Commending hir to Iohnne þe ewangelist:
    Scharp bludy teris hir cristell eyne out ran.   44
Suollit wer thy syddis for scurgis bla and wan;
    Naikit and paill, ded on þe croce þou hang—

27 þin] MS. þ⁹.

Thy wanis burssin, þi senouis schorn, þan
　Crownit with thorne for scorne,—twa thevis amang.　48

My wofull hert is baith reiosit and sade,
　Thy corps, lorde Iesu christ, quhen I behalde.
Of my redempcioun I am baith blyth & glaid;
　Seand þi panis, sorelie weip I walde.　52
Cryand 'hely', þi gaistlie spreit þou ʒalde;　[fol. 161ro]
　To longus hande þi blude ran in ane rest;
Thy wofull moder swonit stif and calde,
　Quhen þou inclynit with consummatum est.　56

Dyrk wes þe sone fra þe sext hour to nyne;
　Montanis trymblit, hillis schuke & rochis claif.
Centurio said, 'þou art goddis sone dewyne';
　Ioseph de-curio spicit þe in þi graif　60
With myr and must, most vertuis & suaif—
　Thai gert þe de and forgaif berrabas.
My saule with sanctis, saluiour, resaif,
　Sen þat þi passioun purgit my trespas.　64

　　　　Explicit.

92.　　*Thy Blood Thou Shed for Me*
　　Henry E. Huntington Library, MS. HM 142

I Hū, that alle this worlde hast wroghte,　[fol. 48ro]
　And of a clene virgyn so take oure kynde,
And with thi blode oure soules hast boughte,
　My loue to þe I pray þe to bynde,
　In werk, in worde, in þought of mynde.　4
　　My soule, my body, I yeue alle to the;
　So kynde a frende schal I noon fynde,
　　ffor-why þi blode þow sched for me.　8

　　　47 MS. brurssin, *with the first* r *cancelled*.
　　　49 MS. glade, *cancelled, before* sade.

fferst, ihū lord, sone after þi byrthe,
The .viii. day, named þi Circumcisyoun,
Thow wepte in stede of yoles myrthe,
    And in a maner began thi passion;   12
    So was þou kutte for oure transgressyoun,
        With a stone knyf aboue thi kne.
    I loue þe, lord, with trewe affeccioun,
        ffor þus þi blode thow schedde for me.   16

The same nyght, lord, þat þou was take,
    After þi soper and wasshyng of fete,
Warnynge discyples þat þei schulde wake,
    Thou prayed þi fader with dropes ful wete,   20
    Swetyng þi blood þat is so swete.
        ffor drede of deth þou wolde not fle—
    A cause of loue þis is ful grete—
        ffor þus þi blode þou sched for me.   24

Aftir þi takynge, lord, þou was bounde
  Vnto a pyler, & scourged ful sore;
They leyde on þe wounde on wounde,
    ffor thi fayre body was alle to-tore;   28
    Noon ynche ther-of was kept in store.
        Thus was þou bounde to make us fre,
    Mikel am I bounde to þe þerfore,
        ffor þus þi blode þou sched for me. [fol. 48ᵛᵒ] 32

A clothe of purpure on þe þe[i] cast,
    And before pylat on þe next morne,
The to crucifye, þei cryed ful fast,
    Puttynge on þi hede a croune of þorne   36
And callyd þe 'kynge' with iape & scorne—
        The kynge of heuen, of erthe & see.
    So witht þi body, þi hede was torne,
        And þus þi blode þow sched for me.   40

Then, berynge þe Cros to caluarie,
  Vn-to þe mount þou cam at last;
Thi bodyly wounde were woxe al drye,
  The purpure þer-to was cleued ful fast.   44
  They rente it of with a grete haste,
    And þat was, good lord, more peyne to þe
  Than al þe scourgynge þat was now past,
    And þus þi blode þou sched for me.   48

Lord, to þe cros then was þou nayled,
  Handis & feet, & lyft-up on hye,
Hangenge þer-on tyl þi lyf fayled.
  All þis þou suffird us for, to bye   52
  Oure soules to lyue when oure flessche schal dye.
    What myght þou schewe more charite?
  'Graunt mercy, good lord, & mercy,' I crye,
    ffor þus þi blode þou sched for me.   56

Whan þou was deed, þorou a blynde knyght
  Wyche claf þi hert with a scharpe spere—
And with þi blode he gate his syght,
  Askynge þe mercy & mercy was there.   60
  Euer in my hert this wille I bere.
    Of alle þi kyndenes blessit mote þou be!
  If I forgate þe, ful vnkynde I were,   [fol. 49ro]
    ffor .vii. tymes þi blode þou sched for me.   64

Oracio

Now, now, Ihū, for thi Circumcisioun,
  When þou was kut so in fleshe & skyn,
Make with my soule suche a conclusioun,
  That I falle neuer in fleshly synne;   68
  And for þe grete drede þat þou stode inne,
    Prayinge thi fader yf deth myght passe,
  Conforte my soule, þat I may wynne
    Hope of þi mercy & drede þe lasse.   72

And for þi skourgynge, bounde with a corde
  Vnto þat pylour, al for our sake
Graunt us þat blode, o mercyful lorde,
    Oure soules to washe fro synnes so blake;   76
    And for þe thornes þei dide the take,
      Crounynge þin heed in-to þe brayne,
    Yeue us þat croune þat þou dide make
      In heuen for us, witht al þi payne.   80

And for purpure, þat cleued so faste
  Whan it was drawe fro þe drye blode,
Off al þi peynys gif us a taste,
    Þat þei may be oure goostly food;   84
    And with þo naylis, so stronge & good,
      That peresshid þrou both handes & feet,
    Ioyne all oure hertis vnto þat roode,
      That we þi kyndenes neuer forgeet.   88

Now, last we pray, lord, of þi grace,
  And for þat spere þat opynde þi syde,
That we may se þi blisful face
    Whan we schal here no lenger abyde;   92
    And in þis pryson sle al our pride
      With charite, mekenes & pacience,   [fol. 49ᵛᵒ]
    That, in þat kyngdom þat is so wyde,
      We may reioyce euer thi presence. AmeN.   96

93.   *The Hours of the Cross*

Cambridge Univ. MS. Ee. I. 12

I Hard a maydyn wepe   [fol. 1ᵛᵒ]
  ffor here sonnys passyon;
yt enterd into my hart full deipe,
  wyth grete contricion.   4

77. þe . . . . the] MS. þe the.   81 purpure] Harl., Douce: þi coote.

Patris sapiencia,
  The sonne off god almyght,
off fals judas be-trayd he·was,
  The maker off all lyghte.   8

Hys discipulis fled a-waye,
  And fast from hym they went.
Hys body bare was scorgyd ther,
  Hys flesche was all to-rent.   12

Hora prima, dominus
  be-fore pylate was browthe,
Wyth fals wytnes hym to dystres
  A-gaynst hym ther was sowht.   16

In the neke they smote hyme sore,   [fol. 2ro]
  And bownde hys handdis fast,
And at the last—þat grevyd hym worst—
  They spyt in-to hys facys.   20

'Creuce-figi!' clamytant
  The Ives, in the thyrde owre;
Hym for to scorne, wyth purpull clothyng
  They cledyd owre savyowre.   24

Vppon hys hede a crowne of thorne
  To set they wolde not spare.
Ryght pytyusly to caluery
  The crosse hym-selfe he bare.   28

Hora sexta, dominus
  Vppon the crosse was naylyde,
And as a theffe, for manys greffe,
  To dethe he was be-trayd.   32

They gaue hym to drenke
  Aesell myngelyd wyth gall.
Owre sowllis to þe blysse to bryng—
  In heven he ys a king.   36

Ora nona, dominus   [fol. 2ᵛᵒ]
   Hys spryt he dyd vp-yelde,
Into hys fathers holey handis,
   the vyctory of the felde.   40

Lungius, þat blynd knythe, wyth a sharpe spere
   He smote owre sauyor into the harte ;
and than be-gan the yerth to quake,
   the sun dyd lese hys lythe.   44

Hys mother wepte water & blode,
   Standyng here dere sone by ;
I can not tell wheder of them
   More Rufull was to see.   48

De cruce de-ponitur
   Was takyn from the crosse,
And in-to the sepullture
   Hys body beryd it was.   52

Wyth spices swete in-bracyd,
   the scrypter to fulfyll—
Hys passion kynd to haue in mynde,
   As yt was euermore hys wylle.   56

94.   *The Dolours of Our Lady*

Arundel MS. 285

Heir followis þe houris of oure ladyis dollouris   [fol. 141ᵛᵒ]

QUhat dollour persit our ladyis hert,
   Quhan scho hard hir sone was tane & bund,
Syne led to Annas, þat of syn had na part,
   Quhair fals witnes agane him sone wer fund.   4

At prime

At prime scho followit him to pilotis place,
   With sobing, siching, lik to fall in swone;   [fol. 142ro]
Thair the Iowis spittit in his face
   And fals witnes spak fast to put him doun.   8

At terce

At terce, 'crucify him!' þe Iowis can cry;
   The quhit coit and purpour claith gaif him for scorne,
Thai scurgit him; and our lady þat stude by,
   Saw him beir þe croce and crownt with thorne.   12

At sext

At sext þai him nakit nalit on a tre,
   For drink þai gaif him bitter gall;
The blud droppit doun on his moder mary;
   The erd trimblit and cragis begouth to fall.   16

At none

At none he commendit his moder to Sanct Iohnne,
   Syne with gret dolour scho saw him decese.
The sone tynt licht fra þe sext till none—
   His passioun betuix god and ws maid peace.   20

At ewinsang

Oure lady saw his syd oppinnit with a speir
   At ewinsang; syne his body þai tuk doun,
And laid him with mony salt tere
   In our ladyis bosum, of glore þe crowne.   24

At compling

Our lady saw þame to graif his body beir,
   And clois him þairin with a gret stane;   [fol. 142vo]
To keip him þe Iowis put men of weir—
   And þe faith of crist remanit in our lady all[ane].   28

O mary, moder of mercy & of grace!
  Thir houris to þi honour I refer;
To be my aduocat in euery cais,
  And stand with me at þe bar.   32

Grant me of þi sonne to haue compassioun,
  And ay be ane seruand to þe;
And for my synnis do Satisfactioun,
  Syne be tane to þe blis of hevin finalie.   36

Heir endis þe exercicioun for Setterday. And begynnis þe exercicioun for Sonday:

95.   *Behold Jesus on the Cross*

MS. Douce 126
(Sum. Catal. No. 21700)

G Odys sone þat was so fre   [fol. 90ᵛᵒ]
  In-to þis world he cam,
And let hym naylyn vp-on a tre,
  Al for þe loue of man.   4
His fayre blod, þat was so fre,
  Out of his body it ran—
A dwelful syȝte it was to se.
  His body heng blak & wan.   8
      Wiþ an o & an I / His coroune was mad of þorn,
      And prikkede in-to his panne / Boþe byhynde &
      a-forn.

To a piler y-bowndyn,
  Ihū was swiþe sore,   12
And suffrede many a wownde
  þat scharp & betere wore.
He hadde vs euere in mynde
  In al his harde þrowe;   16

31 MS. aduoat.

And we ben so vnkynde
  We nelyn hym nat yknowe.
    Wiþ an O & an I / But ȝif we loue hym trewe,
    Houre peynys ben in helle / Ȝarkyd euere newe.   20

Who-so wele loue trewe,
  Byhold ihū on þe croys,
How he heng pale of hewe,
  And cryde wiþ mylde voys—   24
'Me þristiþ' he gan to kalle—
  þe iewis herdyn þys;
Eysel meynt wiþ galle,
  þey bedyn hym y-wys.   28
    Wiþ an O & an I / His þrist was to seyȝe,
    ffor loue of manys soule / Hym longede for to deyȝe.

Who-so be proud in herte,
  þynk on god al-myȝt   32
And on his wowndys smerte,
  How rewly he was a-dyȝt.
Godys sone in trone,
  þat heyȝest is of myȝt,   36
Tok batayle a-lone
  ffor oure loue to fyȝt.
    Wiþ an O & an I / þe batayle was so stronge,
    At many a betyr wownde / þe ryche blod out
      spronge.   40

Trewe turtyl, corounyd on hylle,
  þat heyȝest art of kynde,
þy loue chaungyþ my wille,
  Whan þu comyst in my mynde.   44
þe fend I forsake anon
  ffor on lady so hende—   [fol. 91ro]

To seruyn þe lady þan wil I gon,
  ffor ʒhe is of my kende.   48
    Wiþ an O and an I / Ich am on of þo,
    þat þy sone bouʒte dere / He schal me nat for-go.
        A – M – E – N

96.   *The Seven Words from the Cross*

Arundel MS. 285

Heir followis ane deuoit orisoun To be said in the   [fol. 163ro]
  honour of þe sevin wordis that our saluiour spak
  apoun þe croce.

      O Lord God, O Crist Ihū,
        O sueit saluiour, I þe salewe!
    The quhilk sevin wordis of maist vertu,
    Off þi life þe last day,   4
    Thou said on þe croce in þi passioun

   .   .   .   .
    The quhilk I beseik the with supplicacioun
    To haue þame in mynd we may.   8

    Throu vertu of þir wordis, we pray þe,
    Quhair I haue synnit þat þou gif me

   .   .   .   .   .   .
    The sevin deidly synnis,   12
    Prid, Cowatice, Ire, Inwy,
    Lichery, Sueirnes, and glutony,
    I ask forgevinnes þat cum may I
    In hevin, quhair now þou wynnis.   16

    And as þou prayit to þi fader but faile,
    Apoun þe croce hingand full paile,
    To forgif þi crucifyaris al haill   19
    Thair mis and thair mysdeid,   [fol. 163vo]
        1 MS. Ihū Crist.

Grant me sa þat I may spaire
And forgif all man, les and maire,
Hes done me noy or caire,
That for thy blude couth bleid.   24

And as þou said vnto þe theif,
Quhilk hang besyid þe, for releif—
To the his saule wes leife—
Said, 'into paradice   28
Thou sal be with me þe samyn day,'
God grant me to leif sa ay
That to me þe samyn þou may say,
'Cum to my palice of maist price.'   32

And as þou said to þi moder deir,
Quhilk dulit and murnit & maid gret beir,
Said to hir þan, 'woman, Lo! heir
Sanct Iohnne, thy sone to be,   36
And þou his moder, mary meik.'

.   .   .   .   .   .

To þame me follow I þe be-seik,
Throu verray lufe and cherite.   40

And as thou said þan 'elay'
Vnto þi fader þan in hy,
That Is to say, 'quhy left am I   43
And leifis me þus on þe rude',   [fol. 164ʳᵒ]
Sa grant me in perrell & tribulacion
In all anger, noyis & vexacioun,
Lorde, helpe me & geve me consolacioun,
That redemit me with þi blude.   48

And as þou said þan, 'I thrist',
The heill of saulis quhilk þou wist
Wes in þe Lymbe in myrknes & mist,
Bydand þi cumyng, O kyng   52

Of erde, hevin and of hell,
That I þe luf, grant me þi-sell,
O well of weilfair, of vertu well,
In hevin with þe to ryng.   56

And as þi body was extendit
Apon þe croce, þi spirit commendit—
Vnto þi fader, þe quhilk ascendit
And broucht ws fra all baill—   60
ffor þat blist wourde, grant me þe Ioy
Off paradice & me convoy
Quhair þat þou rignis, o ryall roy,
Quhen þat I pas but faill.   64

In hevin euer with þe to ring,
To þe quhilk conwoy me, o cumly queyne, [fol. 164ᵛ]
With Sanctis in solace,
Euer mair þat I may sing   68
And þair se thy fair face   Amen.

97.   *The Mourners at the Cross*

Trinity Coll. Camb. MS. 601

Sequitur Meditacio de Passione Domini nostri Ihū   [fol. 276ᵛᵒ,
Cristi   col. 2]

THere stood besyde the crosse of Ihū
    Hys modyr, hyr sustyr and also Iohne,
Beholdyng his woundes bledyng all new.
    They syghyd, þey sobbyd euer in on;   4
    His modyr þus mornyng made her mone:
        'Dere sone, delyuer vs out of pyne,
    Take me with the, my ioyes be gone.
        Lat bothe be lyke, thy deth and myne.   8

59 ascendit *corrected from* discendit.   61 Ioy *corrected from* day.
65 *Following this line the scribe repeated lines 57–64; also he
omitted the seventh word*, consummatum est.

'Thy peynes to me they be so smert,
  My sorow so sore hit wyll nat slake,
That as a swerde they perse my hert
  And euer wyll do tyll dethe me take,   12
  The peyne wherof hit maketh me quake
    But well I wote to com to the
  And euer ioy and myrthe to make—
    Full long therto now thynketh me.'   16

She lokyd vp hygh vnto the crosse,   [fol. 277ro,
  She saw her son opon hit hyng.   col. 1]
How myght þat may haue had more losse
  Than lese her son, þat was a kyng?   20
  She myndyd well, he made all thyng
    And myght haue sauyd hymsylf fro wo.
  Therfore sorow to her hert dyd thryng,
    That he suffred suche wreches to sle hym so. 24

'Allas! dere son, thynkest þu nat on
  How thow thyne aungell to me sent,
And seyd þu wold become a mon
  To saue mankynde þat þan was shent?   28
  He gret me with grace & good entent,
    And seyd I shuld conceue with ryght
  The lord on whom my loue ys lent,
    For thow art my son and god of myght.   32

'Gabryell gret me all with grace,
  And all with myrthe he myngyd my mode;
And now I loke opon thy face,
  And se the hyng there on the rode,   36
  Spoylyd and sprynkelyd all with blode,
    Scornyd and scorgyd & all to-shent.
  Now may there nothyng do me good,
    For sorow and care so hath me hent.   40

11 as] MS. ys.

'Somtyme I lappyd the in myne arme,
  And thought full kyndely the to kysse;
I weryd the wyll fro all kyn harme,
  On the was all my ioy and blysse.   44
  But now methynke hit ys all amysse
    To se thy blood renne from thy hert.
  But I most take hit as hyt ys,
    And sofre sorow with peynes smert.   48

'Dere son, thow sokyd vppon my breste,   [col. 2]
  And coueryd me well fro all kyn care.
I know well þu made bothe man and beste,
  Heuyn & erthe & mekyll mare;   52
  But now þu lernyst another lare
    And suffrest dethe withoutyn skyll.
  Allas! dere son, how shall I fare?
    Rewle me & gyde me euen as þu wyll.   56

'I lappyd the, I lullyd the, I layde the soft,
  I kyssyd the oft opon my kne;
And now thow makest me syng full oft,
  To se the thus hang on thys tre,   60
  'Allas! wyll hit no better be?
    Shall all my Ioyes þus fro me go?'
  Make here my ende, take me with the,
    And lat me neuer abyde thys wo.'   64

Than spake þat lorde wordys full mylde
  As he hyng vppon the tre:
'Woman, take Iohne here to thy chylde.'
  And þan anone to Iohne seyd he: 68
'Lo here þy modyr, þow may her se.'
  And euer aftyr with all hys myght
He socoryd þat lady, blessyd mot she be!
  And seruyd her truly bothe day & nyght.   72

59 syng] ? *read* sygh.

Yet mornyd that mayden in her mynde,
  When she saw þat her chylde was slayne.
Blame her nat, hit was but kynde.
  Yet was ther oo þyng made her fayne,   76
  She wyst that he shuld ryse agayne.
    But for all that she was full wo
  To se her chylde suffre suche payne,
    And hang there dede, boþe pale & blo.   80

Euer she syghyd & seyde, 'Allas!   [fol. 277ᵛᵒ,
  A carefull woman, what shall I do?   col. 1]
My ioy, my comfort in euery cas,
  My owne dere chylde ys slayne me fro.   84
  Why wold þese wyked Iewes do so,
    To sle my son withoutyn cause?
  Wyte me nat þaugh I be wo,
    For I may neyther bynde ne lause.'   88

That blessyd lady, chosyn for chaste
  To bere þat lord þat all thyng wrought—
Heuen and erthe, wode and vaste,
  Water and wynde & all of nought—   92
  Her sorow was suche þat she ne rought
    To dy, for dole of her son dere;
  Hyr sorow so suyd here vnsought
    That nothyng myght amende here chere.   96

O lorde, syth þu wolde nat her spare,
  That of her body toke flesshe & blood,
But as a caytyf let her haue care
  When thow hynge nakyd on the rood,   100
  Why shuld we wreches, þat neuer dyd good,
    Groge with peyne or aduersite,
  But thanke & blysse the with myght & mood
    In ioy or sorow, whether that we be?   104

Remembre, lord, of thy goodnes,
　Howe with thy blood þu bought mankynde,
And brought hym frely out of dystres
　Fro the foule fende, þat dyd hym bynde   108
　Where euer for syn he shuld haue ᴅynyd,
　　But þat þu for hym dethe wold take.
　Let neuer þat sorow renne fro oure mynde,
　　That thow wold suffer for oure sake.   112

And late þy godhede graunte vs grace   [col. 2]
　That we may mekely, with all oure myght,
Thanke þe & looue whyle we haue space,
　Serue þe & blesse boþe day & nyght   116
　And at owre [dethe] com to þat lyght,
　　Wheryn þu art & euer shalt be,
　And euer abyde þere in þy syght.
　　Amen Amen, for charyte.   120
　　　　Explicit.

98.   *For Thy Sake Let the World Call Me Fool*

Henry E. Huntington Library, Ellesmere MS. 34. B. 7

A goode praier   [fol. 82ʳᵒ]

O Ihū, lett me neuer forgett thy byttur passion,
　That thou suffred for my transgression,
ffor in thy blessyd wondes is the verey scole
That must teche me with the worlde to be called a fole.   4
O Ihū, ihū, ihū, grauntt that I may loue the soo,
Þat the wysdom of the worlde be cleene fro me A-goo,
And brennyngly to desyre to come to see thy face,
In whom is all my comford, my joy and my solace.   8
　Amen — Ihesus — maria — Iohannes.

99.   *The Child that Died for Us*

MS. Rawlinson C. 86
(Sum. Catal. No. 11951)

I saruyd oure lady bothe nythte and day   [fol. 51ʳᵒ]
    the louyr that I may

OUre lady hade a childe bothe fryssh and gaye,
    wiche ded for wus on goode fryday,
and allso a childe good   3
þat dede for wus oppon the Rode,
and allso a childe good and free,
that ded for wus oppon the Roode tre.   6

100.   *The Wounds, as Wells of Life*

Arundel MS. 286
(written as prose)

IHesus woundes so wide   [fol. 3ʳᵒ]
    ben welles of lif to þe goode,
Namely þe stronde of hys syde,
þat ran ful breme on þe rode.   4

ȝif þee liste to drinke,
to fle fro þe fendes of helle,
Bowe þu doun to þe brinke
& mekely taste of þe welle.   8

101.   *An Alphabetical Devotion to the Cross*

MS. Rawlinson B. 408
(Sum. Catal. No. 11755)

Here begynneth þe A.B.C. of deuocion   [fol. 3ʳᵒ]

✝ OF ihū criste be euer oure spede,
    And kepe vs from perel of synnes and payne!
Blessid be þat lorde þat on þe crosse dide blede,

No. 99. 5 MS. frere.

Crist, god and man, þat for vs was slayne,   4
Dede he was and rose vp agayne.
    Euer helpe us, crosse, with hym to a-ryse
    ffro deeth to lyue and synne to dispise!

Gracyous crosse, now grawnt us þat grace   8
    Hym for to worship with al oure mynde,
In wordes, in werkes, and in euery place,
    Knelyng and kyssyng þe where we þe fynde.
    Late us be neuer to hym unkynde,   12
        Mercyfully þat made vs to be men,
        No more to kepe but his heestis ten.

O blisful crosse, teche us al vertu
    Plesyng to god, for oure saluacion,   16
Quenchyng alle vices in þe name of ihū,
    Raunson payng for oure dampnacion.
    Sende us such grace of conuersacion
        That we may stye and glorified be,   20
        Where crist is kyng þat dyed on tre.

Crist, þat dyed on þe holy roode,
    I pray þe, good lorde, with al my myght
Sende us sume part of al thy goode,   24
    And kepe us from yuel euer day and nyght,
    Contynuyng þi mercy, sauyng al ryght
        Titulle of þi passion, *Poynt* us saue
        As to thy ☩ reuerence we may haue.   28

102.   *'Thou Sinful Man that by Me Goes'*
Arundel MS. 285

The Dollorus complant of oure lorde   [fol. 164ᵛᵒ]
Apoune þe croce Crucifyit

NOw herkynnis wordis wunder gude,
How Ihū crist hang on þe rude;
With lufly speche and myld mude,
        He schew till man   4
        How he fra hell,
        With panis fell,
        Oure saulis wan.

'Thow synfull man þat by me gais,   [fol. 165ʳᵒ]   8
Ane quhyle to me þou turne þi face!
Behald my body, in euerylk place,
        How it is dicht,
        All to-rent,   12
        And all to-schent,
        Man, for thy plycht.

Man, fra me þou ga not ȝit!
Behalde my handes & my feit,   16
How þai ar knaggit with nalis gret
        Wnto ane tre;
        Thir depe woundis,
        Þir harde stoundis,   20
        I tholit for the.

Behald my croun of thornis kene,
The Iowis thrang on my heid in tene,
Tua theifis I was hangit betuen   24
        With gret dispyte,
        This mekill vnseill
        Þou seis me feill,
        Man, I the wyte.   28

            26 MS. vnsteill.

Behald hertlie vnto my syde;
Thair ma þou se ane wound full wyde,
That maid was with ane speir full reid
  Wnto my hert—   32
  This anger, þis wa
  Þou seis me ta,   [fol. 165ᵛᵒ]
  Thy syn it gart.

Behalde my schankis and my kneis,   36
Body, heid, armes and theis;
Behald, on me na thing þou seis
  Bot sorrow and pyne—
  Thus was I spylt,   40
  Man, for þi gylt
  And not for myne.

Me Rewis for mary, my moder mylde,
That murnis so sair for me hir chylde; 44
ffor sche me saw þusgait revylde,
  In alkin thyng
  Leid as ane tyke,
  & theif-lyke,   48
  On gallowis to hyng.

Behalde how, with þair rapis teuch,
The Iowis fell my lymmes oute dreuch,
ffor þat na lymme was meit aneuch 52
  Unto þe bore.
  This anger, þis wa,
  Þou seis me ta,
  I tholit þe for.   56

Man, vnderstande eik þou sall,
In-steid of drink þai gaif me gall;   [fol. 166ʳᵒ]
Asaill myngit þair with-all
    Thai Iowes fell.   60
    Man, sickerly
    Þir panis thole I,
    To saif þi saule fra hell.

Behalde my corps, how Iowis it dang   64
With knoppit quhippis, with scurgis lang;
As stryndis of wellis, my blude oute sprang
    On euerylk syde,
    Weill ma þou wit,   68
    Quhair knoppis hit
    Maid wondis full wyde.

ffor þè, man, þou sall vnderstande,
In body, heid, fute and hande,   72
ffyve hundreth woundis, & fyve thousande,
    And þairto sexty
    And fyftene,
    Was taulde & sene   76
    On my body.

Behalde, on me not hale was left—
And ȝit, fra me or þou war reft,
All thir panis, I wald tholl eft   [fol. 166ᵛᵒ] 80
    And for the de.
    Heir may thou se
    Þat I lufe the
    Moist hertfullie.   84

57 MS. sell.   73 MS. woindis.   80 MS. And all.

Sen I throu lufe hes bocht þe deir,
As þou thy-self þe suth seis heir,
I pray the hertlie, with gude cheir,
    Luffe me agane   88
    That it like me,
    Þat for þe
    Thollit all this pane.

Gif þou þi life in syn hes led,   92
To ask me marcy, be þou nocht dred,
ffor þe lest drop I for þe sched
    May clenge þe sone,
    And all þe syn,   96
    þis warld within,
    That þou hes done.

I wes wraithar with Iudas
ffor he wald me na marcy as,   100
Than I wes for his gret trespas
    Quhen he me sauld.
    I wes reddy
    to gif marcy—   104
    Ask he nocht wald.

Cayam, þat his brothir sleuch,   [fol. 167ʳº]
Mycht haue had marcy weill aneuch,
Bot wanhop him fra mercy dreuch—   108
    He wald ask nane.
    Thairfor in hell,
    euer to duell,
    His saule Is gane.   112

Sanct peter, þat me thris forsuke
Apoun a nycht, as sayis þe buke,
Vnto my mercy he him tuke—
    My marcy gat he—   116
    In hert had cair
    Þat he sa sair
    Had grevit me.

Paule, Magdalen and mony ma,   120
That in þis warld wrocht mekill wa,
Without marcy past nocht me fra,
    Quhen thai It aste.
    But þair askyng   124
    in alkin thing
    Thai had als fast.

The theif þat hang on my rycht syid,
Ane littill quhile befor he deit,   128
Efter mercy sa fast he cryit
    On reuthfull wise.   [fol. 167ᵛᵒ]
    Thairfor with me
    þe day Is he   .132
    In paradice.

I wer full laith for-suth to tyne
Thy saule, I wane with mekill pyne,
All þe defalt it salbe þin   136
    Gif I þe þarne.
    Now ask mercy,
    þi fader am I,
    And thou my barne.   140

---

123 aste] MS. aske.   124 MS. asknyng.
134 for-suth] MS. full suth.   137 MS. ȝarne.

Now luke þat I find þe kind,
And haue my passioun in þi mynd,
And sickerly þou sall me find
　　Kindle the to,　　　　　　　　　144
　　Helpand in neid
　　in alkin deid
　　Thou hes ado.

I[n]steid of luf nocht ask I the,　　　148
Bot faynd þe fast fra syn to fle;
Pane the to leife in cherite
　　Baith nycht and day.
　　Than in my blis,　　　　　　152
　　þat neuer sall mys,
　　Thou sall duell ay.

Now, Ihū, for thy gret gudnes,　　[fol. 168ʳᵒ]
As thow for man thollit herdnes,　　156
Grant ws to lef in cleynes,
　　And marcy send.
　　And grant ws grace
　　to se thy face　　　　　　　160
　　In hewin but end. Amen.

103.　　　　　*Woefully Arrayed*

Harley MS. 4012

Ho-sumeuer saith þis praier in þe worship of þe　　[fol. 109ʳᵒ]
　　passion shall haue .C. ȝere of pardon

W Ofully araide,
　　My blode, man, ffor the ran,
　　hit may not be naide,
My body blo and wanne,
　　Wofully araide.

Beholde me, I pray þe, with all thyne hole reson,
and be not hard hertid, for this encheson
þat I, for thi saule sake was slayne, in good seson,
Begilid and be-traide by Iudas fals treson,　　　　　4
　　Vnkindly intretid,
　　With sharp corde sore fretid,
　　Þe Iues me thretid,
　The mowid, they spittid and dispisid me,　　　　8
　Condemned to deth as þu maiste se.

Thus nakid am I nailid, O man, for thi sake.
I loue þe, þenne loue me. Why slepist þu? awake!
Remember my tender hert-rote for the brake,　　　12
With paynes my vaines constrayned to crake.
　　This was I defasid,
　　Thus was my flesh rasid,
　　And I to deth chasid.　　　　　　　　16
　like a lambe led vnto sacrefise,
　slayne I was in most cruell wise.

Of sharp thorne, I haue worne a crowne, on my hed,
　　　　　　　　　　　　　　[fol. 109ᵛᵒ]
So rubbid, so bobbid, so rufulle, so red,　　　　20
Sore payned, sore strayned, and for þi loue ded.
Vnfayned, not demed, my blod for þe shed,
　　My fete and handis sore,
　　With sturde naylis bore;　　　　　　24
　　What myght I suffer more
　þen I haue sufferde, man, for þe?
　Com when þu wilt, and welcome to me.

DEre brother, non other thing I desire,　　　　28
But geue me thi hert fre, to rewarde myne hire.
I am he that made þe erth, water and fire.
Sathanas, þat slouen and right lothely sire,

Hym haue I ouer-caste,   32
  In hell presoune bounde faste,
  Wher ay his woo shall laste.
 I haue puruaide a place full clere
ffor mankynde, whom I haue bought dere.   36

Who-sumeuer saith this deuotely hathe grauntid be diuers
Bisshopis saing at the laste ende fiue pater nosters and fiue
Aues .CCCCCC. dayes of pardon.

104. '*Unkind Man, Take Heed of Me*'

Harley MS. 4012
(written as prose)

VNkinde man, take hede of mee!   [fol. 94ʳᵒ]
  Loke, what payne I suffer for the.
sinfull man, to the I crie,
only for the I die.   4
beholde, the bloode of *my handis downe renneth,
not for my gilte but for youre sinnes,   *[fol. 94ᵛᵒ]
fote and hande with nailes so ben faste,
that sinoes & vaines alto-berste.   8
The blood of myne hert rote,
Loke, how hit stremyth downe by my fote.
Ouer all theeis paines þat I suffer so sore,
With myne herte hit greuith me more,   12
þat I vnkindnes finde in the
þat for thi loue hongid vpon a tree.

> 5 *Read* rinnes *and restore the rime.*
> 8 *Read* alto-braste *and restore the rime.*

105. 'Why Art Thou, Man, Unkind?'

MS. Rawlinson C. 86
(Sum. Catal. No. 11951)

LAte as I wente one myne pleynge   [fol. 65ʳᵒ]
  I set my herte all in solase.
Criste one a crosse I sawe hangynge,
That dyede for mane withoute trespas.   4
To mane he cried and sayde, 'alas!
Why art þu, mane, vnkynde to me?
And now I dye to geve þe grace,
    Quid vltra debui facere?'   8

Criste Ihū þies wordes may saye
To euery creature þat is vnkynde:
'What shulde I more, mane, I þe praye,
Haue do for þe þat is be-hynde?   12
Thou art þe fayrest creature in kynde,
ffor I þe made ouer, lyke to me,
And gave þe reason, with witte & mynde,
    Quid vltra debui facere?   16

'I love þe, mane, a-boue all þynge,
Therfor for þe I wolde be bore,
And all for I wolde þe to blisse brynge.
What shulde I þanne for þe do more?   20
ffor Adam synne þu were forlore,
And lyke for euer perisshid to be,
Yt I woll to blisse þe restore,
    Quid vltra debui facere?   24

'I muste love þe, I maye none oþer,
Therfor love me a-gayne,
Or ellys þu art an vnkynde broþer.
My love to haue þu shuldest be fayne: 28

In nede I þe helpe with myght & mayne,
And now one þe crosse I dye for the,   [fol. 65ᵛᵒ]
And suffir þornes to perich my brayne.
  Quid vltra debui facere?   32

'My hondes for þe on þe crosse bene spredde,
To shew þe mercy yf þou wilt craue.
Me to offende þu shuldest be adrad,
ffor yf þu do wel I wol þe saue.   36
Whane þu art dede and lefte in grave,
[And all thy frendes from the flee,]
Yt þy sowle I seke to save,
  Quid vltra debui facere?   40

'Whane I made þe to my lykenesse,
I made þe lorde Above all þynge,
And gave to þe all plentousnesse
Of fisshes þat arne in þe see swymmyng;   44
And ouer all bestes þat are crepynge
On erthe I made þe lorde to be,
And ouer all fovles in þe eyre fleynge.
  Quid ultra debui facere?   48

'I made þe sonne with sterres of hevene,
The mone also with bryght shynynge,
And sette þe sterres with planetis vije—
All þis I did for þy plesaunce.   52
And of þe erth I made to sprynge
Erbis and treis in þer degre,
Her frute to bere to þy norishynge.
  Quid vltra debui facere?   56

'Ther myght neuer creature one me pleyne,
And seye þat I was vnkynde,
ffor to helpe þe I haue ben fayne,
But yt one þis þu hast no mynde.   [fol. 66ʳᵒ]

---

38 *Supplied from Douce Fragm. f. 48.*   48 MS. debiui.

To save mane yt was devyned   61
That I shulde dye vpone a tre;
Wherfor for þe I was pyned,
    Quid vltra debui facere?   64

'Grete love I shewid whanne I þe made
Of erth, a creature most excellent.
Yf kyndnesse þanne in þe þou hadde,
Thow shuldest love me with good entent.   68
Mane, thy soule I made represent
To þe lykenesse of þe trinite,
ffor þou shuldest love as I went.
    Quid vltra debui facere?   72

'Though þou haue synned, yt come to me
And aske mercy with mekenesse,
ffor mercy to geve I am redy,
Thus shewith experience by expresse.   76
ffor I shewid neuer yt no orȝelnesse
to synfull mane þat askyth mercy,
Yt euer þu shewist vnkyndnesse.
    Quid vltra debui facere?   80

'I gave þe Reasoun and eyene clere,
To teche þe flee from all evyll;
And also erys þu hast to here,
And in þy sovle I sette fre vill.   84
And now I hange on caluery hill,
Naylid one crosse with naylys thre.
To save þe, mane, þu shuldest not spill,
    Quid vltra debui facere?   88

'Whanne mane had synned, to hym I sende [fol. 66ᵛᵒ]
Patriarkes, profettes and postels also,
Trwe prechours to teche him to Amende,
That mys had done to twynne me fro.   92

        77 MS. orvelnesse.

And to save from endles woo
I ordeyned of penaunce partys thre.
Why hatist þu me, mane, why art þu me foo?
   Quid vltra debui facere?   96

'Rather þan thou dampned shulde be,
I from hewene agayne wolde discende
And grevouser deth yt to suffir for þe.
Why wrathis þu me? I nouȝte offende,   100
All þat þe nedeth to þe I sende;
And now one þe crosse, as þu maiste se,
My body is scourged and all to-rente.
   Quid vltra debui facere?   104

'I haue not trespasid, why art þu me foo?
Why wratthis þu me þat am þy frende?
Thow hast no cause to fle me fro;
I covet to kepe þe from þe fende,   108
loo! euer to þe I am hende.
Yf þu aske mercy with humylite,
I wyll be for þe at þynne ende.
   Quid vltra debui facere?'   112
       ffinis

106. *What More Could Christ Have Done?*

MS. Ashmole 189
(Sum. Catal. No. 6777)

Quid vltra debuit facere
Þat lorde þat dyed for þe & me?

CRyste made mane yn þis maner of wyse: [fol. 104ʳᵒ]
 Lyke vnto þe trynite he deyd þe dewyse,
By resoun, vertue And orygynall Iustice,
And set þe in þe plesant place of paradyse. quid vltra
  etc.   4

He made þe all-so to be boþe lorde and kynge,
Off erþe & off all creatures þat beth þeryne levyng,
Sonne, moone & sterrys, contynuall shynynge,
ffor thy sake fynallye he made All maner thynge. quid
    vltra etc.   8

Wyth these grete gyftis þu cowdyst not be content,
Butt by grete presumpsioun Assentyst to þe serpent;
by-cause þu woldyst be lyke god omnipotent,
thane All thy grete vertues A-none Away þey wente.
    quid vltra etc.   12

Cryst þene, beholdynge þy grete & grewous fall,
Perseywynge þe spoyled off thy gyftis naturall,
Was Anone meked with pyte paternall,
the to make fre that by synne was thrall. quid vltra etc. 16

The to redeme He founde sone remedye,
Vsynge humylite to þi pride clene contrarye,
ffor, where-as by pryde thou nere fall dedelye,
[he] by hys humilite restored the full hylye. quid vltra
    etc.   20

ffor where-as by pride þu were made dede,
with grete humylyte he toke one hyme manhede;
Off A vyrgyne was I-bore þe to restore in-dede,
Off Iesse-ys lyne and off hys kynrede. quid vltra etc. 24

By frute of A tree þu felle to dampnacyoun,   [fol. 104ᵛᵒ]
thane, be-holde & see thy makers provysyoun:
howe by A tree [he] restoreed þy saluacyoun,
one the crosse whene he suffred hys passyoun. quid vltra
    etc.   28

15 meked] *read* meved.
18 MS. remedy *struck through after* Vsynge.
19 nere] *read* were.

þane were þu delyuerde fro þe captyuyte.
And by feythe And baptyme restored þe,
Remyttynge þe blame of orygynall Iniquite,
And þe restored Agayne to þy fre lyberte.   quid vltra
    etc.   32

Sethe cryste hathe þe honoured þus by hys natyuyte,
Conueynge yne one persone þy nature with þe deyte.
by merytes of hys passyoun browȝt þe to felicite,
to þis for-seyde questyoun Ane Awnswere nowe geve me:
    quid vltra etc.   36
                 Explicit.

107.   *A Dialogue Between Natura Hominis and Bonitas Dei*

Caius College Camb. MS. 84

    S Aluator mundi domine,   [page 180]
      to þe, Ihesu, make I my mone,
    to haue mercy Thorow þi pyte;
      gracius god, now here my bone.   4

Natura   If I haue done owte of þo way
hominis   of ryghtfulnes thorow my foly,
    Or dethe me kache & close in clay,
      mercyful god, I crye mercy!   8

Bonitas Man, qwat haue I done to þe?
dei   qwy art þu, man, to me vnkynde?
    Qwy has þu, man, for-sake me?
      qwy flese þu, man? I am þi frynde.   12
    ffurst, I þe made to my lyknes
      & put al þis world in þi bayle,

30 MS. restored þe Agayne.
34 *Read* Conioynynge.
 1 Saluator] *small s with space left for an illuminated initial.*
 5 done] *interlined above.*
 7 kache] chake *written first and cancelled.*

And, for to hele al þi sekenes,
  I lost my myght & toke mercy.   16

Natura   Þu maduste me, lord, to þi lyknes,
hominis   And to þin ymage þu me schape
          Þo makynge, lord, of þi godnes
            let not me, lord, thorow fowle warke.   20
          My flesche is frele & redy to fall,
            þo world, þo dele, a grete enmy.
          With meke hert þer-fore I cal,
            Mercyful god, I crye mercy!   24

Bonitas   Man, þo rede see I partud in too,
  dei   owte of egypte qwen I browghte þe;
          I was þi frynde, þu was my foo,
            þu in deserte haste for-sake me;   28
          With awngels methe þer I þe fedde,
            my luf to þe þu fonde ay redy;
          þer þu were worthy hell pyne to haue had,
            I left my myght & toke mercy.   32

Natura   Þat mercy, lord, take þu to mynde,
hominis   þat þu wold schewe to Maudeleyn;
          Thynke þat þu art of owre kynde,
            let noght mane-kynde þoro synne be sleyn. 36
          Opone my synful sole þu rew,
            as þu hit boght with þi body.
          ffor dedly syne has chawngude þo hewe,
            mercyful god, I cry mercy!   40

Bonitas   Mane, my prophetus I sent to the,
  dei   my lawe þe for to preche & take,
          And þem þu kylduste, in spyte of me.
            my-selfe, I come downe for þi sake,   44

16 lost] *probably an error for* left *as in ll. 32 and 64.*
26 MS. þe browghte.
28 MS. for-sake me haste.

I sowghte þi luf & þu me slowe—
  be-holde, my body is all blody.
I myghte hawe distryde þe wel, & wold noght,
  I lost my myght & toke mercy.   48

Natura   Lord, of þi mercy fygur I fynde,
hominis   on Petur qwen I caste my thoghte;
How þat he was to þe vn-kynde,
  & seyde þat he knewe þe noghte.   52
þu lokudste one hym with mýlde mode,
  aftur mercy hertly can he cry.
As þu for vs wold schede þi blode,
  mercyful god, I cry mercy!   56

Bonitas Man, þe erthe I can do qwake,
  dei   for al þis word is in my hande;
Vengans also may I take,
  qwere me luste, one watur or lande.   60
Be synus, tokunus & spekynge to,
  my luf al-way þu myghte a-spye;
And for þu schulduste take hede þer-to,
  I lefte my myghte & toke mercy.   64

Natura   ffor þat I haue don wrong,
hominis   ryghte as þi chylde, þu schalte me bete.
More is þi mercy þen my mys,
  gracius god, þu hit for-ȝete!   68
I sob, I sorow, I clepe, I call,
  with sory hert & wepyng eyȝe.
As mercy passus þi werkus all,
  mercyful god, I crye mercy!   72

47 *Both rime and meter are defective.*
48 lost] *probably an error for* left *as in ll. 32 and 64.*
59 MS. Vegans.

Bonitas
dei

Mane, for þe my blode I bled,
   & for þe was I al to-schente;
All þat me luffud fro me þai fledde,
   & all my frendus fro me þai wentte.   76
If þu can fynde a-noþur frynde,
   to do so mycul for þi foly,
Leue now me & with hym wende,
   of me aske þu no more mercy.   80

Natura
hominis

So sykur a frende was newur non borne,
   to do so mycul for luf of me.
ffor any oþur frenschyp, I had bene lorne,
   had þi passioun, lorde, ne be.   84
Syn þi frenschyp þus has me boght,   [page 191]
   so dulfully with þi body,
Let not þin ymage now go to noght,
   Mercy-ful god, I cry mercy!   88

Bonitas
dei

Man, my byddynge þu breycus al day,
   as holy kyrke wyl þe schewe;
With þi grete oþus þat þu swerus ay,
   my body þu wonduste euur-more newe.   92
Ʒyt leue þi synnus, & turne to me,
   & for þi gylte be þu sory,
And now as welcum schalte þu be
   as he þat nedud neuur any mercy.   96

Natura
hominis

Gramercy, gracius god of myght,
   þat one my sowle wyl haue mercy.
To luf þe, both day & nyghte,
   I ame now bowndone sycurly.   100
Here, al my syne now I for-sake,
   & to þi mercy I wyl me hye
Gracius god, þi grace me take.
   mercyful god, grawnte me mercy!   104

89 *After* man b *written and cancelled.*   96 MS. euur.

Bonitas   Now, swete sole, welcum to me,
  dei   with me in blys schal þu ewur-more dwell;
        I blesse þe tyme þat I boghte þe,
          þe tyme þat I wente for þe to hell.   108
        Into my kyndam, cum now with me,
          into þe blysse of hewun one hye,
        ffor þere in ioy schal þu now be
          & ewur-more, thorowe my mercy.   112

108. Querela Divina: Responsio Humana
B.M. Addit. MS. 37049

Querela diuina   [fol. 20ro]

O Man vnkynde / hafe in mynde
  My paynes smert!
Beholde & see, / Þat is for þe
  Percyd, my hert.   4

And ȝitt I wolde, / Or þan þu schuld
  þi saule forsake,
On cros with payne / Scharp deth, agayne
  ffor þi luf take.   8

ffor whilk I aske / None oþer taske,
  Bot luf agayne.
Me þan to luf, / Al thyng a-bofe,
  þow aght be fayne.   12

Responsio humana

O lord, right dere, / Þi wordes I here
  with hert ful sore;
Þerfore fro synne / I hope to blynne,
  And grefe no more.   16

108 tyme] *interlined above.*

Bot in þis case / Now helpe, þi grace,
  My frelnes;
Þat I may euer / Do þi pleser,
  With lastyngnes.   20

Þis grace to gytt, / Þi moder eeke
  Euer be prone,
Þat we may alle / In-to þi halle,
  With ioy, cum sone. Amen.   24

At the top of the page, partly trimmed away: 'Beati mundo corde qui ip[si Deum] vident.'

109.   *Brother, Abide*

Helmingham Hall MS. LJ. I. 10
(In an early XVI-cent. hand, at the end of Hardyng's *Chronicle*)

Here begynnyth a lamentable complaynt of our saviour cryst kyng eternall to sinfull mane his brother naturall.

BRother, a-byde, I the desire and pray;   [recto]
A-byde, a-byde and here thy brother speke.
Be-holde my body in this blody aray,
Broysed & betyne wyth whippis that wold not breke.
This ferefull force, this wo, this wrongfull wreke,   5
ffor the I sufferd, what canst thou do, then, lesse agayne,
But stonde a while and harke how I complayne?

A-bove the sterrys, in hevyne emperiall,
Crouned, I satte, thi lorde and thi soverayne,
Servide wyth bodies of nature ymmortall,   10
In Ioyes that euer shall endure & remayn.
hevyn, erth, & hell, and all thei contayne,
To me dyde owe dewe obedyence,
As to theyr prynce, most hygh in excellence.

21 eeke] *between the first and second* e *a letter blotted out.*

I raynyng thus in full felicite,   15
Thou lyveddyst in erth, subiecte to the fende,
Wrappyd in wo & grett aduersite,
Woyde of socoure, woyde of comforde for any ffrende.
And worst of all, thou knewest no tyme nor ende
Off thy distresse; thou knewest no remedy   20
A-gaynst thy greffe and mortall mysery.

Pety I hade, beholdyng the this wise
Be thin enmy oppresside, in distresse;
And, of grett love, a-noone, I dyd devise
The to delyuer out of this wrechidnese.   25
And by and by, with-out longe procese,
I lefte my trone and regall mageste
And hither I came, a maydyns childe to be.

Borne in bedlem, lappyd and laide in strawe
Ine a powur howse wher bestys ete ther mete,   30
Brought to the temple after the Iues lawe
And circumcysed—this ys not to forgette,—
I lede my yought wyth children in the strette,
Poorly a-rayed in clothes bare and thyne,
Suche as my mother for me dyde make & spyne.   35

Myn age encresed, & then a-bought I wentt,
Prechinge scripture; & wher-sumeuer I came
I movyd the people for to be penitent,   [verso]
And that I saied, was in my fathers name.
Some praysed my preching, some said I was to blame, 40
Some toke my techyng, sum wold nott of my scole,
Sum held me wyse, some said I was a fole.

Thus longe I lyvid, passyng frome place to place,
Bare-fotyd, caplese, wythout syluer or gold.
Payne of my traveylle a-pered in my face;   45
Men myght perceyve yf thei listed to be-hold.

Watch & grett labur, sharpe honger, thurst & cold
ffull ofte me brought so feble & so lowe,
That myne owne mother sum tyme dyd me not knowe.

Thus, & mych more, for the endured I.   50
Therfor, brother, make thou no hast to starte
Nother of my speche be thou no-thing wery,
ffor yf thou be, to blame thou arte.
To whom shuld I disclose or brek myne harte,
To whom shulde I complayne my greffe mortall,   55
but to the, my brother most naturall?

Harke now therfor! hark now, & take goode hede,
And of my troble a-noone thou shalt here more
To shewe my-self as god & mane in deede,
lasar I raysed, buried fowre dayes be-fore.   60
The people I cured of euery maner sore—
Some deffe, some dome, sum full of dropsy,
And some sore enhawnted wyth ferefull frensy,

And some lame, of lidernes þat myght not goo nor crepe,
And sum blynde borne, by ympedyment of nature,   65
And some vexed, they cowde nevyr reste ne slepe,
And sum that fell dede by sodene adventure.
Bothe powur & ryche I holpe & toke to cure,
Vsyng to them noone other medycyne
But my holy worde, full of vertue divyne.   70

Then myn enmys begane to rage & rayle,
And said I hade the devyll at my demayne;
Some said I vsed arte magike wythought fayle,   [recto]
And some said I coude not longe contynew ne rayne.
Al this I hard and litle I said a-gayne;   75
All that myne ennymes dyd I sufferd paciently,
And to ther wordis no countraury speche hade I.

Then they came to me, flamed wyth Ire fervent,
And said the people by me deceyvid were.
Many blynd reasons & miche froward argument   80
To me they made, and bade I shuld answere.
Answere I dyde, wher-to they leyed good ere,
And specyally thei gave sure attendance,
To take me wyth some fawlte in vtturaunce.

But to my saying they cowde no-thyng replye;   85
My resouns wer so playne and apparentte.
Never-the-lesse, so miche was ther envy,
That styll they murmorde & wold not be contente.
Cownsell they toke and, by secrett assentte,
They were a-greed to dethe me for to bete,   90
Wyth cloddys of erthe & stone hard & grette.

I me wyth-drewe & dyde lette theire fury passe
And, for a seasone, fro them I dyd me hyde.
Neuerthelese, a-gayn a-brode I wase,
All there malys redy for to abyde.   95
And by this tyme thei had gotene them a gyde—
One that I trustyd, & Iudas was his name—
Which me betrayed & hynge hyme-self for shame.

Then, to conclude ther cruell appetyght,
Thei gatherd them in a great companye,   100
Wyth byllys & battys, wyth torch & lanterne lyght,
me to dystresse; and so takyne was I,
And leede to prysoun wyth clamor & ought-cry,
ffast bownde in roppys, & left my-self alone—
ffor all my frendis were fro me flede & goone.   105

Petur, my frend, that said wyth wordis bolde
In my quarell he wolde bothe lyve & dye,
Stode by the fyere to warme hyme-self for colde,
And for his master thrise he dyde me di-nye.

Thus was I lefte no frende to stande me by,   110
Thus was I lefte in fere and grett danger,
A-monge myn enymys a wofull prisoner.

Be-fore pylate erly they dyd me brynge,   [verso]
He as a Iuge, to here what shuld be sayde.
And too stode forth, a-gaynst me witnessyng,   115
And a fals mattur vnto my charge they layde.
'Speke, manne,' qd pylate, 'how ys thy lyf convayed?'
And wyth that worde, wattur to whasche he callde,
And I stode styll, seke and sore appalled.

Then sodenly the folke feelle in roure,   120
And wyth one voyce they cryed, 'hang vp this theff!'
Pylate stode forth & openly he swoure
He cowde lay no-thyng to my repreff.
Neuer-the-lesse, fering his propur greeff,
And wyllyng also noyse to a-pease & stylle,   125
He badde them take & do wyth me ther wyll.

Then they layde hande & lede me forth that day,
Wyth shotyng & crying, wyth mokry & mych dysdayne;
Some pulled me forwarde & tare my powur a-ray,
And by the here some plukkyd me bake a-gayne.   130
Often I stomelled & felle to the grounde for payne
And, wythout pyte of my grevance or hurte,
They spornned me vp, all betrodene in durte.

And, as people most cruell & vnkynde,
When I for woo blode & water swette,   135
Vnto a pylar nakyd thei dyde me bynde
And wyth sharpe scorgis thei dyde my body bette
Vnto the bonnes—the synues dyd freete—
And on my heode sharpe thorns thei dyd dystayne
Thorowgh skyne & skulle, that rane vnto my brayne. 140

    113 MS. be brynge.   134 MS. As as.

Thus bete, thus rentte, and all to-tore,
Wyth a great crose thei dyd me charge & lade,
Which on my shuldure vp to an hill I bore,
In steppys of blode as depe as I cowde wade.
A-bowt me rennyng, myche tyrany thei made,   145
And as wood men thei dyde me dryve & chace,
Wyth mobbys & knockys & spettyng in my face.

This crosse soo sade a-pone my shulder ley
That bake & bone it made to bowe & bende.
Often I stomeled, & fell downe by the way   150
As I labored the mounteyn to ascende;
When I came vp my breth was at an ende,
I cowde not speke, in me no powur ther was,   [recto]
But as in a mane redy for to passe.

Then one this crosse thei dyde me strecch & strayn, 155
And nayled me faste wyth naylles gret & longe,
And hyng me vppe betwene false thevis twayne,
Most shamefully, wyth moche rebuke & wronge.
I called for drynke, my thurst was grevous strong;
Thei gave me aysell, tempred wyth bitter galle,   160
Which I did taste & dranke therof but smalle.

My visage changed to pale & blew as byse,
My fleshe be-ganne to styff & waxid drye,
My hart lokyd lyke a plomett of Ise,
My lyff was spent, myne owre was come to dye.   165
Vnto my father I cryed, 'heli, heli!'
And wyth that worde, I layde myne hede a-syde,
And dolfully gave vp the spret & dyed.

Ther honge I dede, a pytefull fygure,
And mene in harnesse were sette the place to kepe, 170
And, by-cawse of me thei wold be sure,
Wyth a sharpe spere my hart thei lawnsed depe.

My mother stode, but what cowde she doo but weepe?
And weepe she dyde, terrys both whight & rede,
Wrynging her handys, & fill downe by me deede. 175

Now, gentyll brother, be-holde this matur welle,
And myndfully make this rufull reknynge,
Loke one this processe, consider it euery delle
fro the furst to the laste, consider euery thynge:
ffurst, consider I raynyd as a kynge; 180
Seconde, considere, as a frend moost fre
To make the ryche, I died in pouerte.

What cowde one brother more for a-nother doo
Then my complaynte presently dothe a-pere & expresse?
What canst thou adde, or putte eny thyng þer-too, 185
That myght be done by brotherly kyndnesse?
Se what I suffred, thy grevanse to reddresse!
What canst thou aske or more desire of me,
Thy feythfull brother, dyeng in pouerte?

Off tendure love, all this I dyd endure; 190
Love dyde me lede, love dyde me thus constrayne;
And, for my dede & grevouse adventure,
More aske I nott but love for love a-gayne.
Brother, be kynde, & for a good certayne,
by-side all this, rewardede shalt thou be 195
in the blysse of hevyne, where ther ys no pouerte.

110. 'Have All My Heart and Be in Peace'

Trinity Coll. Camb. MS. 263. Part II

Querimonia Xi languentis pro amore. [fol. 31ᵛᵒ]

TRewloue trewe, on you I truste,
Euermore to fynde you perseuerawnt,
Ellys wolde my herte yn sondir brest,
Bot I cowde love yn expyrant. 4

Loke þat youre chere change for no chaunce,
Ne kepe noman youre sorow see;
If I may not do you plesance,
Myne herte hath holly noone but ye.   8

Therfor, haue alle myne herte & beon yn pees,
& þynke I love you soueranly—
ffor þat I say hit is no lese—
Wolde god ye wyste as wele as I.   12

ffor wele I se, bothe day & nygth   [fol. 32ro]
That trew loue wyle me neuer cese.
Haue mercy on me, worthly wiygth,
Haue all my herte & be yn pese.   16

Ye haue all myne herte where-euer ye go,
Herte, body & all my richez;
I am bot dede & ye go me fro,
There was neuer þynge I louyd so moche.   20

Therfor, dere herte, loke ye be trewe,
& loue me wele withouten lese;
I wyll neuer change you for no newe,
Haue all myne herte & be yn pees.   24

ffor where I love I kan not leve,
Ofte tymes hit doeth myn herte gret wo;
A preuey peyne hit is to preue
To loue & be rygth longe þer-fro.   28

ffor—& ye wyste ye wolde say so—
A lovere wolde his love ay se.
Therfore, I morne rygth ofte I-wys,
& so doeth oþer loveris mo.   32

14 m *struck through after* wyle.
18 mygth *crossed out after* my.

My herte hath noone but ye yn folde;
A! dere herte, whan dyde I ylle,
But euer wrougth rygth as ye wolde,
Or euer was vntrewe you tylle?   36

III.   *Christ Triumphant*

Advocates MS. 19. 1. 11

I Haue laborede sore and suffered deyȝth,   [fol. 179ᵛᵒ]
and now I Rest and draw my breyght;
but I schall come and call Ryght sone   3
heuene and erght and hell to dome;
and thane schall know both devyll and mane,
What I was and what I ame.   6

112.   *Aloft is Risen the Great Illuminer*

Arundel MS. 285

Off þe Resurrectioun of crist.

O Mothir of God, Inuolat virgin mary,   [fol. 174ᵛᵒ]
Exult in Ioy and consolacioun!
On loft is ryssyn þe gret Illumynar,
The lampe þat lichtnes euery regioun.   4
Thy glorius birth, þe blisfull orient sone,
With Ioy is partit fra þe subtell nycht;   [fol. 175ʳᵒ]
His bemes persit hes þe skyis doun,
Quhois blyssit vp-rissing glades euery wycht. 8

Be glaid, ye angellis and ye archangellis cleir!
Ȝoure wailȝeand prince, victorius in battall,
Met with all hevinlie melody and cheir;
And to ȝoure king ȝe sing, 'haill, victour, haill!' 12

33 hoolly *struck through after* hath.
No. 112. 5 MS. blifsull.

That hes in erd ourecumyn with gret travell,
And hes of hell þe power put to flicht,
And þair strang portes priulie done assale,
Quhois glaid vprissing blithis euery wycht.   16

Be blicht, mankind, and gif god Laude & glore,
That hes þi lyne relaxit of þe Lymbe
Quhilk   .   .   .   .
                into presoun sumtyme dirk and dym.   20
Honour with houres and with antane & hyme
The saikles lorde, þat slane was for þi slycht,
The pasche lambe, þat on þe croce did clym,
Quhois blith vprissing glaides euery wycht.   24

The mychty, strange, victorius campyoun,
With hie Imperiall Laude, hes done returne,   [fol. 175ᵛᵒ]
With palme of glory and with Lawre croune,
With his all-weilding father to soiorne,   28
Quhois palice hie schynes abone saturn,
Off quhome etheriall sternes takis Lich[t],
Quhome hevin and erd dois honour & adurn,
Quhois glaid vprissing blithis euery wycht.   32

Wnto his trone, with hie tryvmphald tryne,
Is gone þis glorius prince of most degre,
With sang of all þe angellis ordouris nyne,
Off sound excellyng in suavite—   36
To quhois incomprehensable maieste,
Superlatyve and Innosable mycht,
Be infynite laude in tyme & vnite,
Quhois glaid vprissing blithis euery wycht.   40

                        ffinis

19 *This line omitted in MS.*
21 MS. y hyme *with the first letter crossed out.*
27 MS. *after* of *is written* Lav *and crossed out.*
30 MS. Lichnyng *with last four letters crossed out.*

113. *The Lord is Risen from Death to Life*

Arundel MS. 285

Off the Resurrectioun.

THow that in prayeris hes bene lent [fol. 175ᵛᵒ]
     In prayaris and in abstinance,
ffor thy trespassis penitent,
Confessit and cleyne of all offence,   [fol. 176ʳᵒ]
Ris with þe Lambe of Innocence   5
To den þat did þe dragoun drif
This day, with hie mangnificence.
The Lord Is rissin fra deth to Life.   8

The sing triumpand of þe croce
Schew, to confound þe feindis feid,
And quhen he fechtis with maist force,
Wi⁺h confessioun hald doun his heid.   12
Ris with thy ransonar fra dede,
And the of all þi synnis schrife.
Thow Rew apoun his woundis reid,
That for þe deit and rais on Live.   16

And þou þat art in hert so dour
That nocht for his gret passioun growis,
Behald þi meik, sueit Saluiour,
The to enbrace, how þat he bowis.   20
Se how he mertirit wes with Iowis
And how he stud for þe in strife.
Hes he þi lufe, all he allowis
That for þe deit and Rais on live.   24

6 MS. *after* To *is written* dey *and crossed out.*
9 MS. trumpand.

And þou þat art in errour dirkit,   [fol. 176ᵛᵒ]
ffollow thy Lord—the way Is plane—
And off his futsteppis be nocht Irkit
That tuke þi gidschip with sic pane.   28
Quhen þow gois wrang, returne agane
And with þi ransoner rewife.
Lang in syn þou ly not plane,
Bot Ris with him fra ded to life.   32

O man, þat wes in syn disparit
Tak now gude hope and haue contricioun.
ffor [þow] þat Rebell was declarit
Hes of þi realmes Restitucioun;   36
Now blindit Is þi Inhibicioun
With the blud of cristis woundis five,
And seillit agane Is thy remissioun,
To Ris with him fra ded to life.   40

114. *The Bread Come from Heaven*

Sloane MS. 2593

Worchyp we boþe more & leste   [fol. 21ᵛᵒ]
crystes body in furme of bred.

IT is bred fro heuene cam,
ffleych & blod of mary it nam;
ffor þe synnys of adam
    he sched his blod þat was so red.   4

'he þat onworþi þis bred ete,
þe peyne of helle he xal gete;
my swete body awey to lete
    & makyn his sowle to be ded.   8

28 MS. pyne.   30 MS. rewis.

'he þat þis bred haȝt in mynde
he xal leuyn withoutyn ende;
þis is bred to ȝeuyn a frende,
   withoutyn qwyt, withine red'—   12

On schyre þursday al at þe messe
to hese desipel he seyde þisse—
'Etyȝt þis bred, myn body it isse;
   lok þer-of ȝe han non dred.'   16

Aftyr-ward at here soper,
he tok þe wyn þat was so cler   [fol. 22ro]
& blyssid it with mylde cher:
   'þis is myn blod þat is so red.'   20

þe Iuwys wern boþe wylde & wode,
he puttyn Ihū vp-on þe rode,
ffor to spyllyn his herte blode—
   ffor manys synne he sufferid ded.   24

Ihū, lynd vs þis bred to ete,
& alle our synnys for to forȝete,
& in heuene a place to gete,
   þrow þe vertu of þis bred.   28

115. *An Orison of the Sacrament and Creed*

Challoner MS.

Als oft as men says þis orisoun   [page 404]
Betwen agnus dei & þe leuacion
Twa thowsande wynter of pardon
Mon þai haue to þe crōñ.

IHū, my lord, welcom þu be!
In flesch & blode I þe see,
Bath god and man veraly
As I trow witterly.   4

Þis haly flessh and þis blode,
Of a mayden mylde of mode,
Þou resaued for oure gode,
And þat þu kid opon þe rode.   8

Quhan þat blode ran fra þi syde,
Out of a wounde wonder wyde
For to safe witt all man-kynde,
And þe to haue ay in mynde.   12

And so þu died as me say
And rayse ogayne þe thrid day,
An þis same flesch wyth woundes fyfe
Þow rayse ogayne fra deed to lyue ;   16
And efterward til heuen þu stegh
To mak us sitt wyth þe on hegh ;
And sone her-after þu sall come
To þe drede-full day of dome,   20
All man-kynde to deme sone
Efter þai hafe sayed or done.

Als sothely, lorde, als I trow þis,
Lat me ner lose þi blyss   24
In vertu of þis sacrament,
Lorde, lat me neuer more be schent.
In wyrschipe of þi haly name,
Scheld þu me fra synne & schame,   28
Fra all perels þu kepe me,
And gyf me grace to won with þe,
Thurgh vertu of þi body here
Þat þe priste handels in þe auter.   32
And ay þu kepe me with þi grace
And graunt me in heuen a place.

13 MS. did.

Ihū criste, þat it so be,
Lorde, þu graunt par charite! 36
And euer þu do mercy witt me
In worschipe of Trinite.

Aue et gaude maria mater domini nostri ihū Xp̄ī regina celi
domina mundi imperatrix inferni miserere mei et tocius populi
Xp̄iani.

116. *By a Chapel as I Came*

Porkington MS. 10

Mery hyt ys in may mornyng   [fol. 199ʳᵒ]
Mery wayys ffor to gonne.

ANd By a chapell as y Came,
  Mett y wyhte Ihū to chyrcheward gone
Petur and Pawle, thomas & Ihon,
And hys desyplys Euery-chone. 4
        Mery hyt ys.

Sente Thomas þe Bellys gane ryng,   [fol. 199ᵛᵒ]
And sent Collas þe mas gane syng,
sente Ihoñ toke þat swete offeryng,
And By a chapell as y Came. 8
        Mery hyt ys.

Owre lorde offeryd whate he wollde,
A challes alle off ryche rede gollde;
Owre lady, þe crowne off hyr mowlde,
The sone owte off hyr Bosome schone. 12
        Mery hyt ys.

Sent Iorge þat ys owre lady kny3te,
He tende þe tapyrys fayre & Bryte—
To myn y3e a semley sy3te,
And By a chapell as y Came. 16
        Mery hyt ys.

15 MS. my ny3e.

117.   *The Mystery of the Incarnation*

B.M. Addit. 20059

Mervell nothyng, Joseph, thaȝ mary be with child.   [fol. 6ᵛᵒ]
she hath conceyved verre god & man & yet she vndefiled.

COnceyved man, how may that be by reasoun broght
    abowte ?
By gode reason aboue all reasons hit may be withowten
    dowte,
For god made man above all reasonȝ of slyme erthe most
    wyld.
Wherfore, Joseph, mervell not thaghe mary be withe
    chyld.   4
   Mervell nothyng, Joseph, &c.

Mary was bothe wyf & mother & she a verrey mayde,
And conceyued god, our brother, as prophettes bifore
    hade saide.
Sithe god made reason why may not reason of his werkes
    be begyld ?
Wherfore, Joseph, mervell not though mary be with
    chyld.   8
   Mervell nothyng, Joseph.

The erthe, ayer, sonne & mone, fyre, water & every sterre
bi gode reason that aboue all reasonȝ shuld passe our
    reasonȝ ferre.
To reason with hym that made reason our reasonȝ are
    but wyld,
Wherfor, Joseph, mervell not though mary be with
    child.   12
   Mervell nothyng, Joseph.

The hye & holy sacrament in verrey forme of bred   [fol. 7ʳᵒ]
Is God and man, flesshe & blode, he that was quyck & ded.

Did reason this dede? nay, nay, reason is ferre begylde.
Hit is gode reason aboue all reason3 Mary to be with
    child.   16
  Mervell not, Joseph.

God, Angell, soole & devyll lett all clerkes determyne,
By reason they be, but what they be, reason cannot defyne.
Then serve the fyrst, & save the thrydde, the forte let
    be resyled.
And mervell no more but fast beleue, Mary was maide
    with child.   20
  Mervell not, Joseph.

118.   *Three Things Against Nature*

Helmingham Hall MS. LJ. I. 10

A carolle   (fly-leaf at end)
By resone of ij and powur of one,
This tyme god [&] mane were sett at one.

GOd a-geynst nature iij thyngys hath wrought:
  ffirst of the vyle erth made mane with-out mane,
Then womane with-out woman of man made of nought, 3
  And man without mane In woman than.
  Thus god and man to-gether be-gane
    As ij, to yoyne to-gethyre in one;   6
    As one, this tyme to be sett at one,
  This god be-gane
  This world to forme, to encresse mane.   9

Angellis in hevyn for offence was dampned,
  And also man for beynge variabyll;
Whether these shulde be savyd, it was examyned,   12
  Man or angell; then gode was greabyll
  To answer for man (for man was not abyll)
        18 MS the . . . . the.

And seid, 'man hade mocyon & angell hade none;   15
Wherfore god and man shulde be sett at one.'
Thanke we hyme thane,
That thus lefte angell and sauyde mane.   18

119.   *Faith is Above Reason*

A. Sloane MS. 3534

Hoc mens ipsa stupet quod non sua ratio cernet   [fol. 3ᵛᵒ]
Quo modo virgo pia genetrix sit sancta Maria
Ac Deus almus homo sed credat ratio miro
Namque fides superest cum perfida ratio subsit.

Pecok

WItte hath wondir that resoun ne telle kan,
      How maidene is modir, and God is man.
Leve thy resoun and bileve in the wondir,
For feith is aboven and reson is undir.

B. MS. Lat. Liturg. e. 10
(Sum. Catal. No. 32942)

WYtte hath wondyr þat Reson tell ne can,   [fol. 22ᵛᵒ]
      Houh a mayde bare a chylde both god & man;
Therfore leve wytte & take to the wundyr—
ffeyth goth a-bove, & Reson goth vndyr.

C. Harley MS. 541

WYtte hath wonder how reson telle can   [fol. 207ᵛᵒ]
      That mayd is mother and God is man,
Oure noble sacrament, yn thre thinges on.
In this leeve reson, beleve thou the wondre—
There feith is lord, reson gothe undre!

Gregorius: 'Fides non habet meritum, ubi humana ratio probet
experimentum.'

120.   *The Divine Paradox*

MS. Rawlinson B. 332
(Sum. Catal. No. 11670)

A God and yet a man?   [first fly-leaf ᵛᵒ]
  A mayde and yet a mother?
Witt wonders what witt Can
  Conceave this or the other.   4

A god, and Can he die?
  A dead man, can he live?
What witt can well replie?
  What reason reason give?   8

God, truth itselfe, doth teach it;
  Mans witt senckis too farr vnder
By reasons power to reach it.
  Beleeve and leave to wonder!   12

121.   *God Bids Us Use Reason and*
Evidence

Porkington MS. 10

Why, why, what ys þis? why, hit ys   [fol. 201ʳᵒ]
Non nodyre sekurely but weritus were-by domini.

WHane no-þing whas but god alone—
  The fadyre, þe holly gost & þe sone—
Whone ys iij and iij ys whone.   What

Heyuyn & erthe furst he wroȝt,   4
And odyre creaturs he made of noȝt,
All þing dyspossid lyk as he þowȝt.   What

Mane for an appull of lyttyll prys,
He lost þe blys of parradys,   8
ffor he dessyryd for to be wys.   What

Tell me þis ressoun, yeve þat þu cane,
how goddys sone be-came a mane
be lynnag of dawyt and nassone?   What 12

Marwell I have þat pure wyrgyne   [fol. 201ᵛᵒ]
Myȝt consayfe sappyens dewyne;
I trow hit passyt all wyttus þine.   What

The grettust lord of sofferantte   16
ys god him-selfe in his humannyte,
ffor man-kynd he dyid wppon a tre.   What

Man, þu art but corrypptybull,
Tell me how hit may be possibull   20
That he schall lyue euer, as sayth þe bybull? What

Man, þu art but in faynyt
To comprehend nor to indyte
All þis matters se in sennyt.   What 24

God hym-selfe byddyt vs by his senttens
To so vse owre resoun and owre efydens,
And to his wordys yef wholl credens.   What 27

122. *An Orison to St. John the Baptist*

B.M. Addit. MS. 39574
(The Wheatley MS.)

To Seynt Iohn   [fol. 58ʳᵒ]

SEynt Iohn, for grace þou craue,
 Þat of his mercy he wole us saue,
   As þou nexst hym were boren beste.   3
And whanne we schulen fro hens weende,
Thou gete us grace to make good eende,
   In heuene blis wiþ hym to reste.   5
                A – M – E – N

26 MS. eyfdens.

123. *The Martyrdom of St. Thomas*

Caius Coll. Camb. MS. 383

A a.a.a. nunc gaudet ecclesia.　　　[page 68]

HErkenud lordyngus, grete & smale,
　ych wole ʒow telle a wondur tale,
how holy churche was brout in bale
　　cum magna iniuria.　　　　　　4

Knytus werone sent fro harry kyng,
Wyckede men wyt-out lesyng,
þere þey dedone a wondur þyng
　　ffrementes insania.　　　　　　8

þe chef clerk of al þys lond,
of Kaunturbury ych vndur-stonde,
he was slay wyt wyckede hond
　　Demonis Potencia.　　　　　　12

þey soutone þe byschop al aboute,
in hys paleys wyt-inne & wyt-oute;
Of ihū cryst þey haddone no doute
　　In sua Superbia.　　　　　　16

Wyt her mouþus þey ʒendone wyde,　[page 69]
& seyde to hym wyt gret prude,
'traytur, þu here schal a-byde
　　ferens mortis tedia.'　　　　　20

He ansuerede wyt mylde chere,
'Ʒyf ych schal dye in þys manere,
lat hym go þat ys here
　　absque contumelia.'　　　　　24

5 MS. knyg.　　　9 MS. clrek.　　　19 MS. a-bucge.

turmenturus abouten hym gon sterte,
wyt wyckede wondis hey hyn herte;
þer he dyede, on hys modur churche,
　　Optans celi gaudia.　　　　　　　　　28

　Clerk, mayde, wedede & wyf,
Werchepud thomas in al her lyf,
for fyftene tokenus of gret strif
　　Contra regis consilia.　　　　　　　32

124.　*Prayer to Mary and All Saints*

MS. Bodley 939
(Sum. Catal. No. 27691)

[M]Ary, moder of mercy & pyte,　[fol. 117ᵛᵒ]
　　And seynt Kateryn, pray for me
To the blyssidfull & ryghtwous iuge on hy,
That ihū on me haue mercy.　　　　　4

Seynt Michael & seynt gabryell,
And all good Angels als wele,
　Praye for me to owr lady,
　　That ihū on me haue mercy.　　　8

Holy patriarchis & prophetis,
To yow I pray and besech,
　Pray for me wyth owr lady,
　　That ihū on me haue mercy.　　　12

Petir & palle & postils alle,
To yow I cry & hartili calle,
　Pray for me wyth owr lady,　　　[fol. 118ʳᵒ]
　　That ihū on me haue mercy.　　16

16 MS. Tthat.

Seynt steuyn & seynt laurence,
All ma[r]terys that suffryd turment,
   Pray for me wyth owr lady,
   That ihū on me haue mercy.   20

Seynt marteyn & seynt nicholasse,
And alle good confessors þat euer wasse,
   Pray for me wyth owr lady,
   That ihū on me haue mercy.   24

Seynt Kateryne & sent margaret,
And alle virgynys good & swet,
   Pray for me wyth owr lady,
   That ihū on me haue mercy.   28

Alle the halowys, that euyr ware
Wyth ihū cryst both leff and dere,
   Pray for me wyth owr lady,
   That ihū on me haue mercy,   32

And for all quik and dede.
Pater noster Aue and Crede.

125.   *A Prayer of the Holy Name*

Cambridge Univ. MS. Ff. 1. 6

O Cryste Ihū, mekely I pray to the,   [fol. 146ᵛᵒ]
   To lete thy name, wedyr y ryde or gone,
In euery parell & in euery aduersite,
Be my defence a-ȝenste my mortall fone   4
To make them stonde styll as eny stone;
And that castene me falsly to werray,
Make thow here malyce to-to obey.

18 MS. turnament.

To thi name, & make hem stond a-backe,   8
Or thay haue poure to yoy here cruel myght ;
And wicked spretus so oryble & blake
That besy bene to wayte me day & nyghte,
Let thi name dryue hem owte of syghte   12
And, in my fored when I 'Ihū' empresse,
Make me of grace theyre malyce to oppresse.

ffor to þi name hoolly y me commende,
Myn lyf, deth, my body, herte & all,   .   16
My sowle al-so when I hense wende,
O cryste Ihū, o lorde ynmortall !
Praying to the, whene thow me deme schall,
That thow me saue from eternall schame,   20
That haue full feght & hole truste in þi name.

Explicit.

126. Keep Me To-day from Shame and Sin

Sloane MS. 3160

[I]Hū crist, I the be-seche   [fol. 152ʳᵒ]
Thow here my prayere & myn speche,
And haue it in þi mynd,
As þu boghtis me with þi blod,   4
And raymett was one þe rod
ffor me and all man-kynd.

Derworthe god, I the pray   .
ffrom shame & shenship kepe me to-day,   8
All perrell put me fro.
lord, to þe I crye & call,
lett me to-day no myssechefe fall,
But fend me frome my fo.   12

Kepe me, lord, frome dedly syne,
þu lett me not fall þer-in
   Thrughe þe fendis falsyng,
But gyf me grace wyll to sped,   16
In word, in wytt & thoght & dede,
   As þu art heuen kyng.

I shryue me to the kynge of heuen,   [fol. 152ᵛᵒ]
Gylti in the synnys seuen,   20
   lord, þu me amend!
Thow lene me grace to lyf with wyne,
Without dett and dedly syne,
   When I shall make an end.   24

The .x. comaundementis I haue broken,
With body wroght, and mowthe spoken—
   lord, I aske þe grace!
ffadur and sone and holy gost,   28
One god of myghtis most,
   ffor-gif me my trespace!

Mare, goddis modur dere,
qwene of heuene, þu me here,   32
   And kepe me to-daye,
lady, for þi Ioyus fyve.
As þu art modur & maydene & wyfe,
   Thow socur me al-waye.   36

Al-myghty god and mare myld,
ffro syne & shame ȝe me shild!
   Sent Myghell, I the be-seche,
Kepe & socur þu me send;   40
ffrome temptacione of þe fend
   Thus day þu me safe & kepe. Amene.

127.   *An Evening Prayer, I*

Harley MS. 541

(written as prose)   [fol. 228ᵛᵒ]

VPon my Ryght syde y me leye,
  blesid lady, to the y pray,
ffor the teres that ye lete
vpone yowr swete sonnys feete,   4
Sende me grace for to slepe
& good dremys for to mete,
Slepyng, wakyng, til morowe daye bee.
Owre lorde is the frwte, oure lady is the tree;   8
Blessid be the blossome that sprange, lady, of the!
In nomine patris & filij & spiritus sancti
                                    Amen.

128.   *An Evening Prayer, II*

MS. Ashmole 61
(Sum. Catal. No. 6922*)

IHc̄ lord, well of All godnes,   [fol. 22ʳᵒ]
  ffore thi grete pety i þe pray;
ffore-gyffe me All my wykidnes,
    Where-with I haue greuyd þe to-dey.   4

Honour & praysing to þe be,
    And thankyng four thi gyftis All,
That I þis dey reseyuid off the;
    Now, curtas cryst, to þe I calle.   8

This nyght fro perell thou me kepe,
    My bodely rest whyll þat I take;
And als longe as myne evyne sclepe,
    Myn hert in thi seruys wake.   12

11 evyñ] *i.e.* eyen.

ffore feryng of þe fend owre fo,
    ffro fowll dremys & fantasys,
Kepe þis nyght; from synne also
    In clenes þat I may vp-ryse.   16

Saue my gode doers fro greuans,
    And quyte them þat þei on me spend;
Kepe my enmys fro noyans,
    And gyffe þem grace forto Amend.   20

Mercy, Ihū, & grante mercy
    My body, my soule I þe be-kene,
In nomine patris & filij
    & spiritus sancti, Amen.   24

129.   *A Morning Prayer*

MS. Ashmole 61
(Sum. Catal. No. 6922*)

IHū, lord, blyssed þu be!   [fol. 22ro]
    ffore all þis nyght þu hast me kepe
ffrome þe fend & his poste,
    wheþer I wake or þat I slepe.   4

In grete deses & dedly synne
    Many one þis nyght fallyn has,
That I my selue schuld haue fallyn In,
    Hadyst þu not kepyd me with thi grace.   8

Lord, gyffe me grace to þi worschype
    This dey to spend in þi plesanse,
And kepe me fro wyked felyschipe,
    And frome þe fendis comb[er]ance.   12

Ihū, my tunge þu reule all so
    That I not speke bot it be nede,
Hertly to pray fore frend & fo,
    And herme no mane in word ne dede.   16

Cryste, gyffe me grace, off mete & drynke
    This day to take mesurably,
In dedly synne þat I not synke,
    Thorow out-rage off foule glotony.   20

Ihū my lord, Ihū my loue,
    And all þat I ame bond vnto,
Thi blyssing send fro heuyn A-boue,   [fol. 22ᵛᵒ]
    And gyffe þem grace wele to do.   24

My gode Angell, þat arte to me send
    ffrome god to be my gouernour,
ffrome all euyll sprytis þu me defend,
    And in my desesys to be my socoure.   28

        Amen qd Rate.

130.   Speed Our King on His Journey

Lambeth MS. 344

KYryeleyson, Kp͞eleysone   [fol. 8ᵛᵒ]
  Pater de celys, deus, to the we crye,
Goodyse sone that bought vs, the secund persone,
Spiritus sancte, deus, one vs haue mercy!   4
Holy trynyte as god, beleue we fully.
Spede oure kynge and [spare] thy servant fre,
Wyth contynuell grace hym mvltyplye.
    Salvum fac regem domine.   8

Sancta maria, mylde medyatryce,
Avdi [nos] rogantes seruulos!
Dey genitryx, to thy flovyr de-lyce,
Pray for owre kyng where-so he goose.   12

  6 thy *is written over an erasure. A word of 4 or 5 letters (be-*
ginning with o *?) has been scraped out.*
  11 thy] MS. hy.

O virgoo virginum, lete hym never loos
That hath the kepyng of thy doware fre,
But be port and prynce yn hys pvrpose.
   Saluum fac regem domine.   16

Sancta Anna, genytryce of marye,
ffunde preces thy doughtur to praye,
That ys crystes moder of mercye,
To speed oure kyng yn hys yournay,   20
That he may well speed yn hys vaye,
And kepe ys ryght as yt shold be.
Moder and doughtter, as ye well may
   Saluum fac regum domine.   24

Seynt mychaell, prynce, archangel and knyght,
And the .ix. ordres of angles alle,
And gabryel that glyded from good almyty
To owre blessyd lady that ys to calle,   28
Beth medyatours yn the heven halle
To oure gracyose lord yn mageste,
In enemyes fortune that he never falle.
   Saluum fac regem domine.   [fol. 9ro] 32

Precussor dnī, seynt ihon̄ bapttyst,
Patryarkes, prophetys, pray for our kynge
That god of hys goodnesse gyf hym hys lyste
Of power and strenght that ys to hys plesyng—   36
Abraham, ysaak and jacob reynyng
Patres, senyores o seynt moyse—
ffor owre lyege lord that ys lyvynge.
   Saluum fac regem domine.   40

23 MS. may well, *but marked for transposition.*
36 MS. hys ys to plesyng: *corrector has cancelled* hys *and marked it for insertion after* to.   38 Patres] MS. Peter.

Seynt petre, prynceps Apostolorum,
Seynt poule, seynt andrew and yames by name,
Seynt iohne, crystes derelyng, sociusque vestrorum,
Seynt tomas and the lasse seynt yame,   44
Seynt phylyp, seynt barthelemewe ful tame,
Seynt matthew, synt symoun, and tadee
Seynt mathy, seynt barnbe, prayeth all yn same.
    Saluum fac regem domine.   48

Seynt luke, seynt marke,—ewangelers
Enforced to the apostoles ye are—
Alle crystes dyscyples and hevenly feres,
Prayeth for owre spede and oure welfare.   52
Alle the holy nombre that passyone bare,
Innocentys for crystes natyuyte,
Defende oure kyng from hys enemyes snare!
    Saluum fac regem domine.   56

Seynt stevyne that was wyth stones pynede,
Seynt oswalde kynge and martyr clene,
Seynt thomas, flovre of england shrynede,
Alle myghtful martyres on yow y mene!   60
Thorugh yow and the prayer of heven quene,
Send to owre kynge humanyte,
Beth hys tvtors yn travayle and tene.
    Saluum fac regem domine.   [fol. 9ᵛᵒ]   64

Seynt george, oure ladyes knight
On whom alle englond hath byleve,
Shew vs thy helpe to god almyght,
And kepe oure kyng from all myscheve.   68
Thu art oure patronesse knyght y-preve
To defend wyth fyght oure ladyes fe,
Seynt george, by oure helpe yn all oure greve,
    Saluum fac regem domine.   72

       47 prayeth] y *interlined above by the corrector.*

Thu precyose pastour, seynt erkenwalde,
Helpe and here thy nacyoun,
Seynt edward, kyng and confessor called,
ffor thy provynce put orysoun.   76
Alle confessours and the congregacyoun
Of monkes and heremytes yn alle degre
ffor oure ryght make supplycacyoun.
    Saluum fac regem domine.   80

Thu blessyd womman, marye magdaleyne,
The better part to the thu chees,
Seynt kateryn and seynt eleyne
And all the virgynes yn hevenly prees,   84
Prayeth ye to cryst to send vs pees.
Omnes scī et scē orate,
That grace wyth vs may ever encresse.
    Saluum fac regem domine.   88

Propicius esto et parce nobis,
Ihū, lord god of myght and grace,
Alle-though we erre and do amysse,
Mercy we crye for owre trespace!   92
As penytentes we wyle purchace
The precyose yndulgence and thy pyte,
To saue thy peple yn every place.
    Saluum fac regem domine.   96

Swete seynt george, take to oure kyng heed,   [fol. 10ʳᵒ]
To hys lynage and to other lordes all yn fere,
They mowe haue grace well to speed
And couere hem alle vnder thy banere.   100

91 MS. Alle thought.
93 *Corrected from* penytes.

To that gloryose gemme that shyneth so clere,
Gooddes moder and mayd of pyte,
Devoutly seyth all that bene here,
  Saluum fac regem domine.   104

131.   *Mary, Take in Your Hand this*
Dread Voyage

Arundel MS. 249

Mercyful quene, as ye best kan and may   [fol. 6ᵛᵒ]
  after your sone, of wreches take pyte,
send your confort nowe on your blessed day
to sory folke in gret aduersite.   4
Make me to fele your swete benyngnyte,
Sterre of þe see, as botefull ys your name!
Behold me now in your hye mageste,
Most swete lady, an deffend me fro schame.   8

Moder of god, virgine most meke and pure,
With entier hert y pray you deuoutly,
Take in your hond and in your blessed cure
This dradd voyage, so as your grete mercy   12
ffor oure pourpose may schape the remedy.
And, as ye know I mene the comone wele
Bothe of my frend and of myn enemy,
Graunt my request party or euerydele.   16

And al worschip that schal come by your grace
To god mote tourne with you his moder dere
Besechyng hym for-geue myn olde trespasse
Graunt me gode spede for your most swete prayere 20

101 MS. shynetht.

And you .I. pray in most humble manere,
Quene of heuen, wel of myserycord,
As ye be sterre most feyre schynyng and clere
Wyth my desyre your grace ye wel accord.   24

Prouost of heuen, Archangel Michael,
Deffend me now be powayr most mythye
Of god the fader, and holy gabriel
Geue me counsayl of the sone most wyttye,   28
And raphael, guyde vnto thobye,
Be my confort and lede me to gode cost,   [fol. 7ʳᵒ]
By the uertu of blessed holy gost.

Dere spouse of god, holy seynte Kateryne,   32
Whose stedfast loue myght chaunge for no tourment
Nor feyre promes, martyre and pure uirgyne,
I beseche you to faueur myn entent;
And lyke as mylke oute of your feyre nek went   36
In stede of blode vppon your dying day,
Here my prayer and be with me al-wey.

Prynce of knythode throwoute the grete breteyne,
Noble of blode, large of hospitalyte,   40
Holy seynt Albon, thou settest but in veyne
Al worldly pomp for hym that died for the;
Now in my nede, gode lorde, remembre me,
As of martyres thou hast begone oure daunce,   44
ffirst in oure lond oure bonechief to auaunce.

Blessed seynt Gorge, most in oure remembrance,
A-geynyst oure fone haue us alwey in mynde;
Pray for oure grace, oure spede, and oure gode chaunce, 48
As to englond thou hast be euer kynde.
And, þow fortune hath cast vs late be-hynde,
Yet fayle vs nat whan þat we crye thi name,
ffor with thyn helpe we hope recure gode fame.   52

Holy marye, O blessed magdeleyn,
Ye with oure lord fonde gret loue and mercy
ffor that tourment, rygthe gret longynge and peyn
Þat your hert felt after ye saw hym dye,   56
And for þat Ioy and confort bodylye   [fol. 7ᵛᵒ]
That he gaue you with his first apparence,
Geyn al euel be ye my sure deffence.

Derest Lady and moder gracyouse,   60
Blesse me this tyme with þat uertu dyuyne
To you geuen, for me most desyrousse
To obey you vntyl my lengest fyne.
Pray ye oure lord with his moder virgyne   64
That my werkes may tourne to thy preysyng,
And I schal pray the botefull kateryne
To pray for youre and myn Ioyfull metynge.

132. *Lovely Angel, Keep Me Day and Night*

Cambridge Univ. MS. Ii. 6. 43

Oracio ad proprium angelum.

[I] Praye þe, spirit, þat angell arte   [fol. 98ᵛᵒ]
      To whom .y. ame be-take,
That þu me kepe in clene lyf,
      Wheþer .y. slepe or wake.   4

God of hys grace haþ me þe sende,
      To kepe me boþe daye & nyȝt,
Tyde and tyme me to defende,   [fol. 99ʳᵒ]
      And with þe fende for me to fyȝt.   8

57 þat *interlined above.*
7 MS. defendee.   8 fende] *altered from* fynde.

Louely angell, counforte me
  In what desese þat y be ynne,
Helpe with grace þat y maye flee
  In wyll and dede & deedly synne.   12

Alle temptacions þu put me
  ffro þe fendes þat wyll me drede.
Where-euer y goo my fere þu be
  That y maye knowe þy helpe at nede.   16

Þow y haue be to þe vnkynde,
  To þe mercyfull kynge for me þu praye,
Þat no gylt in me be founde,
  Whan y schall ryse at domesdaye.   20

Whanne þu seest me goon with wronge,
  ffor hym þat haþ me wroȝt,
To hym a-ȝey þu me wysse,
  Ellys y lese my blys for noȝt.   24

What sorowe or what desese,
  Helpe me with þy prayere,
My lordes face þat y may see   [fol. 99ᵛᵒ]
  at domys daye with-outen fere.   28

Also y praye þe, myn angell swete,
  Ȝyf yt maye be by anye waye,
Þat þu do me to wete
  Of my lyuyng or þe last daye.   32

Suffre not the fende blake,
  With [s]cornis ne with wanhope,
Neyþer my mynde fro me to take,
  My sowle to see.   36

21 wronge] *read* mysse *and restore the rime.*
28 fere] MS. feree.   29 swete] MS. free.
Lines 35 and 36 transposed in MS.

Whan y schall owte of þys worlde goo,
  ffor-sake me noȝt tyll þu brynge
me hym to that my sowle came fro,
  Euer in ioye with angeles to synge.   40
                              AmeN.

133.   *My Keeper so Sweet*

B.M. Addit. MS. 31042

HAile! holy spyritt, & Ioy be vn-to the!   [fol. 101ᵛᵒ]
  My keper so swete, myne Aungelle so fre,
In-to thi handis I pray the to take
My fastyng, my penance, my prayers þat I make,   4
My ympnys, my psalmys, my syngyng for syne,
My knelynge, My louynge, My charite þat I ame Ine,
My wakynge, my wepynge & my deuocyoun,
My pacience, my angyrs & my tribulacioun,   8
My werkes of mercy & my almus dede,
And offere þame to Ihū, & gete me some mede.
And alle my gude dedis, gyffe þay littill be,
I pray þe to presente þame bifore þe trynyte,   12
And to my lorde, Ihū, þu me recomende,
& thanke hym of alle gudnesse þat he hase me
      sende.
And if I haue seruede & worthy be to payne,
Ȝitt some drope of his mercy þu brynge me agayne,   16
His pite & his gudnesse in me for to schawe,
Þe wrethe of myne Enemy þat I may with-drawe.
And alle þat me sekis to angyre & to ill,
To lufe & to charyte þu conuerte þaire will;   20
And my gastely enemys, all þat fandys me ay,
Dystrowye þu þaire myghtis by nyghte & by day.

And so þat all spirittes, þat me will assaile
In fandynge, be feble & of strenghe faile,   24
With þe blyssynge of his righte hande he me defende,
Þat regnys god in trynyte, in worlde withowtene ende.
Amen.

134. O Sweet Angel, Bring Me to Bliss

Henry E. Huntington Library, Ellesmere MS. 34. B. 7

A praier to the goode Angell.   [fol. 81ro]

O Swete angell, to me soo deere,
  that nyght and day standithe me neere
    ffull loueyngly with mylde moode,
Thankyng, loueyng, loue & praysyng,   4
Offer for me to Ihū, our kyng,
    ffor his gyfftes greate and goode.

As thow gothe betwix hym and me,
And knowethe my lyffe in euery degre,   8
    Saying it in his presence,
Aske me grace to loue hym truly,
To serue my lorde with hertt duly,
    With my dayly diligence.   12

Keepe me from vice and all perells,
Whiles thowe with me dayly trauells
    In this worlde of wyckednesse;
Sett me my peticions grauntede   16
By thy praier dayly haunted,
    Yff it please thy holynes.

The versicull

O swete Angell, that keepith me,   20
Bryng me to blysse, I pray the!

*135. O Heavenly Star, Most Comfortable
of Light*

Chetham Library, Manchester, MS. 6709
De Sancta Maria contra pestilenciam.   [fol. 281ro]

(1) O Hevenly sterre, most Comfortable of lyght,
    Which, with thy goostely gracyous Influence,
Haste Claryfyed and put vnto flyght
Alle mysty wedrys parlyous for pestylence,   4
Preseruyd thy peple from all olde vyolence,
Plantyd be Adam whan he fyrst gaff asse[nt]
To evys Councell, take of the serpent.

(2) Thow art the sterre, with brestis softe as sy[lke], 8
That gave owre lorde at his Natyvyte
ffull offte sowke of thy Celestyall Mylke,
Whos gracyous Condyte had Angelyke plente,
Tryacle, & Bawme Ageyne all Mortalyte,   12
Plantyd be Adam when he fyrst gaffe Assent
To evys Councell, take of the serpent.

(3) O gloryous Sterre, do not now disdeyne
Contraryous planetis to Appeese & Represse,   16
Whos dredefull werrys do men full Mortall peyne,
Be vnholsome Eyres Cawsyng greete sykenesse,
Roote & Begynnyng of eche ffeverus Accesse,
Toke his Orygynall when Adam gaff assen[t]   20
To evys Councell, take of the serpent.

(4) O loode sterre of this [tempestuous] se,   [fol. 281vo]
In which we be fordryve with many a [wawe]
And forpossed be Many aduersyte,   24
Be owre freele flessh to froward lustis drawe,
Ageyne all such pereyles lette þi lyght a-dawe
On all thy peple that serue the of Intent
And children of Adam, disseyved be a serpent.   28

Parts of ll. 22 and 23 are illegible.

(5) Sterre of the poole, bryghtest of sterrys alle,
Whos bryght beames all derkenesse doth enchase,
Be thow owre socowre when we to the Calle,
Crying for helpe, knelyng Afore thy face.   32
Helpe, noble Pryncesse of pyte & of grace,
Be pestylence eyre that we be not shent—
We chyldren of Adam, deceyued be a serpent.

(6) Sterre of Iacob, owre myschevis to Releve,   36
Caste down thy streemys, thi seruauntis to socowre
Ageyn blake nyghtis, owre Esperus at Eve,
Day sterre A-morowe, for folkys þat labowre
Helpe that karybdis owre vessell not devowre   40
With froward Rokkys, þat it be not to-Rent
Be noo false Treynys of the olde serpent.

(7) . . . . Adam the secounde,   [fol. 282ʳᵒ]
Affter [. . . . .] be a tree.   44
Wounded wel ofte be many bloody wounde,
Off owre harde dispoylere, bought vs Ageyne parde.
O Rose of Iericho, O virgula Iesse,
Ageyn owre thre Enymyes be with vs presen[t]—   48
The freyle flessh, the worlde, & the serpent.

(8) Be these iij. foon suffre vs have no losse,
Off thy Chaste mylke make owre preseruatyffe,
Holde vppe the Baner of thy sonnys Crosse,   52
Vs to defend ageyn all mortall stryff.
In worldely daungerys of this present lyff,
Preserue thy seruauntis, þat be dylygent
The for to serve, mawgre the olde serpent.   56

(9) All gostely myschevys of new & olde poyson
ffyrst of A Tre tooke ther Orygynall;
Syth from A tre Cam owre Saluacyon
Ageyn the lustis of Ane Appyll small.   60
Cryste on the Crosse dranke þ'Eysell & gall

ffor owre Redempcyon, he hath his blode all spent
Ownly to owtray owre Enymye the serpent.

(10) Affter Adam was ow . . . .   [fol. 282ᵛᵒ] 64
When he was exylyd and [. . . . .] boode.
ffrom Cristys passyon the thefe be parlay axid grace,
Conveyid was his Raunsom made with bloode.
O blessyd vyrgyn, so wyse, so feyre, so goode,   68
Lyght bode Aungil Adam be þe holy gost down sent,
Be owre proteccyon Ageyn the olde serpent!

(11) Wyff & Mayde, moder of Cryste Iesu,
Thys dyrge made In thy Reuerence   72
Receyue at gre, & be thy Grete vertu
Preserve thy peple from gostely pestylence,
And from Infeccyon of worldely vyolence,
Whan we shall passe—Mawgre the serpent—   76
Off grace & Mercy be with vs present. Amen.

> Explicit Secundum lydgate
> God graunte vs grace quod
> Willelmus Cotson Canonicus.

136.   *Stella Celi Extirpavit*

Chetham Library, Manchester, MS. 6709

Stella Celi extirpavit que lactavit Dnm Ipsa(?).

(1) THow hevenly quene, of grace owre loode sterre,
[fol. 279ᵛᵒ]
With thy Chaste mylke plentyvous of plesaunce
Gave Ihesu sowke, puttyst Away the werre
Off Pestylence to Appese owre grevaunce,   4
Owre well of Mercy, owre Ioy, owre suffysaunce,
fflowre of vyrgynyte, Moodyr of moste Pryce,
Racedyst vppe all surfetis of myschaunce,
That owre forne fader plantyd In paradyce.   8

(2) [Thow] same sterre—of sterrys noon so bryght!—

[fol. 280ʳº]

Celestyall sterre, of bewte most souereyne,
To the we pray, on vs Cast downe thy syght
Oonly of Mercy, that thow not disdeyne   12
Of Infecte Eyres the Mystes to Restreyne,
That be thy Gracyous most holsome Influence,
We have no Cause on hasty deth to pleyne,
Which sleyth the people be swerd of pestyl[ence].   16

(3) Owre trust Is fully, and owre Confidence
Vndespeyryd, In owre Opynyoun
Ageyn all wedrys of Corrupte Pestilence:
Be thy Requeste and Medyacyoun,   20
And be thy soonys gloryous passyoun
And Remembraunce of thy Ioyes all,
Gayne frowarde Eyres Causyng Infeccyoun,
Diffend vs, lady, when we to the Call.   24

(4) ffor, as Phebus Enchasith Mystis Blake
Toward Midmorowe with his beemys Cleere,
Lucifeere byddyth sluggy folke Awake
In the Oryent, fyrst when he doth Apeere.   28
Ryght so mayst thow, In thy Celestyall speere,
O sterre, of sterrys most of excellence,
Mayd & moder, be Meene of thy prayere,
Save all thy servauntis fro strooke of pestylence.   32

(5) On vs wrecchis, of Mercy to Recorde,   [fol. 280ᵛº]
Emperesse of the hevynly Consystory,
Callyd ffons & well of Myserycorde,
The Goldene Crone, bastell of owre Victory,   36

9 Thow] MS. *illegible.*
16 MS. pestyl . . . *rest of word illegible.*

And Crystall Paleys of owre gostely glorye,
Gladdest Aurora of most Magnificence,
Mayde & Moder, have one thy Men memory!
And them preserue from strooke of Pestylence.   40

(6) Grounde & begynnyng, honowre of owre kynrede,
Temple of the Trynyte, most blessid & most benygne,
Where the hooly goste his golde dewe lyst down shed,
In-to thy Closette moste Competent & condigne,   44
With sevyn sealys, thy Breste he lyste Consigne
Paraclitus to have ther Residence.
As thow were born vnder the vyrgynall sygne,
Save all thy servauntis fro stroke of pestylence!   48

(7) O blessid Ihesu, for thy Moders sake,
lyke as thow lyste, of Mercyfull Pyte,
Sent from thy ffader, owre Nature for to take
In her þat flowryd In Pure Vyrgynyte—   52
ffor mayde & Mooder was nevyr noon but she,
Gayn all Infeccyoun she Is owre Cheef dyffence—
O lorde Above, Callyd oon & two & thre,
ffor her Meryte, save vs fro Pestylence!   56

Amen & Explicit
scdm lydgate

137.   *Parce Mihi, Domine*

MS. Ashmole 189
(Sum. Catal. No. 6777)

FAdyr & sone & holy gost,   [fol. 105ᵛᵒ]
  Grete god in trinite,
As þu art lorde of grete host,
  Parce mihi, domine!   4

Fadyr of heuene, I make my mone,
  With contryte hert I pray to þe:
Off my synnes euerychone,
  Parce mihi, domine!   8

In þy seruys I haue mysdo,
  And oftyne tyme offendet þe,
Mercy! lord, I wyll no more soo,
  Parce mihi, domine!   12

As clerkes tellene to vs I-wys,
  Mane was made, for thynges thre,
To wurshyp þe, kynge of blysse—
  Parce mihi, domine!   16

I-wurshyp goddys false haue I,
  I-seruyd creaturis more þen þe,
I-loued synne & eke foly—
  Parce mihi, domine!   20

But þu fro reuerence me spare,
  I-lost foreuer schall I be.
Lorde, haue mynde of mannys care,
  Parce mihi, domine!   24

138. *All Ten Commandments I Have Broken*

MS. Rawlinson liturg. e. 7
(Sum. Catal. No. 15839)

Here bygynnythe the .X. comaundementis.

THe ten comawndementis I haue broke [fol. 14ʳᵒ]
  Many a tyme with wickede skylle ;
To falce goddus I haue spoke
And wrowghte, a-gaynes my lordis wille.   4

1 MS. that I haue.

Many tyme I haue take
Goddes name in Idylsheppe,
There-fore I tremell, drede and quake.
Mercy! god, for thi lordshepe.   8

Myne holidai I haue myspent,
Ther-for myne herte it is ful sore;
ffadur and modur I haue forfende—
Now mercy! lord, I wylle no more.   12

Mansleer I was with all my myƷt,
In thouƷte, in worde and eke in dede;
Befowlyd womman bothe day and nyƷt,
There-of toke I litil heede.   16

To do thefte wolde y noƷt reste,
WrouƷt I haue aƷens thy lore;
To bere fals wytnesse wold I ay preste—   19
Now mercy! lord, I wole[*] no more.   *[fol. 14ᵛᵒ]

ffor to desyre my neyƷborus howse—
Lytil hede there-of I rowƷte—
Also his wyfe that was his spouse,
And odur catelle that he owƷte.   24

Thus haue I my lorde forsake,
And alle his comaundementis I-broke;
To thi mercy I me take,
ffor-sothe I can no bettur grope.   28

139.   *I Have Lived After My Lust*

Royal MS. App. 58

Now marcy, Ihe-su, I wyll amend   [fol. 23ro]
and neuermore displease the,
yff grace thow wylt me send.

MY thoght ys full hevy
and greuith me Ryght sore;
my synnys be pesy,
 whych repentyth me euer-more.   4
my flesh fast swetyng
 my paynys to Renew,
my body besely boylyng
 with hetys—lord Ihesu,   8
This haue I full surely
 for that I was vniust
to god, the sune off mary,
 and leuyd after my lust. Now mercy, Ihesu.   12

My fete, sume tyme more
 and lesse, they do swete;
my hert ys very pore,
 and besyly doth bete;   16
my hed ys all macy,
 and meruelowsly dothe werke;
my[n] yene dyme and dasy,
 my neke ys full sterke;   20
Thys haue I full surely
 [for that I was vniust
to god, the sune off mary,
 and leuyd after my lust. Now mercy, Ihesu.]   24

8 lord Ihesu] *not clear in MS. Flügel reads:* for A Ihesu.
21 *After this line* vt supra *is written in MS.*

My hondys do me no good
  ne-dys must I ly so
and take no erthly fode

.   .   .   .   28

now helpe me, goode lorde,
  my stomake ys full faynt;
I make to the acorde
  Vppon payne off a-taynt;   32
I wyll no more suerly
  to the be so vnjust
butt kepe thy lawes truly
  And put a-way false lust. Now mercy Ihe[s]u.   36

140.   *Out of Sin My Soul Unbind*

Cambridge Univ. MS. Kk. 1. 6

ALmy3ti god, maker of Heuene,   [fol. 197ro]
  Erthe & Eyre, Water & Wynde,
to þe I calle with myld steuene,
  That flesche & blode tokyste of mankynde.   4
Out of synne my sowle vnbynde
  That for me deydiste apon a tree!
To rekene, y am ful fer be-hynde,
  But, Ihū, þy grace, & haue mercy on me!   8

ffor yff y scholde ry3twyse rekenynge make
  ffro þat tyme þat y was bore,
Then woldest þu vengeaunce take,
  Than were y loste for euer more.   12

28 *A line skipped by the scribe; no gap in the MS.*

Thow haste ordeyned salue for euery sore   [fol. 197ᵛᵒ]
  And mercy, sowles leche to bee ;
That þu haste bouȝte, lette neuer be lore.
  Wherefore, Ihū, have mercy on me.   16

ffor with-out þe no man hath myȝt,
  Pore ne ryche, lough ne hygh.
Thenke how þu haste mercy be-hyȝt
  To all tho þat aske hit mekelygh,   20
  With woful herte & wepynge ye.
    I ȝilde me, lorde, now thus to the,
  And for my mysdedes merci I crye,
    That, lord Ihū, þu have mercy on me.   24

Mercy! for þy comaundement
  That I have ofte tymes y-broke,
And in þy seruyse be neclygent,
  And mony a wylde word haue spooke.   28
  What were to þe to ben a-wrooke
    On hym þat may noþer fyȝt ne fflee ?
  Lette neuer thyn Eris fro me be loke,
    But euer, good Ihū, haue merci on me.   32

Now merci! I am in wyll no more
  ffrom hennes forth to do trespase.
Now mercy, lord, I be not lore,
  But part with me al of þy grace,   36
  That I may se þy swete fface,
    As þu art god in trynyte,
  In Heuene þer to haue a place
    Wher, Ihū, þu haue mercy on me. Amen.   40

Here endith þis preyere to our lord Ihū, And begynneth the
ymne, Vexilla regis Prodeunte.

16 Wherefore] MS. Where.

141.   Thy Gifts I Have Expended
Unprofitably

MS. Hatton 73
(Sum. Catal. No. 4119)

O Lord allmyghty, blissid thou be,   [fol. 121ʳᵒ]
  That hast me formyd and redemyd;
And whenne y was dampnable thou suffrid me,
And to penaunce reseruyd that synne flemyd.   4
I knowlych, lord, thy mageste be quemyd,
All that to my helth y had of thi gyfte,
Vnprofitably, as to thy sight hit semyd,
I haue expendid thurgh dampnabill schyfte—   8

That is to say, the tyme of my penaunce
In vanitees, and in superfluite
My body also, in pride and distaunce
The grace of my baptyme; but allthyng worldle,   12
My lord, y haue louyd more than the,   [fol. 121ᵛᵒ]
My redemptour, my noryssher and my conseruatour.
Therfor mercy y axe, as a wrecch in degre.
And for y knew not, blyssid savioure,   16

Thy benigne pacience that thou had to me;
Thy gastfull Iugement, lord, y ne drade,
Ne lernyd what answer y shuld gyf the
ffor the innumerable godes that y had,   20
But contrarie, fro day to day ayenst my furst vowe,
With wikked dedis prouokid the.
Therfor, but oon word y haue to the nowe,
That is forto say, domine miserere!   24

22 MS. *After* the *scribe* wrote *thus* and then crossed it out.
24 MS. dn̄e *interlined above the line.*

Haue mercy, god, of my mysdede!
ffor thy mercy, that mychell is,
latt thy pitee spryng and sprede,
And graunte that nevir here-after y do amys.   28

Below these verses is written in another hand:
'Thys is my lady more boke
And sumtym it was Quene margarete boke.'

142. *Though I Have Been a Wretch, I Hope of Mercy*

MS. Bodley 850
(Sum. Catal. No. 2604)

O Blissed god, þat art al-miȝti,   [fol. 87ᵛᵒ]
  þu arte ful of goodnesse, euer full of mercy.
how curteys and howe mercyfull þu art to mankynde,
how louly & piteful, may no man haue mynde.   4
for mankynde thowe tokist both flesshe and blood,
of þe blessed virgyne mary, which euer was meke and
     good.
  for this good and many oþer, I thanke þe,
  mekely euermore seyng hertly, mercy & gramercy!   8

With hard peynes þu woldist by us vpone þe rode tre,
but many dispites and repro[*]ues þu sofredist for me,
                              *[fol. 88ʳᵒ]
Angry wer the wordis which þu sofred for mane;
But angeryer were þe betyng þen I may tell or kan.   12
A pytefull Ihū, in peynes blessed mote þu be,
þat þu woldist such dyseases sofre so for me.
  Lo! ihū, I can non oþer but lift vp myn hert only,
  and euer sey with louly chere, mercy and gramercy! 16

1 *Initial* E *in MS. through mistake of the illuminator.*
15 MS. list.

Thyne hede þu bowdist all a-downe to here me full
    mekely,
Thowe spreddist thyn armes all a-brode to take me to
    mercy,
Thowe schewdist thyn hert thurgh þi syde vpone þe rode
    tre.
Thi blissed loue þu graunte vs, þat euer is so fre.   20
In tokne þu wilt wissche vs, in dedes and in thouȝtis,
To þe crosse þi fete were nayled, whith greet and full
    sore peynes.
    A! good ihū, what schall I sey to þe, þat art so
      goodly?
    But euer I cry nowe louly, mercy and gramercy!   24

Ȝit lorde almiȝt, blessed mote þu be!
ffor many are þe benefetys þat þu haste yeuene to
    me,
ffor riȝt wittys and riȝt lemys, my lyfelode also,
ffull many oþer vertues and ȝiftes many moo.   28
But [*] sori may I be, if I spend not deuli   *[fol. 88ᵛº]
All thise ȝiftes ȝeuen to me freli.
    And, lord, to ȝeue mercy euer þu arte redy,
    Therfor trustly I sey, mercy and gramercy!   32

Witte and kunnynge haue I none, þat goodnesse for to
    telle,
Howe plentefull þi mercy is, may no man rede ne spelle.
To them is mercy nedefull þat haue þe falsely serued,
As seruauntis vnkynde, which haue them-selfe de-
    ceyued.   36
    But nowe, for þer is none so vntryisty, so vnthende, I
      hope, as I,
    To þe I ȝelde me gylty, for euer I hope in mercy.

To be to the a trewe seruaunt, With bitter deth þu
    bouȝtist me,
And in thi seruyce recheles, fals and vnthende I a[m]
    to þe.   40
A mercyfull ihū, what shall I, suche a wrecche, þen do?
That haue ben so synfull, so proude and wykkyde also.
    But though I be wrecchyd, ȝit I clepe and cry
    To þe, almiȝti ihū, for euer I hope of mercy.   44

I haue also misspendede my witt, þu hast ȝeue to me,
With many dyuers thouȝtis, I haue ofte misplesede þe.
What þu hast me forbode, þat haue I do;
Aȝenst, lorde, þi commandementis I haue done also.   48
                                        [fol. 89ro]
    ffor all thise defautis, peynes though I be worthi,
    Ȝit, lord, shewe me grace, for euer I hope in mercy.

Synned I haue in pride, wrath & enuy,
In slouthe of þi seruice, couetyse, gloteny & lechery.. 52
ffor thise synnes and oþer moo, If riȝt dome should be do,
As a wrecche as I am, euer I shoulde dwelle in woo.
    But mercyfull iuge, to yeue grace euer þu art redy,
    I put me therfor in þi dome, for euer I hope of
    mercy.   56

A pyteful ihū, longe tyme it were, I wote well,
my synnes, my freelte, to shewe þe nowe euery dell,
Also, lord, sith it is so that all thyng is knowe to the,
ffor the may no thyng be hidde, priuy or pert wheþer
    it be,   60
    But ȝit, lord, whath cometh to mynde, To þe I know-
    leche mekely.
    ffor thoughe a wrecche I haue bene, ȝit I hope of mercy.

45 witt] MS. whith.   56 me] MS. my.   59 sith] MS. sich.

Nowe, lord, I haue shewed þe my freelte & synnes all;
To þe, crist, good ihū, wepynge I crye and calle.   64
Though thus falsely I haue lyuede, nowe me repent [*]
    sore.   *[fol. 89ᵛᵒ]
  What I þe pray with sorouful hert, grawnt me nowe gostly,
  ffor euermore, lorde ihū crist, trustly I hope in mercy.

Grace nowe me grawnte my synnes to forsake,   68
And fro hens forward neuer them to take.
But euer in leuyng, by nyȝt and day,
What is to thi plesyng and most to thi pay,
That geue me grace to do to my lyues ende.   72
And when I shall hens goo, to thi blisse þu me sende.
  And though I turne aȝen to synne, as euer þe flesshe
    is redy,
  Ȝit graunt me þat I hope to wynn, good ihū, thy mercy.

Nowe, lord, for hem þat ben deed, mercy I aske dewly,   76
And for hem whiche ledde her lyfe ofte also synfully.
ffast for þi modir loue, and oþer that be in blisse,
To me, synfull, and alle oþer, A riȝt wey þu vs wisse.
And, good lorde, suffre thow vs oure tyme not for to spille, 80
But euer, ihesu, to do þat what is þi wille.

Graunt vs also in oure ende to take thi sacramentis
  worthily,
and oure synnes forsake, And þen to dye   83
with full [*] feythe, With mekenesse and chastite, *[fol. 90ᵣᵒ]
ffrom hens þu graunt vs to wende with charite.
  To þe soules whiche mercy abyde, in peynes ful strong,
  Graunt hem, lorde, som remedy for they thynke wel
    longe.

    65 MS. Tough.   69 MS. fro hens for hens.
    82 MS. to take *repeated after* worthily.
    85 MS. gaunt. MS. wende with full beleue and charite.

And though they be in peynes strong, ȝit mercy they hope
    to haue, 88

And aftir þer sorowes they hope þat thowe wilte hem
    saue.

Therfore lorde of pyte, ihū, þat dydest one þe tree,

Sore sighyng, I pray to the with bitter teris, as þu mayste
    see.

Besechynge also mekely, nowe for oure synnes we be
    sory, 92

That fully what we hope, trustely graunt vs þat
    graciously.

Ihū þat art almiȝti, Nowe and euer, þi mercy.

                        Amen, ihūs.

143. *O Redeemer, Purge Me of My Vices*

MS. Douce 1
(Sum. Catal. No. 21575)

O Glorius god, redemer of mankynde, [fol. 54ᵛᵒ]
  whiche on the crosse hyng full of compassyon,
Graunt of thi grace, within my herte and mynde [fol. 55ʳᵒ]
Holly to remember the armes of thy passion. 4

Enrote, good lorde, thi greuous paynes stronge,
Depe in my thought, auoydynge all synne,
and purge the vyces þat hathe ben in me longe,
with contrite herte these verses to begynne. 8

Enclyne alowe, of mercy, now thyne ere, [fol. 55ᵛᵒ]
Contemplynge thy paynes, vnto my peticion,
And graunt me grace so to serue the here,
Affter this lyfe to be in thi tuycion. Amen. 12

144.   Jesu, Mercy for My Misdeeds

Chetham Library, Manchester, MS. 6690

Incipit oracio deuota ad dominum Ihesum Orō.   [fol. 133ro
(col. 1)]

IHū, Ihū, mercy I cry!
myn huge synnes þou me forgyf!
þe werld, my flesch, þe fend, felly
þei me be-sette boþe strong & styf;   4
I haue ful ofte to hem consent,
And so to do, it is gret drede:
I aske mercy wiþ good entent;
Ihū, mercy for my mysdede!   8

Þe werld þurgh his fals coueytis,
Þe fend wiþ pryde, wiþ Ire, enuye,—
I haue, Ihū, ben fyled oft-sythis—
Mi flesch, wiþ slauthe & leccherye,   12
And oþer manye ful grete synnes:
Wiþ repentaunce, Ihū, me fede,
ffor euere þe tyme vpon me rynnes;
Ihū, mercy for my mysdede!   16

Turne nouȝt þi face, Ihū, fro me,
þowh I be werst in my leuynge;
I aske mekely mercy of þee,
ffor þi mercy passeth alle þinge.   20
In þi fyue woundes þou sette myn hert,
Þat for mankynde on crosse wolde blede.
And, for þi ded vgly and smert,
Ihū, mercy for my mysdede!   24

To þi lykenes þou hast me made;
þee for to loue, þou ȝeue me grace!
þou art þe loue þat neuere schal fade;
Mercy, I aske, to haue tyde & space.   28

I trost Ihū of forgyfnesse
Of alle myn synnes—þat is my crede;
I me bytake to þi goodnesse,
Ihū, mercy of my mysdede! 32

As touching grace, but aske & haue— [fol. 133ᵛᵒ
þus hast þou hyght in þi beheste. (col. 1)]
Þerfore some grace of þe I craue;
Wiþ-outen grace I am but a beste 36
And, were þan beste, defyled wiþ synne;
þou graunte þat grace may in me brede,
Þat I þi loue, Ihū, myȝt wynne:
Ihū, mercy for my mysdede! 40

Al werldly loue is but vanyte,
But loue of þe passeth alle þinge;
þer is no loue wiþ-outen þee,
[& þe to lufe I aske syghynge. 44
Ihū, me graunt lufe þee for-thy,]
And in þi lawe, Ihū, me lede.
þat I myslouede, I aske mercy:
Ihū, mercy for my mysdede! 48

It is of þee for to forgyue
Al kynnes trespas, boþe more & mynne;
It is of me, whiles I here lyue,
Or more or lesse ylke day to synne; 52
It is of þee fende to dwelle þer-Inne.
þou ȝeue me grace to take good hede
þat I þi loue, Ihū, myght wynne:
Ihū, mercy for my mysdede! 56

31 MS. guodnesse *with the* u *closed at bottom.*
35 I] *omitted in MS.* 37 þan] MS. þat.
*Lines 44 and 45 left blank in the MS.; supplied from Trin. Coll.
Camb. MS.*

Dispyse me nouȝt, swete lord Ihū,
þat am þee werk of þin hande hende;
þowh I haue be to þe vntrew,
Ihū, þou canst me sone amende;   60
þou hast me made to þi lyknesse,
þurgh synne I haue lost heuenly mede;
Now, lord, I aske of þi goodnesse,
Ihū, mercy of my mysdede!   64

Þou woldest ben born for synful man,
And suffir ded vp-on a tre;
I preye þee, for þat kyndenesse þan,   (col. 2)
ffor synne þou take no wreche of me;   68
Me counforte be þi passyoun,
Ihū, þer-of haue I gret nede;
ffor synne graunt me contricyoun,
Ihū, mercy for my mysdede!   72

After my dedys þou deme nouȝt,
After mercy þou do to me;
If þou me deme as I haue wrouȝt,
In bytter peynes I drede to be.   76
My lyf to mende þou haue mercy,
My lord ihū, þou be my spede,
Loue þee and drede, þat syttes on hy:
Ihū, mercy for my mysdede!   80

If I haue done yche cursed wark,
And alle manere synnes were wrouȝt in me,
þou may hem slake, as is a spark
Whan it is putte in myddis of þee see;   84
Þer may no man, lord, slake my mysse
But þou, Ihū, of þi godhede;
Whom þou wolte sauen, þou sone forgeuysse:
Ihū, mercy for my mysdede!   88

58 *Trinity MS.:* þin aghen hende.

Who schal þe loue in fynal blysse
But mankynde & aungel so fre?
Myn herytage for sothe þat isse.
Þurgh good lyuynge & grace of þe,   92
þou me restore vn-to þat blysse;
Beholde þe frelte of myn manhede
Þat me maketh ofte to don amysse:
Ihū, mercy for my mysdede!   96

Þou wylt nouȝt þe ded of synful man—
þus seyst þou, lord, in holy wrytt.
fful wel wote I þou coueytis þane,
He torne his lyf and sone mende It.   100
þou ȝeue meg race my lyf to mende,   [fol. 134ro,
Besoyled in synne as wicked wede;   col. 1]
Graunte me þi loue wiþ-outen ende:
Iesu, mercy for my mysdede!   104

Þou art my god, I þe honoure,
þou art þe sone of mayden & moder;
In my dysese þou me socoure,
þou art my lord, þou art my broþer;   108
þou schalt me deme, my creatoure,
Whan vp schal ryse euereylke a leede:
Mercy, Ihū, my sauyoure,
Ihū, mercy for my mysdede!   112

þou helpe me, lord, in my dysese,
Þat woldest Susanne help in hire tyme;
fful gret clamour þan gunne þou pese
Whan sche accused was of cryme.   116
þou sette myn soule, myn herte, in ese,
þe fend to fle his falshede,
And souereynly þe forto plese:
Ihū, mercy of my mysdede!   120

Q

In my baptem I made beheste
þe for to serue lellely and wele;
Of þi seruyse ofte haue I seste,
Wiþ synnes þousandes seruyd vnsele;   124
Bot þi mercy nedis moste be sene
þer most synne is & wicked dede;
þe moste synful man am I, i wene:
Ihū, mercy of my mysdede!   128

ffor synful man wolde þou be born,
ffor ryghtwys nouȝt, þou wil recorde;
Whanne man hadde synned he was for-lorn,
þanne hym kyndely þou restorede;   132
þou suffred peynes, crouned wiþ þorne,
Naked, wiþoute cloth or schrede,
Wiþ mykel scorne þi body to-torne: (col. 2)
Ihū, mercy for my mysdede!   136

Þou art myn hope, my way ful sure,
Ay lestyng hele, trewthe and pesse;
þou art pyte þat schal endure,
þou art goodnes þat neuere schal cesse;   140
þou art clennes, boþe mylde & mure,
Me þee dysplese, Ihū, forbede:
As þou were borne of virgyne pure,
Ihū, mercy for my mysdede!   144

Þou byddis yche man ȝelde good for ille,
Nouȝt ylle for ylle to ȝelde ageyne;
þanne I beseke þee þat þou wille
Graunte me mercy for peyne!   148
þou me forȝeue and mercy graunte,
And in my soule þou sowe þi sede,
þat I may, lorde, make myn a-vaunte:
Ihū, mercy for my mysdede!   152

Bot, worþi lord, to þee I cry,
And in my synne stande obstynate;
þerfore þou hers nouȝt me, for-þi
þou wilt nouȝt here me in þat state;   156
þou ȝeue me grace to leue my foly,
And feruently þee loue and drede,
þanne, weel wote I, .I. get mercy:
Ihū, mercy for my mysdede!   160

Nouȝt euery man þat calleþ þe lorde
Or mercy aske, schal haue þi blysse,
His conscience but he remorde,
And werke þi wille & mende his mysse.   164
To blysse schal I be restorede
If I my soule þus-gates wil fede;
Of þi mercy late me recorde:
Ihū, mercy for my mysdede!   168

I me betake to þi mercy   [fol. 134vo,
þat mercy ȝeuest to synful men;   col. 1]
Þou kepe me, lord, I schal dy,
And wote neuere wher, whou, ne when.   172
In þin hote loue me graunte to bren,
And þat lessoun trewely to rede;
Mercy, þou graunte! amen, amen!
Ihū, mercy for my mysdede!   176
Ihē, Amen, Maria, AmeN.

Alia Oracio Deuota

Ihū, þi name honoured mot be
Wiþ alle þat ony lyf is Inne.
Swete Ihū, as þou made me,
Þou kepe me ay fro dedly synne!   4

173 MS. brennen.

Ihū, þe sone of Marye fre,
Þe ioye of heuene þou graunte me wynne!
Mi soule, Ihū, take to þee
Whanne my body & it schal twynne.   8

Ihū, þi name in me besette,
As þou art kyng & lord of lyght;
And graunte me grace ay bet & bette
Mi lyf to mende and lyue aryght.   12
Ihū, þi sydis wiþ blode were wet,
And dolfully for me were dyght;
Þou kepe me out of synne & det,
Swete Ihū, ay most of myght!   16

Ihū, þi name is heygh to neuien,
And ȝet I, caytif, crye & calle:
Þou forȝeue me þee synnes seuen,
ffor I am gylti of hem alle.   20
Ihū, me helpe, & brynge me to heuen
Wiþ þe to wone, my synful saule.
Myghti Ihū, þou here my steuen,
As þou me bought whan I was þralle.   24

Ihū, my loue, my lykyng,   (col. 2)
Euere more blyssed mot þou be.
Mi louely lord, my dere derlyng,
Weel were me I myght see þee.   28
Ihū, my counfort, þou me synge,
A loue-likyng is come to me;
My swete swetnesse of alle þinge,
Myn hope & troste is al in þee.   32

Ihū, helpe euere-more at nede,
ffro þe fende þou me defende;
Set my soule to loue and drede,
And my mysse þat I may mende.   36

Ihū, for þi blode þat þou wolde blede,
ffro þis lyf or þat I wende
Wasche awey al my mysdede,
And graunte me blysse wiþ-outen ende.   40
    AmeN.

145. *Our Three Foes Make Us Mis-*
       speak, Mis-think, Mis-do

B.M. Addit. MS. 39574
(The Wheatley MS.)

GOd, þat madist al þing of nouȝt   [fol. 57ᵛᵒ]
    And with þi precious blood us bouȝt,
  Mercy, helpe and grace!
As þou art verry god and man,   4
And of þi syde þi blood ran,
  fforȝeue us oure trespace!
þe world, oure flesch, þe feend oure fo
Makiþ us mys-þinke, mys-speke, mys-do—   8
  Al þus we falle in blame.
Of alle oure synnes, lasse and moore,
Swete ihc̄, us ruweþ soore,
  Mercy! for þin holy name.   12

146. *A Song of 'Sins'*

Bodleian MS. Add. B. 66
(Sum. Catal. No. 29273)

MAn, sigh & sorw for þi synnes,   [fol. 11ᵛᵒ]
    þan semeþ þi synnes as slayn.
Man, in schrifte schewe al þi synnes,
  þan lyn þei ful dede for certeyn.   4

Man, do penaunce her for þi synnes,
  þi soule schal haue þe lesse peyne.
Þei þat don þus for hir synnes,
  And now3t in wille to turne agayne,   8
Þei ben assoilid for hir synnes
  ffor-soþe as grete clerkis seyne;
And if þou falle a3en in synnes,
  Anon, with al þy myght & mayne,   12
Vnto þi prest telle þou þi synnes—
  Non of hem loke þat þou leyne;
ffor if þou do for-soþe suche synnes,   [fol. 12ro]
  Þei schal turne þe to tene & treyne.   16
And if þou schryue þe of þi synnes
  þei wasche a-way as doþe þe rayne.
þus to be schryuen & soilid of synnes,
  Euery wise man schuld be fayne.   20
þat we mow do þus for our synnes,
  To god mekly, I rede, we pray.
Now god, haue mercy for our synnes,
  þat mercy had of mary mawdleyn,   24
And bringe us to þat blis þat neuer blynnes,
  Almyghti god, lord & souereyne. A[men].

147. *The Day of Life—Night Comes Soon!*

Porkington MS. 10

AS I went one my playing,   [fol. 62ro]
  Vndure an holt vppone an hylle,
I sawe an ovld mane hovre make mornyng,—
  Witt sykyng sovre he sayd me tylle: 4
'Sum tyme þis worde was at my wylle,
  Witt reches and witt ryallte,   [fol. 62vo]
And now hit [is] layd doun ful styll;
  This word ys but a wannyte.   8

3 an] MS. and.

'That one þe morrov when hit [is] fayre & clere,
    After none hit wendys awaye,
And commyth to the nyʒt as hit was ere:
    This word ys but a daye: 12
Soo for ryʒt all owre lewyng heyre;
    ffrow chyldwood vnto mannys degre,
Owre enddyng drawyt nere and nére,—
    This word ys but a wannyte.   16

'I leccone my lyfe vnto the morrow-tyde;
    When I was chyld so bare I-bore,
ffor me my modyr soffyrd gret sovre,
    Witt gronttyng and weppyng was I bore;   20
But þow one me was wem ne hore;
    Sethe in sin I have I-be,
Now I am olde, I may no more,—
    This word is but a wannyte.   24

'At myde-morroo-daye I lernnyd to goo,   [fol. 63ʳᵒ]
    And play as chyldorne done in strete;
As chyldwood me thoʒt & tavʒt I dyde þoo,
    Witt my fellous to fyʒt and beyt.   28
What I dede me þoʒt hit swete,
    Ryʒt as chyldhod taʒt hit me;
Now may I say witt terrus weete,
    This word is but a wannyte.   32

'At vnder-day to skole I was I-sete,
    To lerne good as chyldern dothe,
But when my master woold me bete,
    I wold hym cowrs & wax folle rowthe: 36
To lerne good I was full lovthe,
    I þoʒt one play and gollytte;
Now for to say þe sothe,
    This world is but a wannyte.   40

                36 MS. rovthe.

'At mydday I was dobbyt a kny3te,
  In trvthe I lernnyd for to ryed;
There was none soo bold a wy3te,
  That in battayll durst me abyde.   [fol. 63ᵛᵒ]   44
Where be-commy3t all owre pryd,
  Owre Iollytte and fayre bovtte,
ffrow dethe I may not me here hyd,—
  This word ys but a wannyte.   48

'At nonne I was crounyd a kynge,
  All þis world was at my wylle;
Euer to lyvfe here was my lykynge,
  And alle my lust I wold fulfyll: 52
Now age is croppyn one me ful styll,
  He makyt me hore, blake, and bowe;
I goo all dounward witt þe hylle,—
  This world ys but a wannyte.   56

'At myd-vndure-none wondorly I waxe,
  My lust and lykyng hit went away,
ffrom þe world my chere ys goone,
  ffrom ryalte and ryche a-raye: 60
Owre lewyng ys but one daye,
  A3eynst þe world þat euyre schal be;
Be þis matter I dare well saye,   [fol. 64ʳᵒ]
  This word ys but a wannyte.   64

'At ewynsong tyme I was so cold,
  That now I goo all by a stafe,
There-fore is dethe one me so bold,
  And for his hyre he dothe me crawfe: 68
When I am dede and layd in grawe,
  Then no þing schall save me,
But well and woo þat I done havfe,—
  This word ys but a wannyte.   72

  67 his *deleted between* There *and* fore.
  68 cr *in* crawfe *altered from some other letters.*

'Now ys þis day commyn to þe nyʒt;
   I hawe lost my lewyng;
A dredefull payne ys for me dyʒt,
   In cold claye þere-in to clynge.'   76
As I went on my playing,
   Vndure an holt by a tre,
This hard I an old man mak mournyng,—
   This world ys but a wannyte!   80
In domino confydo. Amen, Dico vobis.

148. *God Send Us Patience in Our Old Age*

Harley MS. 1706

FRom þe tyme þat we were bore   [fol. 212ᵛᵒ]
   Oure ʒouþe passeþ fro day to day,
And age encreseþ more and more;
   And so doþ yt nowe, þe soþ to say.   4
At euery oure a poynte ys lore,   [fol. 213ʳᵒ]
   So fast goþ owre ʒouþ a-weye,
And ʒouþ wylle come aʒen no more,
   But age wylle make vs boþ blake and graye.   8
þerfor takeþ hede, boþ nyʒte and day,
   howe faste oure ʒouþ doþ aswage;
And, boþ ʒounge and olde, lete vs praye
   þat god send pacyence in oure olde age.   12
Age wylle take from vs oure myʒte,
   þat in oure ʒouþ to vs was lente,
And eke þe clernes of oure syʒte,
   And oure herynge schal be feynte.   16
þan schul we be heuy, þat ere were lyʒte,
   By-cause þat ʒoungþe ys from vs wente;
And þan wol men do vs no ryʒte,
   But al contrarye to oure entente;   20

And sykenes wol do vs grete turment,
Whom deeþ wol send on hys message—
fforsoþ þe beste amendement
Is pacyence þan in oure olde age.   24

Oure body wol yche, oure bonys wol ake,
Owre owne flesshe wol be oure foo,   [fol. 213vo]
Oure hede, oure handys, þan wol schake
Owre legges wol trymble whan we goo,   28
Oure bonys wol drye as doþ a stake,
And in oure body we schulle be woo,
Oure nose, oure chekes, wol wex al blake,
And oure glad chere wol vade vs fro;   32
And whan oure teeþ ben goon also,
Oure tunge schalle lese hys fayre langage.
Prey we for vs selfe and oþer moo,
þat god send vs pacyence in oure old age.   36

Oure frendys þat schul loue vs beste,
Þan wol þei haue vs but in hate;
In frendschipes is noon oþer truste,
And þerfor ben we y-ware to late—   40
þan may we synge of had-y-wyste—
Oure feynte frendes han vs for-sake.
And also we schullen goo vnkyste,
Boþ at þe dore and at þe gate,   44
ffor al þe chere þat we can make.
þan ys no ioye of oure vysage,
Whanne oure bewte schal a-slake—   [fol. 214ro]
God send vs pes in oure old age!   48

We schullen be so angrye, euermore
We wold be a-wreke of euery wronge;
þan sume wold scorne vs þerfore,
And sume wold sey we lyue to longe.   52

23 MS. ffosoþ.
26 *This line is also copied above in a later hand.*

Oure sorowe wol sytte vs þan so sore,
Oure stomake wol no mete fonge.
And euery day, more and more,
Of sorowe and care schal be oure songe.   56
But whan we were boþ hole and stronge
We were to wylde and wold outerage.
And þerfor lete vs pray a-monge,
þat god send vs pacyence in oure old age.   60

[For þan wole no þing us availe
but oure bedis and oure crucche,
for wordli welþe wole fade & faile,
And þerfore truste we it not to myche;   64
& þan wole sijknes us assaile
Til it haþ made us lijk a wrecche,
& þan may we do no greet traueile
But summtyme grone, & sumtyme grucche,   68
And sumtyme clawe for scabbe & icche
Whanne age haþ us at his auauntage:
Who-so lyueþ long schal be such;
God sende us paciens in oure olde age!]   72

Al þat we haue lyued here
It ys but a dreme y-mete,
ffor nowe yt ys, as yt neuer were.
And so ys yt þat ys to comynge ȝit—   76
And faste we drawen to oure beere—
In sorowe and drede we schullen be sette.
Of olde men þe ȝounge may leere,
And ȝit fewe þer ben þat don bet,   [fol. 214ᵛᵒ] 80
ffor þe fende haþ cauȝte hem in hys nette,
And hold hem faste in hys bondage
ffor þei schulden not dyspyse her wytte,
To haue pacyence in her old age.   84

þan schul we se þat wordly blysse
Is but þinge of vanyte,
And yt makeþ men to do a-mys
þat ben in welþe and grete bewte;   88
And þerfor, lord, good ry3t yt ys
Wiþ oure owne stafe chastysed to be.
Lord, 3eue vs grace to þenke on þis,
As þou bou3tteste vs alle vppon a tree;   92
And þat we may in charyte
Welle passe, ouer þis passage,
In-to the blysse þat euer schal be
Whan we ben passed oure old age.   A-M-E-N.   96

Lines within brackets supplied from Lambeth MS. 853.

149. *Farewell, this World is but a Cherry Fair*

Trinity Coll. Camb. MS. 1157

FFare well, this world! I take my leve for euere,
  I am arested to apere at goddes face.   [fol. 67ʳᵒ]
O myghtyfull god, þu knowest that I had leuere
Than all this world, to haue oone houre space   4
To make a-sythe for all my grete trespace.
My hert, alas! is brokyne for that sorowe,
[Som be this day that shall not be to-morow]

This lyfe, I see, is but a cheyre feyre;   8
All thyngis passene and so most I algate.
To-day I sat full ryall in a cheyere,
Tyll sotell deth knokyd at my gate,
And on-avysed he seyd to me, chek-mate!   12
lo! how sotell he maketh a devors—
and wormys to fede, he hath here leyd my cors.

Speke softe, ye folk, for I am leyd aslepe!
I haue my dreme, in trust is moche treson.   16
ffram dethes hold feyne wold I make a lepe,

But my wysdom is turnyd into feble resoun:
[I see this worldis joye lastith but a season].
Wold to god, I had remembyrd me be-forne!   20
I sey no more but be ware of ane horne!

This febyll world, so fals and so vnstable,
Promoteth his louers for a lytell while,
But at the last he yeveth hem a bable   24
Whene his peynted [trowth is torned in-to gile].
Experyence cawsith me þe trowth to compile,
Thynkyng this, to late alas! that I began,
For foly & hope disseyveth many a man.   28

[Farewell, my frendis! the tide abidith no man:
I moste departe hens & so shall ye,
But in this passage the beste song þat I can
Is Requiem Eternam—I pray God grant it me!   32
Whan I haue endid all myn aduersite,
Graunte me in paradise to haue a mancyon,
That shede his blode for my redempcion.   35
    Beati mortui qui in domino morivntur
      Humiliatus sum vermis.]

Text within brackets supplied from Balliol Coll. MS. 354, fol. 199ro.

150. *Man Begins and Ends in Wretchedness*

MS. Arch. Seld. B. 24
(Sum. Catal. No. 3354)

THy begyning is barane brutelnes,   [fol. 229vo]
    With wrechitnes wofull away thou w[endis]
The deth certane, the houre vnseker[nes],
   The lyf so schort approching euer th[e end is]   4
   Quho hiest clymbis most sud[danly descendis].
    Quhat is her-of bot cast in god [thy cure]
    And stand content of any avent[ure].

5 MS. Quhy.

Quho will aduert the grete . . .   8
  Off this fals warld and won . . .
The grete vn-es Ingent aduersite
  ffulfild of flatery and fals disse . . .
    And man no wicht content is . . .   12
      And thus but contrair thaim . . .
      Quho leste here traistis I . . .

151.   *Vanitas Vanitatum*

MS. Ashmole 61
(Sum. Catal. No. 6922*)

Vanyte.

O Vanyte off vanytes & all is vanite!   [fol. 156ᵛᵒ]
  lo! how þis werld is turnyd vp & downe,
Now wele, now wo, now tranquilyte,
Now werre, now pese, & now rebilyoun.   4
Iff þu wole daly labour fore renowne,
  ffore profete, plesure, astate, ore grete degre,
  The best þer-of schall ende in vanyte.

Ȝit beldis þu castellus, haulys, townys & towris,   8
Sytis & bourȝes, with wallis stoute & stronge,
With plesand herbours, of chambours & of bouris,
Hangyd with Arras stoutly depe & longe,
With rych presyus stones sete A-monge,   12
  Ennewyd with gold, rych as it may be—
  Ȝit schall all waste & turne to vanyte.

Iff þu seke worschipe all þe werld a-boute,
ffore dede of Armys to Avaunse þi name,   16
So þat þer is not none fond so stoute,
Off ȝonge ne olde, þu toke neuer schame—
In euery place þu beris awey þe fame,
  At euery Iustis þu berys awey þe gre,   20
  Ȝit schall þi werke all end in vanyte.

7 The] MS. Tohe.

ȝe feyre ladis, apareld with plesance
To ȝo, both ȝouth & bewty ben Appendyng,
And many low labours doth ȝour obseruans,   24
And in ȝour courte deyly bene Atendyng.
They spare noþer fore labour ne fore spendyng,
   To do ȝour plesure wer-so-euer ȝe be,
   ȝit schall þat myrthe All end in vanyte.   28

ȝiff þu off byrth here was þe worthyest,
And one þe erth was gretyst off astate,
Kyngis & popys so rych wer, At þe laste
Off þem Aȝene, þu durst do debate   32
ȝit in a whyle þu schall be cheke-mate;
   When deth wyll come & take hys propour fe,
   Than schall þu knaw þi pride was vanyte.

ȝiff þu be wedyde to thyne intente,   36
And haue a wyff full plesant & feyre,
Well borne & also obedyente,
And Also haue chylde forto be þin eyere,
ȝit in a whyle þis plesans schall Apare;   40
   When Age schall come, croke both hand & kne,
   Than schall þu knaw þat was bot vanyte.

ȝiff þu be stronge & ȝonge & fayre of face,
Als sembly of schap as any creatour,   44
louyd of pepull & gouernyd be grace,
lernyd in wysdom be wyse scryptour,
Preuyd in manhed passyd many a wynter,
   And euer in wourschype, both be lond & se,   48
   ȝit schall [all pas] & end in vanyte.

30 one] MS. ōne.
47 a wynter] *?read* aventour.   49 *No gap in MS.*

The well of fortone is so changeabull,
And deyly tournys vpon so slyper a pyne—
And ӡit some tyme it makis men abull   52
To cruell to ryne aӡen All þer ryall kyne—
Onone be vnfortone, þe state þat þei wer In
  Oþer men happis, & þus ӡe may well se
   That state ne reule is not bot vanyte.   56

In ӡouth now styres mekyll wantonys,   [fol. 157ro]
And oft intendyth to lustys & pley,
And lytell remembyrs his awne febulnys;
ho ӡouth schall pas & departe a-wey,   60
And deth schall come, þat is none ney.
  Thou blynd ӡouth, loke vp & se
   Thy pride, þi pley—all is bot vanyte.

lo! here comys ӡouth with myrth & plays Ioly,   64
With-outen thouӡt ore care, fader & moderles,
Bot medyll Age thinkis þat it was foly
And ner peynes hym-selue with werldly besynes,
Bot all his labour is to grete ryches—   68
  Than commys Age & seys þat he must dyӡe,
   Than he knaw ӡought & all was vanyte.

We tyll þe erth, we tourne it to & fro,
We labour ryӡht deuly with grete besynes,   72
We dyge, we delue, we saw, we schere also,
We geder þe corne home fore oþer mens ryches,
We haue full seldome any restfull gladnes,
  Bot labour in pouerte to þe tyme þat we dyӡe— 76
  Ӡit is oure labour not bot vanyte.
         Amen qd Rate.

152. *A Mirror for Young Ladies at Their Toilet*

Harley MS. 116

Cest le myrroure pur lez Iofenes Dames a regardir   [fol. 128ro]
aud maytyne pur lour testes bealment adressere.

MAist thou now be glade, with all thi fresshe aray,
  One me to loke that wyll dystene thi face.
Rew one thy-self and all thi synne vprace!
Sone shalte þu flytte and seche anoþer place,   4
Shorte is thy sesoun here, thogh thou go gay.

O maset wriche, I marke the with my mace.
Lyfte vp thy ieye, be-holde now, and assay!
Yche loke one me aught to put þe in affray;   8
I wyll not spare the, for thou arte my pray.
Take hede, and turne fro synne while þu hast space.

O þoughte, welthe heele to this, thaught ȝe say nay.
My tyme muste nedis comme as I manace;   12
Be lenghte one lyfe may lepe oute of my lace.
I smyte, I sle, I woll graunte no mane grace.
A-ryse! a-wake! amend here while thou may.

              Explicit.

153. *On the Untimely Death of a Fair Lady*

Henry E. Huntington Library, Ellesmere MS. 26. A. 13

HA! cruell deeth, contrarious to creatures in kynde.
                         [fol. 131vo]
Ha! deeth dispitous, who may aduertise
Thi mourther, thi malice who may haue in mende?
The myschief that to mankynde þu dost excercise,   4

11 *? Read:* O þou, wel the hede to this thaugh ȝe say nay.
13 one] *read* none.

Thi rigour, þi rancour, who may deuyse?
The matyng of þi miserie no man may endure,
ffor thi chekkes conclude eueri creature.

Thu art to alle creatures hidous to be-holde,   8
Thu pyllour, thu pirate, cesse of þi prise!
Thi felonye ys multiplied in so many folde
That al the wordle generally of the deþ agrise.
Stynt of þi malice, for, wyth thy malgyse,   12
Loueris ful lykyng and lusty in game
Thu marrest wyth myschief and makest hem lame.

Thu tyraunt vntemperat, wyth thi tene & treson,
The solas of soueraignes þu dost siluestrise;   16
And ladies likyng thu sleest out of seson,
And reuest hem here ryalte wyth þi reprise.
Thyn insaciable malice who may a-complise?
When þat loueli ladies thu leyest so lowe,   20
And here bright beaute þu blemshest in a throwe.

ffor þi malice, me semeth reames sholde arise
To destruye cruell deeth and do hym of dawe.
But oon wynked on me then: 'war', quod þe wyse,   24
'And cesse of þi sentence for symple is þi sawe,
ffor deeth vniuerselly the wordle schal vengyse.
So ys the tyraunt tytled to that victorie
By adam, the alderman of old auncetrie.'   28

Then sorwed I, that sentence recouered by assyse,
And mourned for my maystresse, here marred in molde.
There ys countour ne clerk bounte can decyse,
In vertu here wommanhed was volupid many folde— 32
Discreet, devoute, diligent. deeth, thu mayst agrise
To represse so noble so gentill a creature
In tendir age vntymely, agayn the ordre of nature.

6 The] MS. Te.   16 The] MS. Thi.   26 vengyse] *read* venquyse.

O myghty lord, wos goodnesse neuer schal fynyse,   36
Haue mercy on the soule of my dere maistresse!
The fendis power fro that soule chare & chastise! [fol. 132ro]
Deliuere here, gracious lord, fro peyne and distresse!
Endowe here in thi place of plesaunt paradise,   40
And receyue here, blyssed lord, vpon thi right side,
In thy blysse eternally whyt the to a-byde.

Of lordis lyne & lynage sche was, here sche lyse!
Bounteuus, benigne, enbleshed wyth beaute,   44
Sage, softe and sobre an gentyll in al wyse,
fflorishyng ant fecunde, wyth femenyn beaute,
Meke, mylde and merciful, of pite sche bar þe prise.
Comely, kynde and curteis, in nobleye of nurture,   48
Vernant in alle vertu, plesaunt and demure.

154.   *The Mirror of Mortality*

Harley MS. 116

O mors, quam amara est memoria tua.

O Deth, hough better ys the mynde of the! [fol. 152vo]
That mover arte of moornynge & of moone.
Thou myndly myrrour, in whome all olde may see
The ways of youthe, in which thai haue mysgone,   4
Thou arte the same Remembrance allone,
Whome all astates and euery lawe degre,
With daily diligence owe to awaite vpone,
ffor whome thou clepiste, all muste go with the.   8

Nought may preuaile—pompous prosperite,
Honoure ne heele, gemme ne precious stone,
Renoun, Riches, rent ne rialte—
ffor all that euer haue be of fleshe & bone   12
Thou hast and wolt consume, not levyng oon.
Who is alyve that cane Remembre thre

13 levyng oon] *so Cotton MS.; Harley reads* lyvinge *omitting* oon.

That are preserued ? y finde two allone,
Ennok and Ely—yit shall thai go with the.   16

ffor in the houre of oure natiuite
Thi subtile entre vs preseth euerychone,
With clene continuell chalenginge thi fe ;
And euery day we muste waite here vpone,   20
And while we lyve yit haue we odire foone :
The feende, the flesh, and worldly vanite,
Cotidiane corasy continvinge euire in oone,
Oure cely soule vnceesingly to sle.   24

Popes and prelates stand in perplexite,
and envyus clarkis forth with the thai gone,
Crowned conquerours and odire of law degre,
Knyghtly an hir tymes, thou sparith noone.   28
Marchauntes, men of law, all vndir oone,
Leches, laborers, fayne wolde fro the fle.
ffull wyse is he that cane thinke her vpone   [fol. 153ro]
And for hime-selfe provide, who-so he be.   32

Be-holde this myrroure in thy mynde, & se
This worldis transsitorie Ioy that sone is gone,
Which in effecte is but aduersite,
And of twey weys thou nedis must take oone.   36
Thenk of fre choise god hath the lent allone,
With witte and Resoun to reule thi liberte ;
yif thou go mys, odire blame thou noone—
Thi-selfe arte cause of all that grevith the.   40

O ye that floure in hie felicite,
ffor crystes sake remembreth here vpone !
Thenke that as fresh and lusty as ye be,
Er thei wer war, full sodanly haue gone ;   44

19 clene] *Cotton MS.:* claym.

ffor odire warnynge in this world ys none
But mynde of Deth or sore infirmite.
Whene thou lest wenest thou shalt be calde vpone,
ffor of thine houre thou woste no certeinte.   48

This worthi lorde of veray polyce,
Ser Raufe lorde Cromwell, Remembringe here vpone
ffor alle his lordshipp and gret stately fe,
Knowinge by resoun of oder Rescous none,   52
ffor all his castelles & toures hie of stone,
ffor hime and for my lady, like as ye se,
This towmebe prouyded, ayene that thei shall gone.
In gracius houre gode graunte hir passage be!   56

Muse in this mirrour of mortalite,
Bothe olde and yonge that lokene here opone,
Lyfte vp your hertly eie, be-holde and se
These same right worthi, restinge vndire the stone.   60
Deuoutly pray for heme to criste allone,   [fol. 153ᵛᵒ]
That gyltles for hire gylte sterfe one a tre,
heme to preserue frome all hire gostely foone,
And send heme pees in perpetuite. Amen.   64

155. *Three Lessons to Make Ready for Death*

MS. Laud Miscell. 733
(Sum. Catal. No. 1129)

In my bed liyng on cristis day, half slepyng,   [on front cover]
Sighhis wondrous hevyng, A voice I hard thus spekyng:

Wake, man, slepe not, rise vp and thynk þat erth
    thou art;
And that erth thou shal be, whan the hath cayht deth
    smart.
Com to churche, & serve thy maker with dredefull hart,
lest that thou repent the when thou art owte of quart.   4

    2 deth *interlined above.*
    4 that *interlined above;* not, *cancelled, after* the.

Remember that thou shall dye,
ffor this world yn certentee
Hath nothyng save deth truele.
Therfore yn thy mynde vse this lessone :   8
Liffe so that deth take the yn sesone.

ffor deth to make the ripe, I shal teche the thynges three,
Which and thou vse, owte of sesone thou can not dye.
The furst is a knowlage of the vij synnes dedlye   12
hoole with other to make to thy ffader gostlye.

Secoundly, that thy conscience dayly be well soght
Of wronges to thy neighbor done both in dede and thoght,
And that therof satisfaccioun hastly be broght ;   16
ffor ellis thou shal leese that which, bledyng, thy lord
    boght.

The third lessone vse til thy mouth stopp the cold clay :
ffor thy synnes both wepe & weyle—bere this well away !
In harte be meke and contrite, and than thou shall play   20
In Blys with hym that of A mayde was borne this Day.

156.   Against Death Is no Defence

Univ. of Edinburgh MS. Laing 149

M An, hef in mynd & mend þi mys,   [fol. 87ro
    quhill þow art heir in lyf lyffand ;   (col. 1)]
and think apone þis warldis blys,
    sa oft-syis is variant.   4
for fortonis quheill is ay turnand,
    quhil to weil and quhil to wa,
quhill owp, quhil downe, I onderstand.
    Memor esto nouissima.   8

6 *and* 9 yn *interlined above.*   8 vse *interlined above.*
Day] MS. Days.

Thow seis þi sampil eueril[k] day,
  and þov tak heid withoutyn les,
quhow sone þat yowt may pas away,
  for bald hector and achilles   12
and alex^r, þe prowd in pres,
  hes tane þare leif & mony ma,
þat ded hes drawyne one-til his des.
  memor esto nouissima.   16

Þidder þow com nakit and bayr,
  as bannyst man of kyth & kyne;
so þe behuffis hyne to fayr,
  for al þe ryches þow ma wyne   20
is na defens, be craft na gyne,
  þat ma defend þe fra þi fa,
bot cherite be þe within.
  memor esto nouissima.   24

Þis day thocht þow were hail & feyr,
  as bern baldast, ore kyng with crowne,
Þe morne þow may be brocht one beyr
  for al þi castalis, towre & towne.   28
Þai may nocht al mak þi ransone
  fra ded becumin þat is so thra—
Þow art his pra, but radempsione.
  memor esto nouissima.   32

Quhen þow art ded & laid in layme,
  and þi ribbis ar þi ruf tre,
þow art þan brocht to þi lang hayme—
  adew al warldis dignite!   36

12 bald] *before this word* bl *cancelled.*
23 bot] *one tall letter erased before this word.*
26 baldast] *before this word* bl *cancelled.*

than is to lait forswcht, think me,
  quhen wormys g[n]awys þe to & fra,
now mynd þi mys in al degre.
  memor esto nouissima.   40

Sen it is sa þat þow man fair,
  and knawys nocht þe wayis rycht
Owt of þis warld withoutyn mare,
  quheþer to hel or hewyne so brycht,   44
þow pray to hyme most is of mycht
  þat he þe fra þe dewillis ta,
and schild þe fra þe fendis plycht.
  memor esto nouissima.   48

157. *Devouring Death Makes All Unbold*

Trinity Coll. Camb. MS. 1450

O Mors mordens aspere, yn gyle þou haste noo pere,
                                            [fol. 47ʳᵒ]
Nam sanos in prospere, Thow bryngyst to the bere,
Et tua sentencia, ffallyt bothe yonge and oolde,
Et fallax potencia, Thow makyst all vnboolde.

158.   *Knight, King, Clerk Wend to Death*

A. Cotton MS. Faustina B. vi, Part II
(verses written on scrolls)

I Wende to dede, knight stithe in stoure,   [fol. 1ᵛᵒ]
  thurghe fyght in felde i wane þe flour;
Na fightis me taght þe dede to quell—
  weend to dede, soth i ȝow tell.   4

39 degre] *before this word* dr *cancelled.*
44 brycht] *before this word* bl *cancelled*
No. 158. 1 MS. stirhe.

I weende [to dede], a kynge I-wisse;
What helpis honor or werldis blysse?
Dede is to mane þe kynde wai—
i wende to be clade in clay.   8

I wende to dede, clerk ful of skill,
þat couth with worde men mare & dill.
Sone has me made þe dede ane ende—
beese ware with me! to dede i wende.   12

B. B.M. Addit. MS. 37049

I Wende to dede, a kyng y-wys;   [fol. 36ʳᵒ]
What helps honour or warldis blys?
Ded is to man þe kynde way—
I wende to be cled in claye.   4

I wende to dede, clerk ful of skill,
þat cowthe with wordes men mate & stylle.
So Sone has þe dede me made ane ende—
Bes war with me! to dede I wende.   8

I wende to dede, knyght styf in stowre,
þorow fyght in felde I wan þe flowre;
No fyghts me taght þe ded to qwell—
[   ] telle.   12

C. Stowe MS. 39

I Wende to ded, clerk full of skill,   [fol. 32ʳᵒ]
þat couth with word mate men at will;
Sone has me made þe ded an ende—
Be war with me! to ded I wende.   4

I wende to ded, a kyng I-wys;
What helpes here honur or worldis blys?

B. 12 *Bottom of the page trimmed away by the binder.*

I wende to ded, knyght styffe in stoure,
Thurgh fight in felde I wane þe floure;   8
No feghtis me taght þe ded to qwell—
I wende to ded, soth I ȝow tell.

Be ȝe wele now warre with me!
My name þen is ded;   12
May þer none fro me fle,
þat any lyfe gun led,
kynge, kasere, þeȝn, no knyght,
Ne clerke þat cane on boke rede,   16
Beest, ne foghel, ne oþer wyght,
Bot I sal make þam dedde.

159. *The Lament of the Soul of Edward IV*

Harley MS. 4011

MIseremini mei, ye that ben my ffryndys,   [fol. 169ᵛᵒ]
This world hath enformyd me fforto falle.
How myȝte I endure when euery thinge endes;
    What creature ys made to be eternall?   4
Now ys there no help butt pray ffore my sowll!
    Thus Edward seyth, for latt I was kyng;
xxiijᵗⁱ yeres I reynyd this ymperiall,
    Som men to plesoure, and som men nott to lykyng.   8
fforgefnes I aske fore my nyse doyng,
    What A-vaylyþe it yov to be my foo?
I may nott Resiste nor Amend your compleynynge,
    Quia ecce nunc in puluere dormio.   12

I ly now in mowlde as it ys naturall,
    ffore erthe vnto erthe hath his Reuerture;
What ordeyned god to be terrestyall
    Wyth Recourse off erthly nature.   16

15 þeȝn] MS. þen.   3 MS. I How myȝte.
5 my sowll] *In Lant's print:* me all.

Euyre ffor-to lyve who may be swre?
　What is hit to trust the mutabilite
Off this world whan no thyng may endure?
　I am now gon wych latt was in prosperite,　　　　20
To presumen there vpon hit ys butt vanite—
　No sertayne butt a chery fere full of woo—
Reynyd I nott latt in greet feli[ci]te?
　Et ecce nunc in puluere dormio.　　　　24

Where was in my lyff such one as I
　Whiles my fortune had here continuaunce?
Grauntyd nott sho to me the vyctorie,
　In ynglond to Reygne and to contrybute fraunce?　28
Sho tok me by the hond and led me the daunce,
　And with hure sewger lyppus on me she smylyd;
And for here dyssemblande countenaunce
　I cowd nott be ware tyll I was begylyd.　　　　32
Owtt off this lond sho hath [me] exylyd,
　Whan I was lothest hens for to goo　　　[fol. 170ᵛᵒ]
And I in age, as who seyth, butt a child,
　Ecce nunc in puluere dormio.　　　　36

I se well they lyve that dowbyll my yerys;
　Thus this world delyth with me as hit lyst,
And hath me made, to yov that byn my perys,
　Example to take euyre off had-I-wyst.　　　　40
I stored hucches, cofers and chyst
　With tresore takyng off my commynalte—
ffore there tresore that I toke there prayers I myst—
　Now whom I be-sech with pore humylyte　　　　44
Off forgefnesse, off me to haue pite.
　I was youre kyng and kepte yow from youre foo;
I wold a-mend, butt now hit woll nott bee,
　Quia ecce nunc in puluere dormio.　　　　48

　　　31 MS. continuaunce, *Lant's print:* countenaunce.
　　　33 me *supplied from Lant's print.*

I had Inogthe, I hyld nott me content,
  With-outt Remembraunce that I schuld dy,
More to encresse was myne entent.
  Beyng nott warre who schuld occupy,   ·   52
I mad the towre strong, butt I wyst nott why,
  Nore to whom I purchaced tatersall;
I amendyd dovere one the mowntayne hy,
  And provokyd london to fortefye þer wall,   56
I made notynghame a place Ryall,
  Wynsore and etton & many odur moo,
Westmynster & eltham—yit went I from all,
  Quia ecce nunc in puluere dormio.   60

Where is my gret conquest & vy[c]tory?
  Where be my Rentis & my Ryall aray?
Where be my coursors & my horsys so hy?
  Where is my grett plesure, solas & play?   64
As vanite to nouȝte all ys gon away.
  Lidy besse, for me long may ye call,
Whe be departyd vntyll domus day!
  I lovyd you, lady, my souerayne ouerall.   68
Where be my byldyngis & my castellis Ryall?
  Butt Wynsore off them I haue noo moo   [fol. 170ᵛᵒ]
And off etton ther prayers perpetuall,
  Quia ecce nunc in puluere dormio.   72

Whi schuld ye be prowde & presume so hy?
  Sent Barnard doth þer-off nobly trete,
Seyng a man ys butt a sake of stercory
  And schall Retorne to wormys mette.   76
What cam off Alysaunder the grett?
  And off strong samson who can tell?
Were nott wormys ordeynyd þer fleshe for to frett?
  And Salamon, that off wytt was the well,   80

74 MS. seith . . . noble.

And absolon, proferyd his here forto sell—
  ffor all his beavtes wormys hym ette also.
And I, latte Edward, that dyd excelle,
  Ecce nunc in puluere dormio.   84

I haue pleyd my pagent & now am I past,
  I wyll þat ye wytt I was off no grett elde.
Butt all thing consumeth att the last,
  Whan deth apperith lost ys the feld.   88
Sith this world no lenger vp-held
  Mo, conservyd to me my place.
In manus tuas, domine, my spryte vp I yeld;
  Humbley I be-sech the off thy grace!   92
And ye, corteys commyners, with your hert vnbrace
  Benyngly to pray for me also,
As I forsayd, your kyng I was,
  Et ecce nunc in puluere dormio.   96

160. *The Rich Man's Farewell to the World*

Pembroke Coll. Camb. MS. 248

WOrldys blys, haue good day!   [fol. iiiro]
  No lengur habbe ych þe ne may,
Þe more for þe lasse y haue for-lore;
y-cursyd be þe tyme þat ych was bore!   4
y haue lore for-euer heuun blys,
and go now þeras euer sorow & car ys.

Hic scribitur de diuite qui per malas cautelas et falsas multa adquisiuit et cum esset in extremis querebatur ab amicis quid posset eum magis consolari quibus dixit diuicie qui cum essent coram eo multa et ineffabilia nec possent eum consolari et dixit astantibus in loco anglice vt supra.

83 MS. lotte.   90 *Lant's print:* Nor nought wolde conserue.

161. Beware the Pains of Purgatory

Rylands Lib. Lat. MS. 395

Peas I hier a voyce saith man thou shalt dye   [fol. 119ᵛᵒ]
Remembre the paynes of Purgatorie.

WHy sittist thou so syngyng, þenkyst þou nothyng,
Þat who-so best hoppith at laste ṣhal haue the ryng?
Remembre thy maker and pray to that kyng,
To that blisse that he bought þe vnto, þe bryng.   4
Thou shalt aby, this worlde defygh. Pes, I hier a voice.

I prove þe by Reason that thou art vnkynde,
He that deid afore þe is clene oute of thy mynde.
Thy frendis afore the—why art þou so blynde?—   8
In purgatory paynyng, there shalt thow them fynde.
With doolefull cry, þou shalt aby, þis world defygh. Peas.

Man, compasse in saying, in mynde Every delle,
And pray for the soules so grete paynes fele,   12
In purgatory paynyng their sorowys to keele,
Thy-self in no wors cas and þis it is weele,
This worlde defygh, thou shalt abye. Peas, I hier a.

I haue herd this voice wele, mary, fulle of grace,   16
Spekith it to me, þo I will high me A-paas
To the Chirche, me to amende, lady, pray for space.
Lorde, leste I come to late ye alas, alas! I fere me I,
With doulfull cry, I shall aby. This worlde despygh.
        Pees.   20

A! now am I thorugh þat dey shall I thanne,
But yit, gentil neyghbere, tell me where or whane.
Or where shall I become? why spekist þou not, man?
Is there no Creature þat answere me cane?   [fol. 120ʳᵒ]
Now god me guy, I fere me I, with dulfull cry, I shal
        aby, þis world defygh.   25

Than see I right wele ther is no way butt oone,
Now helpe me, deere lady, Kateryn, and John,
Cristofer & George, myne avowries, echone!   28
Of the nombre dampned see that I be noone.
Pray for me high. Now god me guy, I fere me I,
With dulfull cry, I shall aby. This world defygh,
Pies, I hier.   32

162. *The Testament of a Christian*

Lansdowne MS. 762

Terram terra tegat, demon peccata resumat,   [fol. 3ʳᵒ]
Mundus res habeat, spiritus alta petat.

Terram terra tegat

FFour poyntis, my will or I hence departe,
Reason me moveth to make as I maye:
ffirst, to the erthe I bequeth his parte—
My wretched careyn, is but fowle claye—   4
Like than to like, erthe in erthe to laye,
Sith it is according, by it I woll abide,
As for the first parte of my will, that erthe erth hide.

Demon peccata resumat

Myne orrible synnes that so sore me bynde,   8
With weight me oppresse, that lyen so many fold, [fol. 3ᵛᵒ]
So many in numbre, soo sondry in kynde.
The ffeende by his instaunce to theym made me bold—
ffrom hym they come, to hym I yelde wolde.   12
Wherfore, the second parte of my will is thus,
That the fende receyue all my synnes as his.

Mundus res habeat

Whate availeth goodys, am I ones dede and roten?
Them all and some I leve, peny and povnde,   16
Truely or vntruely, some I trowe mys-goten—
Though I wot not of whome, howe, nor in whate grovnde.

The worldis they been, them in the worlde I founde;
And therfore the thirde parte is of my wille,   20
All my worldly goodis Let the worlde haue still.

Spiritus alta petat

Nowe for the fourth poynte, and than haue I doo.
Nedefull for the soule me thinketh to provide;
Hence muste I nedes, but whother shall I goo?   24
I dowte my demeryttys, which weyen on euery side,
but goddys mercy shall I truste to be my guyde,
Vnder whoes liecens, yet while I maye breth,
Vnto heven on high my Soule I bequeth.   28

163.   *Death, the Soul's Friend*

Cambridge Univ. MS. Gg. 1. 32

THynk, man, qware-off thou art wrought,   [fol. 3ʳᵒ]
   Þat art so wlonk in wede;
Thynk hou þou art hedyr brought,
   & of thyn end take hede.   4
Thynk hou dere god has þe bought,
   With blysful blode to blede;
Thynk for his gylt was it noght,
   bot, man, for þi mys-dede.   8
With an .O. & and .I., thynk on hym, .I. rede,
Þat wroght þis werld to þi be-howe, & heuen to þi mede.

Thynk, man, inwardly on þis,
   & be þou noght vn-kynde;   12
Thynk & forfet noght þat blys,
   þat made es ffor man-kynde;

Thynk qwat þou has don a-myss
  Syn þou hadyst mannys mynde;   16
Thynk þis werld þat wryched es
  will wan o-way als wynde.
With an .O. & an .I., thynk & þou sall ffynde,
Iff þou rekenes ridily, þou ert fful ferre be-hynde.   20

Thynk we wrichid wormys ar,
  & lette no syn þe schend;
Thynk þat þou was born ful bare,
  so sal þou hen wend;   24
Thynk to be ar þat þou fare,
  þi selff þi soule frend;
Thynk & trayst off na man mare
  þan of þi oughen hend.   28
With an .O. & an .I., do so or þou wend,
Þat þou may fynd it efftirward, qware þou sal longest
    lend.

T[h]ynk how dede cummys sudanly,
  als þou may se all-day;   32
Thynk & be noght ferd for-thy,
  bot be wel war all-way;
Thynk & rewyl þe rythwysly,
  or þat þou clyng in clay;   36
Thynk on crist & cry mercy,
  amend þe qwyle þou may.
With an .o. & an .I., thynk qwat .I. þe say,
thynk þis lyf is lyghly lost, þe tothir lastys ay.   40

Thy[n]k þis werld is wondirfful,
  & þat is gret Meruayll;
Thy[n]k þou may noght stand a pull,
  qwen dede þe wil asayll;   44

Thynk þi mekyl muk & mull
   þen may þe noght a-wayll;
Thynk þou wendys qwedyr god wull,
   to rist or to trauayll.   48
With an .o. & an I., þer may na-thyng a-wayle,
Þat here has wroght wrangwysly, him-self to wrathirhayle.

Thynk & dred noght for to dy,
   syn þou sall nedis þer-to;   52
Thynk þat ded is opynly
   ende off werdes wo;
Thynk als so, bot if þou dy,
   to god may þou noght go;   56
Thynk & hald þe payed þer-by,
   þou may noght ffle þer-fro.
With an .O. & an .I., þan thynk me it is so,
Þat ded sal be þi sawl frend, & erthly lyff þi ffo.   60

Thynk þat þou ert ded alway,   [fol. 3vo]
   qwyllis þat þou dwellis here;
Thynk þi lyff be-gynnis ay,
   qwen þou ert layd apon a bere;   64
Thynk & serue þat prince to pay,
   þe kyng of kyng, þat hass na pere;
Thynk I rede, bothe nyth & day,
   on hym þat boght þe so dere.   68
With an .O. and an .I., thynk qwat I þe lere,
Iff þou wil þat solace se þer seyntis syttes sere.
                              Amen.

67 bothe] MS. boght.

164.   *Death, the Port of Peace*

Royal MS. 9. C. ii

HOwe cometh al ye That ben y-brought   [fol. 119ᵛᵒ]
   In bondes,—full of bitter besynesse
of erthly luste, abydynge in your thought ?
   Here ys the reste of all your besynesse,   4
   Here ys the porte of peese, & resstfulnes
   to them that stondeth In stormes of dys[e]se,
   only refuge to wreches In dystrese,
and all comforte of myschefe & mys[e]se.   8

4 reste] *written above* peese *cancelled.*

165.   *Fortune Will Have Her Way*

MS. Tanner 407
(Sum. Catal. No. 10234)

O Ihū, mercy! what world is thys!   [fol. 38ᵛᵒ]
   frendys be feer and feynte at nede ;
Wo is hym hath don a-mys
and lyeth in peyne and may not spede!   4

What fortune will haue, it schal be had
Who-so-euer will say nay ;
therfor lete it passe, and be not sad ;
and thynk vpon hym þat alle amende may.   8

166.   *Fortune Rules Both High and Low*

Cambridge Univ. MS. Ff. 1. 6

When fortune list yewe here assent,   [fol. 53ᵛᵒ]
What is too deme þat may be doo ?

THere schapeth nought from her entent,
   ffor as sche will it goth ther-to ;
All passith by her iugement,
   The hy astate, the pore all-so.   4
         When ffortune.

To lyve in ioy out of turment,
   Seyng the worlde goth too and fro—
Thus is my schort aviseament,
   As hyt comyth so lete it go!   8
         When ffortune.

167.   *Worldly Joy is only Fantasy*

MS. Arch. Seld. B. 24
(Sum. Catal. No. 3354)

THis warldly Ioy Is onely fantasy,   [fol. 138ʳᵒ]
   of quhich none erdly wicht can be content.
Quho most has wit, leste suld In It affy,
Quho taistis It most, most sall him repent.   4
Quhat valis all this richess and this rent,
Sin no man wate quho sall his tresour haue?
Presume nocht gevin þat god has done bot lent—
Within schort tyme the quhiche he thinkis to craue. 8
   Leaulte vault richess.

168.   *Who Trusteth Fortune Will Have*
a Fall

MS. Douce 45
(Sum. Catal. No. 21619)

WHat is this worlde but oonly vanyte?   [fol. 115ᵛᵒ]
   Who trustith fortune sonnest hath a falle.
Ech man tak heed of prodigalite,
Welth that is past no man agayn may calle.   4
The grenowst wounde þat euer man had or schalle
                       [fol. 116ʳᵒ]
Is to thynk on welth þat is gon and past,
And in olde age in mysery to be cast.

169. *Fortune Has Cast Me from Weal to Woe*

Cambridge Univ. MS. Ff. 1. 6

A god whene

M Y-self walkyng all allone,   [fol. 139ʳᵒ]
ffull of thoght, of Ioy desperat,
To my hert makyng my moone,
How I am the most Infortunat,   4
And how ffortune his cruell hate
Hath to me caste, & broght hit soo
That I am kome fro wele to woo.

ffro al gladnesse & comfort   8
Y am now broght in-to distres;
'ffye one myrth & on disport!'
Thus seyth my hert for heuynes,
Seyng þer is no sekyrnesse   12
Of worldly welth, ho takyth hede—
Which ofte causyth myne hert to blede.

And thus I stond, ffulfylde with sorow
With-in my mynd to my gret payne,   16
Wepyng both even & morow
With swollyne hert, when I refrayne
With woofull teris which can nat ffayne:
Soo haue I lost my Countenaunce   20
Of all the world to my plesance.

5 hate] *before this word* ssate, *crossed out.*
20 Soo] *before this word* Now, *crossed out.*
21 *In a different hand, to replace a deleted line:* My hoole
comfort & my plesaunce.

170.   Fortune, Be My Friend Again

Cambridge Univ. MS. Ff. 1. 6

A! Mercy, fortune, haue pitee on me,   [fol. 178ʳᵒ]
  And thynke that þu hast done gretely amysse
To parte asondre them whiche ought to be
Alwey in on; why hast þu doo thus?   4
Haue I offendyd the? I, nay ywysse!
Then torne thy whele and be my frende agayn,
And sende me Ioy where I am nowe in payn.

And thynke what sorowe is the departyng   8
Of ij. trewe hertis louyng feithfully,
ffor partyng is the most soroughfull thynge,
To myn entent, that euer yet knewe I.
Therfore, I pray to the Right hertely   12
To turne thy whele & be my frende agayn,
And sende me Ioy where I am nowe in payn.

ffor tyll we mete, I dare wel say for trouth
That I shall neuer be in ease of herte.   16
Wherfor, I pray you to haue of me sume Routh,
And release me of all my paynes smerte,
Now sith þu woste hit is nat my deserte.
Then torne thy whele and be my frynde agayn,   20
And sende me Ioy where I am nowe in payn.

171.   A Balade by Squire Halsham

MS. Fairfax 16
(Sum. Catal. No. 3896)

THe worlde so wide, th'aire so remuable,   [fol. 195ʳᵒ]
  The sely man so litel of stature,
The grove and grounde and clothinge so mutable,
The fire so hoote and subtil of nature,   4

The water neuer in oon—what creature
That made is of these foure, thus flyttyng,
Mày stedfast be as here in his lyving?

The more I goo the ferther I am behinde,   8
The ferther behinde the ner my wayes ende,
The more I seche þe worse kan I fynde,
The lighter leve the lother for to wende,
The bet y serve the more al out of mynde.   12
Is thys fortune, not I, or infortune?   [fol. 195ᵛᵒ]
Though I go lowse; tyed am I with a Lune.

172. *Good Rule Is Out of Remembrance*

Rawl. MS. poet. 36
(Sum. Catal. No. 14530)

[L]Ord, what is thys world wele!   [fol. 2ᵛᵒ]
     Rychesse, reule, and ryche Aray,
Alday to spende and not to spele,
     Wel sone were-it and wastyth away.   4
Whan plente may no longer pay
     What wyghte wole wythe hym Abyde?
A drede-ful man, bothe nyghte and day,
     Wyth heuye hert hys hede must hyde.   8

Al is for defaute of grace
     That god grucchyth oure gouernaunce;
Whan mesure may not medyl in place
     Good reule is oute of remembraunce.   12
What is to man mor greuaunce
     Than sodeynly fro manhode falle?
In pride is sympyl preueaunce
     Ther pouerte is steward of halle.   16

But who that can in somer sesoun
   Gader or grype or þat he grynde,
In wyntour tyme by wey of resoun
   Shuld not be ferre be-hynde.   20
ffor þer þat mesure is in mynde
   Good reule may not longe fayle;
it is no crafte to be to kynde,
   ffor scoryng on þe countre-tayle.   24

But wele and worshyp with welfare,
   Moche waste and lytyl wynne,
Wel sone bryngyth an housold bare
   Wyth large spendyng wyth-outen and inne. 28
Thanne be a-vysed or þu be-gynne   [fol. 3ʳᵒ]
   That þu haue no nede to pleyne;
Se what estate þu stonde inne
   for pouerte is a preuy peyne.   32

Thogh þu haue helpe and hope of truste
   Of lordys and ladyes wyth þer plesaunce,
Yet be ware of had-I-wyste,
   for envy makyth new dystaunce.   36
In pryde and pouerte is gret penaunce
   And yet is daunger most dysese;
Þer is commorus enquentaunce
   Wen neyþer of them may odyr plese.   40

But had-I-wyst comyth euer to late
   Whan þer lackyth bothe lok and ky;
What nede is it to spare the yate,
   þer no thyng is lefte in the wey?   44
Wyth a penylese purse to pley,
   lete se, who can þe pepyl plese;
Summe man had as lef dey,
   As longe to lyue in suche dysese.   48

A bare berde wyl sone be shaue
  Þer no here is lefte Aboute;
I mene be hym that myche wold haue
  And is not ellys but pore and proude,   52
But redy to ryot in euery route,
  To ley to wedde bothe potte and panne.
Whan the fere is clene blowen oute
  Where shal we go dyne thanne?   56

What nede is it to delue depe
  Whan þer is no sede to sowe?
Þe pot is esy for to kepe
  Þer þe fatte is ouer-blowe.   60
neþer for the kyte nor for the crowe,
  Encombyr not þyn owne neste;
To myche bende wyl breke the bowe,
  Whan þe game is alþer beste.   64

Ensample men may se alday—
  Yet kepe I no man de-fame—
Hye housold and grete aray
  ys lordys lyf and ladyis game;   68
Whan gladness growyth into grame
  And thanne for nede begge and borowe,
Þer pryde is be-fore and after shame,
  ffro solace into sodeyne sorowe.   72

And that is hevy for to here   [fol. 3ᵛᵒ]
  Of hym alwey that man hath be,
And may no lenger make good chere.
  By my trouth, it is gret pite!   76
Yet shuld worshyp know and se
  And help hevy herte at nede,
Lest he falle in þat same degre
  For happis is euer worse than drede.   80

55 clene] MS. chene.   59 MS. kpe.   63 MS. bonde.

He that is bothe chek and mate
  It is ful heuy to restore;
Whan al is go it is to late
  To weshe and wepe after more.   84
Than be Avysed well before,
  That the fyrst draughte be weel drawe,
for whan the game is lore
  þy part is not worthe an hawe.   88

Now he that worshyp wol haue
  And leue after hys degre,
In manhod his state to saue
  God graunte hym here prosperite!   92
Plesaunce, pouer & plente,
  Wythe al honest ordinaunce,
Þis wolle seruice you bothe and me,
  To be ensample of good gouernaunce.   96

173. The Rancour of this Wicked World

Cambridge Univ. MS. Ff. 1. 6

(1) IN ffull grett hevenesse myn hert ys pwyght,

[fol. 144ᵛᵒ]

  And sadely warpud mony a ffowld;
  Wher [it be]ffore wasse ryght lyght
  And warme, that ys nowe ffull Colde.
  Alle Ioy ffro myn hert ys bowght and sowld,
  Thorow rancoure off thys wekyd worde
  That never agayne hyt may remord.   7

(2) Synglure persone I doo none name,
  But alle the world In generalle
  Swyfte off ffalsnesse, replete off blame,
  lame off trewth, off malese regalle.

86 MS. daught'.   87 lore] MS. lost.

But this I ffynde most In Espescyall,
Beste be trust, wythowghton any nay
Sonest may them-selffe be-tray.   14

(3) But iij. thynges ther bene wryten off record
A mane to be ware a-boue all other:
The pryncypall ffurst ys the world,
A monis hown flechse ys a-nother,
The develle hym-selff, the thred brother,
But who so Euer be to blame
A wold Euerry body wer the ssame—   21

(4) Not ffor tha[t] ne, so god me spede,   [fol. 145ʳᵒ]
Be all the world I sett no talle,
ffor any-thyng that Euer I sed or dede
Vn-to thys owr, securet or aperyalle.
But trust ryght thus wythowghton ffaylle—
And that ys Euer my be-leff—
The trewth In dede hyt-selff well preffe.   28

(5) But the moste parte off my grevaunce,
Ottherly hyt ffor to Exspresse,
ffor to haue In my rememberaunce
Wyth-owtthten Causse that lythe En destresse,
Trustyng to Ihū, off hys Ryghtewyssnese,
Tho send hys grace to subpouell & Comffort
Tho all that ys wyth wronge repourt.   35

(6) And alle wykyd tongyss, who Euer they be,
The whych haue no grace to say wylle—
That I may sse or Euer I dey
The Skene ther-off a-wey to pell

17 MS. ffrust.   30 MS. Exspersse.
32 MS. Endestersse.   34, 35 Tho] *read* To.

And, lord, my prayer ffor to ffull-ffylle
And shurtely shew they grace
Tho Comfort the trewth and all ffalshed deface.   42
                              amen pure cherite.

174.   *If One Only Knew Whom to Trust*
Cambridge Univ. MS. Add. 5943

WEl were hym þat wyst   [fol. 162ᵛᵒ]
    To wam he myȝt tryste,
bote þat ẏs in a wyre,   3
ffor offte men but holde chere;
and trystyt frendes fur an ner
þat walkytt in þe myre.   6

Wol god þat alle suche
had a marke lyte oþer moche
þat al men myȝt y-knowe   9
how here hert & moȝt
stent as ryȝt as norþe & sowþe
to þylke hy but sowe.   12

175.   *Perversities of the Age*
Westminster Abbey MS. 27

WIse men bene but scorned,   [fol. 31ᵛᵒ]
    & wedowȝ eke foryerned,
Grete men arn bot glosid,
& smale men arn borne doun & myslosed,   4
lordis wex euer blynd,
ffrendis ben vnkynde,
dethe is oute of mynde,
Treuth may no man fynde.   8

40 MS. pryer.   41 *Read* thy.   42 Tho] *read* To.
5 MS. trystly.

176. Virtues Exiled—Vices Enthroned

Royal MS. 7. A. vi

LEx is layde and lethyrly lukys,   [fol. 38ᵛᵒ]
   Iusticia is exylde owt of owre bowkys,
Paciencia is plukytt þat mony men hyme Lothys,
ffides is fybled & goys in torynde clothys,   4
Caritas is lowkyde & knokytt full smawyll,
Verus is noght vsyde nothyng att all,
Humilitas is hyde, he wyll noght be seyne,
Castitas is prisonde as mony men weynys,   8
Veritas is demytt to hange one the ruyde,
Verecundia was drownytt at þe laste fluyde,
So þat few freyndys may a mane fynde,
ffor rectum iudicium commys so farre be-hynde.   12
ffraus is fykyll as a fox, & reuys in þis lande,
ffuror is hys freynde, as I vndyrstande,
Decepcio is his chamerlande, haif heire-of no dowtte
Detraccio is of his cownsell—I be-schrew þat rowtte!   16
ffalsum Iudicium is a lordschype of hys,
Violencia berys hys swerde, he may noght mysse,
Inuidia is als vmpeire qwen þai be-gyne to stryfe.
Syche anothyre felyschype, god latt þam neuer thryfe!   20

177. A Series of Triads

MS. Tanner 407
(Sum. Catal. No. 10234)

THer ben iij poyntis of myscheff   [fol. 18ᵛᵒ]
   Þat arun confusion to many man,
Weche þat werkyn þe soule gret gryff,
I schall hem telle ȝou as I can.   4

3 MS. Lukys.   12 MS. faire.   15 is] MS. in.
20 MS. thyfe.

Pore men proude þat lytyl han,
Þat wolden beryt owte as riche men goo;
3yf þei don foly and þan be tan
þei may wytyn hem-self her owyn woo.   8

A Ryche man thef is a-nodyr,
Þat of covetyse wyll not slake;
3yf he with wrong be-gyle his brother
In blis þat he schall ben forsake—   12
be-forun god thefte it is take.
Al þat wit wrong he wynnyt soo;
but 3if he A-mendys make
he may wytyn hym-self his owyn woo.   16

Olde man lechere is þe iijde,
for his complexion waxit colde;
It bryngit his soule peyne in-mydde,
And stynkit on god many a folde.   20
The iij thyngis þat I haue told
arun plesyng to þe fende, oure fo.
Hem to vsyn, hoso is bold,
may wytyn hym-self his owyn wo.   24

Many defautis god may fynde
In vs that schuldyn his seruantis be;
He schewyt vs loue and we on-kynde—
sertis þe more to blame are we.   28
Summe stare brode and may not se—
be many a clerk it faret so—
[Ther] þe dred of god wele not be,
þei may wytyn hem-self her owyn wo.   32

In iij poyntis, I dar wel say,
god schuld be wurchapyd ouer all thynge:
With ryghtwysnesse & mercy—þer be twaye—
þe iijde is clennesse in levynge.   36

19 MS. in mynde.   31 Ther *supplied from Cott. MS.*

To men of holy chyrche þat kepyng
it is her charge & to lordys also,
and whan þei don contrari goddis byddyng
þei may wytyn hem-self her ow[yn] w[o].   40

Wrong is set þer right schuld be,
mercy fro manhod is put A-way,
lecchery clennesse hat mad to fle,
loue dar not bydyn neyther nyght ne day.   44
Thus þe deuyl, I dar wel say,
wolde makyn oure frende oure ful fo.
Man, A-mende the whyl þu may,
or wyte þi-self þin owyn wo.   48

It is no wondyr thow þu be wo,
þi owyn wyl quan þu wolt sewe;
goddis byddyng þu wilt not do—
þu art fals and he is trewe,   52
Syn he sende þe alle thyng newe   [fol. 19ro]
and þu seruyst þe fende & gost hym fro,
but þu mende it schall þe rewe,
þu schalt wytyn þi-self þi owyn wo.   56

In iij degreis þe werd kepis:
with presthod, knyghthod, and labourere.
Þer ar but fewe þat nede don A-mys
þer-for a-byd þei schal ful dere.   60
Be good exampyl þe prestis schuld lere
to on-lernyd how þat þei schuldyn do
and, for þat wurde & werke acordit not in fere,
þei schul wytyn hem-self her owyn w[o].   64

Lordys also, boþe knytis & other,
many arun of consciens lyght;
þei schulde helpe þe pore syster and brodyr
for to streynye hem in her ryght.   68

Pride and coueytyse hat lost here myght,
grace, for lecherye, is kept hem fro;
ȝyf þei be-heldyn her owyn syth,
þei may wytyn hem-self her owyn wo.   72

The labourere schuld trauayle for god and man
ryghtfully in word & dede,
In what degre þat he hath tan,
And resonabylly takyn his mede.   76
Wrongfully summe her lyfe lede—
A-mong ryche and pore it is foundyn so—
þe last ende is to drede,
þei schal wytyn hem-self her owyn wo.   80

Man, take hed what þu arte—
but wormys mete, þu wost wel þis;
Whan þat erthe hat taken hys parte,
heuyn or helle wyl haue his.   84
ȝif þu do weel þu gost to blys,
yf þu do euyl to þi foo;
loue þi lord and thynk on this,
or wyte þi-self þin owyn wo.   88

Glorious god, for þi mercy
þi wretthe gostly þu slake!
to vs þat leuyn here ful falsly
on-to þi mercy euer vs take!   92
Now, ihū cryst, oure saueour,
fro vr foo vs defende;
In al oure nede be oure socour
or þat we schul hens wende,   96

And sende vs grace so to A-mende
þi blysse þat we may come to,
Here to haue so good an ende
þat we be not cause of oure owyn wo.   100
                              Amen.

178. Medicines to Cure the Deadly Sins

Henry E. Huntington Library, MS. HM. 183

A^S I walkyd vppone a day   [fol. 5ʳº]
    To take þe aere off feld and flowre,
In a mery morenynge off may
    When fflowrys were ffull off swete flauowre,   4
I hurd one say, 'O god verray,
    How longe shall I dure yn my dolour!'
And one his kneys he began to pray:
    'Now, good god, send me thy succour,   8
    Maryes sone, most off honour,
        Thatt ryche and poore may po[nyche] and plese.
    Now geve me lyfe yn my langour,
        And yeve vs lycence to lyfe yn ese.'   12

To lyfe yn ese and his lawys to kepe,
    Grawnt me, god, yn blysse so bryght;
And withyn þat cabone lett vs neuer crepe
    Ther as lucifer lyeth, I-lok withowt eny lyght.   16
My dedly wowndis ere derne and depe,
    I haue no place to represse þem aryght,
And smertynge wyll nott suffer me to slepe
    Tyll a leche with dewte haue them dyght.   20
    Hitt most be a curate, a crownyd wyght,
        Þatt knew the querely off bene & pese;
    And els thes medicynys haue no myght
        To geve vs lycense to lyve yn ese.   24

A wykkyd wownde that hath me walt
    And traveld my body fro top to þe too,
This wykkid wordyll hitt is I-calt
    Thatt hath many a blayne bothe blak & blo.   28

    9 suster *cancelled before* sone.   20 MS. them̄.

Hitt hath me hurt and made me halt,
  My hert, my hondys, my hed also,
Nere I had be baptisyd yn watyr and salt
    Thatt fervent ffester wold nevyr me fro.   32
    Thatt lech þat lyssyd lazer and moo,
      David and daniel off ther disese,
    Amend þes wondis thatt doth me this woo,
      And geve me lycence to lyve yn ese.   36

This wownd is noryssher off wowndis sevyn:
  Superbia he is the principall—
Pride pertely yn english stevyn—
  He is more bitter þan venyn or gall.   40
To hym I haue had lechis a-levyn
  And þey haue geve medycyns all;
Butt þe soveraynest medicyn vndyr hevyn
  Hit growith yn grownd noþer yn wall—   44
  Humilitas I hurd a lech hit call—
    Had I hym þan I were att ese.
    God, send [hit] me thatt [am] syke thrall,
      And geve vs lycence to lyve yn ese.   48

Ira is the secund wownd,
  He ramagith sore both raw and rede;
All my cors he doith confownd,
  So sore he swellith yn hert and hed.   52
I know none herbe thatt growith yn grownd,
  Nothir no corsiff, will qwinch his quede;
Butt louage with-yn a litill stownde
  will make hym dry and wex all dedde.   56
  God, yeve me grace to sow sum lovage sede
    Þatt yn my gardyn may rote areyse,
  & els, as seker as men etyth brede,
    shall we neuer haue lycence to lyve yn ese.   60

        29 MS. hurth, *with last* h *crossed out*.
        55 louage *corrected from* bouage.

Inuidia the third wownd is,
  A gritter gnawer þan ffelone or gowte;
A is a wykkid wownd I-wis,
  Þer he hath pour to reyse and rowte.   64
The kynde off the wownde for soth is þis,
  To brenne the brest withyn and withowt;
I askyd a leche how I myght me lys,
  He toke me charitas I-knytt yn a clowte.   68
    He bade me bawme me þer-with all a-bowte,
      And than he wold begynne to water and wese;
    And þen sone after, withowt any dowte,
      Thow shalt haue licence to lyve yn ese.   72

Auaricia is an horribill sore,
  He doth me dere both nyght and day;
ffor evyr he covetith more and more
  Off plastris than I purvay may.   76
I askid a mastir off ffysyke lore,
  How I myght make hyme dry and vanysh away.
Elemosina was a gentyll herbe þer-for,
  I-wis one þe best þat evyr he say;   80
'Take and a-noynte hym ther-with evyr when þou may,
  And thinke how requiem yn thy rent shall sese,
And then sone aftyr with-yn a short day,
  Thow shalt haue lycence to lyve yn ese.'   84

Accidia is a sowkyng blayne,
  He bollith and bladderith with-yn my bowre;
And makith me ffaynt both flessh and vayne,
  And kepith me yn cowch like a cowchour.   88
I hurde off an herbe þatt shold lyse þatt payne,
  Men seith hitt berith a dowbyll flour:
Vigilate & orate. Vse well tho twayne,
  And hitt shall be-nyme the thi dolour,   92

    64 is *dotted for deletion after* þer.

As siker as bred is made off flowre.
  Smyll ham yn seson with þi nese,
And the swetnes off thatt swete savoure
  Shall geve the lycense to lyve yn ese.   96

Gula is a grevys gall,
  He rayvith my rest one my bed;
And straynyth my stomake strayte with-all,
  With many a fest when I am full fed.   100
I walow and weyd as a worme yn a wall
  I may nott slepe tyll I haue shamely shed.
Now mercy, lord, on þe I call,
  Thatt for vs lett his brest be bled.   104
  A leche hath led his hed to wed
    Þatt he wyll make me a playster þatt shall me plese
  Off abstinencia, & I hym hed
    Shold geve me license to lyve yn ese.   108

Luxuria is a lither mormale,
  A mercy! lorde, full of pyte,
My brokyll body he bryngith yn bale,
  And ffrayeth my sowle yn frayalte.   112
Sum tyme a surgeryn told me a tale,
  This was þe lesson þatt he lerid me:
The rote off an herbe I shold vpp hale,
  That clerkis callith castitas fre.   116
  'Pownd hym and temper hym with penitence,
    When þe rebaude will on þe rese,
  Drayne hym & drynke hym with confessioun,
    Than shalt thow haue lycense to lyve yn ese.'   120

And othir iij herbis ther beth also
  Þat shall save þis sorys, þey shall neuer swell:
The ffirst is cordis contricio,
  Þat wasshith the wowndis as doith a well;   124

The secund is oris confessio,
    Þatt wyll nott suffyr no ded flessh dwell;
Operis satisfactio
    Þatt soveray[n] sanatyfe sothly to tell.   128
    Now, lord, as thow madyst hevyn, erth and hell,
      Geve vs grace hym to serue and plese,
    And with-yn his gloryus blysse thatt we all may dwell,
      And geve vs there licence to lyve yn ese.   132

179.   *On Chattering in Church*

MS. Douce 104
(Sum. Catal. No. 21678)

TUtiuillus, þe deuyl of hell,   [fol. 112vo]
  He wryteþ har names soþe to tel,
    ad missam garulantes.

Better wer be at tome for ay,   4
Þan her to serue þe deuil to pay,
    sic vana famulantes.

Þe[s] women þat sitteþ þe church about,
þai beþ al of þe deuelis rowte,   8
    diuina impedientes.

But þai be stil, he wil ham quell,
Wiþ kene crokes draw hem to hell,
    ad puteum autem flentes.   12

ffor his loue þat ȝou der boȝth,
Hold ȝou stil & Iangel noȝth,
    sed prece deponentes.

Þe blis of heuen þan may ȝe wyn;   16
god bryng vs al to his In,
    amen! amen! dicentes.

    7 *Blot in MS. over part of first word.*

180.   *Against Traducers*

MS. Eng. poet. e. 1
(Sum. Catal. No. 29734)

· I pray ȝow all with hert & thovȝt   [fol. 24ʳᵒ]
Amend me & peyer me novȝt.

HOly wrytt sayth no thyng sother,
þat no man shuld a-peyer oþer;
Sythen I am in god þi broder,
    Amend me & peyer [me novȝt.]   4

þis in þe gospell ych man may se:
If þi broder trespace to þe,
Betwen ȝow to corectyd he be,
    Amend me, &c.   8

Yf þu se I do gretly amys,
& no man wott butt þu of þis,
Mak it not so yl as it is,
    Amend me, &c.   12

A-peyer no man with þi word,
Neþer in ernest ne In bord;
Let þe tong þat is þi swerd
    Amend me, &c.   16

Lok þat þu no man defame,
Ne a-peyer no mans fame;
Riȝt as þu woldest haue þe sam
    Amend, &c.   20

Now to a-mend god ȝyffe vs grace
Of repentance, & very space;
And in hevyn to se hys face,
    Wher al thyng amend & peyer novȝth.   24

181. See Much, Say Little, and Learn to Suffer in Time

Royal MS. 2. D. xxxvii

Virtutem primam.   [fol. 153ro, col. 2]

SEe much, sey lytill, and lerne to suffre in tyme ;
empreynt thes thre yn thy remembraunce.
lyke as the mone chaungyth a-for the prime
so faryth thes world, replete with variaunce.   4
Oft lewyd langage causyth grete distaunce,
Werfor wyse Catoun seyth to old & ȝong:
'the fyrst chefe vertu is to kepe owr tong.'

Werfore, wold god thes fals tongys all—   8
meuyng and clappyng lyk to the leue of apse,
Woys dayly venym more byttur is than gall—
Were boundyn euerchon with a claps[e] !
Tyl trowth and temperance lust them to [vnhapse] ;   12
for fals detraccioun, lesyng & dysclaunder
Hath slay mor peple than dud kyng Alysa[under].

Yf yn thes lyf thu woll encrese and eche
thyn worldly Ioy, thyn ese, and thyn wellfar[e],   16
Be wele avysyd at all tymes of thy [speche],
and saue the sure fro satan & hyse [snare].
Oft yll reportis engenderyth sorw[e and c]are ;
Were-for in spekyng at no tyme [is] he ydill   20
That can hys tong at all tyme wysly bridill.

A lytell spark may set a towne a-fyre,
But wen it brennyth it is nought lyghly quey[nt].
On word myspoken may bryng the yn the myre   24
So depe y-wyss till thu theryn be draynt.
A fals tong may florysch weell & peynt

14 MS. sclay.

as for a cesoun, but euer the end ys schame;
And wo is hym hoys tong h[ath lost hys name].   28

lytill mellyng causyth [meche reste];
Ouer besy was [neuer] yit commend[able].
loke were thu art yn dowt, and deme the [beste];
Dele nogth with dowblenesse, ne be nogth descey-
    uable;   32
Rechelesse & racle [are] oft tymys repreuable;
Werfor, thysylf and thu wollt kepe fro crime,
See much, sey lytill & lerne to suffyre yn tym[e].

182.   *Think Before You Speak*

Trinity Coll. Camb. MS. 1450

What euer thowe saye A-vyse the well.   [fol. 48ᵛᵒ]

ALmyȝty godde, conserue vs fram care!
    Where ys thys worle A-way y-wente?
A mane that schold speke had nede to be ware,
    ffor lytyl thynge he may be schente;   4
    Tonggys beth y-turne to lyther entente,
        Hertys they beth bothe fykel and felle.
    Man, be-ware leste thow repente,
        Whate euer thow sey, A-vyse the welle!   8

A-vyse the, mane, yn whate place and whare
    A woord of conseyl thow doyst seyne;
Sum mane may ley there-to hys ere—
    Thow wenyst he be thy frend; he ys thy foo cer-
        teyne—   12
    Paraventor aftyr A ȝere or tweyne—
        Thow trowyst as tru as eny stele,—
    Thys woord yn wreth thow schalt hyre A-gayne,
        Whate euer thow sey A-vyse the welle!   16

Meny mane spekyth yn hastenys,
  Hyt hyndryth hym and eke hys frende;
Hym were well beter hys tonge to sese
  Than they both there-for be schende.   20
  Suche wordys beth not to be had yn meynde,
    Hyt maky3t comforte with care to kele:
  Man, yn the begynnynge thenk on þe eynde;
    Whate euer thow sey, A-vyse the welle!   24

To sum mane thow mayste tel a pryuy tale:
  When he fro the ys wente A-way,
ffor a draw3t of wyne other ale,
  He woll the wrey, by my fay,   28
  And make hyt worse—hyt ys noo nay—
    Than euer hyt was, A thowsend dele.
  Thys us my songe both ny3t & day,
    Whate euer thow sey, A-vyse the welle!   32

Be ware of bagbytynge, y the rede;
  ley flaterynge vndyr thy foote,
Deme the beste of euery dede
  Tyll trowth haue serchyd truly þe roote;   36
  Rrefrayne malyce, cruell & hoote;
    Dyscretly and wysly speende thy spelle;
  Boost ne brage ys worth a Ioote;
    Whate euer thow sey, A-vyse the welle!   40

Dysese, wharre, sorowe and debate,
  ys causyd ofte by venemys tonge;
Haddywyst comyth euer to late
  Whan lewyd woordis beth owte y-spronge,   44

34 *After* foote *MS. adds* loke, *perhaps to call the reader's attention to the line.*

The kocke seyth wysly on hys songe,
  'Hyre and see and hold the stylle!'
And euer kepe thys lessoun A-monge,
  Whate euer thow sey, A-vyse the welle!   48

y dere well swery by the sonne,   [fol. 49ro]
  Yf euery mane had thys woord yn thowȝt,
Meny thynggis had neuer be by-gunne
  That ofte yn Ingelond hath be y-wroȝt.   52
  The wyse mane hath hys sone y-tawȝtte:
    'Yn ryches, poorte, woo and welle,
  Thys worthy reson for-ȝete thow noȝt,
    Whate euer thow sey, A-vyse the welle!'   56

Yf that thow wolte speke A-ryȝt,
  Ssyx thynggis thow moste obserue then:
What thow spekyst, & of what wyȝt,
  Whare, to wham, whye and whenne.   60
  Thow noost how soone thow schalt go henne;
    As lŏme be meke, as serpent felle;
  In euery place, A-monge all men,
    Whate euer thow sey, A-vyse the welle!   64

Almyȝty god yn personys thre,
  With herte mylde, mekly y praye,
Graunte me grace thy seruant to be
  Yn woorde and dede euer and aye!   68
Mary, modere, blessyd maye,
  Quene of hevyn, Imperes of helle,
Sende me grace both nyȝt and daye—
  Whate euer thow sey, A-vyse the welle!   72

        Explicit.

183. *Counsels of Prudence and Patience*

Cotton MS. Calig. A. ii

ffor þe bettur a-byde   [fol. 67ro]

I See A Rybane Ryche and newe,
  Wyth stones and perles Ryally pyght,
Regalles, Rubies, Saffyres blewe;
The grownde was alle of brent gold bryght,   4
Wyth dyamandes full derely dyght;
Ryche Saladyneȝ sette on euery syde,
Wher-on was wrytyn A Resoun full Ryght,
And all was for the better A-byde.   8

Vppoun that Resoun I studyed þat tyde,
And ther-to toke I good entent,
How kynde wytte setteth sorow be-syde,
Wyth eche a mone ther he ys lent;   12
Good suffraunce ys full syldene schent,
Whene weyle and woo a-wey schun glyde;
Hasty mene often tymes harmes hent,
Whene they were bettere to A-byde.   16

I haue harde sungone wyth a harpe,
That haste mene sholde wante no woo;
They kone notte shylde heme fro showres scharpe,
Nayther kene here freende frome here foo.   20
Sum mene says þat hyt ys soo,
Who-so kone suffer, heyle, and hyde,
May haue hys wyll ofte tyme y-doo,
And he wyll for the better A-byde.   24

He that wyll not drede no schame
Ys putte owte of mone & oneste place;
Let neuere thy tonge defowele thy name,
But be kynde and trewe in euery case;   28

26 mone &] *?read:* mony an.

And pray to god to gyffe the grace   [fol. 67ᵛᵒ]
In lond, where-sere thow goo or Ryde,
All wyked werdes A-way to chase,
And euer more for the better a-byde.   32

And thy luffe be yn a place,
Haue hyt in mynde & holde þe styll;
A foles bolt ys sone schote in case,
Whoo speketh mykyll sum he most spylle;   36
Lette neuere þy luffe be on an hylle,
Ner thy councell at þe crosse be cryde;
Lette but fewe mene wytte þy wylle,
And euere more for þe better A-byde.   40

ffor the best þu holde the stylle
And for þe bettere þy spech þu spende;
Though þu haue not to-day þy wylle,
Thy wyll to-morowe god may þe sende;   44
Grucche not agayne hyme, y þe defende,
ffore pouerte or sekenes in any tyde;
Godde wyll see tyme and hyt amende,
And euer more for þe bettere A-byde.   48

I haue wyste mene in prysoun be caste,
And lyve ther-in sex yere or seuene;
And ʒyt be holpene owte at þe laste,
ffor ofte mene mete at vn-sette steuene;   52
Wyth freend & foo god makes euene,
That for vs suffered woundes wyde;
And brynge vs to þe blysse of heuene,
ffor the better ther euer to A-byde.   56

Explicit.

34 MS. hʒt.
45 þe] MS. de.

184.   *Every One Finds His Match*

A. Harley MS. 2251

THere is non so wise a Man / But he may wisdam leere,
[fol. 80vo]
And ther is none so stronge a man / But he may
fynde his peere,
Nor there is none so false a man / But sum man wil hym
leeve,
And there is none so meke a man / But sum man may
hym greve.

B. Trinity Coll. Cambridge MS. 1157

THere is no man so myghty but som man may hym
dere,   [fol. 29vo]
Nor no man so witte but some man may hym lere,
Nor no man is so variaunt but som man wil hym leve,
Nor no man is so pacient but some man may hym greve.

185.   *Neither Too Humble Nor Too Proud*

Cambridge Univ. MS. Add. 5943

lord, how scholde I roule me of al men I-preysed to be. [fol. 145vo]

IF y halde the lowe A-syse
And take a-ray of lytel pryse,
Then men wil say, 'he ys now3t wyse,
He ys a fow, let hym be!'   4

And 3yf I take the mene Astate
& wyth non man maky debat,
Than men wil sey, erly & late,
That I am worth no maner fe.   8

1 holde] *interlined above* take, *crossed out.*

And yf y take gryte A-ray,
Hors & hondes & clothes gay,
Than men wel say euery day
    That I passe my degre.   12

Then take thow hede of the oxe,
Go now3t to lowe for the ffoxe,
Nether to hey tyl thow be wox,
    ffor the kyte that wolde they sle.   16

Ther-for loke that thow be scley,
ffor no thyng hew thow tow hey,
last they falle don in-to thy ey,
    The spones that Above they be.   20

186.   *Measure is Best of All Things*

B.M. Addit. MS. 32578

IN a semely someres tyde,   [fol. 140ᵛᵒ]
   Als I gan walke in a wilde woude,
Vndre a bowe I sawe a-byde
A company of clerkes gude;   4
In a stody als þai stode
Þus þai gan mene in þaire spekynge:
'In ilke manere of mans mode
    Mesure is best of all thynge.'   8

Crist þat all thynge has vndre cure,
Heuene & erthe and also helle—
All he made vndre mesure,
As holy writte wytnes welle.   12

        16 *and* 20 they] *read* thee.

Þu spare no pont of þaire spelle,
Bot leue wele in þis lernynge;
And take þis tale as I þe telle,
Þat mesure is best of all thynge.   16

To litill or to gret excesse,
Bothe arne wike and vicyous
And greue god bothe, as I gesse,
ffor bothe þe partise arne perillouse;   20
Þen were a mene full vertuouse
And proued prisse in prechynge,
And þer-fore, bothe in hille & house,
Mesure is best of all thynge.   24

God graunt þat his grace so grete
Be wele mesured till ilka man;
And to his grace he take hym mote,
With crafte to kepe hym as he kan.   28

187.   *Inordinate Love Defined*

Copenhagen MS. Thott 110

Dicam quid sit Amor: Amor est insania mentis, [fol. 163ro]
Ardor inextinctus, insaciata fames,
Dulce malum, mala dulcedo, dulcissimus error,
Absque labore quies, absque quiete labor.

Y Shall say what ynordynat loue ys:
   The furyosite and wodnes of mynde,
A instynguyble brennyng fawtyng blys,
A grete hungre ynsaciat to fynde,   4
A dowcet ylle, a yvell swetness blynde,
A ryght wonderfulle sugred swete erroure,
Wyth-owte labor rest, co[n]trary to kynde,
Or wyth-owte quyete to haue huge laboure.   8

188.   *What Profiteth this World's Labour?*

Harley MS. 2251

LOng wilbe, water in a welle to keche,   [fol. 78ᵛᵒ]
    A vessell made of yerdis that wil nat holde.
No wounder is it, though it be leche ;
To fille another, I note how it shulde.   4
Right so thus this worldis labour wolde
Man to gadre goode and grete Riches,
But ware of th'ende to hym be no distresse.

Who-so that in suche a vessel these tranes shulde,   8
Rest he ne may, day nother nyght,
Ete nor drynk whan that they wolde,
Therfor in labour thus they do her myght.
Right so this worlde wylle that euery maner wight 12
Goode to gete in trowth from oure to oure,
That in tyme of nede hem to help and socoure.

Goode god! what doth this occupacioune?
We trow thus to level the see—   16
It may nat be by none ymagynacoune!
But the world wil it, as ye may se,
That in yowth euery man laboryous to be
To gadre Riches, hym to supporte and vpholde   20
In age, whan he wexith fieble and holde.

189.   *A Song of 'Goods'*

Univ. Coll. Oxford MS. 33

WHile þou hast gode & getest gode,   [fol. 70ʳᵒ]
    for gode þou miȝt be holde ;
Who haþ no gode, he can no gode—
    a gode man so me tolde.   4

16 MS. two.

Hit is noȝt gode for no gode
   of gode forto be bolde;
But þi gode to god be gode
   þi gode wil fail & folde.   8
Wiþ an .v. & an .I. gode wil come & goo,
but þi godes grounde be gode, þi gode wil worche þe woo.

That is gode þat doth man gode
   When he goth to þe grave;   12
Oþer gode was neuer gode,
   but gode þat wil man save.
Ȝif þi gode while þou hast gode,
   gode þan miȝt þou crave;   16
ffor hit is gode to worche gode
   for god þat doth hit have.
With an .v. & an .I. gode is gode to wisse,
for with gode þou miȝt be gode, & bygge hevene blisse. 20

To doo gode god ȝaf þe gode,
   for þi gode & noȝt hisse;
Doo gode for þi sowle gode,
   & þat is gode ywisse;   24
If þou hast gode & dost no gode,
   þat gode is gon amisse;
for evil gode is cleped gode,
   for wham man left his blisse.   28
Wiþ an .v. & an .I. gode is þat gode doth,
oþer gode was neuer gode for certeyn & forsoth.

A sliper gode is erthli gode,
   for þat gode wil away;   32
goddis gode is euer gode,
   & oþer gode is fay;

ken þi gode & know þi gode
   & doo gode wel alway,   36
for hit is gode to worch gode
   for gode þat lasteth ay.
With an .v. & an .I. in gode is gode ende,
for al is gode which endeis gode & þerto Crist vs sende. 40
                         Amen.

190.   *The Law of Kind*

Cambridge Univ. MS. Ii. 1. 2
(written as prose)

LEerne, þou vnkynde man, to be kynde   [fol. 127ʳᵒ]
  of a beest þat haþ no skille of kynde.
Hou þou doist schame to þi kynde,
but þou to ihū crist be kynde!

       2 MS. a *interlined with red ink.*

191. *For Each Inch God Will Require*
Thee a Span

Cambridge Univ. Ms. Kk. 1. 5. Part 6

SEn trew vertew encressis dignytee,   [fol. 5ʳᵒ]
  and wertew floure and rut is of noblay,
Of ony weill, of quhat esstat yow bee,
  His steppis sew, and dreid the non affray: 4
  Exill all wyce and folow treuthe al-way:
    Luf most thi god, that fyrst thi lust begane,
    And for ilk ynch he wyll the quyte a spane.

[Be not our prowde of thy prosperitie;   8
  ffor as it cumis so will it pass away.

    Lines 8–14 are supplied from the Bannatyne MS., fol. 58ᵛᵒ, as printed in the Scottish Text Soc. ed., ii. 145.

The tyme to compt is schort, thow ma weill se;
  ffor of grene gres sone cumis wallowit hay.
  Labor in trewth quhill licht is of the day;   12
    Trust most in god for he best help the can
    And for ilk inche he will the quyt a span.]

Sen Word is thrall and thot is only free,
  þow dant thi twnge, that powar has & may.   16
Thow set thine Ēnē fra warldly vanitee;
  restren thi lust, and harkyne quhat I say:
  Stramp or yow slyd, and crep furth one the way;
    Kep thi behest one-to thi lord, and thane   20
    ffore ilk ynch he wyll the quyt a spane.

192.   *The Summum Bonum*

B.M. Addit. MS. 37788

THe law of god be to þe thy rest,   [fol. 87ᵛᵒ]
  The flesh þy sacrifice, þe world exile,
God thi love & thi tresour best,
Hevyn þi contre thorogh euery while.   4
Repentaunce þou take In-to þi brest
for þyn vnkynnesse & wikkidnes vile,
And abide at þi selff withinne þi nest
lest vndir pite thow be trappid with gile,   8
Except at som-while as a hasty gest
þu stert to do good but thorogh no long mile.
Haue do, glutoun, fle to this fest!
for here-In of al wynnyng lyth crosse & pile.   12

    11 MS. ? gaytoū.

NOTES

1. *Dear Son, Leave Thy Weeping*

NOT heretofore printed from the Porkington MS. Stanzas
1–6 are found in Laud Misc. 683, fol. 105vo (printed by
H. N. MacCracken, *MLN* xxiv, 225). The sixteenth-century
MS. Balliol 354, contains an expanded text, in which extra
stanzas have been inserted (one after the first stanza and
two after the seventh), and a 2-line burden, 'Now synge
we w^t angelis / Gloria in excelcis,' is added. The Balliol
text has been printed repeatedly (by Flügel in *Anglia*, xxvi.
247, 8, by Pollard, *XVth Cent. Prose and Verse*, pp. 90, 91,
by Dyboski, EETS, Ext. Ser. ci. 21–3, and by Greene,
Early Eng. Carols, pp. 112, 113). The Porkington MS. alone
alternates with the English song the stanzas of the celebrated hymn, 'Criste qui lux es et dies' (Mone, *Lat. Hymn.
des Mittelalt.* i. 92; Sir Stephen Gaselee, *Oxford Bk. of Med.
Lat. Verse*, p. 18). Material textual differences appear among
the versions of the Latin hymn, but the text in the Porkington MS. agrees with that of the 'Ymnus ad Completorium'
(*Lat. Hymns of the Ang. Sax. Church* (Surtees Soc. xxiii)
12–13).

2. *Here I Sit Alone, Alas! Alone*

Occurs only in this MS.; previously printed by B. Fehr
(*Archiv für das Stud. d. neueren Sprach. u. Lit.* cvi, 59, 60).
In the MS. the text is accompanied by musical score.

3. *It is my Father's Will*

Occurs only in this MS.; previously printed by Greene,
Early Eng. Carols, p. 101. This poem with its 'Lullay'
burden recalls the fourteenth-century dialogue between the
B.V. and her child in the Grimestone collection (*Rel. Lyrics
of the XIVth Cent.*, No. 56). Both are written in ballad metre
with medial rime, but in the fifteenth-century poem a 2-line
refrain has been added.

In ll. 10, 15, and 21 one notes the use of the colloquial
at for *that*.

4. *He said Ba-Bay, she said Lullay*

Previously printed from this MS. by Greene, *Early Eng.*

Carols, pp. 100–1. With the 'Ba-bay Lullay' of the refrain one may compare several carols for Innocents Day:

(1) Sloane MS. 2593, fol. 17vo: The chylderin of Israel cryid "wa, wa!" / The moderis of Bedlem cryid "ba, ba!" (Wright, *Songs and Carols*, Warton Club, p. 52).

(2) Caius Coll. Camb. MS. 383, p. 210: The childron [of Israel] cried "Wa, wa!" / Her wondus smertus sore; / Crist in credul seide "Ba, ba!" (Greene, *Early Eng. Carols*, p. 320).

(3) Douce MS. 302 (Poems of John Audelay), fol. 28vo: Crist crid in cradil, "moder baba;" / Þe childer of Iral cridyn "wa wa!" (ed. E. K. Whiting, EETS, No. 184, p. 189).

This 3-line refrain is lacking in the later version (consisting of only two stanzas) in BM. Addit. MS. 5465, which Greene (p. 99) oddly prints as 'Version A' of this piece. In the Addit. MS. a 7-line burden is prefixed, but the text in this MS. (though showing reminiscences of the Harley text in verbally identical phrases) is in the main a free re-working of the theme and in workmanship is vastly inferior.

47. Loyalty (troth) shall depart (fall out) from all the apostles and dwell in you, Mother, alone. The same idea is expressed in No. 94, l. 28: 'And þe faith of crist remanit in our lady allane.' One may cite also a stanza from an unprinted poem in Caius Coll. MS. 174:

> Whene a yong mayde stode in batayle,
> Oure lady, on whome stode the belew of the Chyrch
> yn tyme of passioun—lo such a-vayle
> And prerogatyfe women sche dyd wyrch.
> Sche to an oke, but a branch of byrch,
> Dyd stande & abyde in that grete affray
> Whene that olde berdyd men dyd fle a-wey

(pp. 482–3)

65. That Judas has sold me to outrage.

5. *She Sang, Dear Son, Lullay*

Occurs only in this MS.; not heretofore printed. MS. Ashmole 189, from which this piece and also Nos. 8, 55, 71, 77 A, 79, and 106 are printed, is composed of several independent sections which have been bound up together.

All the English poems occur in the second section, which consists of fols. 70 to 115. On the upper corner of fol. 70vo, as noted by Black (*Catal. of the Ashmole MSS.*), 'is a distich written in a cypher of Arabic numerals for the vowels, which may be read thus:

> Qui scripsit certe Ricardus nominatur aperte
> Quod si queratur recte Wraxall cognominatur.'

According to the *Victoria Co. Hist. of Somerset*, vol. ii, Richard Wraxall (né Bele) was confirmed as Abbot of Athelney 7 Jan. 1517. He was succeeded in this office in 1518 by John Herte (see also Dugdale's *Monasticon*, ii. 404, note m). The inference is that Wraxall died in 1518.

Another note of ownership appears in the MS. on fol. 115ro, written in a small hand in the middle of a page for the most part blank: ' Dominus ricardus Coscumbe Prior de Muchelney est possessor huius libri.' On the verso of this leaf is written in the same hand: ' Ingenita est nobis uia a notioribus notis ad notiora nature procedere. Primo Primi Phisicorum.' This quotation is identified by turning to the text of *Arist. Physicorum*, Lib. I (ed. Frankfort 1604). Richard Coscumbe, Prior of Muchelney, however, was still living in 1538, as appears from the records of Muchelney printed by Browne Willis (*History of the Mitred Abbeys*, Lond. 1719, ii. 198).

In the opinion of Black both notes of ownership in the Ashmole MS. were written by the same person, but the identity of handwriting in the two entries seems to me questionable; and it is difficult to understand why Wraxall should have changed his name to Coscombe, or why he should have resigned the abbacy of Athelney to become prior of Michelney. Both Athelney and Michelney, however, were in Somerset, and the two entries, therefore, combine in offering testimony as to the provenience of this important collection of English verse.

6. *Filius Regis Mortuus Est*

This piece occurs in four MSS.: Lambeth 853, p. 74; Harley 3954, fol. 90ro; Rawlinson C. 86, fol. 74vo; and Douce 78, fol. 3ro: the text of the first two has been printed by Furnivall (*Pol. Rel. and Love Poems*, EETS, Orig. Ser. 15, rev. ed. 1903, pp. 233–42). The Harley version runs parallel with the others for only the first two stanzas and then digresses into an account of the resurrection, interspersed with theological discussion, in which it is not always clear who is speaking. Accordingly, in considering the relationship of the MSS. Harley may be disregarded. If we leave out of account also the 8-line conclusion, peculiar to Douce, giving assurance to the Virgin that her Son 'is a-lyve et non mortuus est', the stanza arrangement of the three MSS. is as follows:

Douce	1, 2, 3, 4, 5, 6,		7, 8.
Rawl.	1, 2, 3, 4, 5, 6, 7, 8,	9,	10, 11.
Lamb.	1, 2,	3, 4, 5, 6, 7, 8, 9, 10, 11, 12.	

Despite the peculiar omission by Douce of three stanzas, Douce and Rawl. agree in almost every case in their readings where Lamb. differs. In fact the only point which I have noted in which Rawl. and Lamb. agree against Douce is at l. 111, where Douce reads 'þen schall ye curse' (: þusse) but Lamb. and Rawl. read 'whider wole ȝe trus'. Otherwise the Douce-Rawl. readings appear to preserve the most authentic textual tradition. In stanzas 2 and 3 Lamb. changes the *b*-rimes from those in Douce-Rawl. and in stanza 4 the *a*-rimes. Also Lamb. omits stanza 3 of Douce-Rawl.—one of the finest in the poem—and on the other hand inserts two rather feeble stanzas (8 and 10) lacking in both the other MSS.

Very possibly the three stanzas lacking in Douce (consisting of rhetorical apostrophes to the elements, the cross, and the scourge) represent later additions. In that case Douce would be taken as supplying the original draft of the poem, and the texts of Rawl. and Lamb. would illustrate successive stages in its elaboration. At all events the superiority of the text here offered over the only one previously printed makes it in effect almost another poem.

106. Though the form *sest* supplies a proper rime for *est*, the grammatical construction is impossible. The grammar would be corrected by reading 'or thou hadest sest'.

123. The rimes *lorde* and *recorde* show that in this line the poet must have written *worde*, a dialect form of *worlde*.

7. *An Appeal to all Mothers*

Of this Marian lament there are three MSS.: (1) Camb. Univ. Ff. 2. 38 (printed by T. Wright, *Chester Plays*, ii.

207–9), (2) Camb. Univ. Ff. 5. 48 (printed in *Rel. Antiq.* ii.
213–15), (3) Chetham Lib. (Manchester) 8009 (printed by
M. Foerster, *Anglia*, xlii. 167 ff.). In addition there is a
second version, preserved in Rawl. C. 86 and Ashmole 61
(both printed by Prof. Helen Sandison, *Chanson d'Aventure
in Mid. Eng.*, pp. 104–9, Rawl. alone by Miss R. Cords,
Archiv, cxxxv. 300) which prefixes a narrative preface of
three stanzas but omits stanzas 5 and 7 of the text as here
given.

The rimes in stanzas 5 and 6 (hand: bledand: daunsand:
likand) make it certain that the poem was originally composed in the North, although the three MSS. differ among
themselves in dialect colour, and no one of them is entirely
consistent. On the whole the text of Ff. 5. 48 preserves
the clearest traces of the original dialect. In this MS. for
example the refrain line at the end of each stanza reads
'ffor now liggus ded' instead of 'ffor now lyeth ded' as in
the others.

4. kne] Chetham and Ff. 2. 38: skyrte

10. dose] Chetham: settist. Ff. 2. 38: castyst

11. pykys . . . be-holdys] Chetham and Ff. 2. 38: pykist
. . . beholdist

18. dose] Chetham: doth Ff. 2. 38: dere

19. with gret solas] Chetham and Ff. 2. 38: gret ioy thou
mas

26. playes & kisses] Chetham: playn and kys. Ff. 2. 38:
playe & kysse

28. gret gap is] so also Ff. 2. 38. Chetham: many gappis

34. stroke] so also Ff. 2. 38. Chetham: strake (: layke)

36. layke] so also Chetham. Ff. 2. 38: laghe

38. speyre] Chetham and Ff. 2. 38: sere

45. any hande] Chetham and Ff. 2. 38: my hand

57. þu hase] Chetham and Ff. 2. 38: Thou haste

60. & myn ded is he] so also Ff. 2. 38. Chetham: and
dede is he

63. be holdyne] Chetham: were holdyn Ff. 2. 38: were
wele holden

66. lovys] Chetham and Ff. 2. 38: lovith

71. sendis youris] Ff. 2. 38: sendyth yourys. Chetham:
sendith you

73. þat has] Chetham: that hath. Ff. 2. 38: þ^t haue

74. And sees] Chetham and Ff. 2. 38: And se
78. Raþer or] so also Ff. 2. 38. Chetham: Rather than

8. *O Thou, with Heart of Stone*

Occurs only in this MS.; not heretofore printed. For remarks on the MS. see above, Note on No. 5.

9. *Who cannot Weep come Learn of me*

Marquis of Blandford MS., now Rylands Lib. (Manchester) Lat. MS. 395; first printed from this MS. by Joseph Haslewood in *Censura Literaria*, x. 186–7, also by Greene, *Early Eng. Carols*, p. 121. Another text of the same poem is preserved in Trinity Coll. Camb. MS. 1450 (printed by Furnivall, *Hymns to Virgin and Christ*, pp. 126–7, and by Chambers & Sidgwick, *Early Eng. Lyrics*, pp. 144–5).

There is also an elaborate poem in 12-line stanzas with the refrain: 'Who can not wepe come lerne at me' which is preserved in three MSS.: MS. Bodley 423, fol. 192vo (76 stanzas), Harley 2274, fol. 35ro (72 stanzas), and Trinity Dublin 160, fol. 1ro (52 stanzas). This has been printed from the Harley MS. by R. M. Garrett, *Anglia*, xxxii. 270–94.

14. Trinity MS.: Ihesus so my sone ys bobbed.

17–18. she seid to me . . . at þee] Trinity MS.: seyng to the . . . at me.

35. Trinity MS.: this ys the lay.

10. *Our Lady's Imprecation*

Not previously printed from this MS.; occurs also in Camb. Univ. MS. Ff. 2. 38, fol. 55ro (printed by Thomas Wright in his ed. of the *Chester Plays*, ii. 204–7); and in Harley MS. 5396, fol. 283ro.

34–7. The rimes 'robbyd', 'bobbyd', 'sobbyd' seem to be a reminiscence of the refrain in the preceding poem,] where they fit somewhat better.

37. He feld riȝt sore] Ff. 2. 38: Yf he felte sore

57. With sharpe scourgis þei] Ff. 2. 38: W^t balefull buskeys ye

61. Cf. No. 125, line 5: To make them stonde styll as eny stone

66. with a knyfe] Ff. 2. 38: as a knyfe

11. *Stabat Mater Dolorosa*

Occurs only in this MS.; not heretofore printed. As the general basis of the first eight stanzas we may recognize without difficulty the Latin hymn beginning:

> Stabat mater dolorosa
> juxta crucem lacrimosa
> qua pendebat filius
> cujus animam gementem
> contristantem et dolentem
> pertransivit gladius
>
> (Mone, ii. 147; Daniel, ii. 131–54, &c.)

From l. 33 to the end the resemblances to the Latin hymn cease. Also one notes that the second half of the English poem has much repetition and very little substance.

34. The three 'names' of the B.V. are Domina Mundi, Regina Celi, and Emperatrix Inferni. See below, ll. 77–80.
35. Inverted order: Saints call thee Queen of Heaven.

12. *Hail, Mother and Virgin Immaculate*

BM. Addit. MS. 20059 is a small vellum Registrum Cancellariae of the time of Edward II, on the blank pages of which were inscribed (about the time of Henry VII) the texts of this piece and also Nos. 38, 51, 69, and 117. The volume belonged in the time of Charles I to Gabriel Wettinhal of Nantwich (Cheshire), afterward to Wm. Falconer Esq. of Chester, and in 1826 was the property of his nephew, Mr. Tho. Falconer of Bath. A nineteenth-century transcript of these five poems, by Joseph Hunter, is contained in BM. Addit. MS. 24542. BM. Addit. MS. 20059 was first identified as the original of Hunter's transcript by Miss B. N. H. Geary in an unpublished Oxford B.Litt. thesis, 1932.

13. *High Empress and Queen Celestial*

Not heretofore printed from this MS. This poem also occurs in the Asloan MS., fol. 292ro (printed in the Scot. Text Soc. ed. of the Asloan MS., ii. 245). The Asloan MS. lacks the concluding stanza.

6. floure] A. barne
7. spue] A. spyce
14. path] A. pace
16. serving] A. seruand

28. Anournyt] A. Adorned
34. parenes] A. parañ.

14. *Thou shalt Bear the Fruit of Life*

Not heretofore printed from this MS. This poem occurs also in BM. Addit. MS. 34360, fol. 60ʳᵒ (printed by Mac-Cracken, *Archiv*, cxxxi. 45–6).

In stanzas 3 and 6 the sixth line is wanting. The fact that in Addit. MS. 34360 exactly these two lines are omitted would imply a very close relationship between these MSS., and this inference is confirmed by the fact that the first seven items in Harley MS. 2251 occur also in Addit. MS. 34360 in precisely the same order.

A curious difference in metre is to be observed in the several stanzas of this piece. Whereas in stanzas 1, 2, and 6 the lines carry only four accents, in 3, 4, and 5 almost every line shows five accents. The text as it stands plainly suggests that it is the work of more than one person, and one guesses that the 5-accent lines represent a later insertion.

15. *A Salutation to the Virgin*

Occurs only in this MS.; not heretofore printed. A similar poem on the Angelic Salutation in 10-line stanzas, with the Latin text in the margin opposite the first line of each, will be found in Royal MS. 17. A. xvi, fol. 3ᵛᵒ (still unprinted). This text ends imperfectly at l. 87, in the stanza 'In mulieribus'.

29–30. The water and blood of that body which was born of thee washed thy stains. This being quite inconsistent with the doctrine of the Immaculate Conception of the Virgin, suggests that this poem was of Dominican origin, since the Dominicans did not accept this doctrine.

73. With this use of the adj. *fede* ('strong, doughty') compare *Sir Tristrem*, l. 153: 'Þe kny3tes þat wer fade / thai dede as rohand bade.' In l. 2474 the word occurs again, this time with the spelling 'fede'.

16. *Mary, Pray thy Son for Us*

Previously printed from this MS. by Greene, *Early Eng. Carols*, p. 139. Stanzas 2, 3, and 6 are also found (in variant form) in Balliol Coll. MS. 354, fol. 249ᵛᵒ (Dyboski, EETS, Ex. Ser. ci. 49).

17. *Enixa Est Puerpera*

Previously printed from this MS. in *Early Bodl. Music*, ii. 65 (with facsimile) and by Greene, *Early Eng. Carols*, p. 141.

This is a rearrangement in 4-line stanzas of the well-known thirteenth-century macaronic hymn 'Of on þat is so fayr and briȝt'—See *English Lyr. of the XIIIth Cent.*, No. 17 and Notes.

18. *Ave Maris Stella*

Previously printed from this MS. by Wright, *Songs and Carols*, Warton Club, pp. 77–8, by Fehr, *Archiv*, cix. 66, and by Chambers & Sidgwick, *Early Eng. Lyrics*, p. 109.

These lines can hardly be termed a translation of the Latin hymn. Although the first four lines incorporate verbally the opening stanza of this celebrated hymn, from that point the English text departs so widely from the Latin that it can hardly be considered even a direct paraphrase.

9–10. These are, of course, appended lines and not a part of the hymn.

19. *Hail, Star of the Sea*

Not previously printed. B.M. Addit. MS. 37049, which contains the unique text of this piece, was evidently written in a Carthusian monastery, for at fol. 22ro occurs a poem of twenty-nine couplets on the Carthusian Order. From the same MS. are printed, besides the present piece, Nos. 26, 67, and 108.

Despite the Latin line which stands at the head of these verses, they are very loosely related to the hymn, *Ave maris stella*.

20. *Mary, Bright Star of Heaven and Holy Church*

Occurs only in this MS.; previously printed by Stevenson, Scottish Text Soc. lxv. 9.

21. *Hail, Queen of Heaven*

Occurs only in this MS.; not heretofore printed.

22. *Ave Gloriosa*

Occurs only in this MS.; not heretofore printed.

23. fra the spleyne] from the heart (see *OED* s.v. Spleen, *sb.* 2b).

59. After this line the scribe repeated, and then crossed out, the follcwing version of ll. 21–3:

> Haill cleyne virgine
> Ay glemand into glore
> Haill cipros greyne
> Haill cipros greyne fra the spleyne.

Here, as at l. 21, the scribe wrote *cleyne virgine* for *virgine cleyne*. A similar careless repetition of several lines occurs at the top of f. 164vo of this manuscript (see No. 96, l. 65, footnote), where the mistake was left uncorrected.

23. *Ave Regina Celorum, I*

Other texts of this piece are found in Advocates MS. 19.3.1, fol. 65ro (printed by W. B. D. D. Turnbull, *Visions of Tundale*, pp. 145–6), in Lambeth MS. 853, p. 24 (printed in *Hymns to Virgin and Christ*, EETS, pp. 4–5), in Balliol Coll. MS. 354, fol. 147ro (printed by Flügel, *Anglia*, xxvi. 165–6, and by Dyboski, EETS, Ext. Ser. ci. 59–60). The text of Trinity Coll. MS. Dublin has not heretofore been printed.

A comparison of these texts shows interesting diversity of readings. Dublin is wrong against the other three in ll. 3, 5, 15, and 35. Dublin confirms Balliol in ll. 4 and 45 and Lambeth in l. 13 against the others. Dublin *may* be right in its peculiar reading in ll. 7, 26, and 36. The rimes *care*: *sare* (9, 11) and *vertues*: *Ihesus* (41, 43) establish the reading of Dublin against the other MSS.

13. Scil. 'þat' after 'berde'.

24. *Ave Regina Celorum, II*

Occurs in this MS. only; not heretofore printed. This may be compared with the similar poem (likewise in seven 12-line stanzas) in Camb. Univ. MS. Ff. 2. 38, fol. 31vo, and Pepys 1584, Art. 8. See *Register*, No. 649.

25. *Salve Regina*

Occurs in this MS. only; not heretofore printed.

26. *An Expansion of Salve Regina*

Occurs in this MS. only; not heretofore printed. Balliol Coll. MS. 354 contains a macaronic version of the *Salve Regina* in which the English lines begin with a phrase of

the Latin hymn; but there are no verbal parallels between
the two pieces. Also, in Balliol the Latin is incorporated
into the structure of the line, whereas in the text here printed
the Latin is merely placed opposite the corresponding English phrase.

27. *Regina Celi Letare, I*

Occurs also in Harley MS. 665, vol. 296ᵛᵒ, and in Lambeth
MS. 306; printed from the latter in *Pol. Rel. and Love Poems*,
EETS, rev. ed., p. 176. Laud Miscell. 213, from which this
piece is here printed for the first time, is a fifteenth-century
MS. of the *Fasciculus Morum*.

28. *Regina Celi Letare, II*

Occurs only in this MS.; not previously printed.

29. *Regina Celi Letare, III*

Occurs only in this MS.; previously printed by MacCracken,
Archiv, cxxxi. 48–9.

17–19. In regard to these lines Sir William Craigie ob-
serves: '*lyth* (= life) rhyming with *dixit*, seems to imply
the pronunciation of final *t* in Latin as þ, for which there is
other evidence in ME texts.'

30. *The Five Joys of Our Lady*

Previously printed from this MS. by MacCracken, *Archiv*,
cxxxi. 49–50. This poem also occurs in two Shirley MSS.:
B.M. Addit. 29729 (fol. 130ᵛᵒ) and Ashmole 59 (fol. 68ʳᵒ).
In the former it is assigned to Lydgate, and in the latter to
'a holy Ancresse of Mansfeld'.

English tradition down to the end of the fourteenth
century uniformly recognized Five Joys of the Virgin, viz.:
the Annunciation, Nativity, Resurrection, Ascension, and
Assumption, whereas on the Continent the number of Joys
is regularly seven, through the addition of Epiphany and
the Purification.

31. *The Five Joys of Our Lady, with Acrostic*

Occurs only in this MS.; previously printed by W. Heuser,
Anglia, xxx. 547. Holthausen prints the text in a normalized
form in *Anglia*, lix. 319–20.

The acrostic with which these verses conclude affords
trustworthy indication as to the district in which the poem

was composed. Pipwel is in eastern Northamptonshire, and was the seat of a Cistercian monastery. The hymn to St. Catharine of Sinai, which in this roll precédes the hymn on the Five Joys, also contains an acrostic, 'Richard Spaldyng'—no doubt the name of the author. Whether the same person composed both poems is not certain but seems altogether probable.

32. *An Orison to Our Lady by the Seven Joys*

Occurs only in this MS.; not heretofore printed.

33. *A Salutation by the Heavenly Joys*

Occurs only in this MS.; not heretofore printed. The Seven Heavenly Joys—which are wholly distinct from the Terrestrial Joys, whether Five or Seven—do not make their appearance in England before the fifteenth century. Besides the text here presented and Nos. 34, 35, and 36 which follow, other English poems celebrating the Joys of the Virgin in Heaven occur in Lambeth MS. 306 (ed. Furnivall, *Pol. Rel. and Love Poems*, EETS, rev. ed., pp. 174–5) and in Mirk's *Festial* (ed. EETS, pp. 232–3). Also a freer and more expanded treatment of the theme is found in a poem of ten 8-line stanzas in Camb. Univ. MS. Kk. l. 6, fol. 200ᵛᵒ (printed by MacCracken, *Journ. Eng. and Germ. Philol.* viii. 260–2).

All these English poems trace their origin to a Latin hymn, Septem Gaudia Celestia, in 6-line stanzas (Mone, *Lat. Hymnen des Mittelalters*, ii. 176 ff.; Daniel, *Thesaurus Hymnolog.* i. 346–7) printed from Royal MS. 8. E. v by Holmstedt in his ed. of *Speculum Christiani*, EETS, 182, p. cxcii. The numerous texts of the Latin hymn show much variation in minor particulars.

7. my clernes] read: '*þy clernes*'

34. *The Seven Joys of the Virgin in Heaven, I*

Occurs only in this MS.; not heretofore printed.

In several MSS. of the Latin hymn on the Seven Joys (all, however, of comparatively late date), its composition is ascribed to St. Thomas of Canterbury on the basis of what appears to be purely apocryphal legend.

Ll. 1–42 of the present piece agree in their arrangement with the text in Royal MS. 8. E. v and in Daniel.

Ll. 43–52 have no counterpart in the Latin hymn.

35. *The Seven Joys of the Virgin in Heaven, II*

Occurs only in this MS.; not heretofore printed. This macaronic version of the Heavenly Joys differs from versions I and III in that it consists of seven stanzas instead of eight, and is written in 8-line stanzas. It corresponds most closely in content and arrangement to the Latin text in Royal MS. 8. E. v, as printed by Holmstedt in his ed. of the *Speculum Christiani* (EETS, 182, p. cxcii).

8. A dignitate munerum] The reading of Royal: 'Dignitate numerum' is clearly an error. The Latin text printed by Mone (ii. 176) reads 'munerum'; also one may compare the reading of the English in No. 36 (l. 6): 'Thorowh dignyte of thi giftis.'

24. Veneratur in gloria] so in the Royal MS. The texts printed by Daniel and Mone read 'Venerans in gloria'.

36. *The Seven Joys of the Virgin in Heaven, III*

Printed from MS. Harley 372 by Karl Hammerle (*Anglia*, xliii. 429–30) from a transcript by Professor K. Brunner. This is the only version of the Heavenly Joys in rime-royal. It also differs from I and II in adding an eighth stanza. While differing in this respect as well as in the order of the stanzas from the Latin versions printed by Mone and Daniel, it agrees in all points with two fifteenth-century MSS. in Munich and Venice which Mone cites in his Notes (ii. 177–8).

50–6. Compare the text of this stanza with the eighth stanza in the Munich and Venice MSS. as given by Mone:

> O sponsa dei electa / esto nobis via recta
> Ad æterna gaudia / ubi pax est et gloria
> tu nos semper aure pia / dulcis exaudi O Maria.

37. *A Song of the Assumption*

Not hitherto printed from the Cotton MS. This piece occurs also in Lambeth MS. 853, p. 1 (printed by Furnivall, *Hymns to Virgin and Christ*, EETS, pp. 1–3); and the first 50 lines in Harley MS. 2251, fol. 18ro. The English poem is based upon the Antiphon for Vespers on the Feast of the Assumption: 'Tota pulchra es amica mea: et macula non est in te: favus distillans labia tua: mel et lac sub lingua tua: odor unguentorum tuorum super omnia aromata: jam

2025·16

X

enim hyems transiit: imber abiit et recessit: flores apparue-
runt: vinee florentes odorem dederunt: et vox turturis
audita est in terra nostra: surge propera amica mea: veni
de libano: veni coronaberis' (*York Breviary*, Surtees Soc., ii,
col. 476).

The Lambeth text shows more than a score of variants
from the Cotton MS., and in almost every instance gives
the inferior reading.

2. in sete full] Lamb.: þou ȝafe souke so

4. be, & be called] Lamb. (preferably): be callide

9. clene] Lamb.: clenner þan

15. My herytage] Lamb.: Myn hiȝ cage!

21. angelles] Lamb.: seintis

22. þe worshyppe in heuen] Lamb.: honoure þee moder
in my

23. Thow] Lamb.: þat

27. A watur full swete of þe shall] Lamb.: Of þᵉ a watir ful
weel gan

28. Thow shalte aȝeyn] Lamb.: þat schal aȝen alle

33–9. The rimes in these lines are sadly disorganized in
Lamb.: chosen: queene: hiȝ: childe: dwelle: blis: mys.

41. Vox tua to me was full] Lamb. (repeating l. 33): Veni,
electa mea, my moder.

49. lylye] Lamb.: loueli

53, 55. Lamb.: changes the rimes to 'was solde' and 'as
y wolde', thereby spoiling the rime-scheme.

59. þowȝty] Lamb.: deintiest

60. & erbes] Lamb.: þat here ben

61. plenere] Lamb.: pleasure

65. Que] Lamb.: Quid

66. celestyall for oure] Lamb.: euere lastyng for her

38. *The Coronation of the Virgin, I*

Not heretofore printed; a nineteenth-century transcript
of this text is found in B.M. Addit. MS. 24542—see Note on
No. 12.

The close relationship between this and the following
song of the Coronation suggests that they are built upon
a common liturgical basis. Here and there one finds even
phrasal parallels, e.g.

38. 41/42: By the spectable splendure of hir fulgent face
My sprete was rauesched, & in my body sprent.

39. 27/28: So was I enspyred froom the speculat splendure,
   That my spirit wasravysshed, my boody a-bood.
38. 46: Withe the seraphynnes in their solemnyte, solemply
   sang.
39. 34: To synge with Seraphynnes in here suavite.
21. The idea here expressed, that Phoebus resigns his
dominion, may have been suggested by a passage in the
hymn, 'Eterna celi gloria':

Ortus refulget lucifer / sparsamque lucem nunciat /
cadit caligo noctium / lux sancta nos illuminet.
(York Breviary, i, col. 849)

39. *The Coronation of the Virgin, II*

Occurs only in this MS.; not heretofore printed. The
imagery in this piece contains some suggestions of the hymn
for the Feast of the Assumption: 'O quam glorifica luce
choruscas stirpis davitice regia proles sublimis residens virgo
maria supra celigenas etheris omnes.' *York Brev.* ii. 484.

9–10. Cf. the opening lines of a hymn to SS. Tiberius,
Modestus, and Florentia (Chevalier, No. 1620):

> Aurora caeli praevia
> a nocte lucem separat
> divisa divina clare.

13. The day-sterre] see the Note on No. 38, l. 21.
65. One is reminded of Rossetti's 'Blessed Damozel':

> Her hair that lay along her back
> Was yellow like ripe corn.

40. *Fresh Flower of Womanhood*

This 8-line stanza is written on a fly-leaf of the MS.; it
has not hitherto been printed. I am unable to supply any
information concerning 'H. Bowesper' whose name is appended to these lines.

41. *Mary, Be our Succour and Help*

This prayer to the B.V., not hitherto printed, occurs in
a MS. of Lydgate's *Fall of Princes*.

42. *Keep Us a Place in Paradise*

The unique copy of this piece stands in the MS. immediately following Rolle's *Form of Living*. These verses have
been printed by Horstmann (*Yorkshire Writers*, i. 157).

43. *Our Lady and all the Angels, Pray for Me*

This prayer occurs in the *English Register of Godstow Nunnery* (ed. Andrew Clark, EETS, Orig. Ser. 129, p. 11), and was reprinted by F. A. Patterson, *Middle Eng. Penitential Lyric*, p. 72.

44. *Mary, Remember Me at my Last Day*

This orison has not hitherto been printed; it is also found in the Amherst MS. at fol. 12ᵛᵒ.

5. Myrroure without spot] see above, No. 39, l. 44.

45. *I Have now Set my Heart so High*

Occurs only in this MS.; not heretofore printed.

A fourteenth-century song of two stanzas begins with a similar line (*Rel. Lyrics of the XIVth Cent.*, No. 129), but the resemblance extends no further than the opening line. Moreover, the subject of the earlier song is not the Virgin but 'that lord þat louid vs alle'.

13. Tota pulcra] see above, No. 37, l. 25, and No. 38, l. 9.

46. *A Love Message to My Lady*

Occurs only in this MS.; previously printed by MacCracken in *Archiv*, cxxxi. 47–8. As Professor MacCracken points out, the first stanza of this piece shows verbal similarities to the concluding stanza of an acrostic poem of fifteen rime-royal stanzas in MS. Rawl. poet 34, addressed to the B.V.:

> Go lytill balett, and doe me recommende
>   Vn-to my lady with godely countynaunce,
> By-sekyng hur that sche me sende
>   Comfortt ayenst all comberaunce,
>   And me deffend from all myschaunce
>   So that afore my fyniall howre
>   I may hur see to my succour.   Amen.

47. *I will Serve my Lady until Death*

Occurs only in this MS.; not heretofore printed. Although separated into two parts by the 'Amen' after stanza 2, this piece appears to be a unit. The common phrases show that all five stanzas were written by the same author, and all breathe the same spirit.

48. *I Will Have No Other Spouse*

Occurs only in this MS.; previously printed by Halliwell, *Reliq. Antiquæ*, ii. 255–6, and by Wülcker, *Altengl. Lesebuch*, ii. 7.

49. *God in Trinity, Give Me Grace*

Occurs only in this MS.; not heretofore printed.

50. *A Petition to Father and Son and Holy Ghost*

Not heretofore printed; occurs also in five other MSS. The texts fall into two groups: the first (represented by Harley MS. 2406, Camb. Univ. MS. Ii. 6. 43, fol. 99ᵛᵒ, and Camb. Univ. MS. Dd. 8. 2, fol. 5ʳᵒ) consists of five stanzas; and the second (MSS. Bodley 789, fol. 146ʳᵒ, and Camb. Univ. Ii. 6. 43, fol. 20ʳᵒ—written as prose) consists of only four stanzas (lacking the stanza to the B.V.). The text of Dd. 8. 2 is peculiar in the arrangement of the stanzas, in the order of the lines, and in some of the rimes.

4. And fulfill my will] so also Camb. Ii. 6. 43 (B). 'And my desyr fulfille' (Camb. Ii. 6. 43 (A) and Bodley). 'And my desire cause to be goode' (Camb. Dd. 8. 2).

7. He yeue me myght] so also Camb. Ii. 6. 43 (B). 'Of myght and grace' (Bodley and Camb. Dd. 8. 2). 'And for myȝt grace' (Camb. Ii. 6. 43 (A)).

10–16. Camb. Dd. 8. 2 shifts this stanza to the end.

51. *A Prayer to the Three Persons in the Trinity*

Occurs only in this MS. (not counting the nineteenth-century transcript of this piece by Joseph Hunter in B.M. Addit. MS. 24542). For an account of the MS. see above, Notes on No. 12. These verses were printed in a small collection of poems ascribed to Skelton, by Richard Lant (1542–8), and are reprinted in the *Poetical Works of Skelton and Donne*, Riverside ed., i. 162. The occurrence of this poem in a Cheshire MS. during the reign of Henry VII renders its ascription to Skelton improbable.

52. *In One is All*

Occurs only in this MS.; previously printed by Horstmann (*Yorkshire Writers*, i. 161–2). Immediately below these verses is written in a contemporary hand: 'Yt is ordan by þe Constytucōn provincyall þᵗ euere curet þᵗ kepyng has of crystyn' men sawles schall schew emong' þer peryschyns

þe faythe of haly kyrk þᵗ es forto say xiiij. artˀ fidei.' The
mention of the Constitution Provincial seems to indicate
that this was written by a friar. Also one notes that in the
MS. these verses directly follow an English translation of
a chapter of Bonaventura's *Meditationes Vitæ Christi*.

53. *The Pater Noster*

The unique text of these verses is in the 'Makculloch MS.'
(Univ. of Edinburgh, Laing MS. 149); previously printed by
Stevenson, Scottish Text Soc., vol. 65, p. 17.

54. *Our Father, Have Pity on Me*

Camb. Univ. MS. Add. 5943, in which these verses are
preserved, formerly belonged to Lord Howard de Walden.
The contents of this MS. have been printed by L. S. M[ayer],
Music, Songs Etc. from an Early XVth Cent. MS., London,
1906.

55. *Salvum me fac, Domine*

Occurs only in this MS.; not heretofore printed. Immediately following in the MS. is another prayer beginning
with the same two lines, and also consisting of six 4-line
stanzas. In this case, however, the refrain is 'Parce michi
Domine'.

For remarks on MS. Ashmole 189 see above, Notes on No. 5.

56. *God Guides All Things*

For a description of the Hatton MS. see Dr. Henry
Bergen, *Lydgate's Fall of Princes*, pt. iv, pp. 73–6: he prints
these lines on p. 75. On fol. 166ʳᵒ is the name of the earliest
recorded owner: 'Alexander Mather aldermannus Norwici
possessor est Huius Libri.' Mather's name appears in the
Norfolk section of the *Valor Ecclesiasticus* of 1535 (Blomefield's *Norfolk*, iv. 538) and among the Burgesses in Parlia-
ment, 1st Edw. VI (Blomefield, iii. 263) and 1st and 2nd
Philip and Mary (Blomefield, iii. 263). He died 12 Sept.
1558, as appears from the funeral inscription printed by
Blomefield (iv. 357).

The verses 'God is a substance' are carefully copied in
the hand of a professional scribe, though he was not the
same scribe who copied the text of the *Fall of Princes*.
These verses had already been written when the book came

into Mather's possession; otherwise he would have entered his name at the top of col. 2, fol. 168ᵛᵒ. This stanza appears to have had some currency, for a Northern version of these lines is prefixed to the Bannatyne MS. (1568) and is ascribed to George Bannatyne by the editors of this MS. (ed. Scot. Text Soc. ii. 2). However, the appearance of the lines in the Hatton MS. makes their ascription to Bannatyne impossible. I have been unable to identify the 'William Hammer' whose name is signed to these lines.

57. *God Governs for the Best*

This poem has been printed from the Huntington MS. by Karl Brunner, *Anglia*, lix. 332–7. It is found also in Camb. Univ. MS. Gg. 4. 31, fol. 104ʳᵒ, with the title, 'A goodly preaer.' The differences between the two texts are mainly orthographical.

4. freell . . . wrechid] Camb.: wreached . . . freele
11. lovist . . . witness] Camb.: lovedyst . . . wytnessyth
14. and all] Camb.: In all
21. after] Camb.: as
23. worldis] Camb.: worldly
33. deserving, lord] Camb.: my deservyng
34. gret] Camb.: & very
38. or] Camb.: or any
46. scornes] Camb.: sporyng
52. goromercy] Camb.: gramercy
54. hool] Camb.: holly
61. better wer al] Camb.: moche better were grett
64. of this] Camb.: off þi
70. prossperite] Camb.: perplexyte
74. lord] Camb. *omits.*   skyll] Camb.: greate skyll
75. thi wyll] Camb.: þe vntyll
76. kneling] Camb.: dwellyng
81. now . . . ho, lorde] Camb.: lorde who gode nowe
89. worldis] Camb.: worldly
93. bad] Camb.: I had
101. passcioun] Camb.: blood.   is mene] Camb.: meane

58. *The Seven O's of Christ*

Occurs only in this MS.; not heretofore printed. These O's are directly based on the Greater Antiphons of the

Advent Season, the Latin text of which immediately precedes the corresponding stanza of the English paraphrase. On the liturgical use of these Antiphons see Professor Cook's ed. of *Cynewulf's Christ*, pp. xxxvi–xxxix and 71 ff. To the Seven O's of Christ an eighth Antiphon, *O virgo virginum*, was added at an early date. Medieval liturgies exhibit some variations in the number and arrangement of the O's. In the *York Breviary* (Surtees Soc.), i, col. 57–8, the text of these Antiphons will be found in the identical order in which they are arranged in the Harley MS.

The Seven O's are not to be confounded with the 'Fifteen O's of Christ', of which there are at least three metrical versions in Middle English: see *Register of Mid. Engl. Rel. and Didactic Verse*, Nos. 1013, 1464, and 1519.

59. *Jesus, My Lord and Protector*

Occurs only in this MS.; not heretofore printed.

60. *Christ, Defend Me from My Enemies*

Occurs only in this MS.; not heretofore printed. This is a translation of a Latin hymn by Berengar of Tours (999–1088) beginning: 'Iuste iudex Iesu Christe, regum rex et domine' (see F. J. E. Raby, *Christian Latin Poetry*, p. 264; for the text see Mone, *Lat. Hymnen des Mittelalters*, i. 359–61). The English poem is immediately preceded in the Corpus Christi MS. by the text of the Latin original. The Latin text is written in lines of eight accents, arranged in 3-line strophes (*aaa*). The English translator has broken this long line into two, thus making stanzas of six lines (*ababab*).

15. I be noȝt seke] Latin: Vt valeam.
26. Þe ȝate of hellys pitt] Latin: Acherontis ianuas.
39, 40. The Latin reads: 'ffiat illis in ruinam laqueus invidie'. Sir William Craigie suggests emending l. 39 to read: 'ffalle in þair gildre'.
48. Abl. absolute cstr.; Latin: 'Et eisdem superatis'.
56. Latin: sensus meos muniat.
66. gifer of grace] Latin: dator indulgencie.

61. *Jesus of Nazareth, Have Mercy on Me*

Occurs only in this MS.; not heretofore printed.

Notes 313

62. *A Prayer by the Wounds against the Deadly Sins*

Occurs also in Christ Church Oxford MS. 151, and in
Cotton Caligula A. ii. It has not previously been printed
from any MS. In content and arrangement this prayer
closely parallels No. 123 in the *Rel. Lyrics of the XIVth Cent.*
Both are written in 6-line stanzas and show even identical
phrases. Such resemblances would be accounted for if the
two poems were translated from the same Latin original.

Between the MSS. the textual differences are slight, but
in general the readings of the Balliol MS. are metrically
smoother. Only variants which seem to improve the text
are noted.

14. both] *omitted in Cotton.*
17. To clense] *Cotton omits* To.
27. Cotton: Whan þey to þe Rode were nayled.
32, 33. Cotton: At þy feet vpon þe Rod / When þey were
þyrled wᵗ nayles.
36. Thynges] Cotton: þo werkes.
43–8. This concluding stanza is lacking in Cotton.

63. *Let not the Fiend Overcome Me*

Occurs only in this MS.; not heretofore printed. The
appearance of such forms as *luf* (five times), *saule* (twice),
gar (l. 36), *suld* (l. 11), *sall* (l. 19), and the rimes *salde: halde*
and *lele: mele* afford sufficient evidence that these verses
were originally composed in Northern dialect; but the text
as we have it has been written over by a Midland copyist.

64. *Richard de Caistre's Hymn*

Of this extremely popular hymn no less than seventeen
MSS. are known. This hymn, which has been printed repeatedly from several of these MSS., was studied in detail
by Rev. Dundas Harford (*Norfolk and Norwich Archaeo-
logical Soc.* xvii. 221–44), who printed the text of ten MSS.
in parallel columns. For the biography of Richard de Caistre,
vicar of St. Stephen's, Norwich (†1420), the reader is referred
to this paper.

Though de Caistre is credited with the composition of
this hymn, eight of the twelve stanzas already existed in a
fourteenth-century poem (see No. 94, *Rel. Lyrics of the
XIVth Cent.*), and this served as a basis for de Caistre's
more expanded version. De Caistre arranged his text in

two sections, with six stanzas in each. The first section is concerned with personal petitions and the second with petitions for others. As will be seen from the following table comparing the stanza arrangement in the fourteenth-century poem with that in de Caistre's hymn, nearly all the stanzas of the second section are peculiar to de Caistre's version.

Stonyhurst MS. 1, 2, 3, 4, 5, 6, 7, 8.

Vernon MS. 4, 5, 6, 7, 8, 1, 2, 3.

de Caistre 5, 2, 7, 9*, 4, 3, 10*, 11*, 12*, 13*, 14*, 8.

(Stanzas marked with an asterisk have no counterpart in the earlier text.)

The first five stanzas of the earlier version are also interspersed in the 'Psalter of the Passion' in the Gurney MS., although it will be noted that these include none of the stanzas added in de Caistre's hymn.

The text of the hymn in Lambeth 853 (*Hymns to the Virgin and Christ*, pp. 15–17) differs from all the others by including fourteen stanzas instead of twelve. The two extra stanzas (2 and 4 in Lambeth) are, however, identical with stanzas 1 and 6 in the Stonyhurst text, and presumably were borrowed by the Lambeth scribe from some MS. of the fourteenth-century version.

The Harley Charter MS. of de Caistre's hymn (previously printed by Harford) is in several places defective, but it has been selected because it shows more distinct traces of the dialect of Norfolk.

65. *Make Me Loathe Earthly Likings*

In the MS. these lines are scribbled on a fly-leaf in a fifteenth-century hand. They have not previously been printed.

'Swete Ihu', which the scribe placed in the first line, was evidently intended as the heading.

7–9. The arrangement of these lines in the MS. is impossible:

And so w^{t}inne & w^{t}owte
Throw me to be soget alle abowte
Ondir þi wille to alle þ^t is reson Right & soþe.

In the first of these lines there are three accents, but six in the last. By transferring 'throw me' from the second

line to the first and 'ondir þi wille' from the third to the
second the metrical regularity is restored.

66. *Grant Peace to Thy True Lovers*

Previously printed from this MS. by J. W. Legg, *Processional of Nuns of Chester* (Henry Bradshaw Society), p. 28.

22. In support of the restoration of the text in this line
see above, No. 61, ll. 1–2.

67. *Close in My Breast Thy Perfect Love*

B.M. Addit. MS. 37049, in which these verses occur, was
written in a Carthusian monastery. These lines were previously printed by Miss F. M. M. Comper, *Life and Lyrics
of Rolle*, p. 318. These six lines may possibly be a fragment
of a longer devotional lyric. On a fly-leaf in Harley MS.
2406 (fol. 84ᵛᵒ) are five 4-line stanzas, the second of which
runs:

> Ihs my ioye my love me rest
> Thy perfyte loue close in my brest
> Þᵗ I þᵉ love & neuere rest
> Or make myn hert in peces to brest.

68. *Lord, I long after Thee*

In the MS. this piece immediately follows the text of
Rolle's *Ego Dormio*. It was printed from this MS. in the
British Magazine, ix (1836). 502.

69. *Ave Gracia Plena*

Not previously printed. For remarks on the MS. see above,
Notes on No. 12.

70. *Ecce! Ancilla Domini*

This song of the Annunciation occurs also in Advocates
(now National Lib. of Scotland) MS. 19.3.1, fol. 89ᵛᵒ, from
which it has been printed, by W. B. D. D. Turnbull, *Visions
of Tundale*, pp. 141–3; by Karl Breul, *Engl. Stud.* xiv.
401–2; and by Chambers & Sidgwick, *Early Eng. Lyrics*,
pp. 112–14.

71. *Gabriel Came Down with Light*

Occurs only in this MS.; not heretofore printed. For
remarks on MS. Ashmole 189 see above, Notes on No. 5.

72. *My Thought Was on a Maid so Bright*

Previously printed from this MS. by J. A. Fuller Maitland, *Eng. Carols of the XVth Cent.*, p. 7; by Chambers & Sidgwick, *Early Eng. Lyrics*, p. 106; by Padelford, *Anglia*, xxxvi. 95; and by Greene, *Early Eng. Carols*, p. 166.

Other texts of the same piece (with some variations) occur in Sloane MS. 2593, fol. 30vo, in Bodl. MS. Arch. Seld. B. 26, fol. 13vo, and in the sixteenth-century MS. Balliol Coll. 354, fol. 222ro (printed from Sloane by Wright, *Songs and Carols*, Warton Club, pp. 88–9, by Fehr, *Archiv*, cix. 68; from Bodl. in *Early Bodleian Music*; from Balliol Coll. by Dyboski, EETS, Ext. Ser. ci. 12; from all three by Padelford and Greene, *ut supra*).

12. Following this line Sloane has two stanzas not found in the other MSS.:

> Ryȝt as þe sunne schynyt in glas
> so Ihū in his moder was
> & þer-by wyt men þat che was
>   R[edemptoris mater]
> Now is born þat babe of blys
> & qwen of heuene his moder is
> & þer-fore þink me þat che is
>   R[edemptoris mater]

73. *Sapiencia Sent to Redeem Man*

Occurs only in this MS.; previously printed by Greene, *Early Eng. Carols*, p. 60.

74. *Honour to Him Who Descended from Heaven*

Occurs only in this MS.; previously printed by Greene, *Early Eng. Carols*, p. 136.

75. *Mary Bore Both God and Man*

Occurs also in Bodl. MS. Arch. Seld. B. 26 from which it was printed in *Early Bodl. Music* and by Padelford, *Anglia*, xxxvi. 107. Previously printed from the Trinity Coll. MS. by J. A. Fuller Maitland, *Eng. Carols of the XVth Cent.*, p. 3, and by Greene, *Early Eng. Carols*, p. 168.

76. *Born is Our God Emanuel*

Occurs also in Bodl. MS. Arch. Seld. B. 26, from which it was first printed in *Early Bodl. Music*, ii. 104. The Trinity

Coll. text was printed by J. A. Fuller Maitland, *Eng. Carols of the XVth Cent.*, p. 5, and by Greene, *Early Eng. Carols*, p. 13. The text of both MSS. is given by Padelford, *Anglia*, xxxvi. 110–11. The Trinity Coll. MS. in every case gives the preferable reading.

77. *A Maid Hath Borne the King of Kings*

The Latin original of this piece is the *Prosa de Nativitate Domini*, of which the text is printed in Migne, *Patrol. Lat.* 184, cols. 1327–8.

Text A. Occurs only in MS. Ashmole 189. For remarks on this MS., see above, Notes on No. 5. Previously printed by Greene, *Early Eng. Carols*, p. lxxxi.

Text B. Occurs only in Bodl. MS. Arch. Seld. B. 26, from which it has been printed in *Early Bodl. Music*, and by Padelford, *Anglia*, xxxvi. 105.

78. *Verbum Caro Factum Est*

Previously printed from the Advocates MS. (somewhat inaccurately) by W. B. D. D. Turnbull, *Visions of Tundale*, pp. 157–9. The text here presented is based on a collation of the MS. kindly made for me by Professor Anna J. Mill of Mount Holyoke College. Another text occurs in Sloane MS. 2593, fol. 18vo (printed by Wright, *Songs and Carols*, Warton Club, pp. 53–5, and by B. Fehr, *Archiv*, cix. 58).

In arrangement the Advocates is superior to Sloane throughout. Stanza 4 with its exposition of the Shepherds' song directly continues stanza 3. In S. on the other hand the meeting with the shepherds (stanza 3) is followed by the meeting with the Magi; and the exposition of the 'Gloria in excelsis' is transferred from the shepherds to the Magi. Again, in A. the Magi when encountered are returning from Bethlehem, whereas in S. they are on their way thither, and accordingly could not report the events there as represented in stanzas 5 and 6.

Moreover, the alliteration is preserved in A. where it is lacking in S.: e.g. (l. 3) 'semelyour syght', instead of 'fayrere syte'; (l. 38) 'we farred wele at þe fest', instead of 'þei woldyn fare prest'; (l. 42) 'bote hasse broght off all oure bale', instead of 'bote haȝt of al our bale'; (l. 45) 'socourd hym sothly yn hur sale', instead of 'curid þᵗ louely in here sale'.

6. Sloane: 'che seyde in here song not lest'—clearly a corrupt reading.

25–32. In the corresponding stanza of S. (33–40) the *b*-rimes (fleych: wych: mys: Iwys) are impossible, whereas in A. they are regular. Ll. 32, 34, in Sloane recur almost unchanged in ll. 49, 51, thus suggesting that some patching has taken place.

37. In A. it is the leader of the Magi who addresses the poet: in S. the kings speak in unison.

49–56. In S. different rimes have been substituted, in both the *a* and *b* lines.

79. *Make Ye Merry for Him that is Come*

Occurs also in two other MSS.: Sloane 2593, fol. 9ᵛᵒ (printed by Wright, *Songs and Carols*, Warton Club, p. 28, and B. Fehr, *Archiv*, cix. 49–50), and Bodl. MS. Eng. poet. e. I., fol. 20ʳᵒ (printed by Wright, *Songs and Carols*, Percy Soc. xxiii. 18). It is printed from all three MSS. by Greene, *Early Eng. Carols*, pp. 54, 55. For remarks on MS. Ashmole 189 see above, Notes on No. 5.

The Sloane MS. after stanza 2 contains a stanza lacking in the other two:

> Ne mentem sompnus oprimat
> Betwyx an ox and an as
> Cryst hymself born he was
> De virgine Maria.

Each stanza begins with a line borrowed from the Latin hymn *Salvator mundi domine* (see *Sarum Breviary*, ii, col. 226, and *York Breviary*, i, col. 520).

80. *The Lord that Lay in Ass's Stall*

Occurs only in this MS.; previously printed in *Early Bodl. Music*, by Padelford, *Anglia*, xxxvi. 112–13, and by Greene, *Early Eng. Carols*, p. 23.

18, 19. Note the occurrence of the same rimes in Harding's *Chronicle*, cxiii. xvii:

> His barons for cause he was vndigne
> Made hym his crowne for to resigne.

Vndigne (as suggested for l. 19) is, of course, to be taken as modifying 'man-kynde'.

81. *The Maiden Makeles*

Occurs only in this MS.; previously printed by Wright, *Songs and Carols*, Warton Club, p. 30; by B. Fehr, *Archiv*, cix. 50; by Wülcker, *A. E. Lesebuch*, ii. 7; by Chambers & Sidgwick, *Early Eng. Lyrics*, p. 107; and by W. W. Greg, *Mod. Philol.* vii. 166.

82. *Her Son Recovers Us from Adam's Fall*

Occurs in this MS. only; previously printed by Chambers & Sidgwick, *Early Eng. Lyrics*, p. 133, and by Greene, *Early Eng. Carols*, p. 29.

A very similar burden appears in a Christmas carol in B.M. Addit. MS. 5665: 'Tydyngs trew / ther buthe come newe / Blessed be ihesu' (Fehr, *Archiv*, cvi. 272). Cf. also the first line of a Song of the Annunciation in Balliol Coll. MS. 354 (ed. Dyboski, EETS, ci. 39).

83. *Bless the Time the Apple was Taken*

Occurs only in this MS.; first printed by Wright, *Songs and Carols*, Warton Club, p. 32, and frequently reprinted.

84. *A New-Year Song of the Nativity*

Occurs also in St. John's Coll. Camb. MS. 259, fol. 11ro, from which it was first printed by James and Macaulay, *Mod. Lang. Rev.* viii. 83. It has been printed from the Sloane MS. by Wright, *Songs and Carols*, Warton Club, pp. 46–8, and *Specimens of Old Christmas Carols*, Percy Soc. iv. 8–9. It is printed from both MSS. by Greene, *Old Eng. Carols*, pp. 102–3.

85. *A Song for the Epiphany*

Occurs only in this MS.; previously printed by Greene, *Early Eng. Carols*, p. 8.

19. steryde] cf. the Sloane MS. of No. 123 (l. 27): 'He sterdyn the braynys up and doun'.

86. *Angels, Star, and Magi*

Previously printed from the Advocátes MS. by W. B. D. D. Turnbull, *Visions of Tundale*, pp. 139–40, by Karl Breul, *Engl. Stud.* xiv. 402–3, and by Chambers & Sidgwick, *Early Eng. Lyrics*, pp. 134–5. Another version is preserved in

Harley MS. 275, fol. 146vo, first printed in *Notes and Queries*, Second Ser., ix. 439. Both texts are printed by Greene, *Early Eng. Carols*, pp. 16–17.

In the Harley text, after a 2-line burden, 'Ioy we alle yn this feste / For verbum caro factum est' we have as the first stanza:

> Ihū almyghty kyng of blys
> Assumpsit carnem virginis
> He was euer & euermore ys
> Consors paterni luminis.

The Advocates MS., on the other hand, lacks the burden of the Harley MS. and has only the first two lines of what is the opening stanza in the latter. The four lines of this stanza, however, unite to form a perfect sequence so that the arrangement in Harley seems to be correct. In that case we must suppose that the last two lines of stanza 1 (and probably the burden also) were accidentally lost in the Advocates MS.

The second stanza of the Advocates text, on the other hand, is lacking in Harley. But the omission of this stanza, instead of causing any break, really improves the connexion, and avoids the repetition of the phrase 'to save monkynd' (ll. 3 and 7). The rimes in these lines are commonplaces (cf. No. 84, ll. 1, 2, and 10, 11); and hence this stanza may easily have been inserted later.

The Latin lines in this song seem to have been appropriated from several different hymns. For 'consors paterni luminis' (Harley, l. 6) see *Hymns of the Ang. Sax. Church* (Surtees Soc.), p. 18, and *York Breviary*, i, col. 775. 'Pastor creator omnium' occurs in the hymn of Sedulius, 'A solis ortus cardine' (*Hymns of the Ang. Sax. Church*, p. 50). 'Veni redemptor gencium' is the opening line of a Christmas hymn by Ambrose (*Hymns of the Ang. Sax. Church*, p. 43).

87. *The Journey of the Three Kings*

Also occurs in Sloane MS. 2593 (printed by Wright, *Songs and Carols*, Warton Club, pp. 40–2, and by B. Fehr, *Archiv*, cix. 54–5). It is printed from both Sloane and Porkington MSS. by Greene, *Early Eng. Carols*, pp. 80–2.

Stanzas 2 and 9 have no counterpart in Sloane; on the other hand, stanzas 3, 4, and 6 in Sloane are lacking in

Porkington. Of these three stanzas the first two directly
paraphrase the scriptural text, but with some poor rimes:
e.g. *pryse: pryse* (stanza 3) and *wynde* (for *wende*) in stanza 4.
Stanza 6 is identical with stanza 11 of No. 88—which in
the Sloane MS. stands on the page immediately preceding.

2. so fyndythe whe = so we learn.

5. The 'bold steward' in this stanza (lacking in Sloane)
carries an interesting suggestion of the popular ballad.

11. A traditional simile in expounding the conception of
the Virgin (cf. *English Lyr. of the XIIIth Cent.*, No. 4, l. 34,
No. 79, ll. 21–2; *Rel. Lyrics of the XIVth Cent.*, No. 31, l. 22),
though not here appropriate. But the line in Sloane, 'As
bryght as gold w^{t}ine þe glas' seems to be a meaningless
perversion.

25. gryll] 'fierce, angry' (cf. *Rel. Lyrics of the XIVth
Cent.*, No. 30, l. 15). The Sloane reading 'ille'—apparently
a modernization—is colourless.

88. *Balthazar, Melchior, and Jasper*

Previously printed from this MS. by Wright, *Songs and
Carols*, Warton Club, pp. 36–8; by B. Fehr, *Archiv*, cix.
52–3. A later version in Balliol Coll. MS. 354, fol. 222vo,
was printed by Flügel, *Anglia*, xxvi. 239–40, and by Dyboski, EETS, ci. 12–13. Both versions are printed by Greene,
Early Eng. Carols, pp. 79–80. The Balliol version (nine
stanzas) has the *cauda* 'Deo Patri sit gloria'; it does not
name the Magi.

29–40. These three stanzas are built on the same formula
and repeat the same rimes.

10. patriarck] obviously a corrupt reading. Balliol: 'Owt
of Egypt into Bedlem', but the meaning is not clear.

89. *The Three Kings and Herod*

Occurs only in this MS.; previously printed by James
and Macaulay, *Mod. Lang. Rev.* viii. 74–5.

33. cryb] formerly applied to 'a barred receptacle for
fodder, hay', &c. (*OED*). It is still used in this sense in
the compound, 'corn-crib'.

90. *Hostis Herodes Impie*

Occurs only in this MS.; previously printed by Wright,
Songs and Carols, Warton Club, pp. 95–6, and by B. Fehr,

Archiv, cix. 69. In the MS. the text of the Latin original stands above the several stanzas of the English poem. For the version by Friar Herebert, a century earlier, see *Rel. Lyrics of the XIVth Cent.*, No. 12. The 'Hostis Herodes' comprises merely a small section of an alphabetical Advent hymn by Sedulius, of which the complete text is printed in the *Corpus Scriptorum Eccles. Lat.* x. 163 ff. The hymn 'Hostis Herodes' was sung at Vespers on the Vigil of Epiphany—see *York Breviary*, i, col. 160.

91. *The Story of the Passion*

Not heretofore printed from this MS. This poem occurs also in the 'Makculloch MS.', Univ. of Edinburgh, Laing 149, fol. 86ᵛᵒ (printed Scottish Text Soc. 65, p. 10) and in Advocates MS. 1.1.6 ('Bannatyne MS.'), fol. 33ᵛᵒ (printed in the Hunterian Club ed. of the Bannatyne MS., pp. 89–91).

11. nardus-specative] spikenard. This is a pedantic attempt to carry over into English the Latin term in the Vulgate, where the genitive form of this word appears as 'nardi spicati'.

24. Locostratus] A corruption of 'Lithostratus', the reading in the Vulgate (John 19. 13).

25. Scil. *quhilk* before *was*. Cf. 96.23 and 102.35.

60. decurio] councillor; cf. Mark 15. 43: 'venit Joseph ab Arimathia, nobilis decurio'.

92. *Thy Blood Thou Shed for Me*

This meditation on the Passion, consisting of eight 8-line stanzas, followed by an 'Oracio' in four stanzas, is found also in Harley MS. 1706 and in Longleat MS. 30. The Oracio alone occurs in Douce MS. 322 in the Bodleian. This poem has not hitherto been printed from any MS.

In the Harley MS. the poem appears with the heading: 'Howe our lorde ihū seuene tymes bleed for vs.' Immediately above this heading is written (fol. 210ʳᵒ):

'As clerkes seyne and specyally Seynt Anselme þere were vppon þe blessed and moste gloryouse body of oure lorde ihū cryste open woundes by nombre .v. þousand iiij hundred seuenty and fyue.'

This is the number of Wounds as given elsewhere, for example in the riming lines in B.M. Addit. MS. 37049, fol. 24ʳᵒ. The

basis of the computation appears in a statement (Harley
MS. 2869, fol. 204ro) that by saying 15 Pater Nosters and
Aves daily for a year one will have worshipped the full
number of the Wounds: $15 \times 365 = 5,475$.

The number of drops of blood which issued from the
Wounds was stated as 547,500, a sum arrived at by a similar
computation: see Trinity Coll. Camb. MS. 601, fol. 277vo:

> Yef thow wolt worshyp synglerly
> W^t oon Pater Noster deuoutly
> Euery drope of þ^t blessyd blode
> Whyche þ^t oure lorde opon the rode
> Shed for vs then must þ^u sey
> Ane hundred Pater Nosters euery day
> Duryng the space of XV yere.

$100 \times 365 \times 15 = 547,500$. This is the actual number of
drops as stated in a group of four MSS., though MS. Douce 1,
through a scribal error, gives the number as 548,500.

93. *The Hours of the Cross*

Occurs only in this MS.; not previously printed.
18, 20 fast: facys. Non-riming lines.

94. *The Dolours of Our Lady*

Occurs only in this MS.; previously printed by Karl
Brunner, *Engl. Stud.* lxx. 106–9.

95. *Behold Jesus on the Cross*

Occurs only in this MS.; previously printed by Morris,
Legends of the Holy Rood, EETS, pp. 150–2, and by Heuser,
Anglia, xxvii. 304–5.

96. *The Seven Words from the Cross*

Occurs only in this MS.; not previously printed.

97. *The Mourners at the Cross*

Occurs only in this MS.; previously printed by Mac-
Cracken, *Archiv*, cxxx. 305.

98. *For Thy Sake Let the World Call Me Fool*

Occurs only in this MS.; previously printed by Legg,

Processional of the Nuns of Chester (Henry Bradshaw Soc'y), p. 28.

99. *The Child that Died for Us*

Occurs only in this MS.; not previously printed.

100. *The Wounds, as Wells of Life*

These lines, which occur in no other MS., were printed in the *Register of Mid. Engl. Relig. and Didactic Verse*, i. 262.

This figure of the Wounds as wells is further developed in a prayer 'Of the .v. woundes' still unprinted (*Register*, No. 625) in 6-line stanzas: 'Of the Ryght Hande Well of Mercy', 'Of the Lyft Hande Welle of Grace' [one 6-line stanza to each], 'Of the Welle of Lyfe' (*i.e.* the spear-wound) [three stanzas rime-royal], 'Of the Ryght Fote, Welle of Pyte', 'Of the Lyfte Fote Welle of Comforte'.

The same idea occurs in a vision related in Harley 2869 (fol. 204vo–205ro). Our Lord appeared to 'A womman solytary and recluse' and said to her: 'Þei þat seye þese orysouns xv dayes byfore his deþ he schal se my holy body and it receyue, and þerby be dylyueryd from euerlastyng hunger. And I schall him ȝif drynk of my blood so he schal neuer þruste. And I schal put byfore hym sygne of my vyctoryos passyoune in defense & subsydy aȝenst alle hys enmys. And byforne hys deþ I schal come wiþ my dere modyr and I schal take and lede his soule into euerlastyng ioye, & whan I haue þedyr browȝth I schal bryng hym to drynk a drawȝth of þe welle & of þe chaleis of my godhede.'

101. *An Alphabetical Devotion to the Cross*

Occurs only in this MS.; previously printed in the *English Register of Godstow Nunnery*, EETS, p. 4, and by Patterson, *Middle Engl. Penitential Lyric*, pp. 137–8.

There is a fourteenth-century ABC poem on the Passion in Harley MS. 3954 (printed by Furnivall, *Pol. Rel. and Love Poems*, EETS, rev. ed. pp. 271 ff.). An 'Alphabetical' poem in rime royal in honour of the B.V. occurs in Leyden MS. Voss 9, pp. 223–30 (printed by MacCracken, *Archiv*, cxxxi. 56–60). Still another 'Alphabetical' beginning: 'cryste crosse me spede & seynt nycolas' is found in Caius Coll. Camb. MS. 174 (unprinted; see *Register of Mid. Eng. Relig. and Didactic Verse*, No. 412).

22. Crist = X (see *Pol. Rel. and Love Poems*, rev. ed. p. 276).

24. Sende] For alphabetical purposes this should be written Zende (which would be the Kentish spelling).

25, 26. The 'And' and the initial 'C' seem to stand for the 'EtC.' which in the horn-books followed the alphabet.

27. 'Titulle' and 'Poynt' denote, in the first place, signs of punctuation, such as were added in the horn-books. They are also used here as words: 'Title' and 'Appoint'.

102. *'Thou Sinful Man that by Me Goes'*

Not heretofore printed from this MS. A defective text of this piece occurs in the 'Makculloch MS.', Univ. of Edinburgh Laing MS. 149 (printed by Stevenson, *Scottish Text Soc'y*, No. 65, pp. 33–6). A third text, likewise defective, stands in B.M. Addit. MS. 37049, fol. 27vo. This was printed by Dyce in his ed. of the *Works of Skelton* (i. 144 ff.), but F. Brie (*Engl. Stud.* xxxvii. 22–6) has disproved Skelton's authorship.

Comparison of the three texts shows that the Addit. and Edinb. MSS. agree with each other more closely than with Arundel. Addit. and Edinb. omit four stanzas contained in Arundel; on the other hand they contain one stanza not found in Arundel. In its general theme this piece is a development of fourteenth-century lyrics (cf. Nos. 46 and 74 in *Rel. Lyrics of the XIVth Cent.*) which went back for their suggestion ultimately to the scriptural verse, 'O vos omnes, qui transitis per viam', &c. (Lam. l. 12). As George C. Taylor (*Mod. Philol.* v. 26 ff.) has shown, thirteen stanzas of this poem are incorporated verbally in Towneley Play XXVI (ll. 244–321).

26. This mekill vnseill] Cf. Towneley Play XII, 3: 'here is mekyll vnceyll / and long has it last'.

127–9. The rimes in these lines are English, not Scotch.

149. 'Bot faynd þe fast fra syn to fle'—Cf. York Play xviii. 149: 'And fande þe furthe faste for to flee'

103. *Woefully Arrayed*

Not heretofore printed from this MS. The text of these verses ending at l. 27 is copied twice in B M. Addit. MS. 5465 (early sixteenth century) printed by B. Fehr, *Archiv*, cvi. 62–3. Also a fragmentary text (burden and stanza 2) is written on the last leaf of a vellum MS. (fifteenth century) described in Quaritch's Sale Catalogue No. 474, Lot 148. Still another text is written in a sixteenth-century hand on the fly-leaf of Richard Heber's copy of the pseudo-Boethian *De Discip. schol. cum notabili commento* (printed at Deventer 1496). The Heber volume was sold by Sotheby, Nov. 1834 (Catal. of Heber's Lib., Part III, p. 54, Item 810), and its present owner is not known. The Heber text inserts (after l. 27 according to Harley) a unique stanza. It repeats ll. 28–9 of the Harley text, but from that point to the end diverges widely.

The Heber copy of these verses concludes with the ascription, 'Explicit q^d Skelton'. Dyce accepts this ascription and prints the last two stanzas from this fly-leaf copy (*Poetical Works of Skelton*, i. 141–3). The lines peculiar to the Heber copy, however, are distinctly inferior to the rest of the poem. Moreover, Woefully Arrayed represents a tradition which seems too early for Skelton: note the assurances of pardon 'grauntid be diuers Bisshopis' at the beginning and end of the Harley text.

104. 'Unkind Man, Take Heed of Me'

Printed for the first time from the Harley MS. An almost identical text occurs in Camb. Univ. Ii. 1. 2, fol. 126vo.

In the Harley MS. these verses are preceded by the text of the Latin original, 'O homo vide quid pro te patior', here incorrectly ascribed to St. Bernard. The English translator has expanded each of the seven Latin lines into a couplet. In the fourteenth century there was a closer translation of the Latin into five English couplets (*Rel. Lyrics of the XIVth Cent.*, No. 70).

The 30-line English text in Camb. Univ. Dd. 5. 64 (*Rel. Lyrics of the XIVth Cent.*, No. 77) was made by adding 16 lines from some other source to the 14-line translation of the 'O homo vide'. That this fourteenth-century text was a combination of material is shown by the appearance in the fifteenth century of the same 14-line version of the 'O homo vide' *without* the material appended from a different source.

4. the] *read* thi loue as in Camb. Dd.
9. of] *read* owt of as in Camb. Dd.

105. '*Why Art Thou, Man, Unkind?*'

Occurs in no other MS.; but a text was printed (*c.* 1550)
by W. Copland, of which some fragments (ll. 10–24, 33–40)
are preserved in the Bodleian as Douce Fragm. f. 48. This
poem was previously printed from the MS. by Helen E.
Sandison, *Chanson d'Aventure in Mid. English*, pp. 110–13.
The poem in its essential theme is a development of the
'Popule meus, quid feci tibi', of which there are several
examples in the fourteenth century (see especially *Rel.
Lyrics of the XIVth Cent.*, No. 72).

8. This refrain line appears again (with the change from
first person to third) in the burden and refrain of No. 106.
Cf. also ll. 9–10 of No. 107: 'Man, qwat haue I done to þe? /
qwy art þu, man, to me vnkynde?'

13, 14. 'Thou art the fairest creature in Nature, for I
placed thee above, like to myself.' See ll. 41–7.

17 ff. Christ's plea for the love of man, his brother, seems
to contain literal reminiscences of the 'Quia amore langueo'
(*Rel. Lyrics of the XIVth Cent.*, No. 132) in which the B.V.
makes a similar appeal.

23. *Yt* (here and also in ll. 39, 60, 73, 77, 79, and 99) is
a dialect form of the conjunction *Yit* or *ʒit*.

106. *What More Could Christ Have Done?*

Occurs only in this MS.; previously printed by Greene,
Early Eng. Carols, p. 228. For remarks on this Ashmole MS.
see above, Notes on No. 5.

107. *A Dialogue Between Natura Hominis and Bonitas Dei*

Occurs also in Tanner MS. 110 (fol. 238ro) in the Bodleian;
not previously printed.

This is a development into dialogue of the older type of
poem on the 'Popule meus, quid feci tibi' theme. The dialogue form of this theme was expanded to 544 lines in
William Lychefelde's 'Complaint of God' (see *Register*, No.
1672).

20. Tanner MS.: 'lete not be lore throgh synful wrake'. This removes the difficulty in the syntax but still leaves the rime defective.

29, 31. Note the defective rimes—*fedde: had*.

47. Tanner MS.: 'I myght a destroyed the wel inoughe'. This corrects the metre and gives a rime for *slowe*.

108. *Querela Divina: Responsio Humana*

Previously printed from this MS. by Miss F. M. M. Comper, *Life and Lyrics of Rolle*, p. 317. A variant text of these verses is inscribed on the walls of the church at Almondbury, West Riding of Yorkshire. A transcript of this inscription will be found in B.M. Addit. MS. 36505.

Besides the text here printed, B.M. 37049 contains at fol. 24ro a single 6-line stanza beginning 'O man kynde / hafe in þi mynde / my passion smert'. This single stanza (which may have been the basis of the 24-line text) occurs also in Tanner MS. 407, fol. 52vo, and in Trin. Coll. Camb. 1157, fol. 69ro.

109. *Brother, Abide*

Occurs only in the Helmingham Hall MS.; not hitherto printed.

110. *'Have All My Heart and Be in Peace'*

Occurs only in this MS.; not hitherto printed. Following the English verses is a Latin distich here (as often) attributed to Ovid:

Ouidius
Nescio quid sit amor nec amo nec amor nec amaui
Set scio si quis amat iritur [sic!] igne graui.

Ll. 21–4, in which Christ's love for the soul is set forth in erotic terms, may be compared with two couplets in a fifteenth-century hand which occur in an English prose collection of Saints' Lives in Trinity Coll. Dublin MS. 319 (fol. 88ro):

Thynke on me and haue in mynde
How I to the haue be so kynde
And loke thow neuer louer take
But me that dyed for thy sake.

111. *Christ Triumphant*

These lines occur only in this MS.; they have not heretofore been printed.

112. *Aloft is Risen the Great Illuminer*

Occurs only in this MS.; not heretofore printed.

113. *The Lord is Risen from Death to Life*

Occurs only in this MS.; not heretofore printed.

10. feid (< O.Fr. fede, feide, faide) Active hatred or enmity. See *OED* s.v. feud: 'In 14–15th c. the word occurs only in Sc. writers, the form being always *fede*, *feide*, or something phonetically equivalent.'

114. *The Bread Come from Heaven*

Occurs only in this MS.; previously printed by Wright, *Songs and Carols*, Warton Club, p. 60; by B. Fehr, *Archiv*, cix. 62; and by Greene, *Early Eng. Carols*, p. 219.

115. *An Orison of the Sacrament and Creed*

Not heretofore printed. The first line is identical with that of the prayer (six couplets) at the 'levacion' (elevation of the Host) in Myrc's *Instructions for Parish Priests* (EETS, ll. 290–301). And ll. 27–8 also are taken over from this source (ll. 292–3). But ll. 1–12 in Challoner follow more directly a Latin prayer found in the *Horae* of Sarum and York:

In eleuatione corporis Christi.
Ave verum corpus natum / de Maria Virgine
Vere passum, immolatum / in cruce pro homine.
Cuius latus perforatum / vnda fluxit sanguine.
Esto nobis pregustatum / mortis in examine
O dulcis, o pie, / O Iesu, fili Marie.   (Mone, i. 280)

The 19-line prayer at the 'levacion' in B.M. Addit. MS. 27924 (fol. 231ro) appears to be merely an expansion of Myrc's prayer.

13. me say] *me* is a weakened form of *man* = Fr. *on* or Germ. *man*.

116. *By a Chapel as I Came*

Occurs only in this MS.; previously printed by Helen E.

Sandison, *Chanson d'Aventure in Mid. Eng.*, p. 102, and by Greene, *Early Eng. Carols*, p. 223.
6. Collas. Probably Nicholas.

117. *The Mystery of the Incarnation*

Now printed for the first time from the original MS.; previously printed (Greene, *Early Eng. Carols*, p. 185) from B.M. Addit. MS. 24542, a nineteenth-century transcript by Joseph Hunter. A closely related piece—four stanzas (*aaaa*) with refrain: 'Meruele noȝt iosep', &c.—is preserved in B.M. Addit. MS. 5665 (first printed by Wright, *Specimens of Old Christmas Carols*, Percy Soc. iv. 52).

118. *Three Things Against Nature*

Only these two stanzas are found in the Helmingham Hall MS. (written in an early sixteenth-century hand). Cotton Vespasian A. xxv, fol. 131vo (written *c.* 1580) contains five additional stanzas. Greene, *Early Eng. Carols*, pp. 60–2, prints the Cotton text with collation of the two stanzas from the Helmingham MS. These lines in the Helmingham MS. seem complete as they stand, and it is questionable whether the stanzas added in the Cotton MS. formed part of the original poem.

119. *Faith is Above Reason*

The A and C versions were printed from these MSS. in *Rel. Antiq.* i. 127 and 207 (reprinted by Flügel, *Anglia*, xxvi. 174). The B version has not heretofore been printed. The text of these lines in Gascoigne's *Theol. Dictionary* (Lincoln Coll. Oxf. MSS. 117, 118) as printed in the Rolls Ser. ed. of *Pecock's Repressor*, ii. 623, agrees most closely with the A-version. For references to still other MS. texts see *Register of Mid. Eng. Relig. and Didactic Verse*, No. 2672.

120. *The Divine Paradox*

Occurs only in this MS., written on a fly-leaf by a sixteenth-century hand; not heretofore printed. These verses may possibly be subsequent to 1500, but they show verbal dependence on No. 119 which unquestionably was composed by Bp. Pecock.

The paradoxical character of these lines recalls the amazed

perplexity of the demons when Christ descended to Hell:
'Hic si reus esset, tam potens non esset. Si eum aliqua
peccata fuscarent, nunquam nostra tartara suo dissiparet
fulgore. Si Deus, utquid venit ? Si homo, quid praesumpsit ?
Si Deus, quid in sepulcro facit ? Si homo, quare peccatores
solvit ? Numquid cum auctore nostro foedus composuit ?'
(Migne, *Patr. Lat.* xxxix, col. 2060).

121. *God Bids Us Use Reason and Evidence*

Previously printed from this MS. by Greene, *Early Eng.
Carols*, pp. 229–30. The first three lines of this text are parallel
to a song in Bodl. MS. Eng. poet. *e. l.*, fol. 24vo (printed
by Wright, *Songs and Carols*, Percy Soc. xxiii. 30–1, and
by Greene, op. cit., p. 229).

12. nassone] = Naasson (Matt. 1. 4).

22. in faynyt] Some emendation is required: the meaning
would be brought out by reading, 'infirme yn wyt'.

122. *An Orison to St. John the Baptist*

Previously printed from this MS. by Dr. Mabel Day,
EETS, No. 155, p. 74.

123. *The Martyrdom of St. Thomas*

Not heretofore printed from this MS. Other texts occur
in Sloane MS. 2593, fol. 23vo (printed by Wright, *Songs and
Carols*, Warton Club, pp. 66–8, and by Greene, *Early Eng.
Carols*, p. 72—with collations), in Balliol Coll. MS. 354,
fol. 227vo (printed by Flügel, *Anglia*, xxvi. 255–6, and by
Dyboski, EETS, Ext. Ser. ci. 31) and in Chancery Miscel-
lanea, Pub. Record Office, Bundle 34, File 1, No. 12.

9–12. In Sloane and Balliol this stanza precedes ll. 5–8.

24. Following this line the other MSS. insert a stanza
lacking in Caius:

> Beforn his aunter he knelyd adoun
> Ther they gunne to paryn his crown ;
> He sterdyn the braynys up and doun
> Optans celi gaudia.

But this stanza presents manifest difficulties. The scattering
of Thomas's brains should not *precede* the attack upon him
(ll. 25–6). 'He sterdyn' must be plural, since it refers to the

action of the murderers. But 'Optans' is singular, and in any case why should the assassins hope for the joys of heaven?

31. fyftene tokenus] A reference, as Greene (*Early Eng. Carols*, p. 374) points out, to the Constitutions of Clarendon (1164) which were drawn up under 16 heads. The original MS. probably read 'syxtene' with a long *s* which was mistaken for *f*. The Sloane MS. reads 'lii poyntes'; and the MS. in the Pub. Record Office 'fiute i poyttes', which is very similar to the 'fyfte poyntis' in Awdelay's poem on the same subject (Ed. Whiting, EETS, 181, p. 191).

124. *Prayer to Mary and All Saints*

Occurs only in this MS.; not heretofore printed.

125. *A Prayer of the Holy Name*

Occurs only in this MS.; previously printed by MacCracken, *Archiv*, cxxxi. 43.

The Festum Dulcissimi Nominis Jesu (7 August) finds a place in a Durham Kalendar of the end of the fourteenth century (see Hampson, *Medii Ævi Kalendarium*, i. 448), and a number of Latin hymns for this Feast occur in medieval Breviaries (see Daniel, *Thes. Hymn.* i. 315, 317; ii. 262; also Dreves, *Anal.* xi. 16). The hymn 'Exultet cor praecordiis / sonante Iesu nomine' shows some resemblance in stanza 6 to ll. 1–5 of the English poem:

> Nomen tuum nos muniat,
> praeservans a periculis,
> et in bonis perficiat
> amotis culpae maculis.

In general, however, one would say that the English verses are of the nature of a loric prayer, and were not intended for the Church service. See also the 6-line prayer: 'Ihesus Iesu for thy holly name', in MS. Rawl. C. 48, f. 134ᵛᵒ, and other MSS.

7. to-to obey] yield completely.

126. *Keep Me To-day from Shame and Sin*

Occurs only in this MS.; not heretofore printed.

127. *An Evening Prayer, I*

Occurs only in this MS.; not heretofore printed.

128. *An Evening Prayer, II*

This prayer and the one which follows are found together in this MS. and also in Trinity Coll. Camb. MS. 601. Both prayers have been printed from the Trinity MS. by Mac-Cracken, *Archiv*, cxxx. 286–311. They have not heretofore been printed from the Ashmole MS.

1. Trin.: Now Ihū lord.
12. Trin.: late my hert.
14. Trin.: ffoule dremes and fro.
15. Trin.: kepe me this.

129. *A Morning Prayer*

The Trinity MS. prefixes an introductory stanza (= ll. 23, 24, 21, 22 of No. 128).

1. Trin.: Now Ihu lord.
2, 4. Trin.: kept . . wakyd . . slept.
7. Trin.: That myself . . . fall in.
15. Trin.: or fo.
22. Trin.: boundyn to

25–8. This concluding stanza occurs separately in Durham Cath. MS. A. iv. 25—see Rudd's Cat. of Durham MSS.

Amen q^d Rate: This signature appears also after the poem of moral instruction which precedes in the Ashmole MS. This may be the same person who is cited at the end of a long treatise on the instruction of children,

> The quhilk is ratis raving cald,
> Bot for na raving I it hald. (EETS, No. 43, p. 76).

130. *Speed Our King on His Journey*

Occurs only in this MS.; not heretofore printed. This poem and the one which follows relate to the expedition to France made by Henry VI in 1430. The following entries are taken from a Chronicle in Cott. MS. Julius B. i (ed. C. L. Kingsford, *Chronicles of London*, Oxf. 1905, pp. 96, 97): 'In this same year [1429] vpon saint Leonardys day [Nov. 6] was Kyng Herry the vj^te not ffully viij yeer off age, crovned at Westm[inster] . . . and on saint George day [April 23] next ffolowynge he passed ouer the see to Caleys, and the xxiij day of May ayenst nyht byfore the tovne off Compayne ther was a woman takyn y-armed in the ffeld with many other worthy capyteyns, the whiche was called Pucell de Dieux. . . . In this same yere oure lege lorde the kyng was crovned kyng in ffraunce in the citee of Parys [by Cardinal Beaufort at Notre Dame, 16 Dec. 1431] . . . And the same yeer he kom out off ffraunce in to Caleys. And after the ffest of Candelmas he kom ouer the see and in short tyme to London [21 Feb. 1432].' Thus he was absent from London nearly two years.

The present piece may be compared with a litany in twenty-four 8-line stanzas beginning:

> Kyrieleyson haue mercy good lorde
> Xp̄eleyson we crye now to þe,

with the refrain: 'And now & euer ora pro nobis'. Copies of this litany are found in Huntington MS. HM. 142 and in Longleat MS. 30. But, though similar in metre and arrangement, this litany contains no personal references and was not composed, like the other, for a particular occasion.

15. port and prynce] *i.e.* haven and ruler in his enterprise. On 'port' in this sense see the *Pilgrimage of the Life of Man* (EETS, Ext. Ser. lxxxiii. 455): 'that taught me, and was so goode a guyde to aryven vp at so holsom a Port, and at so notable an havene, to ffynde Reffuyt and Refuge.' Here also, it should be noted, the figure is one of a voyage and the reference is to the Virgin.

97–8. 'Henry VI arrived at Calais on the 23d or 27th of April 1430, being accompanied by the Dukes of York and Norfolk, the Bishops of Bath, Ely, and Rochester, seven Earls and eleven Barons' (*Proceedings of Privy Council*, iv. p. x–xi).

131. *Mary, Take in Your Hand this Dread Voyage*

Occurs only in this MS.; not heretofore printed. Whereas the preceding piece was a prayer *for* the King this is a prayer spoken *by* the King before his voyage.

3. your blessed day] *i.e.* Lady Day or March 25, the Feast of the Annunciation. This was some four weeks before the date on which the King embarked for France.

50. A reference to the reverses which the English armies

had suffered from the French under the leadership of Joan of Arc.

60. The King is here addressing his mother, Queen Katharine. Line 64 makes it impossible to regard it as addressed to the Virgin.

67. In other words, for the happy reunion of mother and son on his return from France.

132. *Lovely Angel, Keep Me Day and Night*

Occurs only in this MS.; not heretofore printed.
12. & deedly synne] read: 'al deedly synne'.

133. *My Keeper, so Sweet*

Previously printed from this MS. by Karl Brunner, *Archiv*, cxxxii. 318. Another text of this piece occurs in Magdalene Coll. Camb. MS. 13, fol. 28vo.

134. *O Sweet Angel, Bring Me to Bliss*

Occurs only in this MS.; previously printed by J. W. Legg, *Processional of the Nuns of Chester* (Henry Bradshaw Soc'y), p. 27. Immediately following 'The versicull' is a 'Collect' in prose beginning: 'O my lorde Ihu crist as it hathe pleasede the to Assigne an Angell to wayte on me dayly and nyghtly.'

135. *A Heavenly Star, Most Comfortable of Light*

Occurs only in this MS.; not heretofore printed. A few lines at the top of fol. 282, both recto and verso, have been rendered almost illegible by the use of galls or chemicals.

136. *Stella Celi Extirpavit*

Now first printed from the Chetham MS. MacCracken (*Minor Poems of Lydg.*, pp. 294–5) prints the text from Harley 2255, with collations from four other MSS. but these contain only the first four stanzas. 'Stella Celi extirpavit' appears in the Horae in the prayers to the B.V. against pestilence—see E. Hoskins, *Horae Beatae Mariae Virginis*, &c., pp. 165, 169.

44. 'Competent' and 'condigne' are found together in the same line in the *Fall of Princes*, vi. 618.

137. *Parce Mihi, Domine*

Occurs only in this MS.; not heretofore printed.

138. *All Ten Commandments I Have Broken*

Occurs only in this MS.; not heretofore printed.

139. *I Have Lived After My Lust*

Occurs only in this MS.; previously printed by Flügel, *Anglia*, xii. 268. In the MS. these verses are accompanied with musical score.

140. *Out of Sin My Soul Unbind*

Previously printed from this MS. by MacCracken, *Archiv*, cxxxi. 43–4; also occurs in B.M. Addit. MS. 39574, fol. 52ᵛᵒ, from which it has been printed by Dr. Mabel Day, *The Wheatley MS.*, EETS, pp. 67–9.

25–32. This stanza is lacking in the Wheatley MS. Instead, the Wheatley inserts at this point three stanzas not found in the Camb. MS.

141. *Thy Gifts I Have Expended Unprofitably*

Not heretofore printed; this prayer occurs also in Lambeth MS. 344, fol. 13ʳᵒ (a sister MS. of Hatton).

The text of the Latin original is written at the top of fol. 121ʳᵒ, immediately preceding the English verses:

O Dñe deus omnipotens benedictus sis tu qui me creasti et redemisti. Et cum Dampnacione dignus essem in peccatis tollerasti & ad penitenciam reseruasti, recognosco domine coram magestate tua omnia quecunque dedisti michi ad salutem invtiliter & dampnabiliter expendisse. Videlicet, tempus penitencie mee in vanitatibus, corpus in superfluitatibus, graciam baptismi in superbiis, et omnia delexi plus quam te, creatorem & redemptorem, nutritorem et conseruatorem meum. Et ideo misericordiam tuam peto quia miser sum ex me, et quia non agnoui benignam pacienciam tuam in me. Non tuam horrendam equitatem non attendebam quid tibi pro innumerabilibus bonis tuis responderem, set e contra de die in diem te malis meis prouocabam, propterea non habeo nisi vnicum uerbum ad te, scilicet: Miserere mei deus secundum magnam misericordiam tuam.

A prose translation of this Latin prayer occurs in Lansdowne MS. 381, fol. 60ʳᵒ. The fidelity of the English verses to the original text is noteworthy.

142. *Though I Have Been a Wretch, I Hope for Mercy*

Occurs only in this MS.; not heretofore printed.

21, 22. Non-riming lines.

35, 36. Defective rime.

143. *O Redeemer, Purge Me of My Vices*

Occurs only in this MS.; not heretofore printed.

4. The 'Arms of Christ' were meditations on the instruments of the Crucifixion; see the verses printed in *Legends of the Holy Rood*, EETS, pp. 170–92.

144. *Jesu, Mercy for My Misdeeds*

This prayer has not heretofore been printed from this MS.; it occurs also in Trinity Coll. Camb. MS. 223, fol. 53ʳᵒ (printed by Furnivall, *Pol. Rel. and Love Poems*, rev. ed. pp. 133–8, and by Patterson, *Middle Eng. Penitential Lyric*, pp. 75–80. The 'Alia Oracio', consisting of five stanzas in the same measure, follows in both MSS. and is here treated as a pendent, though with separate line numbers. Patterson detaches it and prints it on pp. 134–5.

141. mure] Cf. *Jacob's Well*, EETS, Orig. Ser. 115, p. 254: 'benignite, þat is to suffer & to be mure & noȝt veniable, ne holde wratthe in herte.' An East Anglian dialect word—see *Engl. Dial. Dict.*

Alia Oracio 30. a loue-likyng Camb. MS. *reads*: a lufely kynge!

145. *Our Three Foes Make Us Mis-speak, Mis-think, Mis-do*

Previously printed from this MS. by Dr. Mabel Day, EETS, 155, p. 73.

146. *A Song of 'Sins'*

Occurs only in this MS.; not heretofore printed.

16. tene & treyne] apparently a variation (for the sake of rime) of the frequent 'tray and teen' and 'teen and tray' = 'pain and vexation'. 'trey' does not properly take an -*n* plural, nor does this phrase elsewhere show a plural form.

147. *The Day of Life—Night Comes Soon!*

Previously printed from this MS. by Halliwell, *Early Eng.
Miscell.*, Warton Club, pp. 9–12. This poem occurs also in
Lambeth 853, pp. 58–61 (printed by Furnivall, *Hymns to
Virgin and Christ*, pp. 83–5), and in Bodl. MS. Lat. misc. e.
85, fol. 81ᵛᵒ.

9–16. This stanza is lacking in Lambeth.

17 and 19 non-riming lines. Lamb. rimes: morewe: sorewe.

54. blake and bowe] Lamb.: & blac of ble.

57. wondorly I waxe] Lamb.: y droupid faste.

59. goone] Lamb.: paste.

148. *God Send Us Patience in Our Old Age*

Not heretofore printed from this MS. It occurs also in
Lambeth 853 (printed by Furnivall, *Hymns to the Virgin
and Christ*, pp. 79–82).

16. feynte] ? read 'shente' and restore the rime.

43–4. Cf. Gower (of somnolence): 'That ofte he goth to
bedde unkist'—*Conf. Am.* iv. 2712.

149. *Farewell, this World is but a Cherry Fair*

Not heretofore printed from this MS. It occurs also in
the later Balliol Coll. MS. 354 (printed by Flügel, *Anglia*,
xxvi. 198, and by Dyboski, EETS, Ext. Ser. ci. 87–8). The
fifth stanza which is lacking in the Trinity Coll. MS. is
found separately in Lansdowne MS. 762, fol. 19ᵛᵒ (printed
in *Rel. Antiq.* i. 268).

8. Cf. *Rel. Lyrics of the XIVth Cent.*, No. 117, l. 85: 'þis
world nis but a chirie faire'.

21. i.e. the summons to Judgement; cf. *Rel. Lyrics of the
XIVth Cent.*, No. 103, ll. 67–8: 'Whon Gabriel schal blowe
his horn / His feble fables schul hym rewe'. See also No. 120,
l. 57.

150. *Man Begins and Ends in Wretchedness*

Not heretofore printed from this MS. The first stanza
only occurs in the Bannatyne MS. (Advocates MS. 1.1.6)
at fol. 74ᵛᵒ (Hunterian Club ed. of the *Bannatyne MS.*,
p. 201).

151. *Vanitas Vanitatum*

Occurs only in this MS.; not heretofore printed. On 'Rate' whose signature stands at the end of this piece, see above, Note on No. 129.

152. *A Mirror for Young Ladies at Their Toilet*

Occurs only in this MS.; not heretofore printed.

153. *On the Untimely Death of a Fair Lady*

Occurs only in these MS.; not heretofore printed. The very remarkable personal tone in these verses (cf. ll. 30–49) distinguishes them sharply from other elegies in Middle English.

31. Cf. *The Siege of Jerusalem* (MS. Cott. Calig.) l. 128: 'Ther is no cownter ne clerke can hem rekyn alle' (ed. EETS, 188).

36. fynyse] here used intransitively; Lydgate has several cases of the word in the transitive sense.

44. enbleshed] Cf. the forms in Lydgate: enbelissche (*T.B.* ii. 5025), t'enbelishe (*Fall. Pr.* ii. 3577).

154. *The Mirror of Mortality*

Not heretofore printed from this MS. Another text occurs in Cotton MS. Caligula A. ii, fol. 57ᵛᵒ (printed by Varnhagen, *Anglia*, vii. 85 ff.).

The Cotton MS. omits ll. 49–56, the stanza which mentions Rauf lord Cromwell, and alters l. 60 to read: 'Thenk, all mankende schall reste under erthe and ston.' Also in l. 63 Cotton changes 'heme to preserve' to 'us to preserve'. The evident purpose in these changes was to efface all personal references.

28. Calig. A. ii: þat were ry3t kny3tly yn hare tyme. . . .

49–56. This stanza enables us to fix definitely not only the date but also the place at which the poem was composed. Ralph, Lord Cromwell, was Lord High Treasurer of the Exchequer from Aug. 1433 to July 1443; and in 1444/5 was appointed Constable of Nottingham Castle and Warden of Sherwood Forest. In 1439 he founded at Tattershall (Lincolnshire) the College of the Holy Trinity for seven priests, six laymen, and six choristers; the chaplains were to maintain divine service continually, and to pray for the King and for the souls of the founder and his grandmother, Dame Matilda Cromwell (*Victoria Co. Hist. of Lincolnshire*, ii. 237). The endowment of the College was further increased between 1448 and 1454 (*Calendar Rot. Char. et Inq. ad quod damn.*, Lond. 1803, p. 389, col. 2). Lord Cromwell died 4 Jan. 1454 and was buried at Tattershall in the tomb to which the poem makes reference. Lady Cromwell's death followed on 15 Sept. of the same year and she was buried beside her husband. The poem must have been composed at Tattershall, and in all probability by one of the Chaplains of the College.

55–6. These lines imply that when they were written Lord and Lady Cromwell were still living. On the other hand, ll. 59–60 refer to them as already resting in the tomb.

155. *Three Lessons to Make Ready for Death*

Occurs only in this MS.; not heretofore printed.

156. *Against Death Is no Defence*

Occurs only in this MS.; printed by Stevenson, Scottish Text Soc., vol. 65, p. 13.

45. Scil. *quhilk* before *most*.

157. *Devouring Death Makes All Unbold*

These lines are found only in this MS.; not heretofore printed.

158. *Knight, King, Clerk Wend to Death*

Previously printed from all three MSS. by Karl Brunner, *Archiv*, clxvii. 21–2. The source of these verses is a Latin poem in thirty-four distiches printed from a thirteenth-century MS. by W. F. Storck (*Zs. für d. Philol.* xlii. 422–8). The distiches which parallel the English lines run as follows:

Vado mori, rex sum, quid honor, quid gloria mundi?
Est via mors hominis regia: vado mori.

Vado mori miles, belli certamine victor.
Mortem non didici vincere: vado mori.

Vado mori logicus, aliis concludere novi.
Conclusit breviter mors michi: vado mori.

159. *The Lament of the Soul of Edward IV*

Not hitherto printed from this MS.; occurs also in B.M. Addit. MS. 29729, fol. 8ro, with the following note at the end of the text: 'Explicit ye Epitaffe of King Edward the fowrth made by *John Lidgate monke of Bury*'. A later hand has cancelled the words in italics and replaced them by the word Skelton. The correction is probably to be credited to Stowe who was the owner of this MS. Stowe would certainly have perceived the absurdity of assigning this poem to Lydgate who died in 1450.

This poem was printed along with five other pieces 'by mayster Skelton Poet Laureat' at London (between 1542 and 1548) 'by Richard Lant / for Henry Tab dwelling in Pauls churchyard at the sygne of Judith'. It was again printed in a collection of Skelton's works in 1568 (I owe this bibliographical information to the kindness of Prof. F. W. Baxter of the University of Belfast). Dyce included this poem in his *Poetical Works of Skelton*, basing his text on earlier prints and also on 'a contemporary MS. in the possession of Miss Richardson Currer'. This MS. appears to be still in existence but Prof. Baxter has not yet succeeded in placing it.

Collation of Lant's print with the Harley MS. discloses some interesting variants. I record only those readings of the print which seem distinctly preferable:

7. reynyd] Lant: rulyd.

10. yov] Lant: freendys.

16. Wyth] Lant: Without.

26. my fortune had here] Lant: lady fortune with me had.

33. Owtt off this lond] Lant: Now from this worlde.

37–48. This stanza is lacking in Lant and other early prints, but is present in the Currer MS.

55 ff. On Edward IV as a great builder see Cora L. Scofield, *Life and Reign of Edw. the Fourth*, II, 429 f.

58. etton] Lant: Eltam.

59. Westmynster & eltham—yit went I from] Lant: Yet at the last I went from them.

64. grett plesure] Lant: myrth my.

65. gon] Lant: wandred.

70. off them] Lant: alone now.

73. ye] Lant: a man.

86. I wyll þat ye witt] Lant: Ye wot well all.

90. Mo, conserued to me] Lant: Nor nought wolde conserve me here in.

94. to pray] Lant: now to pray.

95. As I forsayd] Lant: For ryght wel you know.

160. *The Rich Man's Farewell to the World*

Occurs only in this MS.; previously printed by M. R. James, *Catal. of MSS. in Pembroke Coll.*, and in *Register of Mid. Eng. Relig. Verse*, i. 226.

This is not to be confused with the earlier lyric (22 lines) which begins with the same line (*English Lyr. of the XIIIth Cent.*, No. 58).

161. *Beware the Pains of Purgatory*

Occurs only in this MS.; previously printed in *Censura Literaria*, viii (1808), 401–2, and by Greene, *Early Eng. Carols*, p. 211.

2. A proverbial phrase; cf. B.M. Addit. MS. 37049, fol. 85vo: 'Who so hops þe best sal hafe þe ryng.'

21. The meaning of the line appears to be: 'Ah, now I am certain that I shall die,' but no instance of 'thorugh' in this sense is recorded. If the line is to be read 'Now I am through with that', &c., some emendation is necessary.

162. *The Testament of a Christian*

Previously printed from this MS. by Halliwell, *Rel. Antiq.* i. 260–1. This piece occurs also in Corp. Christi Oxf. MS. 237, fol. 236ro, in B.M. Addit. MS. 29729, fol. 126ro, and in Balliol Coll. MS. 354, fol. 199ro. It has been printed from the Balliol MS. by Dyboski, EETS, Ext. Ser. ci. 86–7.

In the B.M. Addit. MS. these verses are ascribed to 'Robartus poet', a person whom I have not succeeded in identifying.

163. *Death, the Soul's Friend*

Occurs only in this MS.; previously printed by Karl Brunner, *Anglia*, xlii, New Series, p. 290.

The attitude towards death which is here expressed differs from that usually found in medieval poems on mortality, but finds an interesting parallel in the *Prick of Conscience* (ed. Morris, pp. 58–60).

45. muk & mull] Cf. *Pearl*, l. 905: 'I am· bot mokke & mul among.'

55–6. Cf. *Prick of Con.* 2177, 2182–5, 2200–5.

61–2. Cf. *Prick of Con.* 2094, 2108–11.

164. *Death, the Port of Peace*

Occurs only in this MS.; previously printed in the *Register of Mid. Eng. Relig. and Didact. Verse*, i. 363.

165. *Fortune Will Have Her Way*

Occurs only in this MS.; not heretofore printed.

166. *Fortune Rules Both High and Low*

Occurs only in this MS.; previously printed by Ritson, *Anc. Songs and Ballads*, ed. 1877, p. 11.

167. *Worldly Joy is only Fantasy*

Previously printed from this MS. by Skeat, *Chaucerian and Other Pieces*, Suppl. to Oxford Chaucer, p. 449; occurs also in the Bannatyne MS. (Advocates MS. 1.1.6, fol. 74ᵛᵒ), ed. Hunterian Club, p. 202, and the Maitland MS. (Pepys 2553, p. 291), Pinkerton, *Ancient Scottish Poems*, p. 243.

168. *Who Trusteth Fortune Will Have a Fall*

Occurs only in this MS.; not hitherto printed. The first three lines are also found on a fly-leaf in MS. Royal 17, D. vi, fol. 1ᵛᵒ.

169. *Fortune Has Cast Me from Weal to Woe*

Occurs only in this MS.; previously printed in *Reliq. Antiq.* i. 26.

Two or three other pieces in this MS. carry the mysterious legend 'A god whene' which is usually taken to be the name of the author. But, even so, nothing further is known concerning him.

170. *Fortune, Be My Friend Again*

Occurs only in this MS.; previously printed by Mac-Cracken, *PMLA*, xxvi. 180.

171. *A Balade by Squire Halsham*

Previously printed from this MS. by Dr. Helen P. South, *PMLA*, l. 362. These two stanzas occur together also in

Harley MS. 7333, fol. 148ro (*Reliq. Antiq.* i. 234; Flügel, *Anglia*, xiv. 463), in Harley 7578, fol. 20ro, in B.M. Addit. MS. 16165, fol. 244ro, and in Henry E. Huntington HM. 144 (formerly Huth MS.—text printed in *Notes & Queries*, Fifth Ser. ix. 343).

These two stanzas are ascribed to Halsham by Shirley in Harley 7333 and B.M. Addit. MS. 16155. Also the first stanza separately appears under Halsham's name in B.M. Addit. MS. 34,360, fol. 22. Skeat (*Chaucer Canon*, p. 145) believed that the ascription to Halsham was due to an erroneous supposition on the part of Shirley, but see Dr. South's discussion in *PMLA*, l. 362–71. She identifies the author as 'Johannes Halsham, armiger', who died in 1415, 'seized of lands in Sussex, Kent, Norfolk, and Wiltshire'.

It is interesting to observe that Lydgate appropriated the first of these two stanzas in his 'Pageant of Knowledge' (*Minor Poems of Lydg.*, pp. 730 and 734) and the second stanza in his 'Tyed with a Lyne' (*Minor Poems*, p. 832).

11. The easier the permission, the more reluctant to go. With 'lighter leve' compare Heywood's *Proverbs*: 'Ye might have knokt er ye came in, leaue is light.'

172. *Good Rule Is Out of Remembrance*

Not heretofore printed from this MS. A widely variant text (11 stanzas) occurs in Harley MS. 5396, fol. 290ro (printed in *Reliq. Antiq.* i. 73–5; also an extract (ll. 29–36) is found on a fly-leaf in Royal MS. 8, C. ii, fol. 2vo.

This poem is specially interesting for its series of popular proverbs and saws, usually in alliterative phrases.

4. were-it = weriþ.

87. The rime is restored by reading 'lore', the earlier form of the past participle.

173. *The Rancour of this Wicked World*

Occurs only in this MS.; not heretofore printed.

10. replete off blame] Cf. Lydgate, *Troy Bk.* iv. 5129: 'Replet of falsehod'.

12. most In Espescyall] 'above all'; cf. Lydgate, *Troy Bk.* iii. 3901: 'moste in special'.

13–14. Elliptical cstr.: (Those who are) best by trust [i.e. are held in highest esteem] may soonest betray themselves.

29–32. It is my profoundest grief—fully to express it—
when I call to mind those who without cause lie in distress.

35. wyth wronge repourt] unjustly accused: *repourt* is
the past participle.

174. *If One Only Knew Whom to Trust*

Occurs only in this MS.; previously printed by L. S.
M[ayer], *Music, Cantilenas, Songs,* &c., Lond. 1906.

4. but holde chere] only feign friendliness.

5. trystyt] See *OED* s.v. Tryst, *v.* '2. *trans.* . . . b. With
advb. extension: To invite or entice to a place, or to a distance.' Cf. Child, *Eng. and Scot. Pop. Ballad*, No. 217, stanza
8: 'He has trysted the pretty maid.'

6. walkytt] See *OED* s.v. Wake, *v.* "II. 7. *intr.* To come out
of the state of sleep or unconsciousness.' The Scottish dial.
form of the pret. pl. fourteenth–sixteenth century was
'walkytt'.

9–12. That men might know as plain as North and South
how their heart and mouth stand (in relation) to what they
but show.

175. *Perversities of the Age*

These eight lines, which in this MS. are found separately,
actually are ll. 9–16 of The Abuses of the Age in English verses
beginning: 'Gifte hys made domesman' (see *Register*, No. 564).
The corresponding lines of the Latin original are as follows:

> Etas ridetur, mulier pulsatur amore,
> Dives laudatur, pauper adheret humo,
> Prudentes ceci, cognati degeneres sunt:
> Mortuus ignotus, nullus amicus erit.

Other MSS. render these lines in English as follows:

(1) Harley MS. 2251, fol. 153 (printed by Furnivall,
EETS, Ext. Ser. viii. 88)—

Olde men ben skorned / Wymmen ben wo̊wed
Riche men ben pleasid / And pore men ben diseasid
Wise men bien blynde / And kynrede is vn-kynde
The dede is out of mynde / Triew friend can noman fynde.

(2) Ashmole MS. 750, fol. 100ᵛᵒ—

Old man is skorned, / ȝonge women is wowed,
Rich man is glosed, / and poure man is bowed.
Sleght men been blynde / and kyn been vnkynde
The deed is oute of mynde / and freend may no man fynde.

(3) B.M. Addit. MS. 37049, fol. 85vo (printed by Brunner, *Archiv*, clix. 86)—

Old men are oft scorned / And women are oft defowled
Þe ryche men ar belefyd / Þe pore men are reprefyd.

(4) B.M. Addit. MS. 9066, fol. 54 (Engl. *Gesta Rom.*, EETS, Ext. Ser. xxxiii. 360)—

wise men are but scornede / and wedowes be sore yernede;
grete men are but glosede / and smale men borne downe and myslosede
lordes wexen blynde / and kynnesmen ben vnkynde;
dethe out of mynde / and trewthe may no man fynde.

It is obvious that the Westminster Abbey and the *Gesta Romanorum* versions stand together against all the others, and they show peculiar variations from the Latin in 'Wise men' (Lat. *Etas*), 'wedowȝ' (Lat. *mulier*), 'lordis' (Lat. *prudentes*), 'dethe' (Lat. *mortuus*), and 'Treuth' (Lat. *amicus*).

2. *foryerned* is obscure. The *Gesta Rom.* 'sore yernede' (ardently desired) might stand as the equivalent of 'wowed' in two other texts, but is hardly what would be expected with 'wedowȝ'. One is tempted to emend to 'foryemed' (neglected).

176. *Virtues Exiled—Vices Enthroned*

Previously printed in Casley's *Catal. of Royal MSS.*, p. 119. The figure of virtues banished (or imprisoned) and vices in power is found earlier in fourteenth-century verse; see, for example, Merton Coll. 248 (*Rel. Lyrics of the XIVth Cent.*, p. 54):

falsenes, I vnderstande
haues dreuen trwte of lande,
and tort and fort as sworen þar owth
þat law sal lose is ouer-cloþe.

The same idea is expressed in Latin verses which are copied in several MSS. of the fourteenth and fifteenth centuries (accompanied in Grimestone's Commonplace Book by a metrical English translation—see *Register*, No. 1312):

Mvltis annis iam transactis
Nulla fides est in pactis
ffel in corde uerba lactis
Mel in ore fraus in factis.

Notes

347

See also seven lines in Harley MS. 7322 beginning: 'Loue is out of lond i-went' (*Pol. Rel. and Love Poems*, rev. ed., p. 257/8).

In the fifteenth century we find in the Brome MS. and several others lines which seem directly connected with the verses in the Royal MS.—

> *Lex* ys leyd a downe,
> And *veritas* ys but small,
> *Amor* ys owt of towne
> And *caritas* ys gon with all.
>
> (L. T. Smith, *Notes on a Commonplace Book of XVth Cent.*, p. 40.)

177. *A Series of Triads*

Not heretofore printed from this MS. Six stanzas of confession in the first person have been prefixed in several MSS. of this piece: Lambeth MS. 853, p. 226 (*Hymns to Virgin and Christ*, pp. 35–9), Cotton Calig. A. ii, fol. 108ro (*Reliq. Antiq.* i. 197–200), and Rawl. C. 86, fol. 71ro (Patterson, *Middle Eng. Penitential Lyric*, pp. 57–9).

1–24. The 'iij poyntis of myscheff' are three of the 'Twelve Abuses of the Age'. In the Latin text of the 'Duodecim Abusiones' (Schick, *Temple of Glas*, EETS, Ext. Ser. lx. 68) occurs 'Pauper superbus', the original of 'Pore men proude' in l. 6. 'Ryche man thef' (l. 9) and 'Old man lechere' (l. 11) are both found in the list of Five Evil Things in Rawl. poet 32 (printed in *Reliq. Antiq.* i. 316).

25–80. These seven stanzas are omitted in Rawl. C. 86.

66. consciens lyght] i.e. an easy conscience, lacking moral responsibility.

178. *Medicines to Cure the Deadly Sins*

Huntington MS. HM. 183 was formerly owned by Joseph Haslewood, which he 'obtained from the Hawkins library at Nash Court'. These verses were printed from this MS. in *Censura Literaria*, viii. 77–81. A transcript of the text by Haslewood is preserved in B.M. Addit. 11307, fol. 127ro.

This poem occurs also in Camb. Univ. MS. Ff. 1. 6 (printed by Halliwell, *Nugae Poeticae*, pp. 64–7, and by Furnivall, *Pol. Rel. and Love Poems*, rev. ed., pp. 244–8), and in Sloane MS. 747, fol. 95ro. The Camb. MS. confuses the arrangement of ll. 25–96, placing the stanzas in the order: 4, 3, 6, 5, 8, 7. Also, by a manifest error, Camb. in l. 73 reads 'Accidia' instead of 'Auaricia' and in l. 85 'Auaryssia' instead of 'Accidia'.

12. With this refrain line compare the opening line of a fourteenth-century lyric: 'Þe Mon þat luste to liuen in ese' (*Rel. Lyr. of the XIVth Cent.*, No. 103). The line is based on one of Cato's distiches: 'Securam quicunque cupis deducere vitam.'

21. a crownyd wyght] i.e. a tonsured person, a clerk.

22. querely] apparently an illiterate or colloquial spelling of OF *querele* (defined by Godefroy: 'affaire, chose, raison, motif'). 'Bene & pese' is evidently a pun on *bene* and *pax*, so that the line taken as a whole means, one who is familiar with his service-book.

26. traveld] here used transitively: 'afflicted'.

50. ramagith] Camb. MS. ravissheth. The *OED* does not recognize *ramage* as a verb, but Lydgate uses the adj. *ramage*, 'wild, ferocious, violent' (of animals) in the *Troy Bk.* iii. 2878, iv. 3226; and a verb may have developed from this. Less probably, *ramagith* might be explained as a scribal error for *rauagith*.

179. *On Chattering in Church*

Occurs only in this MS.; previously printed in *Reliq. Antiq.* i. 257, and by Heuser, *Bonner Beiträge*, xiv. 223. As printed in *Reliq. Antiq.* the Latin lines in these verses are meaningless. Some of the lines in this piece are much blurred; and in reading them I have profited by a transcript made by E. O. Winstedt and now pasted on the back cover of the MS. In some points, however, I differ from E. O. W.'s readings.

'Titivillus' is introduced as a character in the morality play, *Mankind* (ll. 447 ff.).

180. *Against Traducers*

Previously printed from this MS. by Wright, *Songs and Carols from a MS. of the XVth Cent.*, Percy Soc. xxiii. 29–30. These verses occur also in Bodl. MS. Arch. Seld. B. 26 (printed by Padelford, *Anglia*, xxxvi. 86, and by Greene, *Early Eng. Carols*, pp. 230–1) and stanzas 1–3 in B.M. Addit. MS. 5665, fol. 31ᵛᵒ (printed by Fehr, *Archiv*, cvi. 271).

18. fame] Arch. Seld.: name

24. al thyng] Arch. Seld.: we schull.

Notes

181. *See Much, Say Little, and Learn to Suffer in Time*

Not heretofore printed from this MS.; these verses also occur in B.M. Addit. MS. 29729, fol. 130ro (printed by MacCracken, *Minor Poems of Lydg.*, pp. 800–1), in Corp. Christi Oxf. 203, p. 23 (stanzas 1, 2, 5), and stanza 1 in Advocates MS. 19.3.1, fol. 61vo. The ascription of the poem to Lydgate lacks any authoritative basis, whereas in the Corpus Oxf. MS. these verses are headed 'Prouerbium R. Stokys'. For a discussion of 'Stokys' and his authorship of this poem see *Mod. Lang. Notes*, liv, 131–3.

The theme of the poem associates it with a group bearing very similar titles: 'Suffer in Time and That is Best' (Vernon MS.; *Relig. Lyr. of the XIVth Cent.*, No. 118), 'Lerne say wele, say litel, or say noȝt' (*Twenty-six Polit. and Other Poems*, EETS, pp. 14–22), 'Hyre and see and say not all' (Trin. Coll. Camb. MS. 1450, in Sandison, *Chanson d'Aventure in Mid. Eng.*, pp. 121–3), and 'Ever say Well or hold Thee Still' (Porkington MS. 10, in Halliwell's *Early Eng. Miscell.*, Warton Club, pp. 62–5).

29. mellyng] other MSS.: medelynge. But cf. *mell* (*Minor Poems of Lydg.*, p. 443, l. 31). In the present instance the word may represent OE mǽlan, 'to speak', as in *Piers Plow.*, B. xi. 104.

182. *Think Before You Speak*

Occurs only in this MS.; previously printed by Furnivall, *Early Engl. Meals and Manners*, EETS, Orig. Ser. 32, rev. ed. pp. 244–6.

183. *Counsels of Prudence and Patience*

Previously printed from this MS. by Halliwell, *Lydgate's Minor Poems*, Percy Soc. ii. 222–4; occurs also in Advocates MS. 1.1.6 (printed *Bannatyne MS.*, Hunterian Club, pp. 225–6).

18. haste mene = hasty men (l. 15); OF hasti.

26. mone &] the very easy emendation to *mony an*, suggested by Sir Wm. Craigie, is undoubtedly right. The Bannatyne MS. varies widely in this line: 'He is nocht worthy to cum in a gud place.' The reading of Cotton seems to have resulted from an aural error.

184. *Every One Finds His Match*

Not heretofore printed. The A-version of these lines occurs also in Ashmole 59, fol. 73ro, and in B.M. Addit. MS. 34360, fol. 77vo.

185. *Neither Too Humble Nor Too Proud*

Occurs only in this MS.; previously printed by L. S. M[ayer], *Music, Cantilenas, Songs*, &c., London 1906, and by Greene, *Early Eng. Carols*, p. 237.

B.M. Addit. MS. 5665, contains a very similar song in three stanzas with the burden 'In euery state in euery degre / the mene ys the beste as semeth me' (printed by Fehr, *Archiv*, cvi. 267, and by Greene, op. cit., p. 236).

14–15. Cf. B.M. Addit. 37049, fol. 86vo: 'Be nowþer to hasty ne to slawe / Fle not to hye ne crep not to lawe' (Karl Brunner, *Archiv*, clix. 90).

18–20. Cf. Addit. MS. 5665: 'To hew abow thy hedde hit is but vanite, / Lest in thy yee ther falle a chyppe.'

186. *Measure is Best of All Things*

Occurs only in this MS.; previously printed by W. H. Hulme, EETS, Ext. Ser. c, p. xxx.

See also the verses 'Mesure is tresure', Brome MS. (printed by L. T. Smith, *Commonplace Book of XVth Cent.*, pp. 14–15), and note the first line of Lydgate's poem: 'Men wryte of oold how mesour is tresour' (*Minor Poems of Lydg.*, p. 776).

187. *Inordinate Love Defined*

Occurs only in this MS.; not heretofore printed.

The Latin verses of which the English is a direct translation appear to have circulated widely: for references to other MSS. containing them see *English Lyrics of the XIIIth Cent.*, No. 9, Notes.

At the bottom of the page containing these verses is written: 'Iste liber constat fratri Nc Barkley, Set postea pertinet ad fratrem Nicho^{m} london prefati fratris affmē idō sororis sue filium naturalem.'

4. fynde] satisfy, supply. See *OED find, vb*. III. 18.

188. *What Profiteth this World's Labour?*

Occurs only in this MS.; not heretofore printed.

MacCracken's characterization of this piece as 'A short

mis-metered thing' (*Minor Poems of Lydg.*, p. xliv, note 2)
seems on the whole somewhat severe.

18. wil it = willith. Cf. 'wexith' in l. 21.

189. *A Song of 'Goods'*

The first few lines of this piece occur also in Advocates
MS. 1.1.6, fol. 75ʳᵒ (Hunterian Club ed. of the *Bannatyne MS.*,
p. 202) and in Trin. Coll. Camb. MS. 1450, fol. 39ᵛᵒ, but the
only complete text is in the Univ. Coll. MS. from which
these verses have not heretofore been printed.

190. *The Law of Kind*

Not heretofore printed.

191. *For Each Inch God Will Requite Thee a Span*

Previously printed from this MS. by J. R. Lumby, *Ratis
Raving*, EETS, Orig. Ser. 43, pp. 10–11.

Also occurs in Advocates MS. 1.1.6 (Bannatyne MS.),
fol. 58ᵛᵒ (printed by Skeat, *Kingis Quair*, Lond. 1884, p. 56,
in Scottish Text Soc., ed. *Bannatyne MS.*, ii. 145.

1. trew] B: throw.
2. noblay] B: nobill ray.
3. B: Of ony vertewis stait that evir thow be.
4. B: stoppis persew.
6. lust] B: luve.
17. set] B: steik.
18. restren] B: refrene.
19. stramp] B: Graip.
20. B: kep thi faith thow aw to god and man.

192. *The Summum Bonum*

Occurs only in this MS.; not heretofore printed.

Described in the Catal. of B.M. Addit. MS. 37788, in
these terms:

'On the fly-leaves are scribbled in 15th-cent. hands
(*a*) Twelve lines beginning
    The law of god be to þe thy rest
Followed by other attempts at verse.'

8. Lest thou be trapped by guile in the guise of pity: see
Chaucer, *L.G.W.*, Prol. F, l. 165.

12. crosse & pile]. The 'cross' is the face of a coin; the
'pile' is the reverse side. Together it is used as an inclusive
phrase, like 'all and some'.

GLOSSARY

No attempt at completeness has been made in this Glossary. Only obsolete words are included and those which on account of changes in form or meaning might cause difficulty to the modern reader. Also only a single instance of the same form is recorded—ordinarily the reference is to the earliest occurrence of a given form in these Texts.

Verbs are entered under the form of the infinitive if an instance of the infinitive occurs in the Texts. Where forms of the verb other than the infinitive are cited the fact is expressly indicated. The abbreviations of grammatical terms are too obvious to require explanation.

a, *pron.*; *he* 24. 28, 173. 21, 178. 63.

a, *vb.*; *have* 83. 6.

a, *prep.*; *on* 84. 1.

abdominacioun, *sb.* (apparently a nonce-word); *surrender of domination, abdication* 38. 21. See Notes.

abone, *prep.*; *above* 112. 29.

a-bouun, *adv.*; *above* 78. 26.

a-bucge, *vb.* (OE ábycgan); *pay the penalty, suffer for* 123. 19; aby 161. 5; abyd 177. 60.

abyde, *vb.*; *wait for* 142. 86.

accende, *vb.*; *to kindle* 66. 12.

accesse, *sb.*; *a coming on of illness, attack, fit* 135. 19.

according, *adj.*; *appropriate, fitting* 162. 6.

a-complise, *vb.*; *perform, accomplish* 153. 19.

a-dawe, *vb.* (a+OE daȝian); *dawn* 135. 26.

a-deryd, *pp.* (< OE á-derian); *injured* 15. 40.

ado, *pp.*; *done* 102. 147.

adurn, *vb.* (by confusion of *ador-en* and *adorn-en*); *to adore* 112. 31.

adventure, *sb.*; *mischance* 109. 67.

advertaunt, *adj.*; *turning away* (from) 39. 21.

advertise, *vb.*; *give warning of* 153. 2.

advoyde, *vb.*; *avoid* 12. 19.

a-dyȝt, *pp.*; *put* 95. 34.

aere, *sb.*; *air* 178. 2; ayer 117. 9; eyre 135. 34; (*pl.*) eyres 136. 13.

aesell, *sb.* (OFaisil); *vinegar* 93. 34; asaill 102. 59; ezyl 84. 23; eysell 135. 61.

affiawns, *sb.*; *credence, faith* 77 A. 22; affiance 47. 29.

affray, *sb.*; (1) *attack, assault* 191. 4. (2) *alarm, terror* 152. 8.

affray, *vb.*; *to terrify* 10. 91.

affy *vb.*; *to give faith to, trust* 167. 3.

a-forn, *adv., prep.* (OE onforan); *before* 95. 10; a-for 181. 3.

after, *prep.*; *according* (to) 28. 76; efter 115. 22.

agen, *adv.* (OE ongéan); *back, into a former position or state* 89. 21; a-ȝen 88. 11; a-ȝey 132. 23; *in return* agayne 105. 26.

ageyn, *prep.*; *against* 90. 16; agayne 173. 7; agane 94. 4.

agrise, *vb.*; *to shudder at, be terrified* 153. 11.

alderman, *sb.*; *ancestor, elder* 153. 28.

algate, *adv.*; *in any case* 149. 9.

aliawns, *sb.*; *alliance* 77 A. 24.

alkin, *adj.*; *of every kind* 102. 46; alkynnes 144. 50.

all-day, *adv. phrase*; *every day* 163. 32.

allowit, *pp.*; *hallowed* 53. 2.

all-wielding, *ppl. adj.*; *almighty* 112. 28.

almesful, *adj.*; *merciful* 25. 16.

al-of, *conj.*; *although* 4. 33.

alowe, *adv.*; *downwards* 143. 9.

als, *conj.*; *as* 15. 95.

also, *adv.*; *as* 81. 3.

alther (OE *gen. pl.* eallra); *of all* 70. 10; alþer 172. 64.

althyng, *sb.*; *everything* 86. 15.

a-monge, *adv.*; *therewith, at the same time* 151. 12, 182. 47; emang 36. 41.

an, *prep.* (OE on); *on* 37. 33.

and, *conj.*; *if* 3. 20, 7. 85.

aneuch, *adv.*; see inogthe.

anger, *sb.* (ON angr); *anguish, distress* 102. 33; (*pl.*) angers 57. 36.

anournyt, *vb. pret.* (< OF aörner); *adorned* 13. 28.

antane, *sb.*; *antiphon, anthem* 112. 21.

a-paas, *adv.*; *swiftly, apace* 161. 17.

apare, *vb.*; *grow worse, deteriorate* 151. 40.

aperyalle, *adv.*; *overtly, openly* 173. 25.

apeyer, *vb.* (OF ampayre); *injure, impair* 180. 2.

aplye, *vb.* (OF aplier); *to join oneself, come into contact* 77 A. 11.

apon, *prep.*; *upon* 163. 64; apoun 102. 113.

appele, *vb.*; *to summon before a tribunal, to accuse* 6. 73; apele 60. 36.

approched, *pp.*; *associated, brought into connexion* 51. 41.

apse, *sb.*; *aspen* 181. 9.

areyse, *vb.*; *bring into activity, raise up* 178. 58.

arn, *vb.* (OE earnian); *to earn, win as a reward* 18. 9.

as, *vb.*; *has* 63. 16.

as, *vb.*; *ask* 102. 100; (*pret.*) aste 102. 123.

asaill, *sb.*; see aesell.

a-slake, *vb.* (OE áslacian); *to become feeble, diminish, abate* 148. 47.

assaile, *vb.*; *to asail, assault* 25. 6; asayll 163. 44.

assale, *sb.*; *an assault* 112. 15.

assoilid, *pp.*; *absolved* 146. 9.

assumptyd, *pp.*; *received into heaven* 31. 25.

astate, *sb.* (OF estat); *degree, rank* 30. 17, 35. 46, 185. 5; *pl.* astates 154. 6.

aswage, *vb.*; *grow less, fall off, pass away* 148. 10.

a-syse, *sb.* (OF asise); *seat, position* 185. 1.

a-sythe, *sb.* (Northern form of asseth(e)); *reparation* 149. 5.

at, *pron.* (clipped form); *that* 3. 10, 3. 21.

ataynte, *ppl. adj.* (OF ateint, ataint); *convicted, attainted* 26. 12.

attour, *prep.*; *in spite of* 22. 57.

auavnce, *vb.*; *to advance* 47. 12; avaunse 151. 16.

auter, *sb.*; *altar* 115. 32.

a-vaunte, *sb.*; *boast* 144. 151.

aviseament, *sb.*; *advice, counsel* 166. 7.

avisioun, *sb.*; *vision, dream* 39. 12.

avowries, *sb. pl.*; *advocates* (especially patron saints) 161. 28.

awen, *adj.*; *own* 15. 54; oughen 163. 28.

aw3t, *sb.*; *aught, anything* 48. 19.

a-wreke, *pp.* (OE áwrecan); *avenged* 148. 50; a-wrooke 140. 29.

ayer, *sb.*; see *aere.*

bable, *sb.* (OF babel); *plaything, bauble* 149. 24.

bagbytynge, *vbl. sb.*; *backbiting* 182. 33.

baill, *sb.* (OE bealu); *evil, torment, bale* 96. 60; (*pl.*) bales 52. 11.

baith, *adv., adj.*; *both* 102. 151.

baldast, *adj.*; *boldest* 156. 26.

band, *sb.* (ON band); *pledge, security* 22. 51; bande 36. 22.

barne, *sb.*; *child, bairn* 4. 25, 21. 4.

barne-teme, *sb.*; *child-bearing* 77 B. 17.

bastell, *sb.*; *fortified tower, bastion* 136. 36.

battys, *sb. pl.*; *sticks, clubs* 109. 101.

bawme, *sb.*; *balm for soothing pain or healing wounds* 135. 12.

bawme, *vb.*; *to anoint* 178. 69.

bayle, *sb.* (OF bail); *custody, jurisdiction, power* 107. 14.

be, *prep.*; *by* 35. 51.

becommy3t, *vb.*; *has gone* 147. 45.

bede, *vb.* (OE béodan); *to offer* 15. 75; (*pret.*) bedyn 95. 28.

be-dene,*adv.*;*forthwith,straightway* 60. 10; bedeyne 22. 26.

bedis, *sb. pl.*; *beads, rosary* 148. 62.

beere, *sb.*; *bier* 148. 77; beyr 156. 27; bere 157. 2.

beese, bes, *vb.*; see *beon.*

beft, *pp.* (be+OE haftian); *beaten* 91. 23.

be-goone, *pp.* (OE begán); *beset, placed* 29. 21.

begouth, *vb. pret.* (OE beginnan); *began* 94. 16.

behest, *sb.*; *assurance, promise* 78. 54.

be-howe, *sb.*; *profit, behoof* 163. 10.

behuffis, *vb. pres.* 3 *s.*; *behoves* 156. 19.

behy3t, *pp.*; *promised* 140. 19.

beild, *sb.* (OE béldó); *refuge, shelter* 22. 68.

beir, *sb.* (OE beran); *bear, carry* 94. 12.

beir, *sb.* (OE 3ebære); *clamour, outcry* 96. 34.

beit, *vb.*; *amend, improve* 22. 77.

be-kene, *vb.*; *commend* 128. 22.

bekke, *sb.*; *a signal or gesture, an obeisance* 39. 67.

beld, *vb.* (OE bieldan); *to defend, shelter* 60. 45.

beldis, *vb. pres.* 2 *s.* (OE byldan < bold); *buildest* 151. 8.

beldith, beldyt, *vb. pres.* 3 *s.*; see *bylde.*

belif, *adv.* (be life); *quickly, at once* 4. 10; blyue 31. 7.

bene, *vb. pres. pl.*; see *beon.*

beningli, *adv.*; *benignly* 47. 5.

be-nyme, *vb.* (OE beniman); *take away* (from) 178. 92.

benyng, *adj.*; *benign, gracious* 22. 56.

beon, *vb.*; *to be* 11. 79; (*pres. pl.*) bene 55. 7; (*imp. pl.*) beth 130. 12; beese 158 A. 12; bes 158 B. 8.

berd, *sb.*; see *bryde.*

berde, *sb.*; see *bryd.*

bern, *sb.*; *knight, man* 156. 26.

beryt owte = *carry it off* 177. 6.
be-seke, *vb.*; *beseech* 49. 6;
(*part.*) beseiking 22. 70.
be-sette, *vb.* (OE besittan);
place, bestow 144 Alia 9; *besett* (*pp.*) 3. 19.
best, *sb.*; *beast* 6. 82; (*pl.*) 78.
14.
be-stad, *pp.* (< OE be-stan-
dan); *be-set with* (dangers,
troubles) 23. 20.
besy, *adj.*; *active, busy* 47. 4.
besynesse, *sb.*; *activity* 164. 2.
bet, *adv.*; *better* 171. 12.
betake, *pp.*; *committed* 132. 2.
betere, better, *adj.*; see *bitter*.
beth, *vb. imp.*; see *beon*.
betwene, betuen, *adv.*; *therewith, together* 20. 17, 91. 13.
bewte, *sb.*; *beauty* 148. 47;
bovtte 147. 46.
bey, *vb.*; see *bygge*.
bitter, *adj.*; *bitter* 164. 2; beteɪe
95. 14, betyr 95. 40, better
154. 1.
bla, *adj.*; see *blo*.
bladderith, *vb. pres.* 3 *s.*; *swells
out like a bladder* 178. 86.
blaiknit, *pp.* (< ON bleikr);
made pale 91. 23.
blaw, *sb.*; *a blow, a stroke* 91. 22.
blayne, *sb.* (OE bleȝen); *a blain,
blister, pustule* 178. 28.
blee, *sb.* (OE bleoh); *colour, hue,
appearance* 6. 105; ble 7. 11.
bleid, *vb.*; *bleed* 22. 47; (*part.*)
bledand 7. 35.
blestfull, *adj.*; *blissful* 78. 18.
blicht, *adj.*; *joyous, gladsome,
blithe* 112. 17.
blindit, *pp.*; *hidden* 113. 37.
blising, *sb.*; *blessing* 22. 51.
blithis, *vb. pres.* 3 *s.*; *gladdens*
112. 16.
blo, *adj.* (ON blá); *blackish
blue, livid, lead-coloured* 97.
80; bla 91. 45.

blomes, *sb. pl.*; *blooms* 37. 62.
blosme, *sb.*; *blossom* 37. 44.
blowe, *adj.*; *blue* 51. 26.
bloyd, *sb.*; *blood* 75. 11.
blynne, *vb.*; *cease* 108. 15;
blyne 6. 101.
blyue, *adv.*; see *belif*.
bobbid, *pp.*; *beaten* 9. 6.
bocht, *pp.*; see *bygge*.
bocsum, *adj.*; see *buxome*.
bode, *vb. pret.* (OE bodian);
announced 135. 69.
bollith, *vb. pres.* 3 *s.*; *swells*
178. 86.
bonde, *sb.*; *covenant* 35. 25.
bonde, *vb. pret.* (< OE bin-
dan); *bound* 10. 102; (*pp.*)
bond 129. 22; bund 91. 20.
bone, *ppl. adj.*; *prepared to go,
bound* (as in 'homeward bound')
78. 39.
bone, *sb.* (ON bón); *petition,
entreaty, request* 17. 19.
bonechief, *sb.*; *good fortune,
prosperity* 131. 45.
boost, *sb.*; *boast* 182. 39.
bord, *sb.*; *jest* 180. 14.
bore, *sb.*; *hole* (for nails) 102.
53.
boren, *pp.*; *born* 122. 3; bore
6. 128, 105. 18.
boryd, *pp.* (OE borian); *pierced,
bored* 7. 38; bore 103. 24.
bot, *conj.* (OE bútan); *except*
102. 149.
bote, *sb.*; *remedy, relief* 78. 42.
botefull, *adj.*; *useful, advan-
tageous, helpful* 131. 6.
bounte, *sb.*; *goodness, worth,
virtue* 153. 31.
bourȝes, *sb. pl.* (OE burh);
towns, burghs 151. 9.
bovtte, *sb.*; see *bewte*.
bowe, *sb.* (OE bóg, bóh); *bough*
(of a tree) 186. 3.
bowe, *adj.*; 147. 54. See Note.
bowght, *pp.*; see *bygge*.

bowndone, *ppl. adj.*; *bound, under obligations* 107. 100.

brace, *vb.*; *embrace, encircle* 22. 92.

brace, *sb.*; *hostile preparations* 13. 23; brase 20. 15.

brede, *vb.*; *grow, breed* 144. 38.

bredyr, *sb. pl.*; *brothers* 15. 75.

breme, *adj.* as *adv.*; *fierce, raging* 100. 4.

brenne, *vb.* (ON brenna); *to burn* 178. 66; bren 144. 173; (part.) brening 23. 12; (*pp.*) brent 10. 26; (*ppl. adj.*) refined by fire 183. 4.

brer, *sb.* (OE Anglian brér); *briar* 22. 13; breere 39. 11.

brest, *vb.* (OE berstan); *burst* 110. 3.

breycus, *vb. pres.* 2 s.; *breakest* 107. 89.

breyght, *sb.*; *breath* 111. 2; breth 109. 152.

brith, *adj.* (OE beorht); *bright* 71. 2.

brode, *adv.*; *wide, broadly* 177. 29.

brokyll, *adj.*; *brittle, fragile* 178. 111.

brout, *pp.*; *brought* 123. 3.

broysed, *pp.*; *bruised* 109. 4.

brutelnes, *sb.*; *fickleness, insecurity, frailty* 150. 1.

bryd, *sb.* (OE bridd); *a child* 28. 15; byrde 15. 86; berde 23. 13.

bryde, *sb.*; *maiden, bride* 24. 5; berd 72. 2; berde 72. 19; (*pl.*) bryddus 24. 1.

bund, *pp.*; see *bonde*.

bur, *vb. pret.* (OE beran); *carried, bore* 22. 46; (2 s.) bure 91. 38.

burioun, *sb.*; *burgeon, bud* 30. 15.

burssin, *vb. pret.* (Scot. form of *bersten*); *burst* 91. 47.

buskyd, *vb. pret.*; *hurried, hastened* 39. 11.

but, *prep.* (OE bútan); (1) *without* 22. 62. (2) *except* (butt) 159. 70, 180. 10.

buxome, *adj.*; *obedient* 15. 55; bocsum 28. 70; buxum *kindly* 26. 36.

by and by, *advb. phr.*; *straightway* 109. 26.

bydyn, *vb.*; *abide, remain* 177. 44.

bygge, *vb.* (OE bycʒan); *buy* 189. 20; bye 92. 52; bey 76. 6; (*pret.*) boght 163. 68; bowght 173. 5; bocht 102. 85.

bygly, *adj.* (*big* (to inhabit) + ly); *habitable, pleasant to dwell in* 74. 3.

bylde, *vb.* 1 (< OE bieldan); *to embolden, encourage* 42. 12.

bylde, *vb.* 2 (< OE bold); *to lodge, dwell* 37. 37; (3 s.) beldith 45. 16; (*pret.*) beldyt 74. 3.

byll, *sb.*; *letter, note* 46. 1.

byllys, *sb. pl.*; *halberds* 109. 101.

byrde, *sb.*; see *bryd*.

byrdis, *sb. pl.*; *birds* 39. 11.

byse, *sb.* (AF bis); *in English wrongly transferred to blue or green pigments* 109. 162.

by-thute, *prep.*; see *wiþ-outen*.

cabone, *sb.*; *cabin, cell* 178. 15.

cairfull, *adj.*; see *carfull*.

calle, *pp.* (ON kalla); *called* 52. 14.

campyoung, *sb.*; *champion* 112. 25.

can, *vb. pret.* (= gan, OE ginnan); *did* (with inf. to indicate past time) 10. 77.

caplese, *adj.*; *bareheaded* 109. 44.

careyn, *sb.*; (*dead*) *body* 162. 4.

carfull, *adj.*; *sorrowful, anxious* 7. 22; cairfull 22. 27.

case, *sb* ; *instance* 183. 28; *in case = in the case* (of one), *if* 183. 35.

castene, *vb.* ; *plot, conspire* 125. 6.

catelle, *sb.* ; *possessions, chattels* 138. 24.

cayht, *vb. pret.* ; see *kache.*

celestyne, *adj.* ; *celestial, heavenly* 38. 19.

celsitude, *sb.* ; *lofty position, eminence* 22. 83, 45. 20.

cely, *adj.* ; see *sely.*

certayne, *sb.* ; *certainty* 109. 194.

cesoun, *sb.* ; *season* 181. 27.

cesse, *vb.* ; *cease, come to an end* 144. 140.

chalenginge (*pp.*) ; *claiming* 154. 19.

challes, *sb.* ; *chalice* 116. 10.

chamerlande, *sb.* ; *chamberlain, steward* 176. 15.

chare, *vb.* (OE cerran- Vesp. Ps.) ; *turn aside, drive away* 153. 38.

chas, *vb. pret.* ; see *chese.*

chaunte, *sb.* ; *singing* 39. 14.

che, *fem. pers. pron.* ; *she* 81. 2.

chekkes, *sb. pl.* ; *checks* (at chess) 153. 7.

cherable, *adj.* (? < OE cierran +suffix-able) ; *competent, capable* 39. 33.

chere, *sb.* ; *countenance, visage, mien* 4. 31.

chererchy, *sb.* ; see *ierarchies.*

chese, *vb.* (OE céosan) ; *choose* 47. 30; (*pret.*) chese 15. 84; ches 30. 3 ; chas 39. 14 ; (*part.*) chesyng 33. 5.

cheyere, *sb.* ; *chair, throne* 149. 10.

cheyre, *sb.* ; *cherry* 149. 8.

childur, *sb. pl.* ; *children* 7. 2, (*gen.*) 7. 50.

choys, *sb.* ; *a choice or picked company* 39. 33.

chyldwood, *sb.* ; *childhood* 147. 14.

chyldynge, *sb.* ; *child-bearing* 71. 39.

cipros, *sb.* ; *cypress* 22. 23.

claf, *vb. pret.* ; see *cleeff.*

claith, *sb.* (OE cláþ) ; *cloth* 94. 10; (*pl.*) (Scottish) clas, 'clothes', 4. 25.

clandnesse, *sb.* ; *cleanness, purity* 38. 31 ; cleynes 102. 157.

clapse, *sb.* ; *a clasp* 181. 11.

clas, *sb. pl.* ; see *claith.*

cledyd, *pp.* (North. form of infin., *clead, cleed*) ; *clothed* 93. 24.

cleeff, *vb.* (OE cléofan) ; *cleave, split* 39. 9; (*pret.*) claf 92. 58, claif 91. 58.

clenched, *pp.*, *fastened* 25. 30.

clenge, *vb.* (North. form) ; *cleanse* 102. 95.

clepe, *vb.* ; *call* 107. 69; (2 sg.) callest 154. 8.

cleued, *vb. pret.* (OE clifian) ; *adhered, stuck fast* 92. 81.

cleymyn, *vb.* ; *to claim, demand as one's due* 84. 5.

closour, *sb.* ; *enclosure, cloister* 22. 33.

clym, *vb.* ; *climb* 112. 23.

clynge, *vb.* ; 1. *to cling* 147. 76 ; 2. *to shrink up, wither, decay* (of the dead body) 163. 36.

cnellyd, *vb. pret.* ; see *kneled.*

coinquinate, *pp.* (Lat. coinquinare) ; *defiled* 13. 7.

cold, *adj.* ; *chill, gloomy* 63. 14.

colvir, *sb.* ; *dove* 39. 41.

commorus, *adj.* ; *cumbrous, wearisome, annoying* 172. 39.

commynalte, *sb.* ; *the commons* 159. 42.

commyners, *sb. pl.* ; *commoners* 159. 93.

compasse, *vb.* ; *consider, ponder* 161. 11.

Glossary

competent, *adj.*; *fit, proper* 136. 44.

compt, *vb.*; *to reckon, hold* (a thing), *to be* (so and so) 191. 10.

condigne, *adj.*; *worthy, deserving* 136. 44.

conduced, *pp.*; *conducted, led* 58. 9.

condyte, *sb.*; *fountain, conduit* 135. 11.

confortacion, *sb.*; *comfort, delight* 14. 26.

coniunctable, *adj.*; *able to be joined together, in conjunction* 51. 36.

consanguinite, *sb.*; *blood-relations* 38. 35.

consels, *vb. pres.* 3 *s.*; *counsels* 52. 4.

conseyl, *sb.*; *a matter of confidence or secrecy* 182. 10; *councell* 183. 38.

consigne, *vb.*; *to seal, or mark with a seal* 136. 45.

constren, *vb.*; *constrain* 57. 15.

contein, *vb.*; *to remain, continue* 20. 24.

contret, *adj.*; *contrite* 22. 81.

contrybute, *vb.*; *levy tribute on* 159. 28.

contynent, *adj.*; *self-restrained, temperate, chaste* 48. 3.

convayed, *pp.*; *conducted, managed* 109. 117.

conuenable, *adj.*; *consistent, in agreement* 56. 3; *couenabel* 35. 37.

conuersacioun, *sb.*; *a course of action undertaken, a way of life* 14. 35.

conwoy, *vb.*; *convey* 20. 5.

conynge, *sb.*; *ability* (at my conynge = so far as I am able) 71. 37.

corasy, *sb.* (reduced form from adj. *corrosive*); *a cause of trouble, a grievance* 154. 23.

corn, *sb.*; *a seed, a grain* 28. 14.

corruscall, *adj.*; *? shining* 38. 44.

cors, *sb.*; *corpse* 9. 19.

corsiff, *sb.*; *a caustic* 178. 54.

cost, *sb.*; *customs, conduct* 131. 30.

cot, *sb.*; *coat* 91. 25.

cotidiane, *adj.*; *daily, recurring* 154. 23.

councell, *sb.*; see *conseyl*.

countour, *sb.*; *accountant* 153. 31.

countre-tayle, *sb.*; *counter-stroke* (on þe countre-tayle = in the reply) 172. 24.

countryd, *vb. pret.*; *sang an accompaniment* (to a melody or plain song) 39. 15.

coursors, *sb. pl.*; *large horses ridden in battle or tournament* 159. 63.

couth, *vb. pret.* (OE cunnan); *could* 158 A. 10. In 96. 24 *couth* is wrongly used for *can* (= did).

couenable, *adj.*; see *convenable*.

coueryd, *pp.* (OF covrer); *recovered, restored* 97. 50.

coueryng, *vbl. sb.*; *recovery* 63. 14.

cowchour, *sb.*; *one confined to bed, a laggard* 178. 88.

cowrse, *vb.*; *curse* 147. 36.

crache, *sb.*; *manger* 16. 10.

crake, *vb.*; *crack* 103. 13.

crawfe, *vb.*; *crave, beg* 147. 68.

creatour, *sb.*; *creature* 22. 27.

crepe, *vb.*; *creep* 11. 11; (*pp.*) croppyn 147. 53.

criand, *pres. part.*; *crying* 60. 31.

crokes, *sb. pl.*; *crooks, hooks* 179. 11.

crone, *sb.*; *crown* 78. 35.
croppyn, *pp.*; see *crepe.*
crosce, *sb.*; *cross* 60. 60.
crosse, *sb.*; *crossways* 183. 38.
crosse, *sb.*; *the obverse side of a coin* (crosse and pile = the obverse and reverse sides, 'heads and tails') 192. 12.
curious, *adj.*; *attentive, desirous of seeing or knowing* 38. 45.
cuttis, *sb. pl.*; *lots* 91. 25.
cwre, *sb.*; *care, keeping* 20. 22.

dalyaunce, *sb.*; *delight* 45. 22.
dang, *vb. pret.* (ON. dengja); *beat* 102. 64.
dant, *vb.* (OF danter); *to curb, master* 191. 16.
dasy, *adj.*; *in a dazed condition* 139. 19.
daunce, *sb.*; *dance*; begone (*the*) *dance taken the lead, been first* 131. 44.
daunsand, *pres. part.*; *dancing* 7. 42.
dawe, *sb.*; *day* (do hym of dawe = kill him) 153. 23.
dawnse, *vb.*; *dandle* 7. 5.
debate, *sb.*; *contention* 182. 41.
decyse, *vb.*; *expound, resolve* (a dispute) 153. 31.
ded, *sb.*; *death* 16. 13; deed 115. 16; dede 158 A. 3; deid 91. 3.
dede, ded, *vb. pret.*; see *dey.*
dee, *vb.* (Scotch dial.); *die* 13. 20; de 91. 32.
defasid, *pp.*; *defaced* 103. 14.
defende, *vb.* (OF defendre); *forbid* 183. 45.
defygh, *vb.*; *renounce faith or allegiance to* (any one), *reject* 161. 5.
deid, *sb.* (OE dǣd); *deed, action* 102. 146.
deir, *adv.*; see *dere* adv.
dele, *sb.*; *devil* 107. 22.
delle, *sb.* (OE dǣl); *deal, part*

109. 178; del (neuer a del = not at all) 7. 69.
demayne, *sb.* (AF demeyne); *possession, dominion, power* 109. 72.
deme, *vb.*; judge 6. 111 (*pret.*) demyd 10. 5; (*pp.*) demytt 176. 9.
demeryttys, *sb. pl.*; *blame-worthy acts, sins* 162. 25.
den, *sb.* (OE denn); *den* (of a beast) 113. 6.
departyd, *pp.*; *separated* 159. 67.
departyng, *sb.*; *parting* 170. 8.
deprecacione, *sb.*; *petition* 58. 19.
dere, *adv.*; *dearly, at great cost* 4. 42; deir 102. 85; derly 15. 26.
dere, *vb.* (OE derian); *to injure* 60. 21, 184 B. 1.
derne, *adj.*; *secret, dire* 178. 17.
derword, *adj.*; *precious* 36. 8; derworthe 126. 7.
derys, *sb. pl.*; *injuries* 89. 66.
des, *sb.* (OF deis); *dais, seat, bench* 156. 15.
descrive, *vb.*; see *distrif.*
desesse, *sb.*; see *dysese.*
desipel, *sb. pl.*; *disciples* 114. 14; desyplys 116. 4.
deȝyryt, *vb. pres.* 3 *s.*; *desires* 90. 3; (*pret.*) dessyryd 121. 9.
dett, *sb.* (OF dette); *debt, obligation* 126. 23; det 142 Alia. 15.
devidyng, *pres. part.*; (Music) *performing 'divisions', descanting* 39. 35.
devoidyng, *pres. part.*; *leaving* 38. 22.
devors, *sb.*; *divorce, separation* 149. 13.
devyned, *pp.*; *foretold* 105. 61.
dewyne, *adj.*; *divine* 91. 59.
dewyse, *vb.*; *create, frame, fashion* 106. 2; deuyse (*relate*) 153. 5.

dey, *vb.* (ON deyja) ; *die* 161.
21 ; die 104. 4 ; dy 163. 55 ;
(*pret.*) dyyd 87. 37 ; dede 99.
4 ; ded 99. 2 ; deid 161. 7 ;
deit 113. 16.

deyd, *vb. pret.* ; see *don.*

deyte, *sb.* ; *deity* 15. 26 ; deite
51. 11.

dicht, *pp.* ; see *dyght.*

dill, *vb.* (ON dilla) ; *to benumb,
cause dulness* 158 A. 10.

dirk, *adj.* ; *dark* 20. 4 ; derk 11.
70.

dirkit, *pp.* ; *darkened* 113. 25.

dirknace, *sb.* ; *darkness* 13. 12.

discrif, *vb.* ; *describe, set forth in
writing* 20. 10 ; descrive 34. 35.

dirparage, *sb.* ; *despair* (through
confusion with OF *desperer*)
44. 6.

disparit, *ppl. adj.* ; *desperate, in
despair* 113. 33.

disporte, *sb.* ; *sport, pleasure* 26.
26 ; disport 169. 10.

dissauit, *pp.* ; deceived 13. 34.

distaunce, *sb.* ; *quarrel, dissen-
sion, estrangement* 141. 11,
181. 5 ; dystaunce 172. 36.

dobbyt, *pp.* ; see *dubbit.*

doctrix, *sb.* ; *doctress* 22. 17.

dole, *sb.* ; *grief* 97. 94.

dome, *adj.* ; *dumb* 109. 62.

don, *vb.* ; (1) *to do, act* 144. 95 ;
(*pret.* auxiliary 'did') deyd
106. 2 ; dud 181. 14 ; (2 *s.*)
dedest 6. 57 ; (*pl.*) dedone 123.
7. (2) (causative, *make*) do
107. 57 ; (3 *s.*) doeth 110. 26.
(3) *put* (on) (2 *s.*) dose 7. 10.

doun, *adj.* ; *dun, dark, gloomy*
112. 7.

dour, *adj.* (OF dur) ; *hard, stubborn* 113. 17.

doute, *vb.* (OF duter) ; *dread,
fear* 15. 40.

dowcet, *adj.* ; *sweet, dulcet* 187. 5.

drade, *vb. pret.* ; see *dreid.*

draughte, *sb.* ; *a 'move' at chess*
172. 86.

drawe, *pp.* ; (chess) *played,
'drawn'* 172. 86.

draw3t, *sb.* ; *a draught* (of wine)
182. 27.

draynt, *pp.* ; see *dreynte.*

dre, *vb.* (OE dréogan) ; *endure,
undergo* 24. 18.

drecche, *vb.* (OE dreccan) ;
afflict, vex 62. 22.

drede, *vb.* ; *to cause to fear,
terrify* 132. 14.

drede-ful, *adj.* ; *full of dread,
anxious* 172. 7.

dreid, *vb.* ; *to fear, dread* 191. 4 ;
pret. drade 141. 18.

drenched, *pp.* ; *drowned* 57. 58.

dresse (up), *vb.* ; *to set in order,
direct, manage* 25. 13.

drest, *vb. pret.* ; *prepared* 10. 6.

dreuch, *vb. pret.* ; *drew, stretched*
102. 51.

dreynte, *vb. pret.* ; *drowned,
perished* 26. 13 ; (*pp.*) draynt
181. 25.

drife, *vb.* (OE drífan) ; *drive* 10.
69 ; drif 113. 6 ; dryve 109.
146 ; (*pp.*) drove 60. 51.

dubbit, *pp.* ; (1) *dressed, arrayed,
adorned* 38. 27 and 51. (2)
dubbed (a knight) dobbyt 147.
41.

dulcede, *sb.* ; *sweetness* 45. 9.

dulcour, *adj.* (< Lat. dulcor) ;
sweet, pleasant 12. 20.

dule, *adj.* ; *dull, sad, depressed*
91. 30.

dulfull, *adj.* ; *sorrowful* 161. 25.

dulfully, *adv.* ; *drearily, sorrow-
fully* 107. 86.

dulit, *vb. pret.* ; *grieved* 96. 34.

duras, *sb.* ; *constraint, forcible
restraint* 28. 71.

dwelful, *adj.* ; *doleful* 95. 7.

dy, dyyd, *vb.* ; see *dey.*

dyght, *pp.* (OE dihtan) ; *direc-*

ted, treated, disposed, appointed
52. 44, 178. 20; dyghte 15. 26;
dicht 102. 11; dyth 72. 7.

dyre, *adj.*; *dear, beloved* 1. 3.

dysclaunder, *sb.* (AF disclaun-
der, OF esclandre); *slander*
181. 13.

dysese, *sb.*; *distress* 144. 107;
desesse 64. 14; desese 132. 10.

dystaunce, *sb.*; see *distaunce.*

dystayne, *vb.* (error for 'dys-
trayne'); *to press* 109. 139.

dystene, *vb.*; *to deprive of its
colour, cause to look pale* 152. 2.

dyth, *pp.*; see *dyght.*

eche, *vb.* (OE écan); *increase*
181. 15.

effeccioun, *sb.*; *affection* 57. 51.

efftirward, *adv.*; *afterwards* 163.
30.

eft, *adv.*; *again, a second time*
102. 80.

eft-hyr, *prep.*; *after* 78. 22.

eie, *sb.* (OE eage); *eye* 11. 60;
eghe 11. 10; ey 9. 28; ieye
152. 7; (*pl.*) eyne 20. 18; eene
26. 25; ene 191. 17; evyne
128. 11; yes 6. 46.

eke, *adv.*; *also, moreover* 66. 4;
eik 102. 57.

elde, *sb.* (OE éldo); *age of life*
159. 86.

ellect, *ppl. adj.*; *chosen* 39. 13.

ellys, *adv.*; *else, otherwise* 77 B.
34; eyllys 24. 75.

emang, *adv.*; see *amonge.*

empresse, *vb.*; *to imprint* 125. 13.

emprice, *sb.*; *empress* 15. 60;
emprys 24. 54; imperes 182.
70.

enbleshed, *pp.*; *embellished* 153.
44.

enchesone, *sb.* (OF encheson);
occasion, cause, motive 9. 2;
encheson 103. 2; enchesoun
57. 27.

endeis, *vb. pres.* 3 *s.*; *ends* 189.
40.

endurs, *adj.* (ON endr, 'formerly'; cf. 'ender-day': the
added *s* is of uncertain origin);
other 2. 1; endres 4. 1.

ene, *sb. pl.*; see *eie.*

enformyd, *pp.*; *taught* 159. 2.

enhawnted, *pp.* (OF enhanter);
possessed, 'exercised' 109. 63.

ennewyd, *pp.*; *tinted, coloured*
151. 13.

enquentaunce, *sb.*; *acquain-
tance* 172. 39.

entent, *sb.*; *attention, heed* 183.
10.

entre, *sb.*; *entrance* 154. 18.

entreted, *pp.* (OF entraiter);
treated 9. 20.

enþeth, *vb. pres.* 3 *s.*; *endeth*
37. 71.

erbes, *sb. pl.*; *herbs* 37. 60;
erbis 105. 54.

erd, *sb.* (OE eorþe); *earth* 13.
26, 53. 4; erght 111. 4.

erdly, *adj.*; *earthly* 13. 48;
erdely 64. 35.

ere, *sb.* (OE eare); *ear* 20. 19;
(*pl.*) eeris 36. 55; eerys 24. 50.

erght, *sb.*; see *erd.*

es, *adv.*; *as* 60. 507.

ese, *sb.*; *ease, happiness* 114.
117.

eterminable, *adj.*; *what cannot
be terminated* 51. 1.

ethen, *adj.*; *heathen, pagan*
77 B. 30.

ette, *vb. pret.*; *ate* 159. 82; (*imper. pl.*) etyȝt 114. 15.

euerchon, *pron.*; *each one* 181.
11.

euerylk, *adj.* (OE aefre ylc)
every 102. 10; euereylke 144.
110.

evyne, *sb.*; *fellow, companion*
24. 56.

evyne, *sb. pl.*; see *eie.*

ewangelers, *sb. pl.*; *evangelists* 130. 49.

ewen, *adj.*; *equal in rank or power* 15. 57.

ewil, *sb.*; *evil* 53. 8.

ewinsang, *sb.*; *evensong* 94. 22.

excelcite, *sb.*; *height, altitude* 39. 19.

expresse, *sb.*; by expresse = *clearly* 105. 76.

expyrant, *pres. part.*; *expiring* 110. 4.

exill, *vb.*; *exile, banish* 191. 5.

exult, *ppl. adj.*; *exceedingly glad* 112. 2.

eyere, *sb.*; *heir* 151. 39.

eyllys, *adv.*; see *ellys*.

eynde, *sb.*; *end* 182. 23.

eyre, *sb.*; see *aere*.

eysell, ezyl, *sb.*; see *aesell*.

fa, *sb.*; see *fo*.

fader, *sb.* (gen.); *father's* 3. 6 and 12.

fall, *pp.*; *fallen* 106. 19.

falles, *adj.*; *false* 10. 31.

falset, *sb.* (OF falset); *treachery, deceit* 22. 72.

falsyng, *vbl. sb.*; *trickery* 126. 15.

fand, *vb. pret.*; *found, met with* 23. 25.

fandys, *vb.* (OE fandian); (*pres.*) *tempt, assail* 133. 21; (*part.*) fandynge 133. 24.

fang, *vb.*; see *fonge*.

faren, *pp.*; *fared* 78. 21.

faret, *vb. pres.* 3 s.; *happens* 177. 30.

fase, *sb.*; *face* 87. 11.

faunth, *sb.* (apheptic form of OF enfaunt); *child* 75. 19.

fawtyng, *pres. part.*; *lacking* 187. 3.

fay, *sb.* (OF fei); *faith* 6. 137.

fay, *adj.* (OE fǽge); *deadly, fatal* 189. 34.

faynd, *vb.* (OE fundian—see

OED found *v.*[1] and *fand v.*[8]); *hasten, set forth* 102. 149.

fayne, *vb.* (OF feindre); *dissemble, feign* 169. 19.

fayne, *adj.* (OE fægen); *glad* 97. 76.

faynyt, ? see note 121. 22.

fayred, *sb.* (OE fæger+hád); *fairness, beauty* 15. 68.

fe, *sb.*; *fief* 130. 70.

febus, *prop. name*; *Phoebus* 31. 28.

fechtis, *vb. pres.* 3 *s.*; *fights* 113. 11.

fecunde, *adj.*; *fruitful* 45. 3.

fede, *adj.* (see *OED* fade, *a.*); *strong, doughty* 15. 73.

fede, *vb.*; *nourish, sustain* 144. 166.

feer, *adj.* (OE feorr); *far* 165. 2; *fur* 174. 5.

feere, *sb.* (OE gefére); *company* (in feere = in company) 11. 64; fere 29. 31.

feid, *sb.* (OF fede, feide, faide); *feud* (in 14–15th c. only in Scot. writers) 113. 10.

feit, *sb. pl.* (Scot. feyt); *feet* 91. 10.

feith, *sb.* (OF feid, feit); *faith* 119 A. 4; feythe 106. 30; feght 125. 21.

fele, *adj.* (OE fela); *many* 60. 32; fell 15. 38 and 83.

fele, *sb.* (OE fel); *skin, hide* 29. 12.

fele, *vb.*; *feel, experience* 161. 12; feill 102. 27; (*pret.*) feld 10. 37.

fell, *adj.* (OF fel); *cruel, fierce* 102. 6; felle 52. 26; *cunning* 182. 62.

felly, *adv.*; *cruelly, fiercely* 144. 3.

fend, *vb.*; *defend* 126. 12.

ferd, *ppl. adj.*; *afraid, frightened* 163. 33.

ferdnesse, *sb.*; *terror, fear* 11. 74.

Glossary

363

fere, *sb.* (OE geféra) ; *companion* 15. 13 ; (*pl.*) feres 130. 51.

fere, *sb.* (OF feire) ; *a fair* 159. 22 ; feyre 149. 8.

ferr, *adv.* ; *far* 9. 1 ; ferre 14. 20.

ferse, *adj.* (OF fers, fiers) ; *fierce* 85. 18.

ferth, *adj.* ; *fourth* 26. 3 ; forte 117. 19.

fest, *vb.* ; *fasten* 10. 22 ; (*pp.*) 10. 46.

fete, *adj.* (OF fait) ; *becoming, neat* 7. 43.

fete, *vb.* (OE fetian) ; *fetch* 15. 22.

feynte, *adj.* ; *faint, feeble* 165. 2.

filiacion, *sb.* ; *the condition of being a son* 51. 18.

fill, *vb. pret.* ; *fell* 9. 30.

fillyd, *pp.* ; *filled* 15. 25 ; fillit 13. 17.

flagrant, *adj.* (see *OED* flagrant, *a.* 6) ; *fragrant* 22. 31.

flauowre, *sb.* ; *fragrance* 178. 4.

flechse, *sb.* (OE flǽsc) ; *flesh* 173. 18.

fleis, *sb.* (OE fléos) ; *fleece* 22. 60.

flemyd, *vb. pret.* ; *banished* 141. 4.

flor, *sb.* ; *flower* 17. 5.

florysch, *vb.* ; *to embellish, ornament with fine words* 181. 26.

flytt, *vb.* (ON flytja) ; *to remove to another place* 60. 30 ; flytte 152. 4.

fo, *sb.* ; *foe* 126. 12 ; fa 22. 44 ; (*pl.*) foone 29. 20 ; fone 131. 47.

fode, *sb.* (OE fóda) ; *food, subsistence* 6. 83 ; fud 13. 31.

foghel, *sb.* (OE fuȝol) ; *fowl* 158 C. 17.

folde, *sb.* ; *fold, enclosure for sheep* 110. 33.

folde, *vb.* (*OED* fold *v.* † 5) ; *to collapse, fail, falter* 189. 8.

fole, *sb.* (OF fol) ; *fool* 98. 4.

foly, *adj.* ; *foolish* 57. 60.

folyes, *sb. pl.* ; *follies* 15. 38 ; folyce 15. 83.

fonge, *vb.* ; *seize, lay hold of* 6. 68 ; fang 15. 78 ; (*pret.*) fanged 15. 13 ; (*pp.*) fonge 37. 53.

foode, *sb.* ; (1) *child* 6. 7 ; fode 6. 25. (2) *creature, person* 24. ·13.

for, *prep.* ; *in spite of* 107. 83.

fordryve, *pp.* ; *driven about* 135. 23.

fored, *sb.* ; *forehead* 125. 13.

forfende, *pp.* ; *thrust away* 138. 11.

forfett, *vb.* (OF forfaire) ; *transgress against* 57. 72

for-grette, *pp.* ; *exhausted with weeping* 11. 2 note.

forme, *adj.* (OE forma) ; *first, former* 22. 69.

formosite, *sb.* ; *beauty* 38. 14.

forne-fader, *sb.* ; *forefather* 136. 8.

forpossed, *pp.* ; *pushed or knocked about* 135. 24.

forte, *adj.* ; see *ferth*.

for-thy, *conj.* ; *therefore* 163. 33 ; for-þi 144. 155.

for-why, *conj.* ; *because* 92. 8.

forwrecht, *pp.* (OE forwyrcan) ; *exhausted* 91. 40.

foryerned, *pp.* ; 175. 2, see Notes.

fow, *sb.* (Fr. fou) ; *fool* 185. 4.

frayeth, *vb. pres.* 3 *s.* ; *assails* 178. 112.

freche, *adj.* ; *fresh* 24. 2.

free, *adj.* ; *noble, good* 13. 45 ; fre (as *sb.*) 10. 93.

freell, *adj.* (OF frele) ; *frail* 57. 4.

freete, *vb.* ; see *frett*.

frelte, *sb.* ; *frailty* 144. 94.

fres, *vb. pret.* ; *froze* (reflexive) 88. 13.

frett, *vb.* (OE fretan) ; *gnaw, bite into* 159. 79 ; freete 109. 138 ; (*pp.* fretid) 103. 6.

frow, *prep.*; *from* 147. 47.

froward, *adj.*; *perverse* 135. 25.

fruyt, *sb.*; *fruit* 14. 20; frute 15. 73; frout 71. 34; frwte 127. 8.

frythe, *sb.*; *forest, wood* 78. 17.

fud, *sb.*; see *fode.*

fur, *adv.*; see *feer.*

furme, *sb.* (OF furme); *form, shape* 114 heading.

furthe, *adv.*; *forth, onwards* 78. 33.

fybled, *pp.*; *enfeebled* 176. 4.

fykel, *adj.*; *changeable, fickle* 182. 6; fykyll 176. 13.

fylyde, *vb. pret.*; *defiled* 6. 63; fyled 144. 11; (*pp.*) fylde 15. 68.

fyne, *sb.*; *end, close* (of life) 131. 63.

fyned, *vb. pret.*; *came to an end* 39. 12.

fynyse, *vb.* (OF feniss); *finish, cease* 153. 36.

ga, gais, gane (North. dial. forms); see *go.*

gadere, *vb.* (OE gad(e)rian); *to gather* 25. 26; gader 172. 18.

gall, *sb.*; *sore, swelling* 178. 97.

gan, *auxiliary vb.* (*pret.* of OE ginnan); *did* 15. 75; gane 24. 9; gone 37. 43; gun 15. 6; gunne (2 *s.*) 144. 115.

gar, *vb.* (OE ʒierwan); *to cause* (to do or to be done) 63. 36; gare 28. 59; (*pret.*) gart 52. 27; gert 91. 62.

garlong, *sb.*; *garland* 84. 26.

gastfull, *adj.*; *dreadful* 141. 18.`

gate, *sb.* (ON gata ME 'gait'); *way, road, course* 15. 17; (*pl.*) gates 15. 80.

gate, *vb. pret.* (ON geta); *got, received* 92. 59.

gayne-stand, *vb.*; *withstand, resist* 60. 46.

gent, *adj.*; *courteous* 38. 4; gente 45. 6.

gesse, *vb.*; *think, suppose* 186. 19.

gidschip, *sb.*; *guideship, guidance* 113. 28.

gildre, *sb.*; *snare* 60. 39 (see Notes).

glades, *vb. pres.* 3 *s.*; *gladdens* 112. 8.

glem, *sb.*; *gleam, light* 89. 3.

glemmand, *part. adj.*;. *gleaming* 22. 22.

glood, *vb. pret.*; see *glyde.*

glore, *sb.*; *glory* 22. 22.

glosid, *pp.*; *flattered* 175. 3.

glyde, *vb.* (OE glídan); *pass away* 183. 14; (*pret.*) glood 39. 26; glode 89. 30.

go, *vb.* (OE gán); *go* 3. 4; gone 87. 34; *walk* 125. 2 (wedyr y ryde or gone = *in all circumstances*); ga 102. 15; (*pres.* 3 *s.*) goose 130. 12; gais 102. 8; (*pp.*) gane 102. 112.

goid, *adj.*; *good* 86. 21; goude 70. 29.

gollytte, *sb.*; see *iollytte.*

goodly, *adv.*; *graciously* 57. 26.

goromercy, *exclam.*; *God have mercy* (meaning 'God reward you') used as a mere expression of thanks 57. 52.

gost, *sb.*; *soul* 28. 64.

goostly, *adj.*; *spiritual* 92. 84; gastely 133. 21.

gotene, *pp.*; *begotten* 69. 6.

goude, *adj.*; see *goid.*

gouernaunce, *sb.*; *government, control* 172. 10; gvuernance 40. 7.

goyd, *sb.* (see *OED* good *sb.* C III. 7 b); *property, possessions* 76. 8.

grace *sb.*; *fortune* 6. 35; *favour* 57. 26.

graif, *sb.* (OE græf); *grave* 94. 25; grawe 147. 69.

grame, *sb.*; *grief, sorrow* 172. 69.

grane, *sb.*; *grain, seed* 22. 3.

grase, *sb.*; *grace* 32. 10.

graunth, *pp.*; *granted* 75. 17.

grawe, *sb.*; see *graif*.

gre, *sb.* (*OED* gree *sb.*[1]); *supremacy, mastery*; *hence the prize for a victory* 151. 20.

gre, *sb.* (*OED* gree *sb.*[2]); *favour, goodwill* (at gre = in good part) 135. 73.

greabyll, *adj.* (OF greable); *willing, compliant* 118. 13.

gref, *vb.*; see *greve*.

greffe, *sb.* (OF grief); *suffering, grief* 109. 21; gryff 177. 3; greve 130. 71; *offence* 93. 31.

grenowst, *adj. supl.*; *greenest* (of a wound), *unhealed, raw* 168. 5.

gres, *sb.*; *grass* 191. 11.

grete = greet *þe* 18. 9.

grett, *vb. pret.*; *greeted* 70. 3; gret 97. 29.

greve, *vb.*; (1) *provoke to anger* 184 A. 4. (2) *cause pain to*, grefe 108. 16; gref 4. 79; (*pret.*) greuyd 10. 54.

greyne, *adj.*; *green, flourishing* 22. 23.

groge, *vb.*; *grudge, be discontented with* 97. 102.

gronttyng, *vbl. sb.*; *groaning* 147. 20.

gronys, *sb. pl.*; *groans* 28. 35.

grope, *vb.* (*OED* grope, *v.* 4, fig.); *to apprehend* 138. 28.

growis, *vb. pres.* 2 *s.* (*OED* grue, *v.*); *shudderest, feelest horror* 113. 18.

grucche, *vb.* (OF groucier); *murmur, complain* (*of*) 148. 68; grucchyth 172. 10.

gryff, *sb.*; see *greffe*.

gryll, *adj.*; *fierce, angry* 87. 25.

grynde, *vb.*; *grind* (grain) 172. 18.

grype, *vb.*; *grasp* 172. 18.

gryte, *adj.*; *great* 70. 20.

gudenace, *sb.*; *goodness* 13. 10.

gvuernance, *sb.*; see *gouernaunce*.

guy, *vb.* (OF guier); *direct, guide* 161. 25.

gyne, *sb.*; *device* 156. 21.

gytt, *vb.* (ON geta); *obtain, get* 19. 8.

ʒalde, *vb. pret.*; see *ʒilde*.

ʒare, *adv.* (OE ʒearwe); *certainly, well* 15. 69.

ʒarkyd, *pp.* (OE gearcian); *prepared, made ready* 95. 20.

ʒarne, *vb.*; 4. 25; see *þarne*.

ʒate, *sb.* (= E ʒeat); *gate* 15. 19; yate 172. 43; (*pl.*) ʒatis 10. 93.

ʒelde, *vb.*; see *ʒilde*.

ʒendone, *vb. pret.*; *yawned, gaped* 123. 17.

ʒerdis, *sb. pl.*; *rods, twigs* 188. 2.

ʒernynge, *vbl. sb.*; *yearning* 15. 21.

ʒeyt, *adv.* (OE ʒíet); *yet* 24. 1; ʒhit 33. 27; ʒĩt 102. 15; ʒyt 107. 93; yt 105. 23, 39, &c.

ʒhe, *fem. pers. pron.*; *she* 95. 48.

ʒyf, *conj.*; *if* 123. 22; gyffe 133. 11; gif 102. 137; yeve 121. 10.

ʒilde, *vb.* (OE ʒieldan); *yield, return* 140. 22; gyld 52. 27; ʒelde 144. 145; (*pret.*) ʒalde 91. 53.

ʒoungþe, *sb.* (young + th); *the state of being young* 148. 18.

ʒouþe, *sb.* (OE ʒeoʒuþ); *youth* 148. 2; yought 109. 33; yowt 156. 11.

had-y-wyste, *phrase*; *had I known* 148. 41.

haʒt, *vb. pres.* 3 *s.*; see *haue*.

halde, *sb.*; *keeping* 63. 20.

hale, *adj.* (OE hál); *whole, sound* 102. 78.

hall, *adj.*; *all* 4. 47.

halowes, *sb. pl.*; *saints* 25. 14; halowys 124. 29.

halsit, *pp.* (OE halsian); *hailed* 91. 22.

ham, *pron.*; *them* 178. 94.

han, *vb. pres.*; see *haue*.

hang, *vb. pret.*; see *hyng*.

hap, *vb.*; *to wrap, protect* 4. 9; (*pret.*) happid 2. 7.

happe, *sb.* (ON happ); *hap, fortune* 60. 58; (*pl.*) happis ('mishaps') 172. 80.

happys, *vb.* (impersonal with dat.); *happens* 7. 31; happis 151. 55.

har, *poss. pron.*; *their* 179. 2.

hard, *vb. pret.*; *heard* 89. 51.

harlit, *pp.* (OED harl, *v.*); *dragged* 91. 20.

harnesse, *sb.*; *armour* 109. 170.

harrowid, *vb. pret.*; *harried, made a raid on* 10. 99.

hass, *vb. pres. 3 s.*; see *haue*.

hastenys, *sb.*; *hastiness* 182. 17.

hate, *vb.* (OE hatian); *to despise* 15. 21.

haue, *vb.*; *have, hold* 148. 38; havſe 147. 71; hawe 147. 74; (*pres. 3 s.*) haȝt 90. 4; hat 177. 43; hass 163. 66; hes 96. 23; (*pl.*) han 114. 16; (*pret.*) hed 178. 107.

haunted, *pp.*; *practised, exercised* 134. 17.

hawe, *sb.*; *haw* 172. 88.

hay, *sb.*; *hay* 191. 11; hey 89. 33.

hayme, *sb.*; *home* 156. 35.

hed, *sb.*; *head* 103. 19; heode 109. 139; heid 102. 72.

hedus, *adj.* (OF hidous); *frightful* 52. 41.

hedyr, *adv.*; *hither* 163. 3.

heer, *sb.* (OE (Anglian) hér); *hair* 39. 65; here 7. 11; herre 6. 8.

hef, *vb.* (OE hebban); 1. (*trans.*)

to raise 20. 21. 2. (*intrans.*) *to be stirred* 156. 1.

heill, *sb.* (OE hǽlu); *well-being, safety* 96. 50; heele 27. 4.

hen, *adv.* (OE heonan); *hence* 163. 24; hens 177. 96; hyne 20. 21.

hend, *sb.* = *end* 163. 28.

hende, *adj.*; *courteous, gracious* 15. 1; hend 78. 19.

heng, *vb. pret.*; see *hyng*.

hente, *vb.* (OE hentan); *to seize* 89. 54; hent 183. 15; (*pp.*) 97. 40.

heos, *poss. pron.*; *his* 11. 15.

her, *adv.*; *here* 146. 5; heir 102. 82; here 147. 47; heyre 147. 13; hire 4. 23.

herbere, *sb.*; *arbour* 78. 2.

herde, *sb.*; *shepherd* 64. 44.

here, *poss. pron.*; *their* 114. 17; hir 146. 7.

herkenud, *vb. imper. pl.*; *hearken* 123. 1.

herme, *vb.* (OE hearmian); *to injure, harm* 129. 16.

hernis, *sb. pl.* (ON hjarni); *brains* 91. 26.

herre, *sb.*; see *heer*.

hertfullie, *adv.*; *heartily* 102. 84.

hertly, *adv.*; *earnestly* 142. 8.

hery, *vb.* (OE herian); *exalt, honour* 52. 54.

hes, *vb. pres. 3 s.*; see *haue*.

hestis, *sb. pl.*; *commands* 58. 2; heestis 101. 14.

hethin, *vbl. sb.* (OED hething); *scorn* 91. 22.

heuynesse, *sb.*; *heaviness, sorrow* 8. 8; heyuenys 1. 12.

hew, *sb.* (OE híew, híw); *colour* 78. 5; hewe 35. 18, hwe 82. 18.

hey, *sb.*; see *hay*.

heygh, *adj.* (OE héah); *high* 144. Alia 17; hyþe 24. 65; hye 131. 7; hy 166. 4; (*supl.*) heyȝthyst 24. 63.

heyle, *vb.* (OE helian); *keep a secret, keep silence* 183. 22.

heyre, *adv.*; see *her.*

hid, *sb.* (OE hýd); *hide, skin* 91. 39; hyde 35. 18.

high, *vb.* (reflexive); *hie, hasten* 161. 17; hy 60. 53; hye 107. 102; (*pret.*) hyit 91. 31.

hight, *vb.* (OE hátan); (*pres.*) art called 23. 3; hyȝth 71. 7; hyȝth (*pp.*) 5. 1; hyght (*promised*)144. 34; (*pp.*) hote 58. 23.

hingand, *part.*; see *hyng.*

hir, *poss. pron.*; see *here.*

hire, *adv.*; see *her.*

hit, *3 pers. pron.*; *it* 147. 7; hitt 178. 21; hyt 166. 8.

ho, *rel. pron.*; *who* 169. 13; hoys (= whose) 181. 28.

ho, *exclam.*; *cease!* 57. 81.

holde, *adj.* = *old* 188. 21.

holden, *pp.*; *esteemed* 15. 60; holde 189. 2.

holdyn, *pp.*; *held* 10. 82; holdyne (bound) 7. 63.

hole, *adj.*; *whole* 103. 1; holl 7. 57.

holey, *adj.*; *holy* 93. 39.

holly, *adv.*; *wholly* 143. 4.

holpe, *vb. pret.*; *helped* 109. 68; (*pp.*) holpene 183. 51.

holt, *sb.* (OE holt); *wood, forest* 147. 2.

home, *rel. pron.*; *whom* 78. 37.

hondes, *sb.* (*pl.*); *hounds* 185. 10.

hong, *vb. pret.*; see *hyng.*

hongid, *vb. pret.* (OE hangian); *hanged* 104. 14.

hoppeth, *vb.*; *dances* 161. 2.

hore, *sb.* (OE horu); *filth, dirt* 147. 21.

hote, *pp.*; see *hight.*

hough, *adv.*; *how* 154. 1.

houre, *poss. pron.* our 16. 21.

hovre, *adj.* (OE hár); *hoary* 147. 3.

houres, *sb. pl.*; *hours, Horae* 112. 21.

hout, *prep.* = *out* 4. 47.

hown, *pron. adj.*; *own* 173. 18.

hoys, *rel. pron.*; see *ho.*

hucches, *sb. pl.*; *chests, coffers* 159. 41.

hwe, *sb.*; 82. 18, see *hew.*

hy, *sb.*; *haste* 96. 42.

hyd, *vb.*; *hide* 147. 47; (*pp.*) hyde 176. 7.

hyde, *sb.*; see *hid.*

hye, hyit, *vb.*; see *high.*

hyght, hyȝth, *vb.*; see *hight.*

hyld, *vb. pret.*; *held* 159. 49.

hylde, *vb.* (*OED* hield, v. 7); *to pour, shed* (lit. and fig.) 42. 11.

hyme, *sb.*; *hymn* 112. 21.

hyn, *prep.* = *in* 123. 26.

hyndynge, *vbl. sb.* = *ending* 24. 79.

hyne, *adv.*; see *hen.*

hyng, *vb.*; *hang* 10. 21, 97. 18; (*part.*) hingand 96. 18; (*pret.*) heng 95. 8; hong 11. 3; hang 52. 25.

hyre, *sb.* (OE hýr); *hire, wages* 147. 68.

hyryng, *pres. part.*; *hearing* 28. 18.

hyt, *3 pers. pron.*; see *hit.*

hyþe, *adj.*; see *heygh.*

i-callt, *pp.*; *called* 178. 27.

i-dyȝt, *pp.*; *prepared* 70. 21.

ierarchyes, *sb. pl.*; *hierarchies* 39. 36; chererchy 31. 20.

ieye, *sb.*; see *eie.*

ilka, *adj.* (orig. two words: ilk = OE ylc, 'each'+indefinite art.) *each* 186. 26.

illicioun, *sb.* (< Lat. illidere, to strike against); *the action of striking against something* 39. 13.

illumynit, *pp.*; *illumined* 13. 41.

i-lok, *pp.*; *locked* 178. 16.

imperes, *sb.*; see *emprice*.

in, *sb.*; *dwelling* 179. 17.

incontynent, *adv.*; *forthwith, straightway* 38. 45.

indeficient, *adj.*; *unfailing, unceasing* 45. 11.

indesinente, *adj.*; *perpetual* 45. 9.

indewed, *pp.* (influenced by Lat. induere); *clothed, endued* 45. 22.

indigent, *adj.*; *deficient, destitute* 13. 35.

indurat, *pp.*; *hardened* 8. 15.

ingent, *adj.*; *immense* 150. 10.

in-grauit, *pp.*; *carved, graven* 91. 5.

in-mydde, *prep.*; *amid* 177. 19.

innosable, *adj.*; not *destructive* 112. 38.

inogthe, *adj.*, *adv.* (OE ȝenóh); *enough* 159. 49; aneuch 102. 52.

instaunce, *sb.*; *urgent entreaty, solicitation* 162. 11.

instynguyble, *adj.*; *inextinguishable* 187. 3.

integrate, *adj.*; *perfect, intact* 44. 2.

intendyth, *vb. pres.* 3 *s.*; *turns, directs* 151. 58.

in-to, *prep.*; *until* 23. 22.

intretid, *pp.*; *treated, handled* 103. 5.

inuolat, *ppl. adj.*; *inviolate* 112. 1.

in-with, *prep.*; *within* 24. 46.

i-plaunth, *pp.*; *planted* 75. 18.

irkit, *pp.*; *wearied, irked* 113. 27; irkyng (*vbl. sb.*) 33. 12.

is, *adv.*; *yes* 4. 78.

isse, *vb. pres.* 3 *s.*; *is* 34. 6.

ix, *vb. pres.* 1 *s.*; *ask* 4. 63.

iangel, *vb.*; *to chatter or talk noisily* 179. 14.

iape, *sb.*; *gibe* 92. 37.

Iewlye, *adv.*; *like a Jew* 9. 20.

iollytte, *sb.*; *jollity* 147. 46; gollytte 147. 38.

ioote, *sb.*; *a jot, a whit* 182. 39.

iounit, *pp.*; *joined, united* 22. 34; ioyned 36. 24.

yournay, *sb.*; *journey* 130. 20.

ioy, *vb.* (*intrans.*); *to rejoice* 36. 1; ioye 36. 15.

yoy, *vb.* (*trans.*); *to enjoy* 125. 9.

yoyne, *vb.*; *to join* 118. 6.

iuge, *sb.*; *judge* 109. 114.

iustis, *sb.* (*pl.* of just, *joust*) *tournament* 151. 20.

kache, *vb.*; *catch* 107. 7; keche 188. 1; (*pret.*) cayht 155. 2.

kalle, *vb.*; *call, name* 70. 25.

keele, *vb.*; *to cool* 161. 13; kele (*to become less violent*) 182. 22.

keist, *vb. pret.*; *cast* (lots) 91. 25.

kelle, *vb.*; *to kill* 28. 55, (*pret.* 2 *s.*) kylduste 107. 43.

kende, *sb.*; *race, kind* 95. 48.

kene, *vb.* (OE cennan); *to ken, know* 183. 20.

kepe, *pp.*; *kept, guarded* 129. 2.

kepe, *vb.*; *to* (*take*) *care* (*that*) 110. 6.

kepis, *vb. pres.* 3 *s.*; *keeps on, is maintained* 177. 57.

kest, *pp.*; *contrived, purposed* 57. 67.

keyne, *adj.*; *keen, cruel* 3. 8.

kid, *vb. pret.* (OE cýðða̱n); *showed* 115. 8; (*pp.*) kyd (made known) 28. 13.

kindle, *adv.*; *kindly* 102. 144.

kitte, *vb. pret.*; *cut* 11. 4; (*pp.*) kut 92. 66; kutte 92. 13.

knaggit, *adj.*; *knobbed, jagged* 102. 17.

knappe, *sb.*; *a knock or blow* 60. 60.

kneled, *vb. pret.*; *kneeled* 38. 37; cnellyd 1. 26.

knokytt, *pp.* (ON knoka); *beaten* 176. 5.

knoppis, *sb. pl.*; *knobs* 102. 69.

knoppit, *adj.*; *knobbed* 102. 65.

knwe, *vb. pret.*; *knew* 82. 12.

kocke, *sb.*; *cock* 182. 45.

kone, *vb.* (OE cunnan); *can, be able* 183. 19; (*pp.*) kouþe (*known*) 11. 37.

konnyng, *sb.*; *ability* 25. 2; kunnynge 142. 33.

kylduste, *vb. pret.* 2 *s.*; see *kelle*.

kyn, *sb.* (OE cyn); *kind* (all kyn = *all kind of*) 97. 43; kyne *kindred* 156. 18.

kynde, *sb.* (OE cynd); *nature* 25. 1; (*adj.*) *natural* 158 A. 7.

kyndely, *adv.*; *according to nature* 28. 56; *lovingly* 97. 42.

kynrede, *sb.*; *kin* 106. 24.

kynrik, *sb.*; *kingdom* 53. 3.

kyte, *sb.*; *kite, bird of prey* 172. 61.

labours, *sb. pl.*; *labourers* 151. 24.

lace, *sb.*; *snare* 152. 13.

lagh, *vb.* (OE Anglian hlæh- han); *to laugh* 7. 83; (*pret.*) lough 2. 7.

laȝyng, *vbl. sb.*; *laughing* 7. 6.

laisar, *sb.* (OF leisir); *leisure, respite* 13. 20.

laith, *adj.* (OE láð); *loath* 102. 134.

lapped, *vb. pret.*; *wrapped* 6. 19; lappyde 5. 3.

larche, *adj.*; *liberal* 32. 10; large 131. 40.

lare, *sb.* (OE lár); *lore, instruction* 97. 53.

lasse, *adv. comp.* (OE læs); *less* 145. 10.

lastyngnes, *sb.*; *continuance* 108. 20.

latt, *adv.*; *lately* 159. 6.

launche, *sb.*; *branch, stalk* 37. 49 (cf. *Pearl* 978).

lause, *vb.*; *set free, release* 97. 88.

lawe, *adj.* (ON lágr); *low* 154. 6.

lawlie, *adv.*; *humbly* 91. 14.

lawre, *sb.*; *laurel* 112. 27.

lawse, *adj.*; *loose, free* 7. 59; lowse 171. 14.

layd, *pp.*; see *leye*.

laye, *sb.*; *song, lay* 9. 35.

layke, *vb.*; *to sport* 7. 36.

layme, *sb.* (OE lám); *loam* 156. 33.

leccone, *vb.*; *liken* 147. 17.

leche, *sb.*; *physician* 6. 133.

leche, *adj.* (OF lasche); *loose, slack* 188. 3.

lede, *sb.* (OE léod); 1. *people* (in lede = *among people, on earth*) 15. 50. 2. *man, person* (leede) 144. 110.

leere, *vb.* (OE læran); *learn* 184 A. 1. See also *lere*.

leese, *vb.*; see *lose*.

lefe, *vb.* (OE Anglian léfan); *believe* 24. 43; leue 77 B. 29; leeve 184 A. 3; (*pret.*) leuyd 10. 43.

leid, *vb. pret.*; see *leye*.

leid, *vb.* (OE lædan); (*pp.*) led, *conducted* 102. 47; led (*spent*) 102. 92.

leif, *sb.* (OE léaf); *leave, permission* 156. 14; leve 171. 11.

leife, *vb.* (OE libban); see *leuyn*.

leife, *adj.* (OE léof); *lief, dear* 96. 27; leff 124. 30.

leifis, *vb. pres.* 2 *s.*; see *leue*, vb.

lellely, *adv.*; *loyally* 142. 122.

lely, *sb.*; *lily,* 23. 7; lille 38. 9.

lem, *sb.* (OE léoma); *ray, gleam, flame* 89. 2.

lemyng, *ppl. adj.*; *gleaming, shining* 28. 2.

lemys, *sb. pl.*; *limbs* 142. 27.

len, *vb.* (OE lænan); *to grant* 6.

129; lene 15. 94; (*pp.*) lent (*devoted, bestowed*) 113. 1.

lende, *vb.* (OE lendan); *to arrive, go, come* 15. 33; (*pp.*) lent (*apportioned, settled*) 10. 28; (*lighted upon*) 97. 31; lente (*descended*) 45. 2.

lenghte, *sb.*; *length* 152. 13.

lere, *vb.* (OE lǽran); *teach* 25. 27. See also *leere*.

les, *adj. comp.*; *less* 96. 22; (*supl.*) lest 10. 78.

lese, *vb.*; see *lose*.

lese, *sb.* (OE léas); *falsehood* 64. 37.

lesyng, *vbl. sb.*; *falsehood, lying* 16. 15.

lete, *vb.* (OE lǽtan); *to allow the escape of* 114. 7; *to forsake* 25. 27; *lette* (*to permit*) 183. 39.

lethyrly, *adv.*; *miserably, wretchedly* 176. 1.

lett, *vb.* (OE lettan); (1) *leave off, desist* 6. 102. (2) *hinder, check*; *let* 180. 15.

leudenes, *sb.*; *lewdness, ignorance* 25. 27.

leve, *sb.*; see *leif*, sb.

leue, *vb.*; see *lefe*.

leue, *vb.* (OE lǽfan); *leave, forsake* 144. 157; (*pres. 2 s.*) leifis 96. 44; (*imper.*) leyfe 1. 3; (*part.*) levyng 154. 13.

leue, *sb.* (OE léaf); *leaf* 181. 9.

leuyn, *vb.* (OE libban); *to live* 64. 28; lyve 166. 5; lyvfe 147. 51; leife 102. 150; leif 96. 30; liffe 155. 9; lyf 126. 22; (*part.*) leuyng 36. 11; lewyng 147. 13.

lewyd, *adj.*; *lewd, ignorant* 182. 44.

leye, *vb.* (OE lecgan); *to lay* 11. 50; ley 65. 2; (*pret.*) leyed 109. 82; leid (*declared, expounded*) 91. 24; (*pp.*) layd

163. 64; layde (*cast down, abased*) 176. 1; leyd (*laid asleep*) 149. 15.

leyfe, *vb. imper.*; see *leue*, vb.

leyne, *vb.* (ON løyna); *to conceal* 146. 14.

lichtnes, *vb.* (*pres. 3 s.*); *sheds light upon* 112. 4.

lidernes, *sb.*; *infirmity, laxity* (*in a physical sense*) 109. 64.

lidy, *sb.*; *lady* 159. 66.

liffe, *vb.*; see *leuyn*.

lifyng, *vbl. sb.*; *estate* 33. 13; *lifetime* 33. 38.

lig, *vb.* (OE licgan); *to lie* 4. 17; (*pres. 1 s.*) ly 159. 13; (*3 s.*) liggus 7. 3; (*pl.*) lyn 146. 4; lyen 162. 9; (*pret.*) lay 9. 3; ley 109. 148.

lighted, *vb. pret.*; *alighted* 50. 6.

like, *vb. impers.* (OE lícian); *to be pleasing* 102. 89; (*part.*) likand 7. 44.

lille, *sb.*; see *lely*.

linage, *sb.* (OF lignage); *lineage, family* 42. 2; lynnag 121. 12; lynage 130. 98.

lof, *sb.* (OE lof); *praise* 15. 93.

loft, *sb.* (OE loft); *air* (*on* loft = *aloft*) 112. 3.

loke, *pp.* (OE lúcan); *locked* 140. 31.

lokene, *vb.* (OE lócian); *look, gaze* 154. 58; (*pres. 3 s.*) lukis 176. 1; luke (*imp.*) *take care,* 102. 141; (*pret.*) lokyd 97. 17; lokyd lyke = *resembled* 109. 64; (*2 s.*) lokudste 107. 53.

lome, *sb.*; *lamb* 182. 62; *lambe* 103. 17.

londe-daye, *sb.* (*cf.* OE lǽndagas); *the days granted to a man to live* 5. 13. Cf. the phrase 'livelong day'.

loos, *vb. intrans.*; *to perish* 130. 13.

lose, *vb.* (OE léosan); *to lose*

115. 24; lese 93. 44; leese 155.
17; (*pp.*) lorne 15. 87; lore
148. 5; lest 10. 78.

loth, *adj.* (with dative); *hateful*
89. 57.

lothe, *vb.* (OE láðian); *to be
disgusted with* 65. 3; (*pres.*)
lothys 176. 3.

lother, *adj. comp.*; *loather* 171.
11.

lough, *adj.* (ON lágr); *low* 140.
18.

louly, *adj.*; *lowly, humble* 142.
16.

loulynge, *ppl. adj.*; *lulling* 37.
50.

louage, *sb.* (OF levesche, lu-
vesche); *the herb love-ache*
(widely used as a remedy)
178. 55.

louyng, *vbl. sb.*; *praise, lauda-
tion* 90. 17; lowyng 33. 34;
loveyng 134. 4.

love-likyng, *sb.*; *affection* 144.
30.

lowkyde, *pp.*; *locked up, imprisoned* 176. 5.

lowse, *adj.*; see *lawse.*

lucern, *sb.*; *a lamp, lantern* 22.
36.

luciant, *adj.* (erroneous form
of 'lucent'); *shining, lumin-
ous* 38. 44.

luf, *vb.*; *love* 7. 85; luff 7. 86;
(*pret.*) luffud 107. 75.

luffe, *sb.*; *love* 183. 33.

lufly, *adj.*; *loving* 26. 25.

lukis, *vb. pres.* 3 *s.*; see *lokene.*

lune, *sb.*; *a leash for a hawk* 171.
14.

lust, *sb.*; *desire, pleasure* 47. 33.

lye, *sb.*; *ally* 77 B. 20.

lyen, lyn, *vb.*; see *lig.*

lyf, lyvfe, *vb.*; see *leuyn.*

lyft, *pp.*; *lifted* 92. 50.

lyghly, *adv.*; *easily* 163. 40.

lykyng, *sb.*; *favour* 58. 45.

lymbe, *sb.*; *limbo* 96. 51.

lynnag, *sb.*; see *linage.*

lynd, *vb.*; *lend, grant* 114. 25.

lyne, *sb.*; *line, snare* 11. 50;
lineage 105. 24.

lynneth, *vb. pres.* 3 *s.*; *ceaseth*
77 B. 27.

lys, *vb.·*; *to relieve* (of pain, &c.),
to comfort 178. 67; (*pret.*)
lyssyd 5. 7; (*pp.*) 178. 33.

lyste, *sb.*; *wish, desire* 130. 35.

lyte, *adj.*; *little* 174. 8.

lyth, *adj.* (OE líðe); *gentle,
meek* 42. 2.

lyth, *sb.* (OE leoht); *light* 72. 5;
lythe 93. 44.

lyth, *sb.* = *life* 29. 19.

lyther, *adj.*; *bad, wicked* 182.
5; lither 178. 109.

lyve, *vb.*; see *leuyn.*

ma, *vb.*; see *may.*

macy, *adj.*; *giddy, dizzy* 139.
17.

mad, maid, *vb. pret.*; see *makyn.*

maire, *adj. comp.*; *more* 96. 22.

maist, *adj. supl.*; *most* 22. 3;
moist 22. 56; mooste 6. 32.

makelesse, *adj.*; *matchless* 30.
18.

makyn, *vb.*; *to make* 114. 8;
maky 185. 6; make 149. 5;
mak 147. 79; (*pret.*) maid 94.
20; mad 159. 53; (*pp.*) maked
52. 2.

malese, *sb.*; *malice* 173. 11;
mallys 24. 55.

malgyse, *sb.*; *perverseness* 153.
12. See Godefroy 'malgesir'.

mamelles, *sb. pl.*; *breasts* 37. 5.

man, *vb.*; *must* 156. 41.

mansuete, *adj.*; *gentle, mild*
28. 19.

mansuetude, *sb.*; *gentleness* 45.
18.

mare, *vb.*; *ruin, mar* 158 A. 10.

mare = *Mary* 24. 13.

372 *Glossary*

mas, *sb.*; *mass* 116. 6.

maset, *ppl. adj.*; *dazed, terrified* 152. 6.

mate, *vb.*; *to checkmate, destroy, kill* 158 B. 6.

matyng, *vbl. sb.*; *checkmating* 153. 6.

mawgre, *prep.* (OF mal gre); *in spite of* 135. 56.

may, *sb.*; *maiden* 33. 13.

may, *vb.* (OE mæg); *may* 3. 2; ma 4. 69; mey 78. 47; (*subj.*) mow 49. 8; (*pl.*) mouwen 16. 1; mown 83. 8.

me, *indef. pron.*; *one* (as *pl.* 115. 13).

meche, *adj.*; see *mycull*.

mede, *sb.*; *reward* 7. 76.

medsyne, *sb.*; *medicine* 38. 17; medicyne 22. 7.

medyate, *sb.*; *intermediary* 11. 43.

medyl, *vb.*; *interpose, take part in* 172. 11.

medyll, *adj.*; *middle* 151. 66.

meene, *sb.* (musical term); *person performing the middle part* 39. 6.

meene, *vb.* (OF mener); *to conduct, manage* 39. 14.

meis, *vb.* (cf. *OED* meek, *v.*: a contracted North. form = to 'mais' from *make*); *appease, calm* 22. 67.

meit, *adj.*; *of the right length, made to fit* 102. 52.

mekle, *adv.*; *meekly* 52. 2.

mekull, *adj.*; see *mycull*.

mele, *sb.* (OE mæl); *time, occasion* 7. 68.

melle, *vb.* (OE mælan); *to speak* 29. 15; (*vbl. sb.*) mellyng 181. 29.

mene, *adj.*; *middle* 185. 5.

mene, *sb.*; *instrument, means* 30. 38, 57. 101, 186. 21.

mene, *vb.* (OE mænan); *relate,*

declare, refer to, mean 22. 5; meene 15. 3; meyne 20. 6 (*pp.*) mente 45. 4.

menskes, *sb. pl.* (ON mennska); *kindnesses* 15. 46.

mere, *adj.* (OE mære); *illustrious* 15. 91.

merwaylede, *vb. pret.*; *marvelled* 71. 13.

mete, *vb.* (OE mætan); *to dream* 127. 6.

methe, *sb.* (OE mete); *meat, food* 107. 29.

meue, *vb.* (OF mover); *to move, persuade* 25. 8; move 9. 12; (*part.*) meuyng 181. 9; (*pp.*) meved 106. 15 note.

meuynge, *vbl. sb.*; *prompting* 15. 91, 45. 18.

mey, *vb.*; see *may*.

meynde, *sb.* (OE ʒemýnd); *memory* 182. 21; mende 153. 3.

meynt, *pp.*; see *myngyd*.

mikel, *adv.*; *greatly* 92. 31.

mis, *sb.*; *fault* 22. 88; mysse 28. 80; mys 105. 92.

misse, *vb.*; *to lack* 42. 3; (*pret.*) myst 159. 43.

mocyon, *sb.*; *instigation, prompting* 118. 15.

moʒt, *sb.*; *mouth* 174. 10.

moist, *adj. supl.*; see *maist*.

molde, *sb.* (OE molde); *earth* 153. 30; mowlde 159. 13.

mone, *sb.*; *complaint, moan* 137. 5; moone 154. 2; (*pl.*) mones 28. 32.

more, *adj.*; *more and less* = *all* 13. 15.

mormale, *sb.*; *inflamed sore* 178. 109.

mornynge, *vbl. sb.*; *mourning* 8. 12.

mortes, *sb.*; *mortise* 6. 76.

morþer-man, *sb.*; *murderer* 6. 67.

most, *adj.*; biggest 7. 45.

Glossary

373

mot, *vb.* (OE mót) ; *may* 53. 3 ;
mote 54. 8 ; mut 89. 68.

mourther, *sb.* (OE morðor) ;
murder 153. 3.

mow, mouwen, *vb.* ; see *may.*

mowid, *vb. pret.* ; *made mouths
or grimaces* 103. 8.

mowlde, *sb.* ; *head* 116. 11.

mowrone, *vb.* (OE murnan) ;
to feel sorrow or grief 11. 22.

mude, *sb.* (OE mód) ; *mind,
thought, feeling* 102. 3.

muk, *sb.* ; *muck* 163. 45.

mull, *sb.* ; *? dust, ashes* 163. 45.

mundificate, *ppl. adj.* ; *purified,
cleansed* 12. 3.

mure, *adj.* (OF meúr, meúre) ;
modest, demure 144. 141.

murth, *sb.* (OE myr(i)ȝþ) ;
mirth, joy 27. 1.

mut, *vb.* ; see *mot.*

mycull, *adj.* (OE micel) ; *great,
many, much* 7. 76 ; mycul 107.
78 ; mekull 24. 53 ; mekill 102.
26 ; mekyl 163. 45 ; mychell
141. 25 ; mych 10. 67 ; miche
109. 87 ; meche 75. 17.

myddell erthe, *sb.* ; *the world* 15.
34.

myde-morroo-daye, *sb.* ; *mid-
morn* 147. 25.

myndly, *adj.* ; *mindful* 154. 3.

myng, *vb.* (OE (ge)mynegian) ;
call to mind, remember 28.
45.

myngyd, *vb. pret.* (OE mengan) ;
mingle ; myngyd with myrthe,
cheered 97. 34 ; meynt, *pp.*
95. 27.

mynistre, *vb.* (OF menistrer) ;
direct, manage 39. 14.

mynne, *vb.* (ON minna) ; *relate*
10. 79.

mynne, *adj.* (ON minne) ; *less*
(always coupled with 'more')
144. 50.

myr, *sb.* ; *myrrh* 87. 18.

myre, *sb.* (ON mýrr) ; *boggy
ground, mire* 174. 6.

myrk, *sb.* (OE myrce) ; *darkness* 91. 30.

myschefe, *sb.* ; *misfortune* 164.
8 ; mescheves (*pl.*) 30. 22.

myslosed, *pp.* ; *dispraised,
blamed* 175. 4.

mythye, *adj.* ; *mighty* 131. 26.

mywet, *adj.* ; *mute, silent* 58. 18.

na, *conj.* (*OED* na *conj.²*) ; *than*
53. 7.

nad = *had not* 52. 47.

naide, *pp.* (OF neier) ; *denied*
103. 3.

nam, *vb.* ; see *nome.*

namely, *adv.* ; *especially* 100. 3.

nardus-specative, *sb.* ; *spikenard* 91. 11. See Note.

nasse = *an ass's* 86. 27.

natheles, *adv.*, *nevertheless* 58.
53.

nay, *sb.* ; *denial* 4. 59 ; ney 151.
61.

nedes, *adv.* ; *of necessity* 162.
24 ; nedis 144. 125.

nelyn, *vb. pres., pl.* ; *will not*
95. 18.

nem, *vb. pret.* (*OED* nim, † 2) ;
went 88. 11.

nempned, *pp.* (OE nemnan) ;
named 14. 25.

neode, *sb.* (OE níed) ; *need* 11.
44 ; neid 102. 145.

ner, *conj.* ; *nor* 48. 16.

ner, *adv.* ; *never* 115. 24.

ner, *adv. comp.* ; *nearer* 171. 9 ;
(*supl.*) nest 33. 22.

nere, *vb.* ; = *were it not* 12. 7.

nese, *sb.* ; *nose* 178. 94.

nest, *sb.* ; *home, lodging* 192. 7.

nevene, *vb.* (Icel. nefna) ; *to
name* 15. 63 ; neuen 19. 14 ;
neuien 144 Alia. 17.

newyng, *part.* (OE níwian) ;
renewing 9. 26.

nobly, *sb.*; *nobility* 153. 48;
noblay 191. 2.
noder, *conj.*; *neither* 3. 4; noþer
178. 44.
nogth, *adv.* (OE nówiht);
nought 181. 32.
noke, *sb.*; *nook* 10. 99.
nolde, *vb. pret.*; *would not* 80.
18.
nome, *vb. pret.* (*OED* nim, *v.*);
took, assumed 25. 31; nam
(*pret.*) 114. 2. (*pp.*) 28. 10.
no nodyre = *none other* 24. 35.
norice, *sb.* (OF norice); *nurse*
35. 23; norse 23. 43.
noried, *pp.* (OF norir); *brought
up* 23. 43.
nory, *sb.* (OF nori); *foster-child,
pupil* 23. 4.
not = *know not* 171. 13; note
188. 4.
noucht, *sb.*; *naught, nothing*
91. 6.
noy, *sb.*; *annoyance* 96. 23;
noyis; (*pl.*) 96. 46.
noyans, *sb.* (gerund); *annoying*
128. 19.
nyre, *adv.*; *close together* 58. 38.
nyse, *adj.* (OF nice); *ignorant,
foolish* 159. 9.

o, *prep.* = *on* 78. 4.
o, *prep.* = *of* 31. 2.
odire, *adj.*; *other* 154. 21; odur
59. 5.
of, *adv.*; *off* 92. 45.
oft-syth, *adv.*; *ofttimes* 52. 8;
oft-syis 156. 4.
oȝt, *adv.* (OE áwiht, áht); *at
all* 7. 61.
on, *indef. art.*; 95. 46; *pron.,
one* 95. 49; in on, *together* 97. 4.
on-avysed, *adv.*; *without warning* 149. 12.
on-brad, *vb.*; *awaken* 23. 18.
onys, *adv.*; *once* 6. 136; oones
57. 32; ones 62. 38.

oo, *adj.* = *one* 97. 76; on 64. 44.
oo, *sb.*; *Omega* 73. 10.
optene, *vb.*; *obtain* 36. 14; optayne 69. 44; (*pret.* 2 *s.*) optayndest 69. 40.
opynde, *vb. pret.*; *opened* 92.
90; (*pp.*) oppinnit 94. 21.
or, *conj.*; *before* 6. 136; or þan,
rather than 108. 5.
ordynatly, *adv.*; *regularly, duly*
39. 59.
ore, *adv.*; *formerly* 63. 36.
orȝelnesse, *sb.*; *pride, haughti-
ness* 105. 77.
os, *conj.*; *as* 33. 6.
ostend, *vb.*; *reveal, manifest* 20.
13.
other, *conj.*; *or* 46. 16.
opus, *sb. pl.*; *oaths* 107. 91.
ottherly, *adv.*; *entirely, utterly*
173. 30.
oughen, *adj.*; see awen.
ought-cry, *sb.*; *outcry* 109. 103.
our, *adv.*; *over* 191. 8.
ouþer, *adj., pron.*; *either* (of
two) 10. 3.
ouer, *adj.*; *superior* 105. 14.
ouer-blowe, *pp.*; *blown off or
away* 172. 60.
overall, *adv.*; *pre-eminently*
159. 68.
ovir-ronne, *pp.*; *passed* 39. 59.
oway, *adv.*; *away* 60. 38.
owe, *vb. pres. pl.*; *ought* 154. 7.
owȝte, *vb. pret.* (OE áhte);
owned 138. 24.
owr, *sb.* = *hour* 173. 25; owre
93. 22.
owterage, *sb.*; *excess, disorderly
action* 69. 17; outerage 148.
58; outray 4. 65.
owtray, *vb.* (AF outreier); *to
overcome, expel* 135. 63.

paal, *sb.* (OE pæll); *a rich cloth
spread over something, a canopy*
39. 51.

pacyonis, *sb.*; *patience* 64. 14.

paill, *adj.*; *pale* 91. 46; paile 96. 18.

pane, *vb.*; *take pains to* 102. 150.

panne, *sb.*; *skull* 95. 10.

parage, *sb.*; *lineage* (esp. noble lineage) 42. 1.

parenes, *sb. pl.* (Scot. dial.); *parents* 13. 34.

parfight, *adj.*; *perfect* 51. 4; perfit 22. 56; (*supl.*) parfytst 31. 4.

parlyous, *adj.*; *perilous* 135. 4.

part, *vb.*; *share* 140. 36.

partise, *sb. pl.*; *alternatives* 186. 20.

pas for pas = *step by step* 87. 9.

pasche, *sb.*; *passover* 112. 23.

passaunt, *adj.*; *surpassing, excelling* 39. 18.

passe, *vb.*; *die* 109. 154.

patryake, *sb.*; *patriarch* 11. 62.

pay, *sb.*; *liking* 142. 71.

payd, *pp.*; *pleased* 78. 53; payed 163. 57.

pecher, *sb.*; *pitcher* 90. 14.

pell, *vb.*; *peel* 173. 39.

pensyfnes, *sb.*; *melancholy* 57. 47.

perich, *vb.*; *pierce* 105. 31; peresshid (*pret.*) 92. 86; (*pp.*) perysshed 8. 5.

perry, *sb.* (OF pierrie); *precious stones, gems* 39. 51.

persawynge, *part.*; *perceiving* 77 A. 14; perseywynge 106. 14.

perse, *vb.* (OF percer); *pierce* 97. 11; (*pret.*) persit 94. 1; percyd 108. 4.

persplendent, *adj.*; *resplendent* 38. 21.

pert, *adj.*; *open, apert* 142. 60; (*adv.*) pertely 178. 39.

pese, *vb.* (OF paiser); *to set at rest, quiet* 144. 115.

pesy, *adj.*; *weighty, heavy* 139. 3.

petuvsse, *adj.*; *full of pity* 6. 113.

peyer, *vb.* (*OED* pair *v.*²); *to make worse, impair* 180. 4.

peynt, *vb.*; *to flatter or deceive with specious words* 181. 26.

pight, *pp.*; *fixed, settled, placed* 23. 13; piyht 36. 38; pyght 39. 1; pwyght 173. 1.

pile, *sb.* (*OED* pile, *sb.*⁴); *the reverse side of a coin opposite to the 'cross' or face* 192. 12.

play, *vb.*; *amuse, divert oneself* 2. 2.

pleid, *sb.*; *controversy, dispute* 20. 9.

plenere, *adj.*; *entire, perfect* 37. 61.

pleser, *sb.*; *pleasure* 108. 19.

pleyne, *vb.*; *bewail, lament* 136. 15.

plomett, *sb.*; *the bob of a plumbline* 109. 164.

plukytt, *pp.*; *robbed, plundered* 176. 3.

plycht, *sb.* (OE pliht); *offence, guilt* 102. 14; *peril* 156. 47.

polyce, *sb.*; *political sagacity, a politic course of action* 154. 49.

pont, *sb.*; *point* 186. 13.

ponyche, *vb.*; *punish* 178. 10.

port, *sb.*; *haven* 130. 15. See Note.

portes, *sb. pl.*; *gates* 112. 15.

poste, *sb.* (OF poeste, pouste); *strength, power* 129. 3; poweste 11. 56.

poure, *sb.* (OF poër); *power* 125. 9.

powaret, *sb.*; *poverty* 4. 4; poorte 182. 54.

powdryd, *pp.*; *spangled* 39. 51.

powur, *adj.*; *poor* 109. 30.

poynt, *vb.*; *to appoint* 101. 27.

pra, *sb.* (OF preie); *prey* 156. 31; pray 10. 106.

praire, *sb.* (OF preiere); *prayer* 56. 5.

prayere, *sb.* (*OED* prayer ²); *suppliant, one who prays* 24. 44; prayowre 31. 4.

precellent, *adj.*; *surpassing, pre-eminent* 69. 29.

prees, *sb.*; *throng* 130. 84; *battle* 156. 13.

preposicioun, *sb.*; *position before or in front* 39. 62.

preseth, *vb. pres.* 3 *s.*; *urges, hastens* 154. 18; (*pret.*) prest 78. 22.

prest, *sb.*; *priest* 10. 86; priste 115. 32.

prest, *adj.*; *alert, eager, keen* 6. 94, 78. 53; (*adv.*) *readily, quickly* 10. 45.

preue, *vb.*; *to experience* 110. 27.

preueance, *sb.*; *provision* (as in the 'Provisions of Oxford' 1258) 172. 15.

preuete, *sb.*; *secret, mystery* 85. 11.

preves, *sb. pl.*; *proofs* 32. 8.

prey, *vb.*; *to pray* 10. 40.

price, *sb.*; *prize* 17. 25.

prime, *sb.*; *the first appearance* (of the new moon) 181. 3.

prisse, *adj.*; *excellent* 186. 22.

priulie, *adv.*; (OF. adj. preu+ ly); *powerfully* 112. 15.

processe, *sb.*; *a narration, story, discourse* 109. 26.

profe, *vb.*; *prove* 52. 24; preffe 173. 28.

proferyd, *vb. pret.*; *proferred* 159. 81.

promes, *sb.*; *promise* 131. 34.

prone, *adj.*; *ready in mind, eager* 108. 22.

propur, *adj.*; *private, individual* 109. 124.

prothoplaust, *adj.*; *first-created* 13. 34.

prowe, *sb.* (OF prou); *advantage, benefit, weal* 42. 14.

prudently, *adv.*; *carefully, wisely* 39. 1.

pruddist, *adj.*; *proudest* 10. 88.

pryce, *sb.*; *excellence, worth* 46. 28.

prys, 121. 7; bers þe prys, *has the pre-eminence* 4. 23.

pull, *sb. bout, trial of strength*; 163. 43.

purpor, *adj.*; *purple* 91. 21; purpure 92. 33.

puruaide, *vb.* (OF porveeir); *provided* 103. 35.

purviaunce, *sb.* (OF purveaunce); *provision* 14. 32.

pwyght, pyght, *pp.*; see *pight*.

py, *vb.*; *buy* 4. 51.

pykis, *vb.* (2 *sg.*); *make trim, comb* 7. 11.

pyler, *sb.*; *pillar* 10. 41.

pyllour, *sb.*; *robber* 153. 9.

pyne, *sb.*; *pin* 151. 51.

pyne, *sb.* (OE pín); *suffering, pine* 52. 46.

pynyd, *vb. pret.*; *suffered* 97. 109.

quha, *pron.*; *who* 20. 10.

qware, *adv.*; *where* 52. 46.

qware-off, *conj.*; *whereof* 163. 1.

quart, *sb.*; *health, tranquillity* 155. 4.

qwat, *pron.*; *what* 76. 9.

quede, *sb.*; *harm* 178. 54.

queer, *sb.*; *choir* 39. 15.

quell, *vb.* (OE cwellan); *to kill* 158 A. 3.

quemyd, *pp.* (OE cwéman); *pleased* 141. 5.

queme, *adj.*; *pleasing* 28. 81.

querely, *sb.*; 178. 22. See Notes.

quheill, *sb.*; *wheel* 156. 5.

quheyne, *sb.*; *queen* 20. 26; qwyn 18. 8.

quhil, *adv.*; *now . . . now* 156. 6.

quhilk, *pron.*; *which* 22. 47.

quhippis, *sb. pl.*; *whips* 102. 65.

quho, *pron.*; *who* 167. 3.

quhyle, *sb.*; *a while, time* 102. 9.

quyte, *vb.*; *to requite* 128. 18.

qwom, *pron.*; *whom* 64. 47.

qwy, *pron.*; *why* 84. 28.

qwyn, *sb.*; see *quheyne.*

qwyt, *adj.*; *white* 114. 12.

race, *vb.*; *to root out* 13. 21; (*pret.* 2 *s.*) racedyst 136. 7.

rache, *adj.*; see *ryche.*

racle, *adj.*; *hasty, rash* 181. 33.

raik, *vb.* (OE racian); *to move forward with speed* 20. 4.

rais, *vb. pret.*; *rose* 113. 16; rayse 115. 14; (pp.) ryssyn 112. 3.

rakkit, *pp.*; *racked* 91. 36.

ramagith, *vb. pres.* 3 *s.*; *rages* 178. 50. See Notes.

ranis, *vb. pres.*; *rain, shed* 91. 7.

ransonar, *sb.*; *redeemer, ransomer* 113. 13.

rasid, *pp.*; *scratched, torn* 103. 15.

rasis, *vb. pres.* 3 *s.*; *raises* 20. 7.

raymett, *pp.* (*OED* raim, *v.*); *spoiled plundered* 126. 5.

rayne, *vb.*; *reign* 109. 74; (*pres.* 2 *s.*) rignis 96. 63; (*part.*) raynyng 109. 15.

rayvith, *vb. pres.* 3 *s.*; *takes away forcibly* 178. 99.

reames, *sb. pl.* (OF reaume); *realms, kingdoms* 153. 22.

rebaude, *sb.*; *knave, rascal* 178. 118.

rebowne, *vb.* (OF rebonder); *bound, spring* 8. 3.

recemande, recommende, *vb.*; *to commit* (oneself) *to a person's care* 40. 8, 46. 1.

rechest, *adj. supl.*; see *ryche.*

rechyles, *adj.*; *negligent, inattentive* 6. 1; recheles 142. 40.

reclame, *sb.*; *challenge, recall* 66. 19.

reclayme, *vb.* (*OED* reclaim, *v.* 7. c); *to protest* 6. 73.

recorde, *vb.*; *attest, declare* 144. 30.

recourse, *sb.*; *course, passage* 159. 16.

recreaunce, *sb.*; *refreshment* 45. 10.

recure, *vb.*; *to recover* 131. 52.

reddure, *sb.* (*OED* reddour); *severity, harsh treatment* 28. 76.

rede, *vb.*; *counsel, advise* 146. 22.

rede, *sb.*; *counsel* 6. 15.

refrene, *vb.*; *restrain, check* 22. 9; refrayne 182. 37.

reft, *pp.*; see *reuys.*

refute, *sb.*; *protection* 25. 23.

regall, *sb.*; *ruler, royalty* 38. 28.

regalles, *sb. pl.*; *precious stones of some kind* 183. 3.

regementis, *sb. pl.*; *supports(?), ordinances(?)* 6. 78.

reherse, *vb.*; *relate* 7. 82.

reid, *adj.*; (*OED* ride, *a.*¹); (of blows) *violent* 102. 31.

reiosit, *ppl. adj.*; *rejoiced, glad* 91. 49.

rekyls, *sb.* (OE recels); *incense* 89. 39.

remeid, *vb.*; *to amend, remedy* 20. 9.

remord, *vb.*; *to feel remorse* 173. 7; (*subj.*) remorde 144. 163.

remuable, *adj.*; *changeable* 171. 1.

renne, *vb.*; *to run, gush* 97. 46.

rentis, *sb. pl.*; *revenues* 159. 62.

renwe, *vb.*; *to return, renew* 82 heading.

repayred, *pp.*; *arrived* (at or in) 42. 1.

repoyse, *vb.* (*OED* repose, *v.*¹); *to replace, restore* 82. 4.

repreff, *sb.*; *reproof* 109. 123.

reprise, *sb.*; *reprisal* 153. 18.

resaif, *vb.*; *receive* 91. 63; (*pret.* 2 *s.*) recewedst 6. 74.

rescous, *sb.*; *rescue, assistance* 154. 52.

rese, *vb.* (OE ræsan); *to rush (on a person), to attack* 178. 118.

respeccyoun, *sb.*; *sight, regard* 8. 2.

rest, *sb.* (medieval armour); *a rest to receive the butt of the lance* 91. 54.

resyled, *pp.* (< Lat. resilire); *recoiled from with aversion, renounced* 117. 19.

resynge, *vb.* (*OED* resign *v.*¹, † 3); *to give over, desist* 80. 18.

reuerture, *sb.*; *reversion* 159. 14.

reuth, *sb.*; see *rewth*.

reuys, *vb. pres.* 3 *s.*; *robs* 176. 13; (*pres.* 2 *s.*) reuest 153. 18; (*pp.*) reft 102. 79.

rew, *vb.*; *to take pity* 107. 37; (*pres.* 3 *s. impers.*) rewis 102. 43.

rewife, *vb.*; *to revive* 113. 30; (*pret.*) revived 9. 32.

rewth, *sb.*; *pity, compassion* 10. 30; rwthe 1. 24; reuth 91. 1.

rewyl, *vb.*; *rule, govern* 163. 35.

reyne, *sb.*; *rein* 57. 17.

rignis, *vb. pres.* 2 *s.*; see *rayne*.

ripe, *adj.*; (1) *timely* 9. 4; (2) *prepared* 155. 10.

rode, *sb.*; *rood, cross* 3. 22; rovde 24. 15.

rone, *vb.* (*OED* roun, *v.* 5); *accost, address* 78. 37.

rore, *vb.* (OE rárian); *roar* 10. 77; (*pret.*) roryd 10. 95.

roure, *sb.* (OE hrór); *confusion, tumult, disturbance* 109. 120.

rowght, *vb. pret.* (OE reccan); (1) *cared, minded* 4. 26. (2) *felt averse to* 97. 93.

rowthe, *adj.* (OE wráþ); *angry* 147. 36.

rowtte, *sb.* (OF route); *crowd* 176. 16.

ruf, *sb.* (OE hróf); *roof* 156. 34.

ruffit, *pp.* (*OED* roove, *v.*¹) *riveted* 91. 33.

rullyde, *vb. pret.* (a forced rime with 'lullyde'); *turned* 5. 4.

rulye *adv.* (OE hréowlice); *ruefully, pitifully* 9. 19; rewlye 95. 34.

ruweþ *vb. impers.* (OE hréowan); *it distresses* (me) 145. 11.

ruyd, *sb.* (OE ród); *rood, cross* 20. 17; ruyde 176. 9.

rwthfully, *adv.*; *pitifully* 1. 19.

rybane, *sb.*; *ribbon* 183. 1.

ryche, *adj.* (OE ríce); *rich* 147. 60; rache 85. 21; (*supl.*) rechest 23. 26.

ryed, *vb.* (OE rídan); *to take part in a raid or foray* 147. 42.

ry3tes, *sb. pl.*; *laws, ordinances* 37. 28.

ryghtwous, *adj.*; *righteous* 124. 3.

rynnes, *vb. pres.* 3 *s.* (OE rinnan); *passes by, elapses* 144. 15.

rysche, *sb.*; *a rush* 15. 31.

ryse, *sb.* (OE hrís); *twig, branch* 30. 34.

ryssyn, *pp.*; see *rais*.

ryte, *adj.*; *direct, straight* 88. 25.

rywlyde, *vb. pret.*; *controlled, guided* 6. 1.

saddely, *adv.*; *firmly, deeply* 34. 34; sadlie 91. 5.

sade, *adv.*; *heavily* 109. 148.

safe, *vb.*; *to save* 19. 2; sawe 77 A. 2; (*pp.*) sawyd 24. 52.

saikles, *adj.*; *innocent, blameless* 112. 22.

sake, *sb.* (OE sacc); *sack* 159. 75.

sal, *vb. pres.*; *shall* 4. 47; (*pl.*)

schun 183. 14; (*pret.*) sud 4. 17; suld 3. 1; schwld 1. 11.

saladyne₃, *sb. pl.* (= celidony); *a stone fabled to be found in the swallow's belly* 183. 6.

sald, *pp.*; *sold* 63. 18.

sale, *sb.* (OE sæl); *a hall or spacious chamber* 78. 45.

salewe, *vb.*; *salute, greet* 96. 2.

sam, *adj.*; *same* 180. 19; samyn 96. 29.

sampil, *sb.*; *example* (given as a warning) 156. 9.

sanatyfe, *sb.*; *a remedy* 178. 128.

sanguinite, *sb.*; *consanguinity, a blood relation* 39. 39.

sapoure, *sb.* (Lat. sapor); *taste, savour* 22. 31, 66. 9.

sauld, *vb. pret.*; *sold* 102. 102; sowld 173. 5.

saunce, *prep.* (Fr. sans); *without* 46. 42.

saw, *vb. pres.* (OE sáwan); *sow* 151. 73.

sawe, sawyd, *vb.*; see *safe*.

say, *vb. pret.* (OE séon); see *see*.

saye, sayed, *vb.* (OE secgan); see *seyne*.

scandaunt, *adj.*; *climbing, ascending* 39. 4.

schere, *vb.*; *reap* 151. 73.

sclake, *vb.* (OE slacian); *decrease, fall off* 35. 53.

scley, *adj.* (ON slœgr); *prudent, wise* 185. 17.

sco, *fem. pers. pron.*; *she* 4. 4.

sconfite, *vb.*; *defeat, vanquish* 14. 21; (*pret.*) scunfett 10. 105.

scoryng, *vbl. sb.* (ON skora); *tallying* 172. 24.

scrycchyng, *vbl. sb.*; *screeching, shrieking* 5. 12.

scuet, scueit, *adj.*; see *sweit*.

se, *sb.*; *sea* 19. 1.

seche, *vb.*; see *seken*.

securet, *adv.* = *secret* 173. 25.

secyn, *vb.*; see *sese*, vb. 2.

secyrly, *adv.*; *without doubt, certainly* 89. 15; sycurly 107. 100; sickerly 102. 61.

seder, *sb.*; *cedar* 22. 21.

see, *vb.* (OE séon); *see* 132. 27; (*pres. 2 s.*) seys 3. 7; seis 102. 86; seyste 6. 58; (*pret. s.*) say 178. 80; see 183. 1; (*pret. pl.*) seo 78. 41; (*pp.*) sayn 6. 21; sene 102. 76.

see, *sb.* (OF sé); *a seat of dignity* (esp. a throne) 30. 4.

seete, *sb.*; *seat* 36. 33; sete 37. 2.

sege, *sb.* (OF sege); *a seat used by a person of rank or distinction* 37. 35.

seid, *sb.* (OE sǽd); *seed* 22. 79.

seillit, *pp.* (OF seeler); *sealed, attested by a seal* (on a document) 113. 39.

seken, *vb.* (OE sécan); *to seek* 71. 38; sekyn 88. 23; seke 88. 19; seik 22. 65; seche 171. 10; (*pret.*) soutone 123. 13; soght (*pp.*) (*examined*) 155. 14.

sele, *sb.* (OE sæl); *happiness, prosperity* 74. 16; selle 28. 53.

selecture, *sb.*; *choice, selection* 39. 45.

selle, *sb.*; see *sele*.

sely, *adj.* (OE (ge)sælig); *happy, blessed, innocent* 171. 2; cely 154. 24.

sembly, *adj.*; (of persons) *seemly, of goodly appearance* 151. 44; semely (of things) *pleasant* 186. 1; (*comp.*) semelyour 78. 3.

sempiterne, *adj.*; *eternal* 28. 4.

sen, *conj.*; *since* 13. 18; sene 4. 18.

senckis, *vb. pres. 3 s.*; see *synke*.

sennyt, *sb.*; *a seven-night, a week* 112. 24.

senonis, *sb. pl.* (see *OED*; obsolete form of sinews); 91. 47.

septure, *sb.*; *sceptre* 58. 23.

seqwens, *sb.*; *a 'sequencer' or sequence-book* 88. 43.

sere, *adj.* (ON sér); *sundry, divers* 163. 70; seyr 33. 20.

sertayne, *sb.*; *certainty* 159. 22.

serten, *adj.*; *certain* 15. 45.

sertis, *adv.*; *certainly* 177. 28.

seruage, *sb.*; *bondage, servitude* 28. 22.

seruand, *sb.*; *servant* 33. 18.

serve, *vb.*; *to deserve, be worthy of* 171. 12; (*pret.*) seruyd 35. 43; seruede 133. 15.

seruice, *vb.*; *to benefit, be of help, advantage* 172. 95.

sese, *vb.*¹ (OF saisir); *to be in possession of, to establish in a place* 178. 82.

sese, *vb.*² (OF cesser); (1) *cause to cease* 182. 19; secyn 76. 4. (2) *cease, leave off* (*pret.*) sest 78. 6; (*pp.*) 6. 106. See Notes; seste 144. 123.

seth, *conj.*; *since* 46. 36; seþ 57. 75; ssyth 46. 7; sethe 106. 33; *adv.*; sethe 147. 22.

sett, *vb. imp.*; *cause to be* 134. 16.

sew, *vb.*; *to follow, pursue* 13. 14; sewe 177. 50; (*pret.*) suyd 97. 95.

sewit, *pp.* (OE siwan); *sewed* 91. 25.

seyne, *vb.* (OE secgan); *to say* 182. 10; saye 147. 63; (*pres.* I *s.*) seie 6. 93; (2 *s.*) seyst 144. 98; (*pl.*) seyne 146. 10; (*imper. s.*) sey 181. 1; (*pl.*) seyth 130. 103; (*pret.*) sed 173. 24; (*pp.*) sayed 115. 22.

shamely, *adv.*; *shamefully* 178. 102.

schapeth, *vb. pres.* 3 *s.*; *escapes* 166. 1.

shaue, *pp.*; *shaved* 172. 49.

schawand, *part.*; see *sowe*.

schene, *adj.* (OE scíene); *fair, bright, beautiful* 35. 50; scheyne 22. 21.

shenship, *sb.* (< shend + ship); *disgrace, shame* 126. 8.

schente, *ppl. adj.*; *ruined, stupefied, exhausted* 6. 6; shent 97. 28.

schew, *vb. pret.*; see *sowe*.

schorn, *pp.* (OE sceran); *shorn* 91. 47.

shotyng, *vbl. sb.*; *shouting, insult* 109. 128.

shoure, *sb.* (OE scúr); *combat, assault* 6. 112; schour 84. 20; showres (*pl.*) 183. 19.

schun, *vb. pres. pl.*; see *sal*.

schurtely, *adv.*; *shortly* 173. 41.

schwld, *vb. pret.*; see *sal*.

schyfte, *sb.*; *evasion, subterfuge* 141. 8.

schyre þursday, *Maundy Thursday* 114. 133.

siching, *vbl. sb.* (OE sícan); *sighing* 94. 6.

siker, *adj.*; *sure, reliable* 35. 50; sykur 107. 81; seker 178. 59.

siluestrise, *vb.*; *banish* 153. 16.

sing, *sb.*; *sign* 113. 9; (*pl.*) synus 107. 61.

sinoes, *sb. pl.* (OE sionu); *sinews* 104. 8; synues 109. 138.

skalys, *sb. pl.* (musical term); *scales* 39. 4.

skene, *sb.* (ON skinn); *skin* 173. 39.

skyll, *sb.* (ON skil); *reason* 37. 47, 57. 74; skill of kynde, *natural intelligence* 190. 2.

slake, *vb.*; *quench* 144. 83.

slay, *pp.*; see *sle*.

sle, *vb.* (OE sléan); *slay* 57. 74; slo 3. 9; (*pret.*) sleuch 102. 106; (*pp.*) slayn 6. 20; slay 123. 11.

slike, *adj.* (ON slíkr); *such* 60. 58.

sliper, *adj.* (OE slipor) ; *slippery* 189. 31 ; slyper 151. 51.

slo, *vb.* ; see *sle.*

slouen, *sb.* ; *knave, rascal* 103. 31.

sluggy, *adj.* ; *sluggish, lazy* 136. 27.

slycht, *sb.* (ON slǽgð) ; *strategy, trickery* 112. 22.

smawyll, *adv.* ; *small* 176. 5.

snobbude, *vb. pret.* ; *sobbed* 6. 43.

snobbynge, *vbl. sb.* ; *sobbing* 5. 11.

so, *adv.* ; *as* 27. 5.

soffarond, *adj.* ; *sovereign* 89. 43.

sofferante, *sb.* ; *sovereignty* 121. 16.

sofre, *vb.* ; *suffer* 97. 48 ; sovere 5. 26.

soget, *ppl. adj.* ; *subject* 65. 8 ; (as *sb.*) sogette 63. 18 ; (*pl.*) suggetis 58. 45.

soilid, *pp.* ; *absolved* 146. 19.

soiorne, *vb.* ; *to sojourn* 112. 28.

soke, *vb. pret.* ; see *sovkys.*

solace, *sb.* ; *joy* 38. 43 ; solase 105. 2.

sole, *sb.* ; *soul* 107. 37 ; soole 117. 17.

solemply, *adv.* ; *sacredly, with due ceremony* 37. 52.

solempnysante, *adj.* ; *celebrated with special ceremony* 12. 12.

soleyne, *adj.* ; *unique, single, solitary* 22. 23.

solistrice, *sb.* ; *solicitress* 12. 27.

solum, *sb.* (Lat. solum) ; *soil, ground* 28. 34.

sonde, *sb.* ; *messenger* 15. 35.

soree, *adj.* (OF sor, 'fauve', 'lustre') ; *tawny, reddish brown* 89. 39.

sotell, *adj.* ; *subtle, obscure* 57. 6 ; subtell 112. 6.

sother, *adj. comp.* ; *truer* 180. 1.

sovkys, *vb. pres.* 3 *s.* ; *sucks* 1.

18 ; (*part.*) sowkyng 178. 85 ; (*pret.*) soke 10. 8.

sovre, *adj.* ; *sore* 147. 4.

soutone, *vb. pret.* ; see *seken.*

soueranly, *adv.* ; *supremely* 110. 10.

sovere, *vb.* ; see *sofre.*

sowe, *vb.* (OE scéawian) ; *show, display* 174. 12 ; (*part.*) schawand 22. 83 ; (*pret.*) schew 102. 4.

sowerov, *sb.* ; *sorrow* 1. 17.

sownedde, *vb. pret.* ; *swooned* 6. 41 ; sownydde 6. 50.

sownyde, *vb. pret.* ; *sounded* 6. 137.

sownyng (*vbl. sb.*) ; *swooning* 9. 30.

spaire, *vb.* (OE sparian) ; *to spare, deal gently with* 96. 21.

spare, *vb.* ; *to fasten with a bolt or bar* 172. 43.

spectable, *adj.* ; *remarkable, worthy of being seen* 38. 41.

speculat, *adj.* (OF speculatif) ; *wonderful* 39. 27.

specull, *sb.* ; *speculum, mirror* 22. 78.

specyous, *adj.* ; *fair or pleasing to the eye* 28. 43 ; specius 28. 61.

spede, *sb.* ; *success, prosperity* 101. 1.

spele, *vb.* (OE spelian, see *OED spele v.*[1]) ; *to spare or save* 172. 3.

spelle, *sb.* (OE spel) ; *speech, discourse* 182. 38.

spelle, *vb.* ; *relate, declare* 142. 34.

spere, *sb.* ; *sphere* 35. 11.

speryd, *vb. pret.* (OE spyrian) ; *inquired* 89. 12.

spill, *vb.* (OE spillan) ; *to destroy* 60. 37 ; spille, *squander* 142. 80 ; *perish* 34. 23 ; spylle 54. 10.

spod, *vb. pret.; sped* 78. 35.

spones, *sb. pl.* (OE spón); *chips* 185. 20.

spornned, *vb. pret.; kicked, spurned* 109. 133.

sprakly, *adv.; actively, speedily* 58. 21.

sprent, *pp.; stirred, leapt* 38. 42.

sprete, *sb.; spirit* 38. 42; spret 109. 168; spreit 91. 5; (*pl.*) spretus 125. 10.

sprongyld, *vb. pret.; struggled, sprawled* 89. 64.

spue, *sb.; spew* 13. 7.

spye, *sb.; observer* 25. 15.

spylle, *vb.; perish* 54. 10.

spythfull, *adj.; spiteful, malicious* 89. 60.

sshe, *fem. pers. pron.; she* 46. 8.

ssyth, *conj.;* see *seth.*

stabyl, *vb.; to make stable, confirm* 55. 15.

stafe, *sb.; staff, rod* 147. 66.

stare, *vb.* (OE starian); *stare* 177. 29.

stede and stall (*in*); *everywhere, continually* 60. 18.

steiien, *vb.* (OE stígan); *to ascend* 4. 69; stye 101. 20; (*pret.*) stey 30. 32; stegh 115. 17.

stent, *vb. pres.* 3 *s.; stands* 174. 11.

stent, *vb.;* see *stynt.*

stercory, *sb.; excrement, filth* 159. 75.

sterfe, *vb. pret.* (OE steorfan); *died* 154. 62.

sterke, *adj.; stiff* 139. 20.

sterne, *sb.* (ON stjarna); *star* 15. 61; steren 21. 1.

sterre, *sb.* (OE steorre); *star* 18. 1; ster 69. 12; (*pl.*) sterren 31. 19.

sterte, *vb.; leap, rush, hasten* 123. 25.

steryde, *vb. pret.; stirred, displaced* 85. 19. See Notes.

stevene, *sb.* (OE stefn, *f.*); *voice, speech, language* 15. 61; stevyn 178. 38.

steuene, *sb.* (OE stefn, *m.*); *a set or appointed time* 183. 52.

stithe, *adj.; stout, stern* 158 A. 1.

stody, *sb.; study, reverie* 186. 5.

stomelled, *vb. pret.; stumbled* 109. 131.

stoundis, *vb. pres.* 3 *pl.; cause a pang* 91. 1.

stoundis, *sb.* (*pl.*); *pains* 102. 20.

stour, *sb.; combat, struggle* 11. 83; stoure 158 A. 1.

stramp, *vb.; to set down the foot firmly, stamp* 191. 19.

strange, *adj.; strong* 112. 25.

streemys, *sb. pl.; rays of light* 135. 37.

streit, *sb.; street* 22. 82.

strem, *sb.* (OE stréam); *stream* 88. 9.

streynye, *vb.* (*OED* strengh, *v.*); *to make strong* 177. 68.

stronde, *sb.* (*OED* strand, *sb.*²); *stream, brook* 100. 3.

stryndis, *sb. pl.* (*OED* strind, *sb.*²); *streams* 102. 66.

stye, *vb.;* see *steiien.*

styf, *adj.; hard, stubbornly contested* 158 B. 9; (as *adv.*) 144. 4.

styff, *vb.* (OE stífian); *to become stiff* 109. 163.

stylle, *vb.; to check the turbulence* (of a person); *to make cease* 158 B. 6.

stynt, *vb.* (OE styntan); *stop, cease* (*imp.*) 153. 12 (*pp.*) 10. 71; stent 58. 17.

styntyng, *vbl. sb.; ceasing* 34. 16.

styres, *vb. pres.* 3 *s.; stirs, becomes active* 151. 57.

subpouell, *vb.* (*OED* † sup-

powell) ; *to support, succour*
173. 34.
subtell, *adj.*; see *sotell.*
suggetis, *sb.*; see *soget.*
suggestions, *sb. pl.*; *temptations*
51. 39.
suld, *vb. pret.*; see *sal.*
sure, *adj.*; *secure* 28. 74; swre
(*confident*) 159. 17.
surfetis, *sb. pl.*; *transgressions,
trespasses* 136. 7.
sueirnes, *sb.*; *indolence, sloth*
96. 14.
sueit, *sb.*; *sweat* 91. 40.
suollit, *pp.* (OF suiller) ; *soiled,
stained* 91. 45.
suth, *sb.*; *truth*, 102. 86.
suyd, *vb. pret.*; see *sewe.*
swappis, *sb. pl.*; *blows* 7. 29.
sweit, *adj.*; *sweet* 4. 55; scuet
4. 10; scueit 4. 16.
swerd, *sb.*; *sword* 136. 16.
swery, *vb.*; *swear* 182. 49.
swiþe, *adv.*; *very* 95. 12 ; swyþe
88. 22.
swonit, *vb. pret.*; *swooned* 91.
55.
swynke, *vb.*; *to gain by labour*
62. 35.
syche = *such* 24. 18.
sycurly, *adv.*; see *secyrly.*
syke, *adj.*; *sick* 178. 47.
sykyd, *vb. pret.*; *sighed* 6. 43 ;
(*part.*) syȝynge 6. 6.
syldene, *adv.* = *seldom* 183. 13.
symple, *adj.*; *foolish* 153. 25.
syne, *sb.*; *sin* 23. 7.
synes, *adv.*; *since, after* 69. 37.
synglure, *adj.*; *individual, particular* 173. 8.
synke, *vb.*; *sink* 62. 34; (*pres.*
3 *s.*) senckis 120. 10.
synues, *sb. pl.*; see *sinoes.*
synus, *sb. pl.*; see *sing.*
syth, *sb.* = *sight, appearance*
177. 71.
sythis, *sb. pl.* (OE síðas) ; *times*

(oft-sythis = oft-times) 144.
11.
sytis, *sb. pl.*; *cities* 151. 9.
sytt, *vb.*; *rest, lie* 3. 22.

ta, *prep.* = *to* 47. 31.
take, *vb.*; (1) *receive, accept* 60.
5; ta 102. 34. (2) (*pp.*)
esteemed, considered 177. 13.
talle, *sb.* (OE talu) ; *tale* (sett
no talle = hold in no esteem)
173. 23.
tane, *pp.*; *taken, captured* 94. 2 ;
tan 177. 7.
taulde, *pp.* (OE tellan) ; *counted*
102. 76.
teme, *vb. pret.* (OE tíeman) ;
brought forth 77 B. 14.
temp, *vb.*; *tempt* 53. 7.
tene, *sb.* (OE téona) ; *distress*
130. 63; *mischief* 153. 15.
tent, *sb.*; *heed, attention* 78. 11.
tente, *vb.*; *give heed to* 45. 8.
tere, *vb. pret.*; *tore* 6. 9.
teuch, *adj.*; *tough, stout* 102. 50.
thaghe, þaugh, þawe, *conj.*;
see *þouȝ.*
þaim, 3 *pers. pron. pl.*; *them*
52. 7.
than, *adv.*; *then* 29. 21.
þare, *adv.*; *there* 4. 43.
þarne, *vb.* (ON þarna) ; *lack,
want* 102. 137; ȝarne 4. 25.
þedir, *adv.*; *thither* 52. 44.
theis, *sb. pl.*; *thighs* 102. 37.
ther-as, *conj.*; *where* 32. 5.
þer-to, *adv.*; *besides* 11. 78;
for that 70. 7.
þie, 3 *pers. pron. pl.*; *they* 89.
47.
þie-of, *adv.*; *thereof* 89. 51.
þir, *dem. pron.* (Northern) ;
these 91. 33; þire 20. 4.
thirle, *vb.* (OE þyrlian) ; *to
pierce* 10. 66; (*pres.* 3 *s.*)
thirlis 91. 2.
þi-sell, *pron.*; *thyself* 96. 54.

þo, *dem. pron.*; (1) as *def. art.* 33. 3, 33. 8. (2) *pl.* 'those' 42. 9; tho 64. 46; thoo 36. 11.

þo, *conj.*; *when* 6. 49.

þoo, *adv.*; *then* 11. 6.

thocht, *conj.*; see *þou3*.

tholl, *vb.* (OE þolian); *to suffer* 102. 80; (*pret.*) tholit 102. 21.

thorogh, *prep.* (*OED* thorough); '*from beginning to end of*' 192. 4; '*over the whole extent of*' 192. 10.

þoroght, *prep.*; *throughout* 78. 17.

þorow, *prep.* (OE þurh); *through* 10. 31; þorowe 71. 43; þoro 107. 36; thoru 62. 33; thurgh 46. 5; þrou 92. 86; thro3 12. 7.

þou3, *conj.*; *though* 57. 74; thow 90. 16; þowe 6. 51; þowh 144. 18; þawe 6. 22; thaghe 117. 4; þaugh 97. 87; thocht 156. 25; *adv.*; *yet* þow 147. 21.

þow3ty, *adj.*; *doughty* 37. 59 (cf. *enþeth* in line 71).

thynk, *vb. pres. 3 sg. impers.*; *seems* (*to*) 4. 16; thynketh long, *desire, yearn* 97. 16; *grow weary* 142. 87.

thra, *adj.*; *stubborn, fierce* 156. 30.

thrang, *vb. pret.*; see *thryng*.

thretid, *vb. pret.* (OE þreatian); *rebuked, reproved* 103. 7.

thrist, *vb. pret.* (ON þrýsta); *pierced, thrust* 91. 41.

þrist, *sb.*; *thirst* 95. 29.

þrou, thro3, *prep.*; see *þorow*.

throwe, *sb.* (OE þrág); *a* (brief) *space of time, a moment* 58. 20.

þrowe, *sb.* (*OED* throe *sb.*); *a spasm of pain* 95. 16.

thryng, *vb.* (OE þringan); *to press, crowd* 97. 23; (*pret.*) thrang 102. 23.

þusgait, *adv.*; *thus-wise* 102. 45; þus-gates 144. 166.

thwarted, *vb. pret.*; *answered* 9. 13.

til, till, *prep.* see *tyll*.

titulle, *sb.*; *title* 101. 27.

to, *conj.*; *till = while* 15. 15.

to, *adv.*; *too, also* 102. 144; tow 185. 18.

toc, *vb. pret.*; *took* 16. 14; tuk 94. 22; tok (*gave*) 178. 68; (2 *pers.*) tokyst (*gavest*) 58. 12.

tofore, *prep.*; *before* 58. 17.

tome: *at tome = at home* 179. 4.

toone: *the toone = that one* 9. 31.

to-rente, *pp.*; *torn to pieces* 6. 8; to-rent 93. 12; (*ppl. adj.*) torynde 176. 4.

to-robbid, *vb. pret.*; *robbed* (with the intensive prefix to-) 10. 39.

to-schente, *pp.*; *ruined, utterly destroyed* 107. 74; to-shent 97. 38.

to-teyre, *vb.*; *tear* (*to pieces*) 1. 22.

tothir: *the tothir = that other* 9. 31.

tow, *adv.*; see *to*, adv.

trad, *vb. pret.*; *trod* 10. 86.

traist, *sb.*; *trust* 13. 18; (*vb.*) trayst 52. 33.

tranes, *sb. pl.* (*OED* train, *sb.*[1] 12); *trains, methods of procedure* 188. 8.

trayng, *vbl. sb.* (OF trair); *betrayal* 10. 18.

treite, *vb.* (*OED* treat, *v.* † 3a); *entreat, intercede* 38. 52.

tremell, *vb.*; *tremble* 138. 7; trymble 148. 28.

treyne, *sb.*; *distress* 146. 16. See Notes.

treynys, *sb. pl.*; *tricks, wiles, schemes* 135. 42.

triumpand, *adj.*; *triumphant* 113. 9; tryvmphald 112. 33.

truele, *adv.*; *truly* 155. 7.

tryacle, *sb.*; (<Grk. θηριακή); *antidote, remedy* 135. 12.

trouth, *sb.*; *troth, fidelity* 170. 15; *trowght* 4. 47.

tryllyd, *vb. pret.*; *rolled, streamed* 6. 59.

tryne, *sb.* (Scot. dial.); *train, retinue* 112. 33.

trystyt, *vb. pret.* (trans.); *enticed to a place or a distance* 174. 5. See Notes.

tryvmphald, *adj.*; see *triumpand*.

tuk, *vb. pret.*; see *toc*.

turtill, *sb.*; *turtle-dove* 28. 52.

tuycion, *sb.*; *protection* 143. 12.

twelwe, *adj.*; *twelfth* 88. 17.

twynne, *vb.*; *to separate* 105. 92.

tyght, *adv.* (ON títt); *frequently* 64. 12.

tyke, *sb.*; *a churl, rustic*, or *a cur* 102. 47.

tyll, *prep.*; *to* 6. 115; *till* 4. 32.

tylle, *vb.*; *reach* 58. 4.

tyne, *vb.* (ON týna); *be deprived of, lose* 102. 134; (*pret.*) *tynt* 94. 19.

tytled, *pp.* (*OED* title, *v.* † 5); *entitled* 153. 27.

typynge, *sb.*; *tidings* 16. 2.

vgle, *adj.*; *dreadful, terrible* 52. 42; *vgly* 144. 23.

vmbelappe, *vb.*; *enfold* 60. 56.

vmpeire, *sb.*; *arbiter, umpire* 176. 19.

vmsett, *pp.*; *beset, surrounded* 60. 32.

vnboolde, *adj.*; *timid, fearful* 157. 4; *on-bolde* 10. 84.

vnbrace, *vb.*; *relent, cause* (the heart) *to relax* 159. 93.

unchoud, *adj.* (OE uncúð); *unfamiliar, strange* 89. 7.

vnder-fonge, *vb.*; *receive, accept* 88. 23.

undigne, *adj.*; *unworthy* 80. 19 note.

vnes, *sb.*; *discomfort, uneasiness* 150. 10.

vnhapse, *vb.*; *'unhasp', disclose* 181. 12.

vnknytt, *vb.*; *disperse, destroy* 60. 28.

vnkyste, *ppl. adj.*; *unkissed* 148. 43.

vnsele, *sb.* (OE unsǽl); *unhappiness, misery* 144. 124; *vnseill* 102. 26.

vnsette, *ppl. adj.*; *not previously appointed* 183. 52; *unsette stevene, by chance, unpreparedly*.

vnthende, *adj.*; *out of condition, weak* 142. 37.

unto, *conj.* (*OED* unto, B. *conj.* † b); *until* 47. 7.

untryisty, *adj.*; *faithless, unreliable* 142. 37.

vntyl, *prep.*; *unto, to* 77 B. 23.

vprace, *vb.*; *up-root, eradicate* 152. 3.

vpriste, *sb.*; *resurrection* 62. 44.

vp-styyng, *vbl. sb.*; *ascension* 16. 14.

vpyn, *adv.*; *open* 10. 93.

vre, *sb.*; *destiny* 47. 17.

vade, *vb.*; *go away, depart* 148. 32.

valis, *vb. pres.*; 3 s.; *avails* 167. 5.

vanis, *sb. pl.*; *veins* 91. 2; *wanis* 91. 47.

vaste, *sb.*; *wilderness, waste* 97. 91.

vaye, *sb.*; *way* 130. 21.

venemys, *adj.* (AF venimus); *venomous* 182. 42.

venym, *sb.* (OF venim); *venom* 181. 10; *venyn* 178. 40.

verey, *adj.* (AF verrey); *true, right* 98. 3; *very* 180. 22; (*adv.*) *verray* 4. 64.

verrement, *adv.*; *assuredly* 38. 2.

vernant, *adj.*; *flourishing* 153. 49.

vilany, *sb.*; *shameful or insulting treatment* ('to put to vilany' = to insult) 60. 59.

vo, *sb.*; see *wa.*

voket, *sb.*; *advocate* 35. 42.

volupid, *pp.* (OF voluper); *wrapped* 153. 32.

voysis, *sb. pl.*; *voices* 39. 35.

vyle, *adj.*; *despicable* 6. 67.

wa, *sb.*; *woe* 22. 50; vo 4. 56.

wailʒeand, *adj.*; *valiant* 112. 10.

wailland, *part.*; *veiling, blindfolding* 91. 27.

wake, *vb.*; *keep awake, watch* 92. 19.

wald, *vb. pret.*; *would* 102. 105.

walkytt, *pret.*; *waked* 174. 6. See Note.

wallowit, *ppl. adj.*; *withered, yellowed* 191. 11.

walt, *pp.*; *cast to the ground, upset* 178. 25.

wam = *whom* 174. 2.

wan, *vb.* (OE wanian); *grow less, wane* 163. 18.

wane, *vb. pret.* (OE winnan); *won* 102. 135.

wanhop, *sb.*; *despair* 102. 108; wanhope 132. 34.

wanis, *sb. pl.*; see *vanis.*

wannyte, *sb.*; *vanity* 147. 8.

ware, *vb. pret.*; see *weron.*

ware, *vb.*; see *were* ('wear').

ware-thrugh, *conj.*; *whereby* 63. 11.

warke, *sb.*; *work, deed* 107. 20.

warld, *sb.*; see *worde.*

warn, *vb.* (OE wiernan); *refuse, deny* 21. 3; (*pres.* 3 *s.*) warns 33. 16.

warpud, *pp.*; *bent, contorted, twisted* 173. 2.

warre, *adj.*; *aware, informed* 159. 52.

wasche, *vb.*; *wash* 144 Alia. 39; wesche 78. 43; (*pret.*) wesche 15. 29; wosche 91. 14; (*pp.*) waschyn 90. 9.

wast, *vb.* (*OED* waste, *v.* II. 12 b); *dwindle or disappear* 34. 40.

wate, *vb. pres.* 1 *s.*; see *wytt.*

wayle, *sb.*; *vale, valley* 26. 20.

wayne, *sb.* (OE wǽn, wǽgen); *carriage, chariot* 31. 28; weyne 22. 26.

wayte, *vb.*; *lie in wait for* 125. 11.

waytyngis, *vbl. sb. pl.*; *ambushes* 60. 28.

weche, *pron.*; see *wheche.*

wedde, *sb.*; *a pledge, pawn* 172. 54; wed 178. 105.

wede, *sb.*; *garment, apparel* 144. 102.

wedrys, *sb. pl.* (OE weder); *weathers, storms* 135. 4.

wedyr, *conj.*; *whether* 125. 2.

weill, *sb.*; *weal, good fortune* 191. 3; weyle 183. 14.

weir, *sb.*; *war* 94. 27; wharre 182. 41; (*pl.*) werrys 64. 39.

weit, *adj.* (OE wǽt); *wet* 22. 81.

welawaye, (OE wei-la-wei); *alas!* 77 A. 27; walaway 3. 14.

welde, *vb.* (OE wealdan); (1 *intrans.*) *to manage, govern* (oneself) 6. 43. (2 *trans.*) wilde 23. 42.

welke, *vb.*; *wither* 60. 38.

well, *sb.*; see *whele.*

welle, *sb.* (OE wela); *happiness, bliss* 10. 107; well 147. 71.

wem, *sb.*; *moral stain, defilement* 15. 5; wemme 16. 17; (*pl.*) wemmes 15. 29.

wemles, *adj.*; *undefiled, immaculate* 15. 82.

wen = *when* 181. 23.

wende, *vb.* (OE wendan); *wend,*

depart 158 A. 1; weend 158 A. 4.

wenyst, *vb. pres.* 2 *s.*; *supposest* 182. 12; (*pl.*) weynys 176. 8.

wepe *vb. pret.*; *wept* 4. 4.

werd, *sb.*; see *worde.*

werde, *vb. pret.* (OE werian); *defended, protected* 15. 36; weryd 97. 43.

werdes, *sb. pl.* (OE wyrd); *fates* 183. 31.

were, *vb.*; *wear* 4. 40; ware 82. 18.

were, *conj.*; *where* 181. 31.

were, *adj. comp.* (ON verre); *worse* 144. 37.

were, *vb.* (*OED* wear, *v.*¹ III. 13); *to wear away, to waste* 34. 40; (*pres.* 3 *s.*) were-it 172. 4.

werke, *vb.*; see *worche.*

werkyne, *vbl. sb.*; *operation* 71. 43.

weron, *vb. pret. pl.* (OE wǣron); *were* 62. 13; *ware* 82. 13; wore 95. 14.

werray, *vb.*; *to make war on* 125. 6.

werre, *sb.* (*OED* were, *sb.*³); *distress, danger, fear* 26. 33.

werrys, *sb. pl.*; see *weir.*

wertew, *sb.*; *virtue* 191. 2.

wese, *vb.* (OE wésan); *to ooze or drip* 178. 70.

wesche, *vb. pret.*; see *wasche.*

weshe, *vb.* (OE wýscan); see *wisse.*

wete, *vb.* (OE witan); see *wytt.*

wex, *vb.* (OE weaxan); *to wax, grow* 148. 31; (*pret.*) wyx 90. 14; wyxyd 87. 25; (*pp.*) woxe 92. 43; wox 185. 15.

weyd, *vb.* (OE wédan); *to rage* 178. 101.

weyen, *vb.* (OE wegan); *weigh* 162. 25.

weyle, *sb.*; see *weill.*

weyne, *sb.*; see *wayne.*

weynys, *vb.*; see *wenyst.*

whake, *vb.*; *quake* 3. 14.

wharre, *sb.*; see *weir.*

whas = *was* 87. 1.

whe = *we* 87. 2, 159. 67.

wheche, *pron.*; *which* 31. 7; weche 177. 3.

whele, *sb.* (OE hweogol); *wheel* 170. 6; well 151. 50.

whelpe, *sb.*; *offspring* 26. 14.

wher = *were* 31. 13.

where-sere = *whersoever* 183. 30.

whight, *adj.*; *white* 109. 174.

whorby = *whereby* 26. 31.

whos, *rel. pron.*; *whose* 135. 30; woys 181. 10; wos 153. 36.

whyt, *prep.* = *with* 153. 42.

wicked, *adj.*; *poor, bad* 144. 102.

wiche, *pron.*; *which* 99. 2.

wiȝt, *sb.* (OE wiht); *wight, person* 9. 21; wyȝte 6. 40; wicht 13. 48; wiygth 110. 15.

wike, *adj.*; *evil, wicked* 186. 18

wilde, *vb.*; see *welde.*

wilfulnesse, *sb.*; *willingness, inclination* 36. 22.

wirche, *vb.* (OE wyrcan); *work, perform* 25. 23; (*part.*) wirk-and 60. 29; (*pp.*) wrot 54. 2; wroȝth 71. 14.

wissche, *vb.* (OE wissian); *to direct, guide* 142. 21; wisse 41. 3; (*pp.*) wyssed 15. 88.

wisse, *vb.* (OE wyscan); *to wish for, desire* 189. 19; weshe 172. 84.

wiþ-outen, *prep.*; *without* 144. 103; wythowghton 173. 12; by-thute 70. 2, 70. 9.

with-sought, *pp.*; *pursued, persecuted* 2. 18.

witt, *prep.*; *with* 24. 8.

witterly, *adv.*; *assuredly* 115. 4.

witt-in, *prep.*; *within* 24. 26; withyn, *less* (*adv.*) 85. 15.

wiygth, *sb.*; see *wi3t.*

wlonk, *adj.* (OE wlonc); *proud, haughty* 163. 2.

wo, *adj.*; *woful* 97. 87.

wodnes, *sb.*; *violence, wildness* 187. 2.

wolde, *sb.* (OE weald); *possession, keeping* 74. 7.

wolt, *vb. pres.* 2 *s.*; see *wylle.*

wome, *sb.*; *womb* 15. 56.

wondur, *adv.*; *wondrous* 52. 26.

wone, *num. adj.*; *one* 24. 2.

wone, *vb.* (OE wunian); *to dwell* 16. 23; wonne 24. 46; wonny 87. 35.

wonynge, *vbl. sb.*; *dwelling* 42. 6; (*pl.*) wonys 28. 33.

wood, *adj.* (OE wód); *wild, raging* 109. 146; woode 85. 18; woyd 76. 9.

woondyn, *pp.* (OE windan); *wrapped, enclosed in* 89. 33.

worche, *vb.* (OE wyrcan); *effect, bring to pass, produce* 189. 10; werke, *ache* 139. 18.

worde, *sb.* (OE worold); *world* 10. 111; werd 177. 57; warld 102. 97; wordle 153. 11; wordill 85. 3; wordyll 178. 27; worldell 32. 2; worle 182. 2.

wore, *vb. pret. pl.*; see *weron.*

worly, *adj.*; *worldly* 55. 18.

worschep, *adj.*; *worshipful* 15. 56.

worschipe, *sb.*; *honour, renown* 151. 15.

worth, *vb.* (OE weorþan); *become, be* 10. 15.

worthly, *adj.*; *worthy* 110. 15.

wos, *rel. pron.*; see *whos.*

wosche, *vb. pret.*; see *wasche.*

wost, *vb. pres.* 2 *s.*; see *wytt.*

woude, *sb.*; *wood, forest* 186. 2.

wox, woxe, *pp.*; see *wex.*

woyd, *adj.*; see *wood.*

woyde, *adj.*; *void, devoid* 109. 18.

woys, *rel. pron.*; see *whos.*

wraichit, *adj.*; *base, contemptible* 91. 19.

wraithar, *adj. comp.*; *angrier* 102. 99.

wrathirhayle, *sb.*; *destruction* (himself to wrathirhayle = to his own destruction) 163. 50.

wratthis, *vb. pres.* 2 *s.*; *provokest to anger* 105. 106.

wreche, *sb.* (*OED* wreche, *sb.*); *vengeance* 64. 27.

wreke, *sb.* (*OED* wreak, *sb.*[1]); *hurt or harm done from vindictive motives* 109. 5.

wreke, *vb.* (OE wrecan); *to drive out or away* 15. 8.

wretthe, *sb.* (OE wræððu); *wrath* 177. 90; wreth 182. 15.

wrey, *vb.* (OE wrǽgan); *beway, expose* 182. 28.

wrich, *sb.*; *wretch* 60. 32.

wri3t, *sb.*; *wright, carpenter* 10. 49.

wrot, *pp.*; see *wirche.*

wull, *vb. pres.* 3 *s.*; see *wylle.*

wundorly, *adv.*; *wonderfully* 147. 57.

wus, 1 *pers. pron.* = *us* 99. 2; ws 22. 50.

wyhte, *prep.*; *with* 116. 2.

wyll, *adv.*; *well* 97. 43; wylle 173. 37.

wylle, *vb. pres.* 3 *s.*; *will* 188. 12; wil 188. 18; wull 163. 47; (2 *s.*) wolt 77 B. 35.

wylle, *sb.*; *pleasure*; wyth wylle; *joyously* 37. 45.

wyn, *vb.* (OE winnan); (1) *to persuade, gain the affection of* 19. 6. (2) *to gain,* wyne 156. 20; wynn 142. 75; (3 *s.*) wynnyt 177. 14.

wyn, *sb.* (*OED* win, *sb.*[2]); *joy, bliss* 15. 14; wyne 126. 22; wynne 24. 30.

wynked, *vb. pret.*; *gave a signi-*

Glossary

ficant glance (as of command or direction) 153. 24.

wynne, *sb.* (*OED* win, *sb.*¹); *gain, profit* 172. 26.

wynnis, *vb. pres.* 2 *s.* (North. variation of 'won'); *dwellest* 96. 16.

wyre, *sb.*; *a state of uncertainty or doubt* 174. 3.

wyte, *vb.* (OE wítan); *to blame* 10. 67; wytyn 177. 8.

wythowghten, *prep.*; see *wiþouten.*

wytnes, *vb. pres.* 3 *s.*; *witnesses* 186. 12.

wytt, *vb.* (OE witan); *to know* 46. 22; wete 10. 75; (*pres.* 1 *s.*) wate 3. 5; (2 *s.*) wost 7. 12; (*pret.* 2 *s.*) wyste 110. 12.

wytte, *sb.*; *understanding* 183. 11.

wyttye, *adj.*; *wise* 131. 28.

wytyn, *vb.*; see *wyte.*

wyx, wyxyd, *vb. pret.*; see *wex.*

xal, *vb.* (OE sceal); *shall* 76. 4, 84. 23.

xe, *fem. pers. pron.*; *she* 18. 2.

yate, *sb.*; *door, barrier* 172. 43.

ych, 1 *pers. pron.*; *I* 160. 2.

ychan = *each one* 10. 6.

yche, *vb.* (OE giccan); *to itch* 148. 25.

y-dyȝte, *pp.*; *disposed, circumstanced* 6. 45.

yerth, *sb.*; *earth* 93. 43.

yftis, *sb. pl.*; *gifts* 46. 20.

yȝe, *sb.* (OE eage); *eye* 116. 15.

yknowe, *vb.* (OE ȝecnáwan); *recognize* 95. 18.

ylke, *adj.*; *each* 78. 4.

yll, *adj.*; *bad, evil* 181. 19; yl 180. 11.

y-mete, *pp.*; *dreamed* 148. 74.

ympnes, *sb. pl.*; *hymns* 36. 41.

ynche, *sb.*; *inch* 92. 29.

ynd, *sb.*; *end* 57. 105.

ynfere, *adv.*; *together, in company* 48. 18.

ynsaciat, *adj.*; *insatiate* 187. 4.

ynvarde, *adj.*; *inward* 32. 15.

yoles, *sb. gen.*; *Yule's* 4. 27.

ys, *poss. pron.*; *his* 130. 22.

yt, *adv.*; see *ȝeyt.*

y-turne, *pp.*; *turned* 182. 5.

y-ware, *adj.*; *aware* 148. 40.

y-wente, *pp.*; *gone* 182. 2.

y-wys, *adv.*; *certainly, indeed* 6. 20; ywysse 37. 54; I-wisse 158 A. 5.

INDEX OF FIRST LINES

PRINTED IN GREAT BRITAIN
AT THE UNIVERSITY PRESS, OXFORD
BY VIVIAN RIDLER
PRINTER TO THE UNIVERSITY

77
79
83
85